BC
Te
(

The Wizard

For J. A. 'Charles' Cuddon who taught me all I know about writing, which is very little of what he knew

The Wizard

The Life of Stanley Matthews

Jon Henderson

YELLOW JERSEY PRESS
LONDON

Published by Yellow Jersey Press 2013

2 4 6 8 10 9 7 5 3 1

Copyright © Jon Henderson 2013

Jon Henderson has asserted his right under the Copyright, Designs
and Patents Act 1988 to be identified as the author of this work

First published in Great Britain in 2013 by
Yellow Jersey Press
Random House, 20 Vauxhall Bridge Road,
London SW1V 2SA

www.rbooks.co.uk

Addresses for companies within The Random House Group Limited can be found at:
www.randomhouse.co.uk/offices.htm

The Random House Group Limited Reg. No. 954009

A CIP catalogue record for this book
is available from the British Library

ISBN 978 0 22 409184 8

The Random House Group Limited supports The Forest Stewardship
Council (FSC®), the leading international forest certification organisation.
Our books carrying the FSC label are printed on FSC® certified paper. FSC is
the only forest certification scheme endorsed by the leading environmental
organisations, including Greenpeace. Our paper procurement policy
can be found at www.randomhouse.co.uk/environment

Printed and bound by CPI Group (UK) Ltd, Croydon, CR0 4YY

Contents

List of illustrations

SECTION 1

1 *t* Jack Matthews in fighting stance (courtesy of *The Sentinel*); *b* Stanley Matthews as a young boy (courtesy of Mirrorpix)

2 *t* Stanley Matthews circa 1937 (courtesy of Popperfoto/Getty Images); *m* Stanley Matthews in action for Stoke City (courtesy of Hulton/Getty Images); *b* The English League team group before the game at Stamford Bridge on 31 October 1934 (courtesy of Colorsport / Wilkes)

3 *t* The English football team give the Nazi salute 14 May 1938 (courtesy of Associated Press/PA Photos); *m* Stanley Matthews grapples with Scottish defender Stephens (courtesy of Getty Images); *b* circa 1945, The United Services team (courtesy of Popperfoto/Getty Images)

4 *t* Stanley Matthews plays a ball over the net of his tennis court in front of his wife Betty and daughter Jean and son Stanley Junior, 1953 (courtesy of Popperfoto/Getty Images); *m* RAF corporal and football star Stanley Matthews takes his daughter and the dog for a cycle (courtesy of Getty Images); *b* Stanley Matthews is pictured running around his home ground with his son Stanley Junior (courtesy of Popperfoto/Getty Images)

5 *t* Stanley Matthews at Ewood Park (courtesy of Colorsport); *b* Training on Blackpool Beach, October 1961 (courtesy of Mirrorpix)

6 *t* Hungary 1953 and *b* Stanley Matthews, England v Hungary at Wembley (courtesy of Colorsport)

7 *t* 1953 FA Cup Final (courtesy of Getty Images); *m* Stanley Matthews dribbles past Bolton's midfielder Barass during the English Cup final (courtesy of AFP/Getty Images); *b* Blackpool Team Group (courtesy of Colorsport/Wilkes)

8 1953 FA Cup Final at Wembley, Stanley Matthews is chaired by team-mates Jackie Mudie, left, and Stan Mortensen after collecting his winner's medal (courtesy of Popperfoto/Getty Images)

Introduction:
The Stanley Show

Stanley Matthews turned matter-of-factly, his stare fixed to avoid eye contact. His expression, washed of emotion, accentuated the slightly sunken, careworn look that made him appear at least as old as his thirty-two years. Time had already gone to work on his hair. It was combed back and still dark but was in the first stages of retreat. In close-up, something seemed to shadow his features, a sadness possibly pleated in the corners of his mouth. No one could have guessed that here was a man at the soaring peak of his powers who had just brought a packed arena to a ferment of excitement.

As Matthews turned, gently hitching the elastic of his loose-fitting shorts on to his hips, the sellout crowd of 75,000 at the Heysel Stadium in Brussels had started to applaud. Moments earlier, England's outside-right had completed a run that even by his standards was exceptional, bewildering Belgium's defence and electrifying the spectators. And that was not the end of this particular piece by Matthews on a pitch made treacherous by a violent cloudburst soon after kick-off. Having wrought havoc with the ball on the turf, he dipped his head, cocked his right boot and lifted the ball over the oncoming keeper. One reporter likened it to a golf shot, Matthews seizing a wedge and lofting the ball in a meticulous arc. All that was left for Tom Finney to do to collect his second goal of the match was to deflect his header into an unguarded net.

Four-two to England, all four goals heavily dependent on Matthews – and a fifth goal would also bear the winger's mark.

'It is Matthews's Night in the old town tonight,' John Macadam wrote in his dispatch to the *Daily Express*, 'and they do say that some more progressive manufacturers are going to make a special lace to the pattern that Matthews wove around the Belgian defence to help England's 5-2 victory at Heysel Stadium today.' Macadam said of the build-up to Finney's second goal: 'Matthews meandered in and out among the defence until the 70,000-odd of the crowd and the other 21 players were hysterical.'

Even Walter Winterbottom, the donnish and pragmatic manager of England who was not alone in regarding Matthews as flawed, particularly as a team player, was unreserved in his admiration when, years later, he reminisced to me about that fourth goal. After England scored three goals early on, Belgium pulled back to 3-2. 'We were looking a bit thin when Stanley decided to put on a show,' Winterbottom said. 'He made a run from the centre of the field. Their centre-half made a dive at Stanley, bringing his shorts down around his knees, but he still went on dribbling through the Belgian defence and finally chipped the ball over to lay on the goal for Finney. It was so spectacular that as he walked back the whole crowd started a rhythmic handclap in time with his walk. Then the VIPs joined in and in the end so did the players of both teams.'

Charles Buchan, the Sunderland and Arsenal player who turned into a prolific writer on the game, said: 'Never was a goal more brilliantly or opportunely made.'

Matthews's own response to the goal was as muted as it was to anything else that he ever did or had done to him on a football field. It was as if self-possession was what nourished him. Naturally introspective, he had allowed his containment to harden because of recent events: the degradation of his relationship with Stoke City, the club that had nurtured him, to a point where in early summer he had moved to Blackpool; and the easing of another bond, that with his first wife. Was this the sadness, rising from deep within him, that was snared in the creases of his face?

He had become the most intractable of competitors. Defenders, even those highly practised in the art of intimidation, grew tired of trying to provoke Matthews, before, in his imperious final years as a professional player, to do so was an act tantamount to treason. Teammates grew to understand that he preferred to celebrate with no more than the merest inflection of his facial mask.

The Heysel match, England's first international of the 1947–8 season, took place on Sunday 21 September. Not so long ago German tanks had been parked on the pitch, their iron-toothed, articulated tracks churning the surface. Repairs had taken longer than expected and England's visit marked the official reopening of the stadium after the war. Little wonder the visitors' fourth goal so enraptured the crowd. Their delight evinced not only their appreciation of a player who by now enjoyed worldwide renown but also their relief that football had so royally reclaimed the national arena.

And Matthews was the gleaming star of the show. When Finney looked back on his own career, he said: 'It would be foolish to try to list all the great things I saw Stan do on a football field – I can't recall a game in which his magic didn't play a key role. If I was to select one game, though, it would have to be the England fixture against Belgium in Brussels in the autumn of 1947. I called it the Matthews Match because he was responsible for putting the fear of God up the Belgians.'

No one suffered more than the left-back, Joe Pannaye, who, Macadam reported, 'took a merciless beating pretty much until the end when his patience wore thin and his elbows began to wear hooks.'

The entertainment in a match that could hardly have risen more spellbindingly to the occasion started early. The England centre-forward, Tommy Lawton, kicked off to Wilf Mannion. The ball then went back to Lawton, on to Tim Ward, on to Matthews, back to Lawton, back to Mannion and then once again to Matthews whose cross Lawton headed into a top corner. England's travelling press corps agreed the goal took twelve seconds and that Belgium's first touch came after they were already a goal down.

After twenty minutes, England were three ahead. Matthews crossed for Mortensen to volley in from twelve yards and then, having been fouled, Matthews looped the free-kick into the goalmouth where Finney's header bounced out of the goalkeeper's grasp and into the goal. Increasingly, said Finney, Belgium 'resorted to tactics of an unpleasant nature' to try to stop Matthews. For a while this altered the course of the game with the home side scoring two goals, one either side of half-time.

Pannaye, of the hooked elbows, was one of those who tried to impede his merciless tormentor however he could. But he and Matthews both knew that this was a capitulation and Pannaye was one of a legion of players who over the years, with intended irony, spoke of the privilege it had been to spend an afternoon or evening being Matthews's dupe. The defender had done reasonably well against Matthews when Belgium lost 2-0 at Wembley in January 1946 but admitted to having been made to look ridiculous by him on this occasion. Pannaye was among those scattered by Matthews as he conjured the fourth goal after, in Finney's words, deciding to break their hearts by waltzing past three challenges. 'He was the best player I've ever seen. A ghost,' Pannaye said, and added: 'I asked some of those close to me to help, but they could do nothing.'

England's fifth goal followed yet another foul by Belgium's

desperate defence on Matthews, who this time played the free-kick short, and tellingly, to Lawton. 'In all his career Matthews has never dominated a game so completely,' Frank Coles told readers of the *Daily Telegraph*. 'He made every one of England's five goals and ran the left flank of the Belgium defence dizzy. The crowd loved the performance of the game's greatest star.'

The year of the Heysel match was the sixteenth of Matthews's career as a professional footballer, which meant it was not even halfway through. He was forty-two when he made his final appearance for England in 1957, more than twenty-two years after his first, and fifty when he played his last Football League match, for Stoke City, in 1965. By then he had long passed into football lore as the game's first player of international renown, a reputation he went on to reinforce with a number of overseas assignments playing, coaching and managing. In 1970, Matthews, at the age of fifty-five, very nearly turned out for the Maltese club he helped to manage, Hibernians, against Real Madrid in a European match in the Bernabéu stadium.

Not all the reporting from Heysel was an unmitigated paean to Matthews. A discordant undercurrent accompanied the eulogising, one that was ever-present during Matthews's playing days but has long since lost its tow, submerged deep beneath the golden reminiscences. Roy Peskett's report from Brussels that appeared in the *Daily Mail* stated: 'Once again the old complaint could be raised that Matthews held up Lawton's attack by not getting rid of the ball until he had beaten one or more men and that he did not come into the game until he was given the ball.'

Despite this recurring theme, Matthews remained on good, if distant, terms with most of his fellow professionals. But his refusal to make concessions, in the way he played and, in some cases, in the way he conducted himself in a wider context, did not always suit the managers he played under. Two of those he encountered at Stoke had had enough of him – and he of them

– by the time he departed; and when he left Blackpool in 1961 he said he no longer saw eye to eye with the manager, Ron Suart.

At international level, too, it seems, fans found it easier to admire Matthews than managers did to manage him. Walter Winterbottom was often exasperated by Matthews's persistence in deploying his gifts as he wished, a privilege of ownership as the player no doubt regarded it, irrespective of the needs of the team. On his side Matthews was irritated by Winterbottom's didacticism. 'I felt Walter Winterbottom never really appreciated my style of play,' Matthews said. 'He wanted a right-winger to track back, tackle and help out in defence. It wasn't my style.'

The sweet-natured Finney would never publicly criticise Matthews. Many tried to goad him into doing so and he was entitled to feel aggrieved given that his own game could be affected by his fellow forward's mode of play. In his report from Brussels after the Heysel match, Frank Coles had written 'as long as we have Matthews I do not think we have room for Finney among the forwards . . . We need a more direct left winger to balance the line.' In other words, having two players who procrastinated on the wing was unacceptable. Finney, grudgingly on a few occasions when he was with close friends, accepted that Matthews's excellence placed him above the expectations that governed others.

This was the dilemma all his critics had to confront eventually. Having upbraided Matthews for aspects of his performance against Belgium, Roy Peskett added: 'But how can you judge by ordinary standards a man who not only gave the crowd and the Belgian defenders something they won't forget in a hurry, but figured in all the goals, four of which were headed from his passes?'

What distinguished Matthews was his speed and skilfulness, which he unleashed with deadly synchrony. Arthur Hopcraft, an outstanding writer on the game, said: 'Matthews did not invent dribbling with a football; he raised it to its highest degree.' He added that before Matthews and throughout his career other players did the same kind of thing, but at a lower level. Dribbling then died after Matthews retired, Hopcraft maintained, until George Best resurrected it nearly a decade later. At times Matthews seemed to be playing in a different dimension from those around him, rendering the game's old formulas meaningless. Regardless of the criticism, his nickname, the Wizard of the Dribble – in Germany they called him *Der Zauberer*, the Magician – was entirely appropriate with his sorcery forever bemusing opponents and bedazzling crowds.

The numerical evidence of Matthews's appeal is staggering. From very early on in his career he would regularly add upwards of 10,000 spectators to a gate. In 1934, during his first spell at Stoke, crowds averaged more than 66,000 during a run of six matches played by the club. The lure of Matthews helped to secure what survives as the highest attendance for an international match in Britain – 149,547 for Scotland v England in 1937 – and for a game played at an English club ground – 84,569 for Manchester City v Stoke City in an FA Cup tie at Maine Road in 1934.

They are numbers that make it almost inconceivable that, for all but the very end of his career, he earned no more from playing than £20 a week, the most allowed just before the upper pay limit was scrapped in 1961. He was quite worldly enough to appreciate the imbalance between his reimbursement and his worth and astute enough to do something about it. One obituarist noted: 'Self-effacing but shrewd, Matthews knew how to market himself at a time when professional players were restricted to a maximum wage.' For some this translated into an unacceptable acquisitiveness; for others it meant no more than a proper claim on his due.

Throughout virtually the whole of Matthews's time as a Football

League player his life was sombrely backlit by a marriage that did not work. This must have had an impact on the way he was, as a footballer and public figure, but, hitherto, has been largely unexplored. It was not something he discussed either with acquaintances or with those close to him.

Soon after he stopped playing his life underwent a dramatic change. In 1967 he met the Czech lady, Mila Winterova – 'the true love of my life', he called her – who would become his second wife. It was a romance that would make Matthews's later years every bit as fascinating as his early ones. Throughout more than three decades together, starting with an elopement that a much dozier media than today's failed to register, Mila kept from Matthews a dark secret from her past – one that I happened upon only towards the end of writing this book.

Matthews's thirty-three years of work as a professional foot-baller is, though, what stands as his monument, an unrivalled body of achievement that, while rooted in England, enhanced many thousands of lives around the world by opening people's eyes to what was humanly possible.

Chapter 1

'Our father never raised his hand to us. He never swore'

Children's excited voices rise and fall in the sweet air of a spring morning. Every so often the sterner tones of a grown man take over, stilling the chatter. The party of four – a father, trim and upright as a Grenadier, and his three sons – arrive at a gate, climb it and set off across the next field. After about twenty yards the father makes them all stop. He gestures the smallest of the three boys towards him and, from a bag, produces a pair of shoes. Spikes protrude from the soles. The other three stand patiently as the boy changes into the running shoes. The father then points to a spot some fifty yards ahead of him and moments later, on a shouted command, the boy, who is no more than four years old, sets off at a sprint. He moves easily over the grass that has been cropped by grazing sheep. The party regroups and again the father and his two older sons look on as the small boy takes off on a second sprint, once again quickly gaining speed on pale, skinny legs.

The walk from Hanley to the village of Werrington and back – a round trip of some ten miles – was a Sunday ritual for the Matthews family. They would do most of the outward journey along the main road before, with a mile to go, cutting up across fields. Sometimes Ada Matthews, who had grown up in

Washerwall Lane, Werrington, went with her husband, Jack, and their three boys: Jack, Arthur and Stanley. So, later, would a fourth son, Ron. He was the youngest by eight years – a span of seventeen years covered the four sons – and sometimes later on he alone would accompany his father on the walk to and from Werrington, a village of just a few houses, much smaller than it is today. Jack had once walked there when he was courting Ada; now the visits were to see Ada's widowed father, Henry Hewitt, and her sister Emmy, a spinster who ran a shop. Ron remembered the old man, who had worked in the now extinct local coal mines, sitting in a rocking chair sucking on a clay pipe.

Jack Senior had detected Stanley's sprinting potential at a very young age. A former professional boxer with firm – cranky, some thought – ideas about physical wellbeing, he observed his sons closely, not simply to discern whether they had athletic ability but also, if they had, to classify what it was. Thus Arthur was spared doing any exercise at all although he later became a keen sprinter; Jack and Ron were simply made to run in ordinary plimsolls; and Stanley alone was coached to sprint. In spiked shoes, what is more. Finding a pair to fit someone as small as Stanley must, at that time, have required a difficult search.

But then Jack Matthews had never been one to take projects lightly, as his lives as a professional boxer and barber testified. The trajectory of his fighting career suggests success based on a strict fitness regime and perseverance rather than the quick realisation of an exceptional talent. He fought at a time when records were kept erratically and often included the results of fights in fairground booths, which were mentioned in British boxing legislation as late as the 1950s. Stanley said in an early autobiography that his father had 350 fights, losing just nine of them, but boxing historians have traced only fifty or so – between 1909 and 1921 – of which he lost at least eighteen. What is certain is that his wins comfortably outweighed his defeats and he achieved a level of proficiency that placed him well above that of 'crowd pleaser', a boxing euphemism for jobbing fighters served up as fodder for those making their way in the sport.

Jack Matthews laid claim to two unofficial titles, the Midlands featherweight championship and the Potteries featherweight championship, and shared the ring with national and European champions. He might well have challenged for a national title himself had not the 1914–18 war interrupted normal life across Europe. When he was much older he was the modest, grey-haired little man who owned a barber's shop, Stanley said, 'but old-timers would address him with the air of folk proud to be familiar with a celebrity'.

Harold Alderman, the boxing historian, described Jack Matthews as an all-round action fighter who was very speedy, had good footwork and hit hard with either hand. He must have had a reasonable defence, too, because photographs show that he emerged from his boxing career virtually unmarked. This was quite an accomplishment considering he was active for so long and his bouts lasted up to twenty rounds. What he lacked in natural ability he made up for in time spent on physical conditioning and in training. His son Jack remembered in later life that he watched with wide-eyed amazement as his father performed one of his party pieces, lining up six chairs and clearing them with a standing jump. His athleticism may help to account for why he avoided the boxer's hallmark, the squashed nose. And his nose must have been quite a target given that just beneath it he sported what was reckoned to be the last waxed moustache worn in the ring by a pro. Many a riled opponent must have wanted to spoil its defiant symmetry.

His greatest fight was undoubtedly the first of his three contests against George Mackness, a renowned scrapper from Kettering, that fifty years later was still being talked about as 'the greatest fight ever'. It was held at the National Sporting Club, the prestigious members' club just off London's Covent Garden.

Founded in 1891 by the 5th Earl of Lonsdale among others, it is credited with having had a huge influence on establishing professional boxing in the form we know it today. Matthews's first bout against Mackness took place there on 13 May 1912.

How Jack Matthews came to be in the ring at all was just one of the remarkable aspects of a fight that *Boxing* magazine said was 'simply astounding from start to finish'. Mackness had been due to box Albert Hough of Stafford, whose manager had been pressing for some time for his man to be allowed to showcase his skills at the NSC. But Hough failed to appear and Matthews, who was there 'to hurl challenges at various featherweights', took his place.

The fight lasted only until the fourth round. The fury with which the two men went at each other must have tested the NSC's tradition of requiring its members and their guests to remain silent during rounds. Both men, eschewing all but relentless aggression, narrowly beat the count on at least two occasions. In total there were seventeen knock-downs, Matthews suffering eleven of them. Matthews, though, triumphed in a climax that turned *Boxing*'s prose a vivid purple: 'Still his [Matthews's] bolt seemed shot, and probably would have been, had it not been determined that the last stage of this miraculous contest would transcend even all the miracles which had gone before. Matthews reeled up weak, and looked a beaten man, but covering well and keeping his head, called up his old guard. Mackness charged in like a tidal wave, and might have got home with a finisher had he not allowed Matthews a clear glimpse of his uncovered chin. This was enough, and the fatal right hook whizzed through the air to connect with the angle of the chin. The punch lifted Mackness from his feet, and, spinning him over, dropped him on the back of his head with a thud which sent the last of his senses to oblivion.'

Neither of the Mackness–Matthews rematches, in November and December of the same year, produced quite the same drama, although both did end eventfully. Matthews dominated the first but was disqualified for a low blow after the ringside doctor 'humanely grasped the situation, and ordered the contest to cease' in the fourth round. Matthews won the final fight, held at the Shelton Drill Hall in Hanley, where in due course he would present himself to enlist in the 3rd/5th North Staffordshire Regiment before going off to war for three years. In the second round Mackness missed with a right uppercut, fell through the ropes and landed heavily on the back of his head. Mackness being unable to continue, the referee awarded the fight to Matthews.

After the war Matthews was no longer the fighter he had been. In September 1919 he and the Scotsman Bob Donati left a bad odour in Manchester's Free Trade Hall. One account said that Matthews, who used 'to hit like a horse', had lost his power. Donati was even worse and his corner threw in the towel in the seventh round, sparing the crowd, as much as their man, unnecessary punishment. Jack Matthews fought only a handful more fights before packing it in in 1921 to spend more time in his barber's shop.

Two stories Stanley Matthews passed down about his father's boxing career are worth retelling even if neither contest is in any official record. Soon after he started fighting professionally, Jack Matthews was approached by a promoter who had accepted a wager to find a novice capable of beating a promising young Manchester fighter called Chambers. The Manchester publican who offered the wager was so unimpressed by Matthews, whom the promoter had spotted in a Hanley gym, that he said he would not pay him for the fight. The publican was further discouraged about the quality of the contest about to take place when Matthews stripped off to reveal a concave, etiolated body with no obvious source of power. Matthews proceeded to dominate the fight, knocked Chambers out in the fifth and so dazzled a group of Mancunians that they offered to set him

up in a hairdressing business in the town. 'But Dad loved the
Potteries,' his son said, 'and could never be persuaded to leave
Hanley.'

The other story concerned a bout at Liverpool Stadium. After
it, Matthews spent the night at a police station while his beaten
opponent battled to regain consciousness. Fortunately for all
concerned he did. If he had died, Stanley said, his father would
have been charged with manslaughter. The fact that the police
became involved and no record exists of the fight suggests the
contest may not have been officially sanctioned.

Jack Matthews's *nom de guerre*, 'The Fighting Barber from
Hanley', was apt given that it was with his fists that he secured
the capital to set himself up in business. With purses and side
stakes, even fighters of Matthews's weight and ranking could
make tidy money. Information about the exact amounts is scant
– inevitably, much of the dealing, particularly in small halls,
was done in dark corners – but enough can be gleaned to get
a good idea of the sums involved. In 1911, Matthews himself
'challenged any 9 stone man in England, for any amount up to
£200'. A few weeks before his second bout against Mackness,
Matthews fought Tommy Mitchell of Chesterfield at the NSC,
standing to win a £75 purse and £50 side stake, but lost despite a
strong finish in a fifteen-round contest. He was more successful
a year later when he beat Billy Gerkin of Newcastle under Lyme
in another fifteen-rounder at the Hanley Skating Rink, this
time picking up £85 – the purse was £60 – for his points win.
Considering how often he fought and won, these sums would
have mounted up to a significant total.

Matthews, whose father Henry had worked as a potter, was as
assiduous in the business of tending heads with scissors and razor
as he was when preparing to belabour them with his fists in the
ring. His shop at No. 7 Market Street – now Huntbach Street –
was a shortish walk from the family's terraced home in Seymour
Street. 'It was quite a big place: four basins, hot towels, the lot,'

Ron Matthews said. Opening was six days a week, sometimes seven: weekdays from 9 a.m. to 7 p.m., except Thursdays, when it shut at 1 p.m. in line with early closing, and Saturdays from 9 a.m. to 9 p.m. On some Sundays he would open from 9 a.m. until noon for Jewish customers, whom he would also serve on Christmas Day. A press photograph taken in his later years shows Matthews Senior standing in the doorway of his shop in a white overall coat, buttoned down the front, and with an immaculately knotted tie. He is still handsome, distinguished even, with strong features and incorruptible expression, the picture of an honest proprietor. His premises shared space with a tobacconist's, which is why the shop window is filled with a range of pipe-smoking paraphernalia. A clearance sale is advertised: 'All pipes, pouches &c in the window 5D. each. Pick which you like. Must sell.'

As well as employing a full-time apprentice, Jack Matthews received varying levels of assistance from each of his sons. Jack Junior eventually opened his own shop, while Arthur stayed on as his father's number two. Before football monopolised Stanley's life, his tasks included sweeping up, brushing the hair from coats and preparing customers for a shave by lathering their chins. He said he enjoyed the work mainly because he liked listening to the yarns his father exchanged with customers. These were invariably about boxing. One tale involved a threat of violence against Jack Matthews unless he threw a certain fight. Stanley said that when he first heard it he was chided by a customer for paying more attention to the story than his lathering, which became increasingly wayward as the plot unwound. In 1964 the BBC made a documentary about Stanley called *Saturday Hero* and filmed him armed with shaving brush lathering up Billy Thompson. Four decades earlier, Thompson had been the first customer the nine-year-old would-be footballer had made ready for his father's cut-throat razor.

*

John 'Jack' Matthews and Ada Hewitt had married on Tuesday 10 July 1906 in St Mark's, the parish church of Shelton in Hanley. He was twenty-one and, as the marriage document certifies, already a 'hairdresser'; she a year younger and a slight figure even beside her featherweight husband, although a little less slight than usual, possibly, on account of her being nearly six months pregnant. It would be hard to imagine someone further removed from the popular image of a pugilist's wife – several degrees of separation existing between her and the boxer's moll beloved of American fiction – and she lived in a state of suppressed anxiety whenever he fought.

The addresses of the bride and groom were given as, respectively, Nos 77 and 88 Mill Street, which was in an area that in the recent past had been described as 'very unhealthy'. A local history talks of 'open middens', or refuse heaps, draining into Mill Street, which soon after the couple married would be renamed Etruria Road. The first son, Jack, was born at No. 77 on 26 October 1906 and by the time Ron arrived in 1923 the family of six fitted rather too cosily into 89 Seymour Street, a small terraced house with no garden. They stayed there, though, until 1934, shortly before Stanley married, when they moved a few doors down to No. 63. This was a superior property with a small garden and greenhouse but still with an outside lavatory.

Seymour Street could have passed for one of many thousands of streets that grew up in manufacturing towns in central England during the country's industrialisation. They had little to commend them bar the fact that the closeness of the rudimentary terraced houses fostered a sense of community, of which, in the case of Seymour Street, impromptu games of twenty-a-side street football were a good example.

Seymour Street is in the heart of Hanley, originally one of the separate towns now joined under the title Stoke-on-Trent. Arnold Bennett, the author who was born a short distance from Seymour Street in 1867, changes Hanley to Hanbridge in his novels and refers to it as one of 'the Five Towns' that make up the Potteries. In fact there are six, Bennett having omitted Fenton apparently because he preferred the literary ring of 'Five Towns'. Bennett's novels gave a romantic, if not necessarily flattering, sheen to the sort of setting in which Stanley Matthews was raised: 'The rows of little red houses with amber chimney pots . . . all netted in flowing scarves of smoke.'

A rather grittier view of Stoke in general and where Matthews grew up in particular comes from Derek Hodgson, who was in charge of administration and publicity at Stoke City Football Club in the 1960s: 'Stanley came from a pretty poor background and of course money has always been tight in Stoke-on-Trent. It's one of the most plundered areas of Britain. When you think of all the craftsmanship that has always gone into the product of the Potteries and how little has come back it's scandalous, absolutely scandalous.'

This heartfelt assessment would have horrified the most famous founding father of Stoke's pottery industry, Josiah Wedgwood, an abolitionist associated with the 'Am I Not A Man And A Brother' anti-slavery medallion. But Hodgson received support for his view after helping to redesign the football club's logo so that it honoured the town's heritage by incorporating a pottery kiln. 'A lot of the supporters won't like that,' he was told. 'It will remind them of being sweated to death for very low wages.' After Hodgson left, the kiln disappeared from the logo.

Jack and Ada Matthews fitted a stereotypical image of working-class parents: he very much in charge, she the homemaker who, although possibly coming across as submissive, was quite capable of mounting effective resistance if she felt it was needed. They were the staunchest of couples. 'My father was devoted to my mother,' Ron Matthews said. 'I don't mean this in the sense that they went around holding hands. Simply that his life was devoted to her.' Among other things he relieved her of some of the household chores by paying for the laundry to be done and employing a Mr Holland to clean twice a week.

Ron Matthews described the barber's shop as his father's second devotion, which was why, given the long hours he worked, the family did not see much of him. Unfailingly, Jack and Ada would go out together on Thursdays, after early closing. A day at Uttoxeter races, a short train journey away – they never owned a car – was a particular favourite. They would always be back around seven o'clock. When Ron was still young, Stanley would be detailed to look after him on the afternoons their parents went out. 'When I returned from school, Stanley would always be there. He told me that all I ever wanted to eat was custard.'

'I've heard people talk and you would think my father was a Victorian or Edwardian type . . . everything black and white,' Ron said. 'It wasn't like that. There were grey areas. He never raised his hand to us; he never swore. But he was of a firm disposition. And not one for jokes. If he cracked more than one I can't remember it.'

When Ron started saying 'Crikey!' in imitation of the comic-book character Billy Bunter, his father admonished him: 'I want a word with you. I'd like you to stop using the word crikey.' Later Ron plucked up the courage to seek an explanation. 'Because it's worrying your mother and me that every time you say it we think you're going to say something else,' his father said. Even in a non-churchgoing household an exclamatory 'Christ!' would certainly have been forbidden.

Apart from boxing and managing his own business, Jack Matthews's only other occupation that we know about was his brief stint as a conscripted soldier in the First World War, when his starting pay would have been a shilling a day and would not have gone much higher.

In March 1915, soon after his third son, Stanley, was born, Jack

Matthews joined up with the 3rd/5th North Staffords. It was a territorial force with headquarters first at Shelton and then at Stoke Drill Hall. The men often trained in Hanley Park. The Victoria Ground, home of Stoke City Football Club, was also used for training and as a parade ground on Sundays before the battalion went to church.

Jack appeared in an exhibition bout in May and, a few days later, refereed two bouts at a professional show in Longton. *Boxing* magazine said at the time: 'By the enlistment of Jack Matthews, the Hanley feather-wt, who now holds the rank of corporal, and his brother, [Private] George Matthews,* the cream of the boxing talent here are serving in His Majesty's Forces.' Jack then fought two bouts at Hoxton in London in February 1916 just days before the 3rd/5th moved to hutments at Catterick Bridge near Richmond in Yorkshire. He did not box again until September 1919 when the war was over.

Apart from this, records of Jack Matthews's wartime activity are not easily found. Nor was it something he talked about at home. 'Looking back, fighting in the Great War did have an effect on my father,' Ron said. 'When I was small I asked him how many Germans he killed and he told me firmly never to talk like that again. He came through unscathed, but he always said that they should have put the generals in the trenches.'

Stanley's birth was at a time when the hostilities were coming perilously close to home and the weapons of war were getting ever nastier. Germany had just carried out the first Zeppelin raids on Britain, while on the Continent the forces of Kaiser Wilhelm, trying to dislodge the Russians from positions west of Warsaw, had introduced poison gas. Delivered into this fracturing world, Stanley could hardly have had a more contrastingly peaceful

---

* Jack's brothers Charlie and George also boxed professionally. George, the youngest of the trio, was reckoned to be the best of them but was seriously injured fighting in the trenches at the Somme.

arrival. Ada was on her own at 89 Seymour Street when the contractions began. Not until Stanley had exercised his lungs for the first time did assistance arrive. The event is recalled by a small black plaque with gold lettering fixed to the front of the house, which reads:

> Sir Stanley Matthews CBE
> Footballer and Gentleman
> Born here 1 February 1915.

Stanley himself remembered a serene early childhood. In later life, he acknowledged how difficult it must have been to raise a large family when the privations of those stringent economic times, particularly for poorer families, were considerable. But there were no signs of hardship that he could remember. 'All I can recall is the support my family gave me,' he said, 'all the help and encouragement a kid could ever wish for.'

His father's influence was what Stanley remembered most vividly; his mother's contribution was also substantial but was not the sort that would have registered with a small boy who led an outdoors life. Several members of the family have attested to how, in the days before there was a cookery book in every kitchen, the untutored Ada improvised and experimented to great effect. 'She was lovely,' Jean, the older of Stanley's children, said, 'and a terrific cook. There was a fireplace with the oven next to it – you can imagine in the summer how hot it got – and she used to make fantastic meals in this oven.'

The Sunday walks to and from Werrington provided Jack Senior with the perfect opportunity to preach the tenets of his philosophy on fitness. Respiratory exercises were what underpinned everything, in particular standing and taking deep breaths, which was central to early morning PE sessions. Generally one son at a time took part in these supervised sessions, which included a series of physical jerks in addition to the breathing. On the weekend walks Jack would elaborate on his theories. He told Ron on one occasion that different types of breathing were needed at different times. 'He said to me, "When you play sport and are tired you shouldn't take deep breaths. You should go like this . . ."' Ron then demonstrated a series of fast, shallow breaths. 'I thought he was telling just me this but when I started to tell it to Stanley he interrupted me and said, "I'll tell you what he told you – he told you to take short breaths when you were tired." He had told us all the same. He also said never squat because it will hurt your knees.'

All the boys led sporting lives, although none came even close to emulating Stanley. Jack was the one in whom his father invested the greatest hope that the family's boxing tradition would be continued. 'Jack was a good boxer and I watched several of his fights at the Palais de Danse in Hanley,' Stanley said. These were amateur bouts that Jack continued with until his mid-twenties, but he disliked the training and admitted he lacked the driven attitude to sport possessed by his father and Stanley.

The evidence suggests that Jack boxed as long as he did only to please his father. Like Arthur, he preferred athletics to any of his other sporting interests. Stanley remembered that both his older brothers were fine sprinters who frequently brought home medals from athletics meetings. Ron came nearest to following Stanley into a life of professional football although he was always amusingly dismissive of his ability. 'I was on the Blackpool staff when I was fifteen. I was in the A team with Stan Mortensen. I reckon I would have been the greatest player in the world if it hadn't been for one thing: I couldn't kick the ball.'

Stanley was comfortably the outstanding athlete of the family, his ability not simply confined to running fast and playing football. He grew up to be at least competent in other sports, including tennis and golf. Jimmy Vallance, the Stoke City trainer who became Matthews's father-in-law, was a keen golfer and he introduced Stanley to the sport while he was still a teenager. Matthews liked the game so much that, once he joined Stoke, he said he occasionally ignored the club rule that the golf course was out of bounds on Thursdays and Fridays. This was to conserve energy for Saturday's game. 'When the club got wind I was breaking this rule,' Matthews said, 'they soon put a stop to it.'*

He liked cricket, too. He might even have made something of himself in that sport at a time when playing both professional cricket and football was possible. The story goes, though, that the promising young wicketkeeper fluffed his chance to progress when, aged twelve, he walked the four miles to Longton for a schoolboy trial. As he approached the ground he saw all the others in white flannels and, overwhelmed by shyness, fled the scene – and that was that. He also became very proficient at tennis, a game that both his children, particularly his son, would play far better than most.**

Under his father's watchful eye, Matthews had little chance to abandon sprinting as he did cricket. It is unlikely he would have wanted to, anyway. The sessions on the walks to Werrington helped to foster a deep love of running in Stanley. He ran everywhere as a kid, he said. 'I never walked when I could trot and never trotted when I could run flat out.' He took to running around the track at Finney Gardens, a recreation ground near

---

* Vallance's tuition and years of practice helped Matthews achieve a handicap of ten in his late thirties. Whether his handicap went any lower is a matter of some conjecture. It has been written that he played off scratch, which was not the case. A report that appeared in the tribute edition of Stoke's local paper after his death may have been a mite more accurate, but still sounds overdone. It said he could have been a top golf professional, having 'once reached a handicap of two, often playing with Bobby Locke and Henry Cotton during his time in South Africa'.

** Matthews, partnered by Jim Westland, once beat Freddie Steele and Frank Soo in the final of a doubles tournament played among Stoke City players at the home of a friend of a club director. And when the England football team toured Europe in 1938, Matthews won a table tennis competition involving all the players, beating Frank Broome of Aston Villa 21-14 in the final.

Seymour Street. His father came along, too, when he could afford to leave work, and brought with him a stopwatch. He secretly timed his son and established that he was exceptionally quick, as fleet-footed as boys nearly twice his age. The next step was to enter Stanley in the August Bank Holiday races at the Victoria Ground, where there was a 440-yard running track made from brick-red cinder around the outside of the football pitch. These races were a popular feature of the late summer in Stoke, with large crowds milling around stalls that sold toffee apples, candyfloss and sweets for the children. Many of the older spectators turned to the bookmakers lined up by the track as the place to fritter away their money. At senior level, international-class athletes were among those who took part, but betting was not confined to their races.

Stanley dissolved into tears the first time his father took him along, overawed by the prospect of performing in front of so many people. A year later, aged six, he conquered his nerves and, with the help of a generous distance handicap for one so young – forty-five yards in front of the older boys on scratch – came first in the under-fifteen 100 yards. The local paper reported he won by 'many yards' with older brother Jack among those panting in his wake. 'On the time this six-year-old winner accomplished – 11sec – an adult champion could not have beaten him off this mark,' the report added.

According to a story passed down by the family, Stanley's father, acting on the evidence of his stopwatch, to which no one else was privy, had backed him to finish first. With some of his gains he bought two goldfish for his son as a reward, conceivably in a lopsided exchange for the watch that was the race winner's official prize. Stanley ran in the 100 yards for the next eight years, coming first four times, including on his last appearance when he was fourteen and had a scratch handicap.

By this age, though, Stanley no longer dreamed of an Olympic gold medal on the running track.

Chapter 2

'If you play the game of life as you played football this
afternoon your success in life is assured'

By the time he reached his teens, Matthews's obsession was
football, a game that embraced his two great sporting attributes:
exceptional speed over a short distance and heightened foot-eye
coordination.

The latter was not a concept that was talked about in the
1930s and is still not fully understood. The evidence is pretty
convincing, though, that areas of the brain respond to repetitive
activity and can be enlarged or diminished depending on how
much you use them. Research has shown, for example, that
inner-city taxi drivers' grey matter enlarges and adapts to help
them store a detailed mental map of the streets they work. As
a rule, the area that controls the arms and hands is larger than
the one that governs the legs and feet, but in Matthews's case
a predisposition, compulsion even, to dribble a football meant
that over time he transformed his aptitude into an extraordinary
skill. Even Arthur, who, Stanley said, rarely had a good word to
say about his younger brother because 'he found me a bit of a
nuisance', was sufficiently impressed to tell friends admiringly
that 'I had trained the ball to obey me'.

Sport, football in particular, had towered over any academic considerations during Matthews's time at Wellington Road School, which was just around the corner from where he lived. While he described himself as a model pupil who was never the source of any trouble during the nine years he was there from the age of five, he also confessed to studying the clock more attentively than books. He reckoned he could be out of the door almost before the fourth chime marked the end of the school day. No doubt he would have been staggered if he had known then that some sixty-five years later a stained-glass window dedicated to him would be installed at the school, now known as Hanley St Luke's CE Aided Primary. The window has eight panels depicting the various stages of his life from schooldays to retirement.

Ada Matthews would admonish her son for a lack of commitment to his studies. She was understandably unaware that his habit of kicking a paper ball, stone or other object in front of him as he hurried home for tea, bread and jam, wolfed down before heading out to play on a patch of ground known as Meakins' Square, was in fact more relevant than any homework he might have done. One particularly touching story, told by Stanley, about his obsession with practising ball skills concerned the time a septic toe kept him away from school. The frustration of not being allowed to kick a football eventually became too much. When his mother went shopping, leaving him alone, he wrapped his foot in a tea cosy and hopped into the garden to do what he liked doing most. His parents chided him for jeopardising his recovery from what could have developed into a dangerous infection – these were the days before the use of penicillin in everyday medicine – but Matthews claimed that from then on his toe healed rapidly even though it was permanently disfigured.

Disfigurement was also a peril of playing on Meakins' Square, which was right opposite the Matthews home and littered with the sharp-edged detritus from a nearby pottery. Matthews believed that despite the dangers, responsible for a lifelong scar on his brother Jack's knee, he learned invaluable lessons from the endless games that up to forty children at a time would play on their make-believe Wembley. Not only did it help to develop his ball control, it instilled in all of them the sense that a good game of football depended on accepting decisions, which in these games they made themselves. Those who continually argued about the self-imposed rulings were made to feel unwelcome until they changed their attitude or went elsewhere.

Matthews's rapid advance as a footballer came to the attention of the local education authority – and landed the school in trouble. Officials felt his promotion to play for an older age group, while still in an infant class, threatened to impede his academic progress. The headmaster received an instruction that Matthews should return to playing with his peers. When, eventually, he was old enough to play for the school's senior team, Matthews's height was regarded as a greater asset than his ball control and he played at centre-half. But he was encouraged by the school's enlightened games master, Jimmy Slack, to push forward whenever the team fell behind or were so dominant that the defence was underemployed. On one occasion he scored eight times in helping to turn a 2-1 deficit into a 13-2 victory, for which the headmaster, Mr Terry, gave him sixpence; on another he contributed eleven goals to an 18-0 victory.

His speed and goal-scoring prowess were what eventually led Slack to play him on the right wing and it was in this position that he was chosen, aged just fourteen, to play for the North against the South in an England schoolboys' trial at Nuneaton. Evidently he did not, initially, like the isolation of being on the wing but he made enough of an impression to be selected in this position for England against the Rest at Kettering Town's Rockingham Road ground on Saturday 6 April 1929. This match, played in warm sunshine, attracted a record crowd for a schoolboy trial of more than 4,000. Matthews responded with a conspicuous performance in a 4-2 victory. His contributions included the first goal after four minutes, when he cut in from the right to put away a cross supplied by West Ham's A. G. Hooper, playing on the opposite wing, and a near miss in the sixteenth minute when he hooked a ball on to a post. He received praise for being, with Hooper, the main threat. The Rest's two goals were scored by Ted Fenton, who went on to play for and manage West Ham. One other feature of the game was commented on by the referee, Captain Linnitt. He noted that 'not a single foul was committed all afternoon'.

After such a performance, Matthews's inclusion in the schools international against Wales at Dean Park, Bournemouth, two weeks later cannot have been a great surprise. Even so, hearing confirmation that he had been picked to wear the England shirt in an international match for the first time gave him almost as big a thrill as any subsequent honour. Years later he recalled the mixture of shock and mind-spinning excitement that overcame him when his headmaster passed on the news. The trip to Bournemouth entailed his first visit to London and his first stay in a hotel. Taking in the size and grandeur of the buildings in the capital was another overwhelming experience. Being waited on by grown-ups in the hotel produced more confusion.

Wales turned the match into an overseas trip by taking a ferry across the Bristol Channel to Weston-super-Mare before travelling on to Bournemouth. It proved a smoother passage than England experienced in the build-up to the game. On the eve of the match, news reached the Grand Hotel, where the England team were staying, that the West Ham players Fenton and Hooper, who had done well in the trial at Kettering, had been in contact with smallpox suspects. The disease was now a rarity in Britain, with endemic cases close to being wiped out, but the unfortunate Fenton and Hooper had to be withdrawn from the team.

One footballer's misfortune is invariably another's big

opportunity and on this occasion Cyril Dean was the beneficiary. A local player disappointed not to make the original selection, Dean came into the side and did not waste the chance to make an impression in England's three-goal win. Matthews caught the eye only occasionally. His main contribution was combining with Dean to lay on the first goal for the centre-forward, Jack Smith of Huddersfield. The second goal was controversial. The visitors claimed it should have been disallowed because the ball struck the higher of two crossbars, which should have meant a goal kick. The lower bar, fitted to reduce the goal to schoolboy size, was the one that counted, but play continued and Dean scored from the rebound.

The occasion also introduced Matthews to the sort of peripheral activities that were part of playing international football. The agenda included a tour of the town and lunch and dinner at the Town Hall, where the deputy mayor greeted the teams. A local paper quoted one of Matthews's teammates as saying: 'Well, we're having a jolly time – but, golly, fancy going to lunch with the deputy-mayor.' The speeches also rang with folksy sentiment. An after-dinner speaker told his young audience: 'If you play the game of life as you played football this afternoon your success in life is assured.'

Matthews received his first England cap, made from red silk with a gold tassel, but it was the only one he collected as a schoolboy. After his so-so performance in Bournemouth, he was not picked for the next match against Scotland schools at Hampden Park. He had not known such rejection before and said that the disappointment he felt was immense.

The first major change brought about by Matthews's facility for playing football was an end to the idea that he might become a bricklayer. His father had found Stanley work with a builder friend, who took him on as an apprentice when he left school in 1929 at fourteen. 'It was hard work but I enjoyed it,' Stanley said. He never lost his fascination for the trade, claiming he always regarded pointing brickwork as his fallback profession, a task about as far removed as it is possible to imagine from the nimble-footed trade that would give his life such content.*

Having instigated the idea of his son entering the building trade, Jack Matthews then took the decision that he should abandon it, reckoning it was foolish for Stanley to risk injury on a building site so close to turning fifteen, the age at which he could join the staff of a club. 'Health and fitness come first. This work will kill you,' he told him. While he waited for his fifteenth birthday, Stanley filled his time subjecting himself to the fitness regime devised for him by his father and playing for Stoke St Peter's, a club that supplied Stoke City with a number of players.

The decision to put aside one set of muddy boots for another could not have been difficult, despite Stanley's professed liking for manual labour. His prospects of making a decent living as a professional footballer were by now pretty obvious. His selection for England schoolboys had given substance to local tittle-tattle about his ability. Around the time of his appearance in the schools match against Wales, Stoke City invited him to join in training sessions at their Victoria Ground where he took part in what the local paper called 'private trials'. Simultaneously, Tom Mather, who was halfway through his twelve years as City manager, started to pay regular visits to Jack Matthews's barber's shop.

Not unusually for a manager in those days, Mather, from Chorley, Lancashire, where he was born in 1888, had an administrative rather than a playing background in football, having been assistant secretary at Manchester City and then

---

* Although he unquestionably enjoyed certain aspects of his recognition, Matthews retained a strong residual yearning for the sort of uncomplicated life led by those close to him during childhood. A first-team colleague at Stoke told of sitting next to Matthews, by now a national figure, in first class on a train. Matthews said he had been watching a porter putting suitcases in a compartment, sweeping the platform, going off to have a smoke. Arguably the world's greatest footballer then turned and said: 'There's something in that normal life, isn't there.'

Bolton Wanderers. Bolton was where, notionally at least, he started out as a manager. Appointed at the start of the First World War, he was called up by the Royal Navy almost immediately and remained manager in name only until 1919. He then went to Southend United where in 1923 he achieved the unflattering distinction of being the first manager to be sacked by the club.

After these two false starts in management, Mather served Stoke well. He still looked more bureaucrat than football club manager, although, again, this was not uncommon in the 1930s. He rarely left his house without first donning a bowler hat. When he entered Jack Matthews's shop he would put aside the bowler for a trim or shave before turning to the real reason he was there, to make the case for young Stanley joining the club. Mather was well aware that Port Vale were also interested in the local lad. At that time Vale still played at the Old Recreation Ground in Hanley, which was even closer to Seymour Street than the Victoria Ground, and were Stanley's initial preference. As a small boy he regularly attended their home matches. Bob Connelly was his favourite player, a Scottish centre-half who was one of those sturdy, pragmatic types whose lives were soon to be tormented by the young Matthews. Despite their different styles, Stanley had an instinctive affinity with Connelly's devotion to the game and the club. 'He carried them on his shoulders for many years,' Stanley said admiringly.*

There was no question that anyone but Jack Matthews would have the final say in which club his son joined. He responded cautiously – brusquely, even – to Mather's preliminary offers. He was far too canny to reveal his preference early on, if indeed he had one. He recognised that Port Vale, who were on the brink of returning to the Second Division from the Third Division North as the 1929–30 season unwound, had their attractions.

---

* Connelly's commitment was indeed impressive. Between January 1927 and November 1929 he did not miss one of a sequence of 127 matches.

Not least Stanley's support for the club, which would survive his decision not to join them.

In the final account Jack Matthews gave high marks to the solicitous way in which Mather had pursued his son's services and so it was that he bestowed Stanley on Division Two side Stoke City FC. With apprenticeships not being introduced until the 1960s, Matthews's employment in the first instance was under a loose arrangement whereby he would work as an office boy while being given time to develop his football. This was agreed without Stanley's knowledge and news of his engagement by Stoke ostensibly to do a clerical job was broken to him by Mather when he visited Seymour Street on the eve of his fifteenth birthday.

Matthews also did menial tasks such as cleaning the dressing rooms. On match days he would help the visiting team carry kit from their bus and run water for the post-match baths. Any sign of familiarity or cockiness by an apprentice, however slight, was liable to be punished by senior players, who would have learned to their own costs during national service the perils of being too confident. On one occasion Matthews's reward for having the temerity to say 'Good morning' to the first team was to be thrown into a bath fully clothed. On another, playing in a match while still a junior, he was told by a grizzled old pro that he had a big head after he beat the full-back, rounded the keeper and then side-footed his shot against a post. 'Young players were not expected to try to be clever,' Matthews said. He was paid no more than a pittance for doing chores in Mather's office and there was only a slight improvement after he started playing regularly in the reserves in 1931, having signed as an amateur for Stoke on Saturday 27 September 1930. His older teammates boosted the meagre earnings he received for his office work by giving him two shillings from their £1 bonus whenever they won. This minimal remuneration early on prepared him for the reality that players of his generation could not expect to gather great riches from playing professional football. Throughout his long career Matthews never earned more from playing in the Football League than a reasonable living wage.

Club boardrooms in the 1930s had priorities other than making players rich. Self-interest may have been one but the money simply did not exist in the game to make anyone wealthy. Football was an entertainment industry with working men representing the vast majority of the fanbase. Admission charges had to be pegged at levels they could afford and this remained the case well after the Second World War.* Even with a maximum wage, not much was left over after paying backroom staff and meeting the general expenses of running a club.**

The only thing that could be said for what players received was that they would not have earned nearly as much in any other job. Football's maximum wage in the mid-1930s meant players could earn £386 a year, not quite such bad money when you consider skilled workers were lucky if they earned £200 over the same period. Matthews recognised he was better off than the vast majority of those he lived among in his early pro days. 'Football cushioned me against the stark miseries of the depression,' he said. 'I earned five or six pounds a week at a time when an unemployed man with a wife and children to support was drawing less than thirty shillings on the dole.'

His father's reaction to the small amount his son earned as an amateur at Stoke underlined his attitude that this was precisely what a working-class lad should expect. 'He would not let me

---

* Receipts for an FA Cup tie at the start of Blackpool's 1953 FA Cup run, when they played Sheffield Wednesday at Hillsborough, were £7,700 for a gate of more than 60,000.

** This is not to say the game's management always acted honourably when it came to wages. After the First World War, the maximum in a player's weekly pay packet was £10. When in 1920 strike action was threatened after the Football League proposed reducing this to £9, a number of players, fearful of the damage withholding their labour might do to their futures, withdrew from the Association Footballers' Union. Not long after this the League drove the wage down still further to £8, where it remained for many years.

handle my own pocket money,' he said, 'and refused me money for my fares.' Quite apart from the cost, Jack Matthews reasoned, taking a bus denied his son the physical benefit of walking the two miles between Hanley and the Victoria Ground four times a day. The journeys included his return home to Seymour Street for lunch. His mother occasionally took pity when the weather was bad and slipped Stanley the bus fare behind her husband's back. 'She was a wonderful ally,' he said. But he said also that although he thought his father was hard with him he was grateful for his lessons in thrift.

Matthews made two appearances in the reserves while he was fifteen. The first of these, against Burnley reserves at the Victoria Ground on the day he signed as an amateur, would be 'forever green' in his memory. He had been surprised and excited to see his name on the team sheet that was pinned to the noticeboard two days earlier. He was apprehensive, too, but acquitted himself well in his first proper examination in the adult game. He liked to recall particularly that he provided the pass from the right wing from which the former miner Joe Mawson scored the first goal in Stoke's 2-1 win. The *Evening Sentinel*, the local newspaper, reported that Matthews had excited the crowd with 'some pretty movements', while suggesting that Stoke would have won the Central League match more comfortably with better finishing by the inside-forwards.

Jimmy Vallance was the greatest influence on Stanley's life in his early days at Stoke. Within a few years Matthews would become a member of the Vallance family, after he formed an ultimately ill-starred alliance with the trainer's daughter. The more immediate impact the disciplinarian Scot had on him was how he conducted himself. Jack Matthews had cultivated in his son a lifestyle that was bordering on ascetic and Vallance did nothing to persuade Stanley that forsaking this would bring any rewards. Whether it was in directing

Matthews to scrub the dressing rooms or in overseeing the players' training and exercise, Vallance was a man who preached extreme rigour.

Vallance had played for Scotland's oldest football club, Queen's Park between 1906 and 1908. He married the twenty-one-year-old Elizabeth Wilson when he was twenty-six and employed as a postman.* Elizabeth Hall Vallance, the future Mrs (later Lady) Betty Matthews, was born the following year.** He had been a reasonably successful athlete, winning 'lots of silverware' and passing on his athlete's genes to his daughter, according to a family member. He was a keen golfer who would eventually give up working in football to become manager of the course at the club near Glasgow where his daughter and Stanley married. By the time he arrived in England in 1920 to start his fifteen years as Stoke City trainer, Jimmy Vallance had an immeasurably wider horizon than Stanley Matthews. When their paths eventually crossed, Vallance started the process of unravelling his young charge's homespun outlook.

Matthews always acknowledged that Stoke had in Vallance a trainer who was a little different from the archetype of the day, the kind who would routinely order players to run laps of the ground before joining them for a few deep drags on a Woodbine. Vallance, Matthews said, was serious about fitness and would tailor routines for individual players, which was particularly relevant to Matthews. He also introduced a lot of ball work into practice, which, bizarrely, was quite a novel idea. 'I was happy to

---

* Some sources have stated that Vallance was the son of Tom Vallance, the first captain of Glasgow Rangers Football Club. This is an error based, almost certainly, on the coincidence that two marriages took place in Glasgow in the first half of the twentieth century between a James Vallance and an Elizabeth Wilson. The second was the one that involved Tom Vallance's son. It was held in 1930, by which time Stanley Matthews's future father-in-law would have been married for some years. Jimmy Vallance, the man who became the Stoke City trainer, was from the Dennistoun district of Glasgow.

** Some years afterwards the Vallances had a son, Tommy, a useful footballer who spent six years from 1947 at Arsenal. Here his main role was filling in on the left wing for Denis Compton, of cricket fame.

be at a club that didn't have a lackadaisical attitude to training,' Matthews said.

Vallance could hardly have been a better mentor for Matthews, whose progress was such that at sixteen he played twenty-two games for the reserves, steadily enhancing his reputation.

This promising start meant that the pressure Mather felt under was increased as the time approached to sign Matthews as a pro. 'Never have I known more anxious days than those preceding the lad's seventeenth birthday,' he said. He resumed his regular visits to the Market Street barber's shop and put in place what he called 'a plan of campaign to repel invaders'. 'I knew, and far too many other managers knew, that Stan was no ordinary footballer,' he said. 'It was obvious he was going to become a genius.'

Huddersfield made the only known firm offer, for £1,000, to prise Matthews from Stoke in the days before his birthday. Others took a stealthier approach. Port Vale remained interested and Birmingham and Aston Villa were among those strongly suspected of casting blandishments Jack Matthews's way.

Mather's plan of campaign included calling up 'spotters' who would pass on information about cars seen in the town with Birmingham number plates and posting 'sentries' in Seymour Street. In addition Arthur Sherwin, the Stoke chairman, a local businessman who would always maintain he was the real mover behind securing Matthews for the club, took an active role in manoeuvres. His contribution at this point was to station himself in a window seat in a pub from where he could keep an eye on visitors to the barber's shop.

The operation to sign Stanley Matthews as a Stoke City player ended at 10.30 on the morning of his seventeenth birthday, Monday 1 February 1932. Tom Mather said he went to the barber's shop in Market Street, where Stanley was waiting with his father. 'I wished Stan many happy returns and got him to sign on the dotted line.'

Chapter 3

'Matthews used his feet like a magician does his hands'

Matthews received a £10 signing-on fee, a sum that made up the first deposit in a savings account that his father insisted he open. Jack Matthews also directed his son to give half his weekly wage, £5 during the football season and £3 in the summer, to his mother and put the other half in his new account. Even his £1 win bonus was subject to the 50 per cent investment rule. Stanley confessed to overlooking this on occasions, keeping ten shillings for himself and handing ten shillings to Ada, who happily colluded in the deviation from her husband's strict code of fiscal management.

The security of still living at home and the fact that he had done office work at the club and played in the reserves when he was an amateur meant Matthews settled in quickly at the start of his professional career. Even so, he was subject to the rituals of being a junior member of a playing staff whose average age was in the mid-twenties. This involved nothing too sophisticated, mostly fully clothed duckings in the communal bath that had already been his lot when he first arrived at the Victoria Ground.

His style of play was, by now, well established, as was his appetite for training. He achieved longevity in his career in large part by supplementing natural athleticism with an obsessive

and unprecedented attention to staying fit.* He had developed
at a young age the habit of practising at times of the day – early
in the morning or late afternoon – when most players were
otherwise engaged. He paid particular attention to basic fitness
and improving his ball skills, for which, even when he was still
playing for the reserves, he knew he had a rare gift.** He devised
a number of routines, such as repeatedly dribbling around
a series of objects spaced in line, all the time keeping the ball
close. At the same time he perfected the exaggerated body lean
that also became an important part of his strategy for confusing
an opponent.

Matthews said it was during the reserve matches right at the
start of his career, one in particular against Manchester City,
that he devised his own way of beating full-backs. Rather than
the traditional method of waiting for the defender to come at
him, he decided to see what happened if he took the initiative
by making straight for his opponent at speed. He would drop
back, receive the pass to his feet in what would become the
most controversial part of his game and then run arrow
straight at his marker. This way he was already controlling the
situation before he brought the prodigious sideways tilt into
play that defenders felt compelled to try to copy, invariably
with disastrous consequences.

Like George Best and Ryan Giggs of later generations,
Matthews's legs were long in proportion to his upper body and

---

* To a certain extent he prospered because his physical conditioning was so superior to that
of his contemporaries and it is unlikely he would have lasted quite as long in the modern
era in which all leading players have to be in peak condition to maintain their status. But
it is perfectly reasonable to suppose that even today he would have played professionally
into his forties.

** Arnold Bennett had foreseen these skills with uncanny prescience in his 1910 novel *The
Card*. In a passage about a match between two Stoke sides which played in the League,
Bennett wrote: 'Dribbling tactics had been killed for ever, years before, by Preston North
End, who invented the "passing" game.' This, though, was about to change. Bennett
introduced a newly signed forward called Callear who dribbled the length of the field to
score the winning goal with a miraculous shot.

the small, rugged full-backs of his day were likely to topple over – some did – if they tried to sway with him. 'He'd murder full-backs because in those days they were built for stamina and strength, not speed,' Derek Hodgson said. 'Whether he would be as effective in the present game where it's one-touch, two-touch at most, I'm not so sure.'

Ron Matthews, who watched his brother play many times, said: 'Most players take the ball away from an opponent. Stanley never did. He took it to the opponent deliberately, and he took it so close to him it was extraordinary. I once asked him why he did it and he said: "I don't know. I just do it because I want to beat them." Opponents were looking at the ball but he still managed to get so close. How was he allowed to do this? I often wonder whether there's such a thing as body hypnosis because it didn't go on for one match with Stanley but for more than twenty-five years. His opponents knew what he was going to do but seemed powerless to stop him.'

He also spoke about his brother's way of creating even more disarray by gazing straight ahead as he ran with the ball. 'When he took the ball to an opponent he looked at the man's chest or face. He might look down after he had beaten the man but not just before he beat him.' It was the pickpocket's art. Look the man in the face while helping yourself to the wallet in his jacket pocket.

The many quotable lines in the poem on Matthews by the English writer Alan Ross include these:

> 'The greatest of all time,' *meraviglioso*, Matthews –
> Stoke City, Blackpool and England.
> Expressionless enchanter, weaving as on strings
> Conceptual patterns to a private music, heard
> Only by him . . .

J. P. W. Mallalieu, the Labour MP and Huddersfield Town director who had been president of the Oxford Union in 1930, conjured a rather different image: 'Have you ever watched a dragon-fly, how it hovers in one spot with its wings vibrating and then apparently, without changing gear, darts away at top speed? Many times I have seen Matthews . . . his whole body vibrating, while his opponent watched. Suddenly Matthews has made his dart to the right, and his opponent has darted with him. It is only seconds later that we and his opponent see that Matthews has in fact darted to the left.'

A remarkable insight provided by Don Ratcliffe, the popular 'Ratter', a left-winger who was at Stoke when Matthews returned to the club in 1961, expanded on why Matthews's body movement was key to his success as a dribbler. It was, he said, because 'when Stan was working the ball he never touched it. He used to move his feet around it, except when helping it on its way. He used his feet like a magician does his hands.' Matthews himself spoke about the importance to his art of 'an easy feinting trick and a natural swerve'. He said he would make a defender run in the wrong direction by 'turning my right foot in, and causing him to believe I am going to turn to his right . . . but without stopping I push the ball forward with my left instep'. 'He couldn't balance a ball, you know,' Ratcliffe said. 'Give me a ball and I can keep it up all day, bouncing it off my feet. Stan couldn't do that. We used to be messing about with the ball and he'd come across, take it off us, put it on the floor and put his foot on it. And he'd say, "That's where you want the ball." He disapproved of keepy-uppy. He didn't like it because he couldn't do it.'

From very early on in his career Matthews was uncom-promising in reserving the right to manage as he saw fit this rare talent for controlling and manipulating a football while moving at speed. The centre-forward John Ritchie, who joined Stoke City in the early 1960s, recalled being taken aside by Matthews, who was well into his forties and coming to the end of his playing days. With avuncular firmness, Matthews issued a directive to the young recruit that he had been passing on for years: 'Son, do not pass the ball in front of me, always pass it to my feet.'

Matthews had been a professional for less than six weeks when, aged seventeen years and forty-seven days, he played his first game in the Football League for Stoke, away to Bury on 19 March 1932. He spun a yarn in his autobiography that he feared he had failed to make any of the teams that Saturday. When the selections were posted on the club noticeboard on the Thursday, he said, he looked at the first-team selection only after scanning all the other sides Stoke were putting out. In fact he was brought into the side on the eve of the match when Bobby Liddle, the regular right-winger, was ruled out with an eye injury suffered the previous weekend against Leeds.

The measly, capped wages at least meant clubs could afford big playing staffs and, with close to forty pros on their books, Stoke had plenty of experience to fill the vacancies left by late-season injuries. Clearly Matthews had been doing well enough in the reserves to be given this early opportunity. His inclusion confirmed Mather was pleased with his progress.

Teams mostly travelled by train then and Matthews, whose memory of that first League appearance remained vivid throughout his life, recalled the change at Manchester's old London Road station on the way to Bury. Having arrived in the town of the host team, the players would often walk from the station to the ground like a classroom of schoolboys with Tom Mather at the head of the crocodile and Jimmy Vallance at the tail.

One of Vallance's duties, Matthews said, was to watch out for players nipping out of line for some refreshment in a pub along the route. The drinking culture was as strong then as it remained for the rest of the century, although the saloon bar and best bitter were as refined as it got. In Stoke, Matthews reckoned,

Mather had all the publicans on a retainer to report players who went on drinking sprees. It was the only explanation for miscreants being summoned to his office whenever they broke the regulations on imbibing, which during the season allowed alcohol consumption only on special occasions. Every player had a rulebook setting out these and other strictures.

Away fixtures that involved overnight stays at hotels severely tested the management's enforcement of their alcohol ban. Matthews, a non-drinker, was privy to one breach of this, when the team were playing Plymouth. The players congregated in the room he was sharing with a teammate for a card school. Beers had been smuggled past Vallance, who used to keep guard by the back door for just such a flouting of discipline. Matthews, feigning sleep, was aware of the players, without bottle openers or glasses, breaking the tops off and pouring the beer into a chamber pot, which was then passed around as a communal drinking vessel. Three or four of the players did not make it back to their rooms, sleeping off the effects of the drink on Matthews's floor, where Vallance found them in the morning.

History does not recount whether the Stoke first team walked from the station to Bury's ground, Gigg Lane, on that March day in 1932. What is recorded is that it was a benign afternoon on which 'about 7,000 spectators paid for admission' to be unwitting witnesses to a major occasion in one of football's great careers.

What was also perfectly apparent on the day was that the match was important for both teams' chances of promotion from the Second Division. The game's only goal came right at the end of the match. Walter Bussey hoofed the ball out of defence for the visitors and Tommy Mills, the Bury goalkeeper, raced out of his area to try to reach it before Stoke's galloping outside-left, Tim Maloney. Caught out by the bounce, Mills was forced to head the ball to avoid being penalised. He succeeded only in giving possession to Maloney who was left with 'an unchallenged path to goal'. Moments later the final whistle blew. Stoke, who had lost 3-0 at Bury in the FA Cup a month earlier, had avenged that defeat.* The opposing local newspapers reacted to the result with time-honoured partiality. According to the *Bury Times*, Stoke were 'much the inferior side on the afternoon's showing'; Stoke's *Evening Sentinel* described it as 'a victory which Stoke deserved'. Both agreed, though, that the goal was hardly a masterpiece of construction. Matthews said that in his many years as a professional player he never again saw a goalkeeper head the ball.

Matthews's contribution to the match appears to have been consequential if not startling. The *Evening Sentinel* based its judgement that it was a fair result on the implied compliment to Matthews that Stoke, having been on the defensive for most of the first half, took command of proceedings 'when they realised the value of their wingmen'. For his part, Matthews said many years later that what really stayed with him from the game at Bury was not so much anything he did, but the physicality of the play compared to what he had experienced previously. He commented on the shirt pulling, obstruction and players using their arms aggressively, all things he had come across but never on such a systematic scale.

A week after the match at Bury, Matthews played his only other first-team game of the 1931–2 season, making his Football League debut at the Victoria Ground in a 2-0 win over Barnsley. Again, what light he cast on the match was perceptible but not dazzling. He started on the right wing with Liddle out of position on the left. The pair switched wings in the second half and it was while playing on the left that Matthews, with a header, came close to laying on his first Football League goal. Joe Mawson, an

---

* The result meant Stoke moved up to third in the table, overtaking Bury who dropped to sixth, both having played thirty-three of their forty-two matches. Stoke, who had not played in the First Division since the 1922–3 season, would finish the season still in third, two points behind runners-up Leeds United, who were promoted with the division winners, Wolves.

ex-miner who was Stoke's top scorer that season, put the ball in the net but was offside.

The *Evening Sentinel*'s preview of the 1932–3 season printed potted biographies of all the Stoke players, including: 'Matthews. S. (outside-right), born in Hanley, 5ft. 9in, 10st. 5lb. Schoolboy international, and afterwards given post on club staff in order to "nurse" his ability. Established himself as reserve right-winger last season and became full-time professional. Is still only seventeen, and justifying high hopes.' The accompanying article said that 'the supporter is entitled to wonder whether, for instance, seventeen-year-old Stanley Matthews will reveal all the talent there is in him and jump into the limelight, all in a few months. He is becoming faster in action under full-time training, and in the later games of last season and the trial games of this, he rarely wasted a ball.'

Injuries to Liddle and Harry Davies early in 1933 produced the openings for Matthews to push for his routine inclusion in the Stoke first team. He played only three times before Christmas, including in September when his first League match in London, a Monday night game on a rain-sodden pitch at Millwall, ended goalless. With Liddle continuing to perform consistently well on the right wing as Stoke built convincingly towards winning the Division Two title, something they had never previously done, Matthews was still consigned mostly to the reserves. But his call-up for the match at Oldham, after Liddle was injured in an FA Cup tie, and then for a home game against Bradford, this time after Davies was hurt, gave him the chance to show how quickly he had matured as a player since his debut season. Stoke won both matches 4-0 with Matthews's performance on the wing against Bradford particularly eye-catching. What, though, was really significant, in terms of Matthews's future, was that for the Bradford game the manager brought back Liddle, but played him in Davies's inside-left position.

If a single performance can be identified as the one when

Matthews 'jumped into the limelight' it was this game against Bradford. The dreadful conditions made it even more admirable. With snow piled up around the Victoria Ground and much of the action taking place in a near blizzard, Matthews gave a display that earned him his first rave review from the local paper: 'Matthews was in sparkling form on the Stoke right wing every time he was in possession, and he never failed to beat a man or two and put in a good centre, giving the Bradford defenders several anxious periods.' Mather was now persuaded to continue with Matthews on the right wing and Liddle at inside left.

Arthur Sherwin, the Stoke chairman, had already started to boast publicly about the young player – not least because he felt Matthews's rapid transition from star-dusted tyro to authentically good player reflected well on him for having sought his signature so tirelessly. After the match at Oldham, Sherwin told those in the boardroom who would listen: 'If certain players are worth £10,000 at twenty-seven or twenty-eight years of age, Matthews is worth £20,000 today at eighteen.' And this was at a time when the record transfer fee in Britain was the £10,890 Arsenal paid Bolton for David Jack, aged twenty-nine, in 1928.

Two weeks after the Bradford game Matthews rewarded the manager's faith in him with his first League goal in what was an away game even though the venue was closer to his home than Stoke's Victoria Ground. Port Vale, the club Matthews supported as a young boy, played on the site now occupied by the Potteries Shopping Centre and it was here, after thirty-two minutes of the local derby, that Matthews scored Stoke's second in a 3-1 win. He killed the ball after it reached him from a goalmouth melee and struck it hard – 'fast and true', the local scribe reported – along the ground from a tight angle.

Come the spring, Stoke had clinched the Second Division title with a point more than Tottenham Hotspur and with Matthews's fifteen League appearances out of forty-two qualifying him for a championship winner's medal. He would not play as few for them again in a complete season until he rejoined the club and was into his forties.

One of the more improbable statistics of the many Matthews generated was that in the twenty-nine seasons in which he appeared in Football League and/or FA Cup matches he scored more goals in the third of these seasons, 1933–4, than any other. And this despite the fact he was still only eighteen at the start of his first season in the top division and hardly played at all before Christmas. He ended up with fifteen goals, eleven from his twenty-nine League appearances and four from as many FA Cup matches. He could be a bit tetchy about this, particularly after Freddie Steele appeared on the scene at Stoke with a rush of goals that threatened to elevate him above Matthews as the crowd's favourite. 'Yeah, anyone can score goals', Matthews said, 'it's making them that's the secret.' Another time, when he reflected on the goalscoring of his England confrere Tom Finney – the forward with whom Matthews has been endlessly compared – he made the startling claim that Finney's more prolific scoring record did not bother him because: 'I didn't enjoy scoring goals.' He said he gained more satisfaction from creating them for others. He even suggested that he changed his style with the specific aim of being a more potent goal provider than producer.

Never again would Matthews score goals more regularly than he did from late December 1933 until the end of the season. Taking his chance at inside-right to start with, before switching to the right wing when the fragile Liddle again succumbed to injury, Matthews averaged close to a goal a match over a stretch of several weeks. He had made an inauspicious start as a First Division player when he featured in a 4-1 defeat at Sunderland's Roker Park in early September – 'Matthews usually worked to advantage when in possession but hardly looked like a match winner' – but he benefited from the extended run when recalled to the side in the depths of winter.

The consistently high quality of his play during this run

was what established him as the first-choice outside-right and projected him to the brink of national selection at a speed that may have surprised even Sherwin. One thing his club chairman had correctly foretold, though, was the interest of bigger teams in Matthews. By the time a dynamic FA Cup run ended in early March 1934 in a 1-0 quarter-final defeat at Manchester City, watched by 84,569, rumours were circulating in the town that Stoke would soon cash in their Matthews chip.

Mather, in the best tradition of managers down the ages, warned their chairman about parting with a precious asset. He issued a 'Not for sale' ultimatum and had the following conversation with a local reporter – Reporter: 'Will you part with Matthews?'; Mather: 'Not a chance.'; Reporter: 'Not even for the £12,000 that Chelsea are going to offer?'; Mather: 'Not even for that.'; Reporter: 'Not even for the £15,000 Arsenal are going to offer?'; Mather: 'Not for any sum any club in the game might offer.'

Accompanying the transfer talk was heightened speculation that Matthews would soon be called on by England. This possibility became a near certainty when on 12 March, less than six weeks after his nineteenth birthday, he was picked for the Rest against England in a trial to take place in nine days' time at Roker Park. The result of the match, 7-1 to the Rest, with Matthews and Raich Carter, the outside- and inside-rights, being praised for their performances, seemed to seal Matthews's selection for the match against Scotland coming up in less than a month. 'Not a single member of the England team could be considered a success,' *The Times* reported, '. . . [while] Matthews was the best of the Rest's forwards.' Charles Buchan said: 'The discovery of the match was the right-wing pair. Matthews exhibited delightful ball control and played with such thoughtful accuracy I think he will be England's outside-right for some years to come.'

His disappointment was huge, then, when the selectors preferred the more experienced winger Sammy Crooks of

Derby County for the Scotland match and the summer tour to Hungary and Czechoslovakia. Crooks, one of seventeen children, was another of the many of this era who had escaped the coal mines of the North-East to play professional football.

Stoke City really began to benefit from Matthews's presence in the 1934–5 season, when he played in thirty-six of the club's forty-two First Division matches. At the beginning of the decade the club's average attendance had been 11,500. Now, with Matthews's bravura displays exciting a local population unused to being spoilt for thrills, the figure was climbing fast to more than double this. On Monday 27 August 1934 Matthews scored four times in an 8-1 win over Leeds United at the Victoria Ground in front of a crowd of 24,555. The following Saturday 29,642 watched the home fixture against Birmingham. They witnessed another command performance by Matthews in a 2-0 victory. Then, in Belfast in mid-September, he played brilliantly, including scoring a goal, for the Football League in a 6-1 win over the Irish League. 'There is probably no cleverer exponent of ball control than Matthews,' one correspondent wrote, 'and there are few who can centre so accurately or hook the ball in so strongly with his right foot from the touchline.'

At the end of October, after twelve matches and with Matthews's form unflaggingly excellent, Stoke went to the top of the First Division. It was the first time in the club's history they had led the League with a season properly under way. A front-page story in the local evening paper on the day Stoke went top, Saturday 27 October 1934, opened with an eight-word intro: 'Stoke City are leaders of the First Division!' The following Monday the paper forwent the exclamation mark but was still singing in excelsis: 'For the first time in their history Stoke City are at the top of the First Division. And they have played only five games out of the twelve at home.

'It has taken a long time to achieve that position, for Stoke can claim to be the oldest football club in the First Division [founded 1863]. The club that has had more ups and downs than any is now definitely "up".

The 2-0 away victory over Chelsea that carried Stoke to first place represented another club record, an unprecedented win at Stamford Bridge. Two players stood out for the visitors: the stalwart defender Bob McGrory and Matthews. McGrory, a Scot who was soon to become Stoke's manager, with profound consequences for Matthews, had served the club as a player since 1921 and had just had his forty-third birthday. He was, above all else, rugged, with a face that looked like the work of a stonemason. He played that day, reported Arthur Simmons in the *Daily Express*, despite having a boil the size of a fist on his neck. Simmons passed on 'salaams' to McGrory, not only for his pluck, but for 'still being able to fool forwards' in his forties.

The same reporter reserved his greatest praise for Matthews, who was the architect of both Stoke's goals: 'Matthews is one of those born players who make close and effective ball control look simple. He is all for economy of effort. Matthews never allowed the presence of a he-man back like McAuley – bang away ball-thumper – to worry him. Matthews has poise.' Bob McAuley was Chelsea's answer to McGrory: a Scottish defender and guardian of that tradition, still not extinguished, that football's main purpose is as an outlet for manliness.

Stoke stood atop the First Division, ahead of Arsenal and Sunderland, with seventeen points from eight wins and a draw – wins were worth two points – out of a possible twenty-four. Vulnerability was evident, though, in their goals for and against, twenty-eight to fifteen, which pointed to a team rather better at attacking than defending. This was borne out a week later when the attack misfired and Sunderland, visitors to the Victoria Ground, knocked Stoke from the summit by scoring three unanswered goals. By the end of the season Stoke had fallen back to tenth in the table. But the club were probably a greater force now than they had ever been. The board of directors issued a self-congratulatory statement trumpeting a net profit of £3,900. Considering they had just spent £4,628 on ground improvements, it was a time of previously unknown plenty.

Chapter 4

'Behind the gentleness was the steel'

Matthews's contribution to Stoke's rise was rewarded on Monday 24 September 1934 when he was picked to play for England, making him the club's first player to be summoned for a full international for more than thirty years. Given the expectation of an earlier call-up, and now with more than fifty League appearances to his name, this might have seemed overdue recognition, but he was still four months short of his twentieth birthday. His debut international would be the match against Wales at Ninian Park, Cardiff, the following Saturday.

The team to play Wales was selected by the thirteen members of the Football Association's international selection committee at their headquarters in central London. One F. W. Rinder had been nominated as the 'member in charge' for the match. Not until Alf Ramsey took over in 1962 were selectorial duties ceded to the manager. Even with the appointment of England's first full-time manager, Walter Winterbottom, in 1947, the selection committee continued to choose the team, much to Winterbottom's frustration.

Winterbottom reckoned England were almost twenty years behind the other footballing countries when they first appointed a full-time manager. Speaking from his own experience, he cast a fascinating light on the crude science that governed selection, which would have been much the same when Matthews was chosen for the first time: 'The chairman would say, "Come on, gentlemen, we've got to pick the team now. Nominations for goalkeeper . . ."' They would choose two players for each position, one of whom would be the reserve. Once, when the selection was all over, Winterbottom said to them, '"Do you mind if I ask you a question? How many of you have seen the two goalies play?" And, you know, none of them had.' Selections could be based on regional preferences, or as a reward for the loyalty of club players. Leslie Compton fitted this latter category, a fringe player who was picked in recognition of his service to Arsenal. All these interests were against the real business of forming a truly strong international side.

Matthews's performance for the Rest in the trial at Roker Park the previous March, and his influential role in the run that took Stoke to the top of the First Division, made it hard even for partisan selectors to ignore him for the match against Wales. The minutes of the meeting showed the continuing rigid adherence to the 2-3-5 'pyramid' line-up that had remained virtually unaltered in Britain since the 1890s, while other parts of the world, notably some South American nations and the so-called Danube countries in Central Europe, experimented with more fluid formations. The minutes recorded: 'The following team was selected Goal: Hibbs (Birmingham). Right Back: Cooper (Derby County). Left Back: Hapgood (Arsenal). Right Half-Back: Britton (Everton). Centre Half-Back: Barker (Derby County). Left Half-Back: Bray (Manchester City). Outside Right: Matthews (Stoke City). Inside Right: Bowden (Arsenal). Centre Forward: Tilson (Manchester City). Inside Left: Westwood (Bolton Wanderers). Outside Left: Brook (Manchester City).'

The highlight of Matthews's first match for England was his goal – the third in a 4-0 victory – at the start of the second half. Ray Bowden provided the pass from which, *The Times* reported, Matthews 'found an opening very cleverly and his shot completely beat John'. Up until a recent move to Preston North End, Roy John had been the Stoke goalkeeper. Matthews was so nervous before the match he suffered a panic attack, wishing he had not been picked at all. Roy John visited Matthews just before kick-off to give the nineteen-year-old some encouragement. Matthews said that when he scored he was too elated to spare a thought for the man who had helped to quell his nervousness.

Despite the goal, Matthews's form against Wales failed to excite the critics. Nor did it, though, discourage the selectors from choosing him for the Football League against the Scottish League, when he did well enough in a 2-1 win at Stamford Bridge to stay in the England side for the visit of Italy, who in June had won the second World Cup.

Highbury staged the Italy match on Wednesday 14 November. The 50,000 crowd witnessed a so-called friendly that was among a number from this era that resonated with more dramatic force and significance than many a competitive match that followed. It left the British press in a particularly splenetic state over the visitors' play.

In a rare piece of political commentary that sounds more like his ghost writer speaking (a journalist friend called Bill Bailey), Matthews said in an early autobiography: 'I am convinced the Italian masses did not want the war, but Mussolini was trying to boost the morale of his countrymen, and if Italy could beat England at football in London it would be a triumph for Fascism.' The story gathered momentum when Mussolini, the self-styled *Duce*, offered the Italy players a range of win bonuses from sums of money to extravagant gifts such as luxury cars.

England won the dramatic match 3-2, a scoreline that seemed unlikely after quarter of an hour. At this point England led 3-0, despite having missed a penalty, while Italy were not only compromising their chances with their overly robust approach but were down to ten men after their captain, the Juventus centre-half Luis Monti, went off injured in the fifth minute. Amid the recriminations that afterwards surrounded Italy's rough play the significance of their second-half rally, during which they scored their two goals, was rather lost. *The Times*'s portentous comment that 'England is still supreme in a game essentially our own' was both ridiculous and spectacularly missed the point. When the depleted Italy side reverted to concentrating on their football they gave an impressive demonstration of the gathering potency of the continental game.

Most of the newspaper comment was reserved for Italy's early play and the injuries suffered by England: Eric Brook needed hospital treatment on an elbow; the captain, Eddie Hapgood, played on with a broken nose, the result of a collision early on with Luigi Bertolini's elbow; and Ted Drake, the centre-forward in his first international, had a badly bruised shoulder.

Otto Olssen, the Swede who refereed the match, said: 'I warned the Italians repeatedly, particularly two defenders. The Italians were too excitable. When they learn to control themselves and not play dirty I think they will be a great side. Their ideas of the rules differ from the English view. They were warned before the game started that it would be conducted according to English laws, but they could not change the style that they have adopted in Italy.'*

English football had already set itself apart from the world game by snootily declining to enter the first World Cup in 1930 and had just skipped the second competition as well. Not until 1950 did England join in. The events when Italy visited Highbury in 1934 convinced several commentators that this standoffishness was not without merit.

---

* Olssen's reference to 'English laws' is interesting. He almost certainly called them this not because the English had their own set of rules but because they were the first to lay down laws of Association Football, in 1863, and these were adopted internationally in 1882, overseen by the International Football Association Board. To this day the board has, contentiously in the view of many, retained a strong British representation. In 1934 Italy may well have felt that the laws were too English for their liking.

'Intolerable Tactics of the Italians', the *News Chronicle* trumpeted in its headline above a report in which Charles Buchan said: 'I thought I knew every conceivable foul in football, but I learned at least a dozen more. The Italians are past masters in the art of obstruction.' The *Daily Express*'s headline called the match a 'A Travesty of Soccer', picking up a line from Arthur Simmons's report: 'Well we have seen the Italian football team. I am sorry to have to write that I have no wish to see them play England again. [The match] was indeed a sorry affair. For the most part a travesty, a tragedy of football. It was quickly evident that a number of the Italians either had a very vague knowledge of the laws of Soccer – as we know them – or that their temperament so got the upper hand that they did not know what they were doing.'

As far as Matthews was concerned the wider ramifications of what happened at Highbury were irrelevant. Understandably, he viewed the match from his own perspective and said the opportunity to prove himself as an international player had turned into a nightmare because of the violence. This may have been why his contribution to the game was minimal, although the tone of much of the press coverage was that this was not entirely his fault. The Stoke paper complained that all the passes supplied to him by Bowden from inside-right were awkward. Arthur Simmons commented: 'Matthews proved to the crowd that, with opportunities that were most difficult, he could play a dangerous game, but he was neglected. Most of the play was on the left or down the middle.'

Matthews openly expressed his distaste at the violence and treachery of the Italy match: 'I have nothing to be pleased about over that game, the roughest in which I have ever taken part,' he said. 'It cost me my place in the England team.'

Right from the start of his career he showed a detachment from the darker arts, which, contrary to the romantic notion that professional football was once played by men steadfastly observing some Corinthian code, had existed since its earliest days. Yet he was also accused of being more merciless and cynical than those who would inflict physical damage on him by using his skills to make fun of his aggressors.

Roy Sproson was one of those who attested to the comedic effect Matthews's sorcery could have. Sproson, a Stoke boy who each morning before going to school would wait for a sight of Matthews striding to the Victoria Ground for training, grew up to play against his hero for Port Vale when they met Blackpool in an FA Cup tie. Many years later Sproson told the *Guardian*: 'Stan was even more of a genius close-up. I fancied myself as a tackler. Suddenly, he's coming at me down the touchline, jockeying, shimmying, his classic situation. Lo and behold he goes and shoves the ball too far in front of him: he's given it me. I smile to myself and think, "Watch this folks, I'm bloody taking the ball off Matthews." Then, bloody hell, unbelievable. Just as my toe was an eighth of an inch from the ball, he's found another gear, two ruddy gears, and his toe comes and sniffs it past me and he's skipping over my sliding leg and is away. I didn't just think I had him, I knew I had him – and now here I was flat on my backside realising genius is really genius, and the crowd all laughing.'

The playwright Peter Whelan first watched Matthews play in the 1940s when he appeared for Blackpool against Stoke in a New Year's friendly at the Victoria Ground. He recalled an incident in that game when Matthews took a pass on the wing and immediately slowed down in an attempt to coax the full-back to come to him. The back, having resisted at first, lunged forward when Matthews calmly put his foot on the ball. 'Immediately Stan seemed to disappear round him in a swaying, bowlegged curve at an angle that no normal human being could possibly sustain,' Whelan said. 'The hapless full-back charged forward into empty air and impaled himself on the corner flag. The crowd was helpless.'

Nature and nurture each played a role in Matthews's reaction to violent play. He had great mental resilience in the face of repeated provocation by those he tormented. Inherently slow to anger, he was also influenced by his father who taught all his boys the virtues of non-aggression. Ron Matthews remembered his pep talk well: 'My father said to me, "You are going to play football at school and don't you *ever* do anything nasty or dirty. If the person kicks you, do not retaliate. And don't you ever object to the referee's decision. If anyone does kick or foul you recognise that you've beaten them and you're now on top." I thought this advice was for me, but again I talked to Stanley and he said he had received the same lecture. He got it into Stanley, "Don't retaliate. If they're dirty you've beaten them."'

On the other hand Matthews was never a benign presence on the field. Good players, great players, who played with him and against him said he was a killer. His brother said: 'Before a game his idea was to destroy whoever was in front of him by fair means.' Matthews would take a cold shower before leaving the dressing room, rarely speaking to the opposition because he said he would lose his concentration. Others have spoken of Matthews being sick before he went on the field. Hughie Kelly, who played alongside him at Blackpool for many years, once said: 'Stan's the most nervous footballer I've ever come across in the dressing room before a game.'

Matthews did develop one way of communicating with the opposition that did not disturb his concentration. He got a teammate to pass on his thoughts. Don Ratcliffe said: 'I got on very well with Stan and used to fire his bullets for him. He was a very quiet fella, but he was funny and used to tell me things to say to their defenders. He'd say, "Tell 'em they can't play. If they were any good they'd be up here with us in the forward line" – that type of thing.'

In the same way, Matthews could dispatch colleagues to administer physical retribution – and smile about it afterwards.

He liked recounting the story of the day he asked Jock Dodds, playing alongside him for Blackpool in 1943, to sort out the Oldham full-back Tommy Shipman, who had been giving him a hard time. Dodds, a rumbustious Scot who was a natural enforcer, duly obliged, and then writhed on the ground himself as if he were the one who was hurt. 'Are you able to walk?' the ref asked Dodds, apparently concerned. 'Yes,' Dodds said. 'Then you can walk off down that tunnel,' the ref told him. Long before red cards, Dodds made such a good job of his play-acting that the press at first reported he went off injured. Only later did they discover he had been dismissed for 'unduly robust play', still unaware, though, that it was at Matthews's behest.

Whelan bore out Ron Matthews's description of his brother as 'a killer'. He said that when he recounted the tale of the crowd falling about after the full-back impaled himself on the flag, Matthews had told him it was never his intention to make a crowd laugh. 'Stan said the first ten or twenty minutes of a match were key to him. Either he was going to destroy and humiliate the defence or, if he let them, they would destroy him and undermine him for the rest of the game. To him, it was dead serious. This spoken by a quiet, gentle, affable man in the broad accent of my hometown really impressed me. Behind the gentleness was the steel needed to put him where he was – at the peak as player and entertainer.'

Jimmy Armfield, who played many times with Matthews at Blackpool, said that although Matthews was never booked or sent off, his psychological approach was unforgiving. 'He used to urge me to impose myself on an opponent, not to show any mercy.' In a clear echo of Peter Whelan's story, Armfield said that late in Matthews's career, during a match at Chelsea in the fifties, he left the field having been repeatedly fouled by a young full-back called Ian McFarlane. The Stamford Bridge crowd taunted him for withdrawing from the fray. But he returned and when Armfield asked him if he was all right Matthews answered with a curt instruction: 'Just get the ball over here.' Armfield and the rest of the Blackpool team did as they were told and Matthews set about embarrassing the opposition. McFarlane suffered the most. On one occasion he unwisely accepted the chance to have another go at Matthews after he had already been beaten once and was used as a stooge a second time. The Chelsea crowd applauded Matthews off the field. He ignored them. 'He never had any communication with the crowd,' Armfield said. 'It just wasn't his style.'

The remarkable point about the flintiness of Matthews's competitive nature referred to by Armfield was that it was not something he developed over his many years of playing the game. So much about his early life suggested he would be far too shy as a young professional to be an arch and uncompromising competitor, but these traits emerged right at the start of his career.

By the start of the season following the Italy game, Matthews was a married man. In his 1989 authorised biography, and two ghosted autobiographies written towards the end of his life, it says incorrectly that his first marriage took place a year earlier, in 1934. One of the most memorable dates in a young man's life, the year in which he becomes a husband, had apparently faded too much for Matthews to recall. Or perhaps his confusion was psychologically induced, the starting date of a marriage that was doomed to fail lost in a fog of unhappiness.

Matthews explained in later years the sequence of events that led to the marriage. He said that one of the first things that happened when he arrived at the ground as a fifteen-year-old was that Betty suddenly appeared and took him to see her father. The friendship blossomed from there and in the summer of 1934, after a scolding from his mother that he was neglecting his girlfriend, Matthews was shamed into hurrying to Scotland. Betty Vallance had gone to join her father because of the lack of attention being shown her by Stanley. Emotions in Scotland were running so high that the young pair married in the clubhouse of the Bonnyton Golf Club near Glasgow within days.

A much earlier autobiography, written when Matthews was still in his thirties, gave the courtship a rather different narrative. In this Matthews said he did not meet Betty until he was nineteen, in 1934 in other words, when Jimmy Vallance invited him to go on a golfing holiday to Girvan in Ayrshire. He was introduced to Betty on this holiday. During it he noted she was a better golfer, by several strokes, than he was. They became engaged and married a year later, he said, making no mention of his mother's reprimand – although this may have been too delicate to air publicly in a memoir published while the marriage was still intact.

This account squares with the marriage certificate, which gives the date of the wedding as 19 August 1935. The Reverend David Langlands Seath, the Minister of Eaglesham and a prominent figure in the local Masonic movement, conducted the marriage ceremony at Bonnyton Golf Club 'after banns according to the forms of the Church of Scotland'. The venue was where Jimmy Vallance now worked, Matthews's father-in-law having the previous month left his job as the Stoke trainer to manage the Bonnyton course.*

The day after Matthews married Betty Vallance a wedding-group photograph appeared on the front page of the *Evening Sentinel*. An accompanying report further contradicted Matthews's later recollection of some of the detail, notably his assertion that it was a simple, spontaneous ceremony 'with just Betty's parents present and one or two officials from the golf club'. The *Sentinel*'s report made it clear it was not quite the

---

* Six years later, Bonnyton would gain notoriety as the course on which the Messerschmitt carrying Rudolph Hess, the Nazi politician, crash-landed. Hess, on a mission to negotiate peace with Britain, parachuted to safety, landing near Eaglesham. He was captured and imprisoned.

impromptu event Matthews implied with no time for members of his family to attend. Not only had Matthews's mother, Ada, travelled to Scotland but she had a dress for the occasion. 'The bridegroom's mother was in beige marocain,' the report said. It added that Betty wore a dress of blue taffeta and carried a bouquet of blue roses and white heather and was attended by a friend, Miss Muriel Smith. In the photograph Matthews is standing like a soldier on parade, a serious look on his face, just behind Ada. Betty is seated at a small table signing the register.

The newly-weds bought a home close to Matthews's parents soon after they returned. Betty signed the mortgage papers because her twenty-year-old husband was below the legal age of twenty-one for doing so. 'When the 1934–5 season started I was very happy and contented and for all my tender years felt well and truly settled,' he said. One of their new near neighbours was Peter Buxton. 'I was a soccer-mad schoolboy, just reaching my teens and he was a rising star,' Buxton said. 'To my utter delight, Stan and Betty bought a house in Ronson Avenue, Trent Vale, a couple of hundred yards from my home. Most days I saw my idol walking to and from the Victoria Ground wearing those baggy plus-fours that were considered to be cool in those days.' Buxton would become a close friend of Stanley's as a sportswriter on the *Evening Sentinel*.

Jimmy Vallance's departure from Stoke in the summer of 1935 was part of a wider change of backroom personnel, which would eventually undermine Matthews's relationship with the club.

For reasons unspecified, Mather, who had been manager since 1923 and had become a friend of the Matthews family, was replaced by Matthews's polar opposite, Bob McGrory, the hard-headed Scot. McGrory's age, forty-three, must have influenced his decision to stop playing, even if he had shown he was still in good shape by being the only Stoke player to appear in all their 1934–5 League games. Why, though, should he oust the increasingly effective Mather? Had he been the much younger man this might have been seen as an advantage, what football clubs like passing off as 'investing in the future'. But the age gap was just three years. A more likely explanation is that as a particularly strong personality he was simply regarded as the right leader to make Stoke a First Division success.

At first the official word was that Mather would stay on as secretary, a job he had done in conjunction with managing. This changed as soon as news of his altered circumstances was made public. Straightaway Mather received an offer to manage Newcastle United, which he accepted. 'I should very much like to have stayed for many years with Stoke,' Mather said, a little darkly. 'But I'm glad I'm leaving it a better club than I found it.' Mather's departure, followed shortly by Vallance's, severed an important 'upstairs' link with the club for Matthews, a break that was never satisfactorily repaired. Vallance's replacement as trainer by Hubert Nuttall and Tom Hancock's promotion to secretary from the assistant's post completed the shuffling of senior staff.

McGrory's first season as manager could hardly have gone better with Stoke City ending 1935–6 in fourth place, in what remains the highest they have finished in the top tier of the English game. With a new boss in place, Matthews had hurried back from his wedding in Scotland to be part of the season's preliminaries. Five days after the wedding he played for the first team against the reserves in a trial match at the Victoria Ground.

Right from the start, when they beat Leeds United 3-1, Stoke remained near the top of the table, although they were soon left behind by Sunderland who would win the title by eight points. Matthews made an immediate impact. Now twenty-one, he had developed rapidly as a player over his first four years as a professional and his form against Leeds, said the local paper, 'suggested that this season he is going to be better than ever'.

Matthews was unsettled, though, because he had lost his England place. After the Italy match, he played in none of the three internationals after Christmas and was left out of the side that played Northern Ireland in the first friendly of the 1935–6 season. Matthews's disappointment grew as the selectors turned to a different outside-right for each of the four matches that he missed. First Sammy Crooks was brought back; then Albert Geldard of Everton, who was less than a year older than Matthews and, like him, a prodigy who had been the youngest player to appear in the Football League at 15 years 158 days; Portsmouth's Fred Worrall, a strongly built forward who had excelled at rugby before choosing to play football, was next to be given a go; and the selectors then turned to the previously uncapped Ralph Birkett, a Devonian who had moved via Torquay and Arsenal to Middlesbrough.

Birkett did well enough in his first international to be picked again for the next match, England v Germany in early December 1935. An injury meant he had to withdraw two days before the game and England never turned to him again. Birkett's misfortune gave what, at the time, must have seemed to Matthews a lucky break. It provided the selectors with the opportunity to recognise his consistently impressive form for Stoke by recalling him for what one national newspaper called 'the most discussed match in the history of Association football'.

One world war had taken place since a German representative team last played in England in 1901 and another global conflict was now looming. The match created considerable unease in Britain, particularly in London where it was to be staged at White Hart Lane. The choice of Tottenham's ground seemed ill judged given the club's large Jewish following. The Trades Union Congress led the campaign for the match to be called off because of the rise of Nazism in Germany, where only recently the Nuremberg Laws had legalised systematic persecution of the Jews.

Matthews's recall of the match contained little mention of the political backdrop against which the game was played, although his observation that 'One had a very uncomfortable feeling about Hitler and the situation over there, even in 1935' could be regarded as quite a sermon for a twenty-year-old professional footballer of any era. One of Matthews's recollections, that for some reason the newspapers never played up the political element surrounding the fixture, was plain wrong.

In fact newspapers gave comprehensive coverage to all aspects of the game. This included a report that large numbers of police were stationed outside White Hart Lane from the day before it took place after posters and graffiti started to appear. The sentiments ranged from 'Stop Wednesday's Match' to, crudely daubed nearby, 'Perish Judah' with two huge swastikas either side. Also reported was that representatives of the FA and the German team met the German ambassador in London to discuss preliminaries to the match. The meeting considered the question of a Nazi salute before kick-off.

The match stirred tremendous interest in Germany with at least 10,000 supporters crossing the Channel in a flotilla of steamers. Seven sailed from Ostend and one from Dunkirk, which would soon be the scene of a rather different exodus. The fleet also included the liner *Columbus*, which brought nearly 2,000 fans to Southampton. Once they arrived in London on the morning of the match, many of the visiting supporters went on a specially arranged two-hour bus tour. For security reasons the bus companies received sealed orders giving details of the route. These were handed to the drivers moments before they set off. Planning even went as far as to stipulate that German fans could bring over no more than sixteen shillings each. Arrangements were made for them to purchase British postal orders for this amount before setting sail.

It seems the police were remarkably successful in keeping troublemakers away from the ground on match day, although

there was trouble afterwards. Fourteen arrests were made –
seven of them at Victoria station from where trains took the
Germans to the Channel ports – as demonstrators excluded
from the game made their feelings felt. No German was arrested,
the problem being the 'insulting behaviour' of the protesters.

Word may well have filtered out that the Germans had been
allowed to celebrate the occasion in what the protesters would
certainly have regarded as an overly jingoistic and provocative
way. The *Daily Telegraph* reported: 'The teams came out on
to the field through the same gate. Universal cheers greeted
them. Then the band played the German National Anthem,
and the whole crowd stood – the German spectators and team
with arms outstretched in the Nazi salute and the Britons bare
headed. A burst of cheering greeted the close of the anthem.'
Maybe the absence of trouble inside the ground helps to explain
why Matthews failed to register the tension the game generated.
It may also be why he and some of his England teammates were
unprepared for the dramatic and highly publicised preliminaries
when they played the return in Berlin in May 1938.

Matthews's memory of the 1935 encounter, which England
won 3-0, was largely confined to what a huge personal disappointment the match was. He made a palpable hash of the
opportunity handed to him after Birkett's withdrawal. As a
consequence the selectors ignored him for the whole of 1936 –
the last time they spurned him for an entire calendar year until
he was into his late thirties.

In later life Matthews dwelt on the part the German left-
back Reinhold Muenzenberg played in his poor performance,
although while most commentators who saw the match agreed
with Matthews's verdict that he played badly none expressed the
view that Muenzenberg was the reason. One even implied the
opposite: 'He would beat Muenzenberg with a polished swerve or
a feint, but there was never any finish . . . [including] a complete
inability to lift the ball into the air when making his centres.'

Another thought Matthews simply lacked the confidence to assert himself. 'He would have done so much better with a little more bustle' given the excellent service he received from the Arsenal half-back Jack Crayston.

All, Matthews and commentators, agreed that he was guilty of a terrible miss early in the game. He called it the worst of his career – 'I was certain I would score. I took a great kick, but kicked the turf' – and said it was the first time he had heard a big crowd, more than 50,000, groan 'like one gigantic voice'. The only excuse, said one report, was that the pitch was a gluepot.

As far as Matthews's father was concerned it was his son's reaction to the bad miss that led to his poor display. Jack Matthews and two of his other sons had borrowed an old car to drive from Hanley to watch the match. Back in Stoke, where Matthews apologised to his club teammates for his limp display, he said his father admonished him for allowing his mistake to have such a crushing effect on his mental outlook. The old pugilist, who knew a thing or two about coming back from heavy blows, said he could ruin his career if he did not toughen up mentally.

Thanks to his father's exhortation, perhaps, Matthews quickly recovered his club form even if this did not convince the national selectors – and a number of critics – that his England future, at least in the short term, was worth resurrecting. They did call him up as a late replacement for a trial game at Old Trafford in March 1936 after Worrall withdrew from the Possibles. On the day of the match he was promoted to the Probables, who won 3-0. 'Ginger' Richardson, the West Brom centre-forward, scored all three goals in the last half-hour. Matthews's performance failed to persuade anyone who mattered that his showing against Germany was simply an aberration.

One group that maintained faith in Matthews's value as a player was Stoke City's First Division rivals. As a transfer deadline approached in mid-March it turned out that Manchester City had been negotiating for Matthews for some weeks, putting a price on him of £9,000. More intriguingly, Tom Mather, Matthews's old boss at Stoke, who would keep chipping away with offers for the rest of the 1930s, persuaded the board of Newcastle United to bid £10,000. The Stoke board held a meeting at which, it was reported, they reaffirmed their decision not to accept any offer for Matthews.

This decision certainly met with the approval of the Stoke fans, who held Matthews in the highest regard as his club form prospered. 'Matthews was the star performer in the Stoke front line and his goal was a masterly effort,' the local paper reported after a top-of-the-table match against Huddersfield ended 1-0. His goal straight from a corner secured a 2-1 success against Everton in early April, putting Stoke in third place with six matches to go, and he was prominent in the 2-1 home win over Liverpool that rounded off the season.

But if Matthews was reaching the peak of his popularity with the public during his first spell as a Stoke player, his relationship with the club showed the earliest signs of fraying, despite what the club's determination to hold on to him might have suggested. In fact the source of the problem was almost certainly not the board but the jutting-jawed manager McGrory. He was finding the conversion of the shy lad of not so long ago into a player whose popularity was transcending that of the team a little irksome.

McGrory's antipathy towards Matthews was almost certainly helped along by the manager's friendship with Bobby Liddle, with whom he had once shared lodgings. Liddle had not only lost his place on the right wing to Matthews but also the affection of Stoke fans. And the irritating thing for an old-style footballing man such as McGrory was the reason why Matthews had found favour with the supporters. Still so diffident most of the time, the young player had the self-belief with the ball at his feet to do things his way. Spectators adored it; McGrory, a martinet figure, preferred people to improvise in their own time. He looked upon Matthews as a show-off.

It would have been hard for Matthews not to take McGrory's dislike too personally, but it was a mistake. The manager disapproved per se of those he regarded as cocky. It did not matter whether their name was Stanley Matthews or Neil Franklin, an outstanding centre-half who would join Stoke in 1939. 'McGrory tended to lose the plot when internationals like Stan and Neil Franklin asserted their independence,' the journalist Peter Buxton said. Dennis Herod, Stoke's goalkeeper straight after the Second World War, said McGrory 'wanted the limelight and was jealous of players like Stan and Neil Franklin'.

Having come under the influence of Walter Winterbottom and his modern ways, the stylish Franklin took to passing the ball out of defence. This infuriated McGrory, who regarded Winterbottom as some southern degenerate. The Scot's canon of how to play football observed only one way of clearing your lines and putting your goal beyond danger: a mighty hoof downfield – and never mind where the ball might end up.

Soon after McGrory's first season as manager ended he found a reason to fall out with Matthews and the man who remained his real mentor, his father Jack. Much later Matthews would date the start of the breakdown of his relationship with Stoke to the early weeks of 1938. In fact it began much earlier, in the early summer of 1936.

Behind the scenes Matthews had been wrangling for days over a loyalty bonus before agreeing in May to re-sign for the 1936–7 season. Matthews asked for £650; McGrory, who latched happily on to the idea that this particular twenty-one-year-old was overreaching himself, told him he could have only £500. The disagreement centred on whether Matthews's time as an amateur should be factored into the years he had served the club. Matthews, directed by his father, held out for the higher sum, while McGrory, on behalf of the club, argued this was due only to players who had been professionals for more than five years. In Matthews's case, McGrory said, this would not be until his twenty-second birthday, more than halfway through the 1936–7 season. In the end, after a Saturday-morning crisis meeting at the club, it was agreed that the figure should stay at £500. The pact was said to be amicable. If it was, the friendliness between the two principals in the quarrel was perilously brittle.

It was not obvious at the time, but, with McGrory settling in for a long stint as manager, Matthews's departure from Stoke was now inevitable, even if the split would still take a while to happen.

Chapter 5

'You can be dead fair to a man and yet kill his soul'

In the summer of 1936, two months before the start of the new season, another conflict beset Stoke City. This time Stanley Matthews was not directly involved but without the club's success on the pitch, in which he played such a significant part, it may never have happened. Had the club not been doing so well, their chairman for the past eleven years, Arthur Sherwin, would in all probability have given up leadership of the board willingly rather than involve them in an unseemly row.

As it was, Sherwin, who as a schoolboy had run messages between the Copeland Arms Hotel, where teams used to change, and the Victoria Ground, decided to try to hang on to the post. The pretext he used for reneging on a loose agreement that he would stand aside was the highly dubious claim that he was the main reason for Stoke's success. When he was voted out of office, losing out to Alderman Harry Booth, he promptly walked out of the board meeting in a huff. He said: 'I resent very much the action that has been taken by the directors.' He maintained that his chairmanship was 'a not unimportant part in the progress and improved status of the club', and by claiming he had done more than anyone else to bring important players to Stoke he managed, implicitly, to bring Matthews into the dispute.

The board countered indignantly. They said Stoke City were not a one-man club and that credit for their success on the field could not be claimed by any one individual. The new chairman said that it was always understood that Sherwin would step down in 1936. He had been kept on only so that he could receive the Football League medal for twenty-one years' service as a director.

Sherwin issued a conciliatory statement the next day, the words somehow forced out between clenched teeth, before going on holiday 'to consider my position'. In July he resigned. His departure provided another piece of evidence, as familiar today as it was then, that success can be as divisive within a football club as failure.

The squabble preceded a curiously uneven season for Stoke, who lurched from periods of poverty to spectacular plenty. They would end up in tenth place in the First Division table, their mercurial form helping to establish them as the League's premier entertainers. Matthews was showman-in-chief with Freddie Steele, emerging as an outstanding centre-forward, and Joe Johnson, an outside left who could, on occasions, outshine his fellow winger, lead members of an impressive supporting cast. The Victoria Ground was no longer simply a place for the long-suffering football fan. It was somewhere to escape the realities of a world in which reasons for thinking war could be avoided were growing rapidly less plausible.

A series of records gave numerical substance to the fanciful notion that amid the pottery kilns could be found some of the best sporting entertainment in the land. In early February 1937 Stoke beat visitors West Bromwich Albion 10-3, on Easter Monday they attracted their biggest League crowd of 51,373 for the game against Arsenal and by the season's end Steele had whacked in thirty-three goals.

In certain respects, notably as a goal provider, Matthews reached the apogee of his first period with Stoke during the

West Brom victory. 'Glory and golden visions were not usually associated with the grimy Potteries of 1937, but they were much in evidence this day,' he said. What was also inescapably in evidence was Matthews's special gift for creating scoring opportunities for others, which was surely a rebuke of sorts to those who had started to question whether he was a team player. Not for the last time a match could be branded Matthews's, even though the most obvious statistic – in this instance five goals by Steele – suggested this made no sense. By his own reckoning Matthews assisted in six of the goals and said it did not bother him that he failed to score.

The local paper described the win over West Brom as 'one of the most sensational football matches seen at the Victoria Ground' and described Matthews's performance as classic. It also reminded readers of an even more comprehensive victory in a home fixture some twenty years earlier, although the circumstances were rather different. Blackburn Rovers, making a wartime visit, arrived with only ten men. A goalkeeper called Underwood was seconded from the crowd, which may well have been a factor in the 16-1 score.

For a while Steele's goalscoring form was fit to stand alongside Matthews's contributions on the wing. The centre-forward, whose career would never fully blossom because of a knee injury, was not as meaty as many of the central attackers of this era but still packed a humdinger of a shot in either foot. Also, he developed an impressive preference for scoring more than one goal at a time. In addition to his five against West Brom, he struck five hat-tricks during 1936–7.

It was Steele's shooting and Matthews's brilliant elaborations of the possibilities of wing play that gave momentum to Stoke's season after a sluggish start. In eight days in mid-September, Steele scored eight goals in three League victories, the third of them a 6-2 win over League leaders Middlesbrough. In another of them, a 4-2 victory over Birmingham that lifted Stoke to second in the table, the defender Willie Steel 'found Matthews almost unplayable'.

Still, though, Matthews had not been forgiven for his failure against Germany. He missed all seven internationals in 1936, despite constructing a powerful case most weekends that he should be restored to the side. What made it worse for him was that Steele and Johnson both found favour with the England selectors while he was ignored. Officials and critics worried about Matthews's temperament. This was considered a problem in two respects: a perceived inconsistency against superior defenders and the view of him as more song-and-dance act than team man. If the second were true, maybe it was also understandable. After all, who wouldn't be inclined to overlook collective responsibility when playing the way he did for Stoke was gaining him a cult following.

Matthews's club form finally regained him favour when he played in an England trial at Burnley in mid-March. The Possibles, with Matthews and Johnson on the wings, lost 2-0 to the Probables but one press report said that 'Matthews was undoubtedly the cleverest winger on view'.

Over the 1937 Easter weekend in late March he continued to press convincingly for international reinstatement. Just as Charlie Chaplin's classic film *Modern Times* had been filling the cinemas, so Stoke's own bandy-legged hero tested the stamina of box-office staff. More than 140,000 spectators turned out for Stoke's three matches, two of them goalless draws against Arsenal. There were nearly 60,000 at Highbury on Good Friday and more than 50,000 at the Victoria Ground for the return three days later. In between Matthews, in scintillating form, undid Sunderland as Stoke won 5-3 at home. Gate money was not yet disclosed for League matches but word was that the Arsenal game generated record receipts for Stoke. The figure, substantial at the time, was reckoned to be £3,000. By today's standards this is, of course, risibly low and a further indicator of just how cheap tickets were – and why players' wages were so modest.

Now even the most sceptical members of the England selection committee were persuaded at least to suspend their doubts about Matthews and recall him for the first international of the new year, against Scotland at Hampden Park on 17 April. With Ted Drake injured and Eric Brook's form considered to have slipped, the selectors also turned again to Steele and Johnson. It meant Stoke had three players in an England side for the first time since 1891, quite a transformation for a club used to cosily fitting the adjective 'unfashionable'.

The match would be the first of nine occasions on which Matthews faced the Scots in a full international, the most times he played against any one country. Over the two decades, 1937 to 1957, he appeared in matches against Scotland he responded to the oldest rivalry in international football – it had all started in 1872 – with particular relish.

His inclusion in the 1937 edition of the fixture did not receive universal approval outside the committee room despite his exceptional League form. Arthur Simmons summed up the misgivings of those newspaper critics who thought his recall was ill-considered. He said that although Matthews had the cleverest feet in football 'the big question of temperament' was one that he had not answered successfully. 'Matthews rose to fame as a lad and had his chance in internationals. He failed to show his best club form.'

In Matthews's time the excitement that preceded England matches against Scotland was immense. It continued to be until 1989 when the overexuberance of fans – most vividly expressed in 1977 when Scottish fans brought the Wembley goalposts crashing down as they celebrated a 2-1 victory – led the football authorities, controversially, to discontinue staging the fixture annually.

'Soccer is obviously a bigger affair in England than in Scotland – but not on that day when the Sassenachs go to Scotland to strive to humble the Scots,' one national newspaper columnist wrote before Matthews's debut in the fixture. He pointed out the anomaly that domestic matches in Scotland attracted relatively meagre crowds – barely 6,000 had just watched Rangers on the same Saturday that 76,000 turned out to see Arsenal – and yet when England travelled north the 'most commodious football enclosure that can be found anywhere' was still not big enough to satisfy demand. 'We of the south are inclined to preen ourselves when 93,000 people congregate at Wembley for the Cup Final [but] it rather pales by comparison with such an event as that which will be staged at Hampden Park, Glasgow, next Saturday.'

How right he was. The crowd that gathered at Hampden that Saturday was 149,547, a world record at the time and still the biggest official attendance for a football match in Britain. Matthews said that when he came out of the tunnel and looked around 'it was all I could do not to stop dead in my tracks'. The steeply rising banks of humanity overawed him. Here, before a tumultuous congregation united by a desire to see him and his teammates fail dismally, was surely the ultimate test of Matthews's temperament.

Matthews would pass the test, although he did not quite achieve the distinction that would dispel all doubts about his international pedigree. In the *Daily Express*, Simmons retracted his reservations. 'Matthew was class: a "real" international for the first time. His dribbling was beautiful, his feints to foil Beattie at close quarters pure football. Beyond question, he enjoyed the match.' Others were not so unequivocal after a match dominated in the first half by England's forward craft, notably Matthews's, but won by Scotland who answered Steele's first-half goal with three after the interval.

Scotland's collective endeavour ultimately trumped England's individual flourishes. 'Though England provided the sheer football craft,' Charles Buchan wrote, 'they were deservedly beaten by a team who took their opportunities.' He admired

Matthews's play but said he was gradually subdued. Frank Coles noted that while Andy Beattie, the highly regarded full-back, had been made to suffer by Matthews in the first half, he 'came into full bloom later'. For some, the song-and-dance rebuke – pass the ball to my feet and I'll show you something frivolous – still held. And for some of these, the theory would harden into a conviction.

Still, the Matthews legend had been furnished with its early chapters – and the season that followed would give a luminous quality to the content. First, though, there was another eruption of the benefit controversy that caused what the press described as a sensational development.

The two parties, Matthews and the club, were interpreting differently what had been agreed a year earlier. On 30 April 1937 the player, no doubt with his father's backing, was reported to have applied to be put on the transfer list. Matthews said that a verbal promise to grant him the higher amount – £650 rather than £500 – was made when the dispute first surfaced publicly in 1936, while the club's position was that nothing had changed since two years ago when the player had asked for £500.

On this occasion it would take four weeks before Matthews re-signed. One immediate consequence of the stand-off was that, the player having failed to re-sign straightaway with Stoke and being, therefore, without a club, the Football Association announced that Matthews, who had been picked for England's tour of Scandinavia in mid-May, would not be going. Another outcome was a stream of letters in the local press. This one was typical:

> SIR – It seems that the deadlock which has arisen between Stanley Matthews and Stoke City may end in the supporters being deprived of the pleasure they have had, and which they had hoped to have for many seasons, of watching this brilliant local lad's exhibitions at the Victoria Ground.

Now it occurs to me that many of the supporters who wish for Matthews to remain at Stoke would be only too ready to subscribe together to find that £150. We should, of course, make it clear that there is no intention whatever of interfering with the business matters of the club, or the player concerned, the only outcome being that we want Matthews at Stoke. Such a suggestion, we trust, would be appreciated by all parties in a sporting spirit.

Anyone interested in such a scheme might kindly communicate with me as soon as possible, with a view to forming a committee.

Yours faithfully, W. Nixon of Oakhills, Stoke-on-Trent

A follow-up from Mr Nixon, this time published on the front page, said he had received a letter from Matthews telling him: 'I could not possibly accept the charity of the Stoke City supporters or the idea of a public subscription on my behalf, as the supporters have supported us well and paid admission for their entertainment.'

One letter agreeing with Stoke's stance, from a George Myatt, of Newcastle under Lyme, had the tone of being from someone connected with the club. Myatt said that Matthews had asked for £500 in 1935 and the club were still willing to honour that guarantee. He added: 'One is of the opinion that, had Matthews not been so hasty then [in 1935] and waited until he had completed five years' service, no doubt the directors would have considered very favourably his request for a full benefit.'

The dispute rumbled on. The Stoke board decided on 18 May, nearly three weeks after the latest episode in the disagreement had broken cover, that they would not budge, Matthews had to accept the £500 benefit 'as included in the player's agreement'. Three days later the local paper reported that Matthews had 'advanced certain suggested terms on which he would be prepared to re-sign'. Presumably having spoken to a board member, the paper added that it was understood that these terms were unlikely to provide the basis for a settlement.

Matters were resolved, for the time being, on 28 May 1937. Reports published at the time suggested the board, almost certainly at McGrory's insistence, had deliberately slowed down negotiations so it did not appear they had been pushed around. Harry Booth, the chairman of the board, said: 'It has only been a question of principle between us and this point, I am glad to say, has now been satisfactorily settled.' Only having made this point did the club announce they would raise the benefits due to all players entitled to them, including Matthews, to £650.

Matthews, whose pay was suspended while he delayed re-signing, said: 'It has been a worrying time for me and I am glad it is all over. I have decided, therefore, to adhere to my agreement with the club and leave my football career, and the question of my benefits, in the hands of the directors.' Intriguingly, he said also that he had received several attractive offers to play for clubs outside the Football League, but he preferred to continue to play in League football.

The dispute did nothing to settle the Matthews argument. Matthews-the-money-grubber tendency claimed it was evidence that he was out for every penny he could get. On the other side, his supporters cited his mounting pecuniary worth to the club as vindication of his stance. 'Think of the salary he was on and then remember this was a man who could put ten thousand on a gate,' Jimmy Armfield said. With his wage pegged at £8 during the playing season, despite the rocketing attendances for which he was chiefly responsible, he was entitled to the maximum bonus on offer.

As if to emphasise the rightness of his benefit cause, Matthews rarely disappointed those who came to admire his flights of fancy down the wing during the 1937–8 season. That Stoke, nevertheless, had a poor season, finishing seventeenth, only two points ahead of the two relegated clubs, was hardly his fault. The break-up of the successful forward line lay behind the decline. Joe Johnson was sold to West Bromwich Albion for £6,500 in what was reckoned to be a good bit of business at the time. It looked a little less shrewd when Freddie Steele, who had been the source of such an abundance of goals, broke down with the knee problems that would blight his career. Matthews alone of Stoke's successful 1936–7 forward triumvirate was a regular presence.

The fortunes of Matthews and Steele started to diverge when Steele was crocked. In early October he damaged his right knee in a collision with the Charlton goalkeeper Sam Bartram. The injury put him out of action for seven weeks. His despair would have been even greater had he known at the time that the knee would never properly recover and his England career was over barely seven months after it had begun. The promise of the eight goals for his country in six matches would not be fulfilled, although he did stay at Stoke until 1949, scoring 140 goals. While Steele was laid up, Matthews received praise for having, in quick succession, mastered three of the best full-backs in the Football League: Arsenal's Eddie Hapgood, Preston's Andy Beattie and Sam Barkas of Manchester City, who was yet another rugged defender rescued from a life at the coalface.

Looking back on his career, Steele would jokingly blame Matthews for the injury that started his decline. The formulaic nature of the English game, which was already being exposed at international level, meant that centre-forwards had only two principal adversaries: the centre-half and the goalkeeper, who received far less protection from referees than he does today. Against Charlton, Steele said, Matthews told him that Bartram was vulnerable to his robust play and urged him to exert even more physical pressure – which he duly did, with dire consequences. Steele then ruefully recollected the moment Matthews left the dressing room after the game. The winger, whose own attitude to robust intervention was to avoid it, was said to have flicked a comb through his hair, airily wished his stricken teammate a speedy recovery and disappeared through the door.

Steele returned in late November before injuring the same knee again in the new year, this time badly enough to require a cartilage operation at a Liverpool nursing home; Matthews, on the other hand, was restored to the national team for matches against Wales at Middlesbrough's Ayrsome Park and against Czechoslovakia, on their first visit to England. He would make even more of an impression than he had against Scotland.

'No one who watched the match will ever again doubt the genius that lies in the feet and brain of Matthews,' F. Stacey Lintott wrote in the *Daily Mirror* after England's 2-1 win over Wales, in which Matthews scored a brilliant equaliser. 'Throughout the first half the Stoke winger had the crowd laughing and cheering when they were not gasping in amazement at the ludicrous ease with which he toyed with such class footballers as Richards and Hughes.' Another national newspaper referred to Matthews 'exploiting just one trick', which he performed 'with such supreme ease that it appeared to be carried out by numbers. First he touched the ball to his left foot and with a sway of the body induced Hughes to follow it. Instantly he brought it back to his right foot, kicked it forward and away he went with the back off his balance.'

The Czechoslovakia match, played on a murky December afternoon at White Hart Lane, turned into a triumph for Matthews after what proved a fortuitous change of position. He had been struggling to make an impression against Czechoslovakia's accomplished full-back Ferdinand Daučík, who was a very different proposition from Hughes, and looked set for a rare afternoon of prolonged frustration. Then an injury to the Chelsea centre-forward George Mills meant Matthews was moved inside. With an altered brief, to head for goal rather than make space to cross the ball against the visitors' best defender,

Matthews paraded his almost forgotten skill as an intuitive goalscorer. He ended with his one and only international hat-trick in a 5-4 victory, all the goals scored with his left foot.

For those who wanted to discern such things – and the distraction of such an exciting match meant there were not very many – the match provided worrying signs for the English game. Its much-vaunted brand of football, which had grown from years of refining something that had limited potential for refinement, was being subverted. England had only scraped home against the Czechoslovaks through a masterpiece of close control by Matthews after the visitors had pulled back from 4-2 to 4-4. One press-box observer, having witnessed something a little different from what the Football League served up, wrote: 'A fine team of footballers, the Czechs . . . In addition to unusual speed and cleverness they believe in working the ball.' Professor R. Pelican, head of the Czechoslovak FA, said that the match showed why England had become vulnerable on the Continent. He referred to the six defeats they had suffered on the European mainland since losing there for the first time against Spain in 1929. 'On a dry ground and with a light ball Continental sides must be feared,' the professor added.

Matthews alone had looked like a continental player – or a selfish one, as his English critics would have it – with the sort of performance that was responsible for making him a figure of national renown. The letters he received grew to an unprecedented number for a footballer, sometimes more than two hundred a day. He answered as many as he could at, he noted, considerable expense.*

If Matthews's life seemed to be blooming under a cloudless sky, with the bonus saga receding into the blue yonder, the

---

* Not all were about football. One woman sought advice on birth control. He ducked giving a direct answer, 'but reminded her that as far as children in our family were concerned, I was the third', proof, surely, that he was a better footballer than agony aunt.

reality was rather different – and it said something for his temperament, still the cause of conjecture, that he managed to play as well as he did at this time. A story was about to break that revealed he had been playing in a state of some distress. On Tuesday 8 February 1938, the *Evening Sentinel* reported in a front-page splash that Matthews had, for a second time, asked for a transfer. The paper called the news 'a bombshell to football circles – and North Staffordshire in particular'. And it soon became clear that, unlike on the previous occasion, this request was backed by real intent.

As soon as the Stoke board received it they summoned Matthews to a meeting. The player had not made public his reasons for wanting to go and, when the board also declined to elucidate, rumour took over.

Speculation about Matthews's discontent did not stop at the friction over the loyalty bonus. Having to carry an attack that had lost Johnson and could no longer rely on Steele being fit was also touted as an issue. And Bob McGrory's unsympathetic attitude towards him was something else that rankled. Accompanying these rumours was one more: that Matthews's success had so divided the Stoke dressing room there had even been fisticuffs.

The letters columns of the local paper were given over almost entirely to comment on developments at the town's main football club. From the terraces, the overwhelming view was that the board would be guilty of a dereliction of duty if they let their star player leave. This observation was typical: 'Matthews has been somewhat discouraged, when, putting across brilliant centres week after week, he has seen them come to naught through the inability of the centre forwards to follow up and score.'

Others developed the point: 'It is unfair to expect Matthews, the finest winger playing football, to play without adequate support. We have watched games this season in which Matthews has been neglected for long periods through the weakness of his partners. It would be a tragedy if Matthews left Stoke City and it is up to the club to see that he remains by buying a first-class inside-forward.'

The paper carried an editorial, which said: 'Without Stanley Matthews, Stoke City would not be Stoke City. He is a star of first magnitude. He cannot be replaced, and some other club would undoubtedly be willing to pay a record figure for his transfer.' A single-line paragraph in bold type followed: 'Stanley Matthews must not be allowed to go.'

The editorial was absolutely right about the interest of other clubs. Everton, Bolton, Derby and Leicester made immediate approaches; Manchester City were reported to be interested; and then Arsenal and Wolves joined the queue. More alarming still for the club must have been a press photograph of Tom Mather, their former manager now in charge of Newcastle, striding into town like some avenging desperado in a western. Mather and one of his directors, A. G. Stableforth, had travelled through the night intent on making a strong bid. Mather said he had a blank cheque in his pocket. It was reported he was prepared to go up to £20,000. If it happened it would be only the fifth Football League transfer involving a five-figure sum and nearly double the previous highest.

By now the story was much more than a little local difficulty. The sports pages of the national press brimmed with speculation – and not just about Matthews's future. Concern even grew for the pottery industry in and around Stoke with output reportedly being affected.

Matthews was constantly exposed to the clamour. Gated refuges and luxury cars with or without tinted windows were still some way from being part of a professional footballer's basic package. Every time he ventured out from his modest home in Trent Vale supporters surrounded him wanting to know his plans. And these excursions were more frequent now that he had opened a sports shop in Stoke.

A second meeting at which Matthews met Harry Booth and McGrory ended with very little fresh official light cast on why Matthews was so restless. An account of this get-together made much of the fact that Matthews had said he was 'uncomfortable' and 'not happy' with the club. This, though, was the effect rather than the cause of his disenchantment and was so self-evident as to be redundant. A letter criticised the club's 'hush-hush policy'; another pointed out that, as Matthews had said there was 'no personal issue between himself and any other player', the grievance must be with the club.

Only much later would Matthews speak and write openly about why he decided it might be better if he started a new life with another club. He cited the talk of the anti-Matthews clique and the squabble over loyalty money as the main things that undermined his wish to remain a Stoke player. 'It was quite untrue there was any ill feeling in the dressing room,' he said, '[but] even when the rumours simmered down it left a nasty taste.' He also expressed amazement the club had been so stubborn about paying him an extra £150 while maintaining they wanted him to stay.

He acknowledged that he suspected McGrory resented him, but did not advance this as a big concern. In the autumn of 1937, he and McGrory, playing golf as a pair for Stoke City, had won two and one in a match against the Stafford golf club Kingston Hill, some evidence that getting on harmoniously was not beyond them.

At the time, with Matthews showing no sign of withdrawing his transfer request, a group of seven influential supporters called a public meeting. An advertisement appeared around the town reserving the biggest type for 'Stanley Matthews must not go!' It called Stoke City supporters to King's Hall, Stoke, on Monday next (14 February) at 7.30 p.m. The motion to be considered by the meeting was:

We, the supporters of Stoke City Football Club present at the public meeting, being concerned for the welfare of the club and the district, earnestly urge the Directors to strive their utmost to secure the retention of Stanley Matthews.

We believe it is possible, if good will is shown by all parties, to satisfy him that it is in his best interests to remain with Stoke City, and convince him that he will be as happy and comfortable with Stoke as any other club.

Further, that the representatives of this meeting be appointed, whose good offices shall be available to both parties to bring about the result so ardently desired by the whole sporting community of North Staffordshire, such representatives to be appointed by the conveners of this meeting; and further, that a copy of this resolution be forwarded to the Directors and Stanley Matthews.

Twelve of Matthews's supposedly feuding teammates, including Freddie Steele, had their say in a statement in the build-up to the meeting: 'We . . . wish strongly to deny the unfounded rumours current in the district that there is trouble in the team. It has even been stated that there has been fighting among the players. These statements are utterly ridiculous and entirely baseless, and are strongly resented by us . . . We wish to state publicly that complete harmony exists among ourselves.'

The players went on to say that they did not wish to discuss the dispute between Matthews and the directors and added, cryptically, 'but we think it only fair to state that it has in no way affected our loyalty to the club, and in particular to the manager, Mr McGrory . . . This is an entirely voluntary statement.'

The public meeting itself was far less well disposed towards McGrory. If anything, antagonism towards him was its dominant theme, despite Matthews's reluctance at the time to speak out against him. The three thousand or so people who made it into the meeting – nearly twice as many tried to get in – rarely wasted an opportunity to make clear they regarded McGrory as a villain in the affair. They received the support of the main speakers who seemed keen to cast the manager as intransigent and unsympathetic.

Ashley Myott, a leading local industrialist, who was one of the conveners of the meeting, drew particular attention to the apparent conflict between a pronouncement by McGrory that he had always done his best to work closely with Matthews and the player's declaration that he was neither happy nor comfortable with Stoke City. Myott said: 'I have been wondering whether it is possible to explain it [the variance] in this way: that Mr McGrory, being a Scotsman, has, in his opinion, given justice and fair play to Matthews as a member of the team.' This one sentence produced two reactions from the audience: laughter at the gratuitous mention of the manager's roots and cries of 'No' at the idea he had treated Matthews fairly.

Buoyed by having what was always going to be uncritical backing, Myott went on: 'Maybe Mr McGrory will say – and say quite rightly – that he has treated the player as fairly as any other member of the team; but, knowing a little about Stanley Matthews, I have been wondering in my own mind this weekend whether the manager has not been a little stinting in that praise and appreciation that no money can replace, and gets the best out of a man. I am wondering whether that may not be one of the solutions of the difficulty.'

Another speaker, Sidney Dodd, questioned whether it was enough for McGrory to say that he had been fair to Matthews. 'Of course I accept Mr McGrory's official statement,' Dodd said, 'but I want to put this point of view: you can be dead fair to a man and yet kill his soul. We are not all built the same way. You can ignore a man and such an act of omission maybe as hurtful as an act of commission. I don't think the whole story is told by the statement from Mr McGrory that he has always been fair. Some men are indifferent to either criticism or praise. Others want handling with sympathy, understanding and appreciation.

I am just wondering whether that has always been extended to Stanley Matthews.' Above the discontented murmuring in the audience some voices called out: 'No, it has not.'

The public meeting agreed unanimously that a deputation should have talks with the board, which the directors had consented to beforehand. The same deputation should also seek an interview with Matthews.

The next day Matthews was adamant he still wished to move. 'I have not changed my attitude,' he said, 'and my previous requests for a transfer still stand.' He did, though, say he was willing to talk to the deputation from the public meeting.

Two days of talking lay ahead before the matter was resolved, for the time being at least. On the Wednesday afternoon, the board met and decided 'not to accede to the player's request to be transferred'. An unconfirmed report said the board felt the reasons Matthews gave for wanting to go were insufficient to warrant them placing him on the transfer list. No doubt having consulted his father, Matthews responded angrily. 'This is a body blow to me,' he said. 'Why should Stoke want to keep a player who is uncomfortable and not happy with the club? I am very disappointed. I expected the club to let me go.'

Crucially, though, the supporters' deputation still had not talked to Matthews. That evening this group spent two hours with him and the next day met the board, after McGrory was asked to leave the room 'to make the discussions as informal as possible'. Matthews would say that he was so touched by the strength of feeling from the Stoke fans – or 'my own townsfolk', as he called them – that he began to have misgivings about leaving the club. Sensing this, the supporters' group asked to meet Matthews a second time on Friday 18 February. Matthews was at the cinema when the request reached him and he agreed to go by car to the North Stafford Hotel. Here he finally succumbed to the pressure of local sentiment, enabling the supporters to issue the following statement:

We have had full and very frank discussions with the directors, as a result of which we have informed Matthews we are satisfied that real and genuine efforts will be made to make him happy and comfortable in future.

Stanley Matthews has authorised us to say that he is extremely glad at this happy termination of the matter and wishes to assure everyone that he will continue to do his best for Stoke City.

The word extremely was almost certainly an exaggeration. A letter from Matthews published in the local paper hardly gushed with enthusiasm: 'As I am to remain with Stoke City F.C., for the present, I shall endeavour, as I have done in the past, to give of the very best that is in me to justify the kindly feeling which seems to exist between the supporters of Stoke City F.C. and myself.' He sounded even less exuberant when a reporter asked him whether he had abandoned his desire to leave Stoke. 'I would rather say nothing about that,' he replied.

Proof of his continuing disenchantment surfaced again at the beginning of May 1938 when, with Stoke involved in a dogfight to stay in the First Division, Matthews initially refused to re-sign for the club.

On the other hand, no one could really argue that he had not been faithful to his word to do his best for the club in the weeks after the public meeting. The day after he changed his mind about wanting to leave Stoke City he served them stoutly in a 1-1 draw against Preston North End and a week later scored a goal in a 3-2 win over the League champions, Manchester City.

This rally in Stoke's fortunes was undermined by injuries to Clement Smith and Tommy Sale, two forwards bought by the club – bought back, in Sale's case, from Blackburn Rovers – in response to criticism that they had not filled gaps left by Steele's injury and the transfer of other players. Nor was Matthews's call-up by England to play against Scotland at Wembley – an undistinguished match won 1-0 by the Scots – particularly helpful. It meant he missed a home fixture against Everton, who, like Stoke, were now in peril of relegation. Everton sneaked a point at the Victoria Ground, adding to Stoke's poor run of results in March and April.

When he was available for club selection, Matthews's contributions rarely flagged. It meant that, even though he had done no more than moderately well against Scotland, England named him in their party for a post-season tour of Europe.

Still, this was of little help to Stoke who, with Matthews in the side, lost 3-0 at Huddersfield on Monday 2 May. Heading for the final Saturday of the season in five days' time, Stoke were fifth from the bottom of the First Division, one of six clubs on thirty-six points occupying the bottom six places. They had to beat Liverpool to be certain of staying up.

News that Matthews was not among the twenty-nine players who had re-signed for Stoke for the 1938–9 season broke the day after the Huddersfield defeat, perhaps giving the impression that he wanted to wait until the club's fate had been decided against Liverpool before committing himself to staying. He dealt perfunctorily with questions: 'I'm very busy in my business at the moment and I have nothing to say about the re-signing matter.'

As it happened Matthews ended the uncertainty two days before the Liverpool game. It was good news for the club only up to a point. His statement announcing what should have been glad tidings for Stoke was heavy with implied discontent. He said he was staying 'because I am particularly keen to make the tour of Germany and Switzerland [and France] with the FA team. I also do not want to miss part of my summer wages, as was the case last season.' In other words his decision was based on beating the FA's deadline for players to re-sign for their clubs in order to be eligible for England's European tour and to ensure he suffered no financial hardship. Allegiance to Stoke and McGrory was apparently incidental. The possibility of his leaving his boyhood club was morphing into a probability. He must have been gratified, maybe surprised, that within twenty-four hours the club released the extra £150 to take his loyalty bonus up to the maximum of £650.

So dawned the day of the Liverpool match and with it one of those stories that firmly roots the Matthews legend in a time when football was not quite so seriously self-absorbed as it is today. On the morning of the game, Freddie Steele, who in a few hours would be a key figure in Stoke's bid to stay in the First Division, married his cousin, Anne Steele.

When the club had given the couple permission to hold their big day on the last Saturday of the season, Stoke had seemed in little danger of relegation and assumed they would be able to make do without their free-scoring centre-forward. As the club's playing fortunes took a steep dive the decision then had to be hastily revisited. Under a new arrangement, the wedding date remained unchanged but not the itinerary of two of the principals. Straight after the morning ceremony, Steele and the Stoke captain, Arthur Turner, who was to give the bride away and was the only other player to attend the ceremony, would head straight for the Victoria Ground, missing the reception.

There was no question, though, of the marriage service being rushed through in a register office in deference to the groom's afternoon appointment. It was a full choral ceremony at Bethesda Church in Hanley, near to where both bride and groom were born. Before the bride arrived, Steele stood chatting with the priest, the Reverend Henry High, and a churchwarden about the afternoon's match. Hotfoot from the church, Steele went on to play a big part in keeping Stoke in the First Division, his fearless diving header sealing a 2-0 win.

The press made little of Steele's pre-match nuptials, the sort of human interest story that today would have them in a froth of excitement.

Four days after the Liverpool match, Matthews left Stoke

to join the England party for their European trip. For once he must have felt relieved to escape the town that had shaped and succoured him. The deterioration of his relationship with the club had now gathered pace to the point where its disintegration was a matter of time, even if superficially all was well.

The idea that Matthews had re-signed for Stoke in May as an act of expedience to safeguard his England place and protect his earnings looked a lot less like speculation when, a few days into the 1938–9 season, he again sought to leave Stoke. It was an indication of just how deep-rooted his discontent was. Also, it cast doubt on his assertion, written in a memoir soon after the war, that the goodwill directed his way at the February public meeting persuaded him to smooth out his differences with the club and stay 'to enjoy a further nine happy years'. Most of these so-called happy years covered the war when Matthews was mostly unavailable for Stoke and, like many players, took advantage of relaxed registration rules to represent other clubs.

By August 1938 Matthews's unrest was so patently obvious that reports of interest in him started appearing once the summer was over. On the last day of the month, Stoke issued what was described as 'an official denial' to a story that Leicester City had made a bid. As official denials go it must rank as one of the feeblest ever put out by a football club. The directors, it said, deprecated persistent reports regarding Matthews's future, because, 'so far as is known, [he] has settled down at Stoke'.

Feeble but honest. Stoke were right to be unsure of the extent to which Matthews had settled down. Two days after the official denial of an approach by Leicester the news leaked that he had in fact put in yet another transfer request. Matthews would keep his mouth shut throughout this latest straining of the relationship between club and player. The club tried to do the same despite reports of seven leading clubs being interested in Stoke's England winger and the record transfer fee of £14,500, paid earlier in the year by Arsenal for Bryn Jones of Wolves, being under threat.

Eventually the board were forced to admit they had held a series of meetings to discuss their response to a request that Matthews had indeed made. The reason for his wanting to leave was presented in the nebulous language that persists today: the player was simply concerned with his football future and a change of club was the only way he could achieve a beneficial outcome. That McGrory was once again the real reason for Matthews wanting to leave was never stated explicitly. It could, though, be inferred easily enough when the board, in once again announcing that they would not let the player go, included in their statement that they had given the manager a unanimous vote of confidence.

How the decision that Matthews should stay was reached was a story in itself – a mystery story, as it turned out. McGrory let slip that Stoke had, before the season started, discussed with Manchester United exchanging him for two players plus a sum of money. Then, after Matthews filed his latest transfer request, the well-informed football correspondent of the local paper reported that in preliminary discussions the board agreed in principle finally to be shot of their manifestly unhappy outside-right. When the board met to confirm this they talked for four hours, breaking off in the middle to watch a reserve-team game. At the time of this break, nothing had changed: five directors, including the board chairman, were still in favour of Matthews's departure and only one was against. No wonder the local paper called the decision that he must stay an unexpected volte-face.

The fact that Matthews did not say anything at the time and, in all his later reminiscences, did not refer to his renewed effort to leave the club at the start of the 1938–9 season nor to why he accepted without a murmur what was apparently a perplexingly late change of mind, means it will remain a mystery. What is certain is that the long-accepted fact that Stoke and Matthews resumed an untroubled relationship after the February public meeting was simply not the case.

And yet at the start of the summer of 1938 all had seemed well. A smiling McGrory had joined a civic send-off party that gathered at Stoke station when Matthews left for the East Anglian port of Harwich, from where the England team would set sail to play Germany, Switzerland and France before the end of May.

Chapter 6

'Not until the match against [Northern] Ireland had fans talked
about him being the best ever . . . If he's not the best,
there certainly never was better'

Matthews did not miss an England match in 1938 – his eight
appearances were the most he made in a calendar year – and
there was no question that he was now the nation's leading
outside-right. What he was not yet was a man of the world. His
seven internationals since his debut against Scotland in 1934
had all been in the British Isles. He could hardly have had a
more tumultuous introduction to representing his country in
a foreign land than the match against Germany at the Olympic
Stadium in Berlin on Saturday 14 May 1938. A game that,
purely in footballing terms, was remarkable enough, would be
accompanied by one of the foreshocks – small but perceptible –
of the outbreak of the rapidly approaching global war.

Teams had started to travel by air – the Germans flew to
Croydon for the 1935 match against England – but the FA had
still to embrace this relatively new mode of passenger transport.
Matthews's rail journey from Stoke to Harwich, where he joined
up with his England teammates, the overnight sea crossing to
the Hook of Holland and then twelve more hours on the train
to Berlin, meant he had been travelling for about thirty hours by

the time the team reached the German capital. At least the ordeal of a big official welcome in Berlin, which had been expected, failed to materialise. Fritz Szepan, Germany's captain, was there to greet the visitors, but he was part of a reception committee that was outnumbered by the party stepping off the train.

Henry Rose, of the *Daily Express*, was a member of this party. In the first of two scene-setting features, he had written about the part English residents played in establishing football in Germany in the late nineteenth century. Rose said they failed to interest the locals in cricket and rugby football before having more luck with association football. One of the first clubs to be formed was Berliner Fussball Club Britannia, who in 1898 won the inaugural Brandenburg championship, one of two regional leagues that launched competitive football in the country.

Rose's second piece said that German football scouts had travelled the country and watched 600,000 players to make sure they chose the best team to play England. The pick of these, several hundred, all of them amateurs, were then gathered together for trials. The exercise seems to have been a success only in public relations terms. In the end, Rose noted, the team selected to play England were old timers with established reputations.

The story neither Rose nor any other correspondent wrote in advance of the match was the one that, in retrospect at least, seems the most obvious: the ramifications of England playing in the capital of a country that a few weeks before had annexed Austria – a takeover euphemistically called the Anschluss, meaning link-up – and whose army would soon lead the Axis powers into a conflict that would engulf the world. One immediate effect of this was that, as far as the hosts were concerned, England would now be playing a team with a new title, Greater Germany, with players from Austria, officially referred to as the Eastern March, eligible for selection.

Rose did wake up to this aspect of England's visit on the eve of the match when he reported that the England players were likely to create a precedent by giving the Nazi salute before the game. He said that he had spoken to Charles Wreford-Brown, a London solicitor who had captained his country as an amateur in the 1890s and was now the FA member in charge of the England party. 'We regard the matter as so important that we are holding a special conference in the morning to decide,' Wreford-Brown said. The quote reeked of moral panic gripping a delegation woefully ill prepared for the predictable diplomatic tribulations that awaited them. The matter was so important that they had waited until the morning of the match to discuss it.

In the end the England team did give the Nazi salute before the match, creating an image that has come to be regarded as one of the greatest moments of infamy in the history of British sport. Joseph Goebbels, the Reich Minister of Propaganda, seized on its implied endorsement of the regime. He instructed all German newspapers to publish the picture.

Who made the decision that the team should salute was told differently – diametrically so – by the officials and players of England, a sure sign that the panic infected both sides and never went away.

Stanley Rous, who was the FA secretary at the time[*] and was with the team in Berlin, said he left the players to decide whether to salute. In other words, the generals resolved their inner turmoil by delegating responsibility to the poor bloody infantry. Helpfully, Rous pointed out to them that whatever they decided would determine whether the match was held in a friendly or hostile atmosphere.

Matthews was adamant that the opposite was true and the players were told they must salute. He said the FA sprung the decision on them just before kick-off. 'We were appalled. I've never known such an atmosphere in an England dressing

---

[*] Rous later became president of the game's world governing body Fifa, for which he gained a knighthood.

room.' Other sources have suggested that it was the Foreign Office which directed the players to give the Nazi salute, almost certainly because it was widely expected that Adolf Hitler, the Chancellor, would be at the match. But the only record of FO involvement is inconclusive. Rous said that the British ambassador, Sir Nevile Henderson, had told him: 'When I go to see Herr Hitler I give him the Nazi salute because that is the formal courtesy expected. It carries no hint of approval of anything Hitler or his regime may do. If I do it, why should you or your team not do it?'

In fact, Hitler did not turn up. Leading figures from the Nazi Party who did attend included Goebbels, Hermann Goering, Rudolf Hess and Joachim von Ribbentrop, all immaculately uniformed and bemedalled – in contrast to Sir Nevile, who sported a shooting hat with hawk's feather and a favourite old pullover. Hitler's absence was reportedly because he had developed an aversion to watching football after Germany's 2-0 defeat by Norway in the quarter-finals of the 1936 Olympic Games. The impending invasion of Czechoslovakia might also have been a distraction.*

Rose reported that before the match, played in front of 110,000 spectators, the England team saluted throughout 'Deutschland Über Alles' and the 'Horst Wessel Song', the anthem of the Nazi Party, but did so 'with some diffidence'. He said that Eddie Hapgood had thought that standing to attention should have been enough. Rose said another player he did not name told him: 'I know that when my father sees a picture of me giving the salute he won't be too pleased.' It has also been reported, but never substantiated, that England dropped the Wolverhampton Wanderers player Stan Cullis because he

---

* Hitler did take an interest, though. Hans Jacob, the German goalkeeper, said the Chancellor had ordered the players' employers to release them for ten days' training immediately before the fixture at a camp in Duisburg.

said he would not salute. Only in his 2000 autobiography did Matthews come up with the story that the players noticed two fans in the crowd waving a Union Jack and assuaged their guilt by, to a man, gazing at the fans and their flag as they stretched out their right arms.

Voelkischer Beobachter gave a German, possibly propagandist, account of what happened. It added to the confusion, particularly with regard to the attitude of the England team. The paper maintained that the apparently disgruntled Englishmen gave one more fraternal greeting to the crowd after the game. It also attributed to them a mentality more usually associated with their twenty-first-century descendants: 'The action of the Englishmen in raising their right arms in greeting during the playing of the German National Anthems and in taking leave of the spectators with the German salute at the end of the game was particularly well received. In itself probably only a gesture of politeness; but when one knows the disinclination of English footballers for every kind of formality, this proof of esteem of comradely feeling should be particularly emphasised.'*

Once again Reinhold Muenzenberg was the Germany defender marking Matthews. While the left-back, in his thirtieth year, had aged to his detriment since subduing Matthews at White Hart Lane in 1935, the twenty-three-year-old Englishman, light-footed and limber, was approaching a prime that would go on seemingly forever. The supremacy Matthews gained over his older adversary was a major factor in an emphatic victory. His performance included a brilliant solo effort to put England 4-1 in front just before half-time. Each of his four fellow forwards

---

* English football extended another gesture of politeness towards the German regime at this time. Aston Villa played a match in Berlin the day after England's victory and their chairman, Fred Normansell, was apparently unabashed in accepting a Nazi badge from Hitler. At the time appeasement was popular among holders of much loftier offices than Normansell's. History would judge the actions of the England players and Villa chairman far more harshly than contemporary commentators did.

also contributed at least one goal in a 6-3 result that Hitler did well to miss.[*]

What merit there was in England's victory over Germany should really be judged in the context of the whole tour, particularly the match against Switzerland in Zurich a week later. The German press was generous in its praise for how England played in Berlin. *Lokal-Anzeiger* said that against a side who 'commanded the art of football in its most complete form' Germany had no chance. *Hamburger Fremdenblatt* described the standard of English professional football as unattainable and said it would probably remain so. Quite what this correspondent would have made of England's 2-1 defeat in Zurich can only be imagined. Some did try to make excuses for it, and there was an element of doubt about the match-winning penalty that the German referee, Dr Peco Bauwens, who, incongruously, wore cycling breeches to officiate the match, awarded the Swiss after the ball struck Alf Young on the arm.

Henry Rose provided the least convincing defence of England's performance. In so doing he showed that even in the press box there were those still inclined to the view that English professionals played on Elysian Fields where, when all was equal, no one could match them. Rose blamed England's defeat on what he called the holiday nature of the build-up to the game and spiced his criticism with patrician indignation: 'No one can convince me that staying in the most expensive hotels and eating rich food, to which they are not accustomed, is the right preamble to a big football match.

'A few hours' flight, a few hours' rest, and then I'm sure our fellows would prove to these Continentals that we are still the masters they tell us we are in the after-dinner speeches.' In fact,

---

[*] Frank Broome, the England centre-forward, completed a notable double. He played on successive days at the Olympic Stadium, giving a Nazi salute each time. Having contributed to England's victory, he scored again for his club, Aston Villa, who beat a German Select eleven 3-2 in front of another crowd of more than 100,000.

he added, that if the match were played over again 'I would mortgage my flat and furniture on a runaway victory for our men'.

Other observers were more perceptive in seeing that Switzerland's victory was not a question of England having an off-day. They noted the home team discomfited the visitors with their 'confusing originality'. In particular, the Swiss disregarded the rigid positioning that the English stuck to as if it would be ill mannered not to. The half-backs spread wide, successfully stifling Matthews and Cliff Bastin on the wings, and the Swiss centre-half, rather than being just a stopper, pressed forward to cut off passes intended for England's front line. Alf Young, England's centre-half, who was used simply to deploying his considerable frame to impede the opposition's No. 9, found himself spinning like a roulette wheel as two light-footed inside-forwards buzzed around him.

Rose said that while the market price of the England team was about £80,000, a huge amount in those days, Switzerland were made up mainly of players from Zurich Grasshoppers, 'a club that would be fighting to keep a place around the middle of our Second Division table, something like the standard of, say, Chesterfield or Southampton'. What he might have added was that Switzerland, by playing the way they did against conservative opposition, demonstrated the difference between price and value. Lauro Amado, who six years earlier was playing for the London side Tufnell Park in a minor English league, was one of Switzerland's biggest successes. An outside-right, here he was upstaging his opposite number, the brightest star in world football. Matthews admitted to playing poorly against a left-back, Gusti Lehmann, who made a living as the leader of a dance band in a Zurich nightspot. Far from being humiliated, as had been predicted, Lehmann not only subdued Matthews but frequently raced across the pitch to help out Sevi Minelli at right-back.

Nor did Rose relate whether England moved to a cheap hotel and eschewed rich food before taking on France five days after their Switzerland defeat. More likely their 4-2 win in front of a record crowd of 65,000 in the Colombes Stadium in Paris was simply a case of the French not having read the Swiss manual on how to beat Matthews and company. England coped comfortably with opponents who stayed loyal to the game's old formulas.

Matthews's contributions at this time were such that he remained an automatic choice for England, in whose colours he produced another of those performances that gave lustre to his reputation. If the fixture against Northern Ireland at Old Trafford on 16 November 1938 had been a stage play rather than a football match, the critics would have chided Matthews for brazenly stealing every scene. As it was he received only bountiful commendations from all who watched.

Matthews's teenage brother, Ron, a very partial critic, of course, remembered the match vividly into old age. He travelled to watch it with the Port Vale team, looked after by the former Stoke forward Harry Davies. It was, said Ron, an extraordinary performance by his brother, 'far, far above the 1953 FA Cup final', the match in which, according to legend, Matthews gave the supreme expression of his skills as a goal provider. In 1938 Willie Hall, the Tottenham forward, was the player who profited, four of his five goals being created by Matthews. It was as if Matthews had deliberately set out to answer criticism that he had ignored Hall ten days earlier when they formed the right side of the English League's attack against the Scottish League. Matthews was accused of having chosen instead to flaunt his sleight of foot in the 3-1 victory.

Matthews said he had been dismayed by the criticism and only after he had corrected this did he put on an exhibition against Northern Ireland, scoring England's seventh goal after a serpentine run from the halfway line. 'Harry Davies turned to me and said, "That was something you were lucky to see, something unbelievable." And it was,' Ron Matthews said. 'It was an extraordinary display.' The journalist John Macadam gave a nice twist to the exercise of valuing Matthews: 'The poker-faced, bandy wizard sent his stock soaring so high that, all personal likes and dislikes apart, you'd have to be a Rockefeller to buy him now.'

Billy Meredith, whose performances, mostly on the right wing, for Wales between 1895 and 1920 had made him as feted a player as Matthews, said: 'Not until the match against [Northern] Ireland had fans talked about him being the best ever . . . If he's not the best, there certainly never was better.'

For many months now footballers like nearly everyone else in Europe had been carrying on their lives hoping that another major war could be averted. Mention of 1939 still resonates with foreboding but the year opened with people nervously trusting that one man's megalomania might somehow be curbed.

The strivings of the footballers of Stoke City were typical of a stolid determination to carry on as normal. They had started the 1938–9 season by winning only once in eight matches but had a productive run in the opening weeks of the new year. Matthews's form remained constant while Freddie Steele returned to his acquisitive best in front of goal. The centre-forward scored nine times in a sequence of five League wins that removed any possibility of another struggle to avoid relegation.

Steele, who had been deeply depressed by his recurring knee injury, said he had definitely benefited from the board's enlightened action in sending him for what the chairman described as psychoanalytical treatment. In time sports psychiatry would become a crowded field. In the 1930s it was pretty much a deserted one. Matthews talked incredulously about Steele's visits to what he called 'a well-known nerve specialist in the Potteries' who would turn the lights down in his study and fix the player with piercing eyes. Steele was encouraged to keep a notebook and pencil at his bedside so he could write down what he remembered of his dreams. 'He convinced me there was no reason I should not recover my form,' Steele said.

Sadly for Steele, while his head was fixed by the shrink his knee proved less susceptible to treatment. In a grim reminder of what was going on in the wider world, Steele, along with other Stoke players, was summoned to a Territorial training camp in Lincolnshire after the end of the 1938–9 season. While there, he twisted his knee in a boxing bout. A few days later it was being operated on in a nursing home in Birmingham.

Matthews seemed to have a monopoly of what blessings were to be had. He and his wife Betty became parents for the first time when their daughter, Jean, was born on the first day of the year and, as he continued to escape the injuries that afflicted his teammates – possibly not so much good fortune as a consequence of his compulsive attention to conditioning – he added an unshakeable consistency to his list of virtues.

Having played so well against Northern Ireland the previous November, Matthews was, once again, an uncontroversial pick for England's visit to Hampden Park in mid-April. The 2-1 victory was England's first in Glasgow for twelve years and Matthews's first success against the Scots in three attempts. With a thumping wind at their backs, Scotland must have feared their 1-0 lead at the interval would not be enough. Matthews, coping sure-footedly with a cloying surface that made conditions doubly testing, did as much as anyone to confirm this. Moments before the end, with the score 1-1, he scooped over a cross from near the corner flag. He fell on his backside from the effort of levering the ball upwards and from his ground-level view watched Tommy Lawton rise from the mud to head it into the net. In the dressing room Lawton said: 'By the way, Stanley, I'm six foot – not six foot two.'

*

For the second successive summer Matthews set off with England for Europe. Matches had been arranged against Italy, Yugoslavia and Romania. As they left the England players could have been excused for feeling more like an expeditionary force than a football team. The German Chancellor's minatory posturing had made the outbreak of war in Europe inevitable. Stoke City had already cancelled a tour of Germany and England's visit to the Continent went ahead only after earnest discussions about its advisability.

Eddie Hapgood's team encountered only conviviality, the warmongering, for the moment, confined to the political classes. Italians, whose fascist leader Benito Mussolini would declare war on Britain just over a year later, gave England a particularly generous welcome when they arrived in Milan by train. Based on this experience, Matthews commented that during the war he could never bring himself to believe that Italy really wanted to fight the Allies.

The pattern of the tour would bear a striking resemblance to the one twelve months earlier: a commendable result to start with, a sobering defeat and finally a win to re-establish confidence.

The 2-2 draw with Italy was less spectacular than the win over Germany that opened the 1938 tour. On the other hand, Italy were a much better side. They were World Cup holders and in just over five weeks would retain the trophy. At times Italy made England look third rate but were lucky their second goal, by centre-forward Silvio Piola, was given after a blatant handball. Matthews maintained that Piola not only punched the ball but his follow-through gave the England right-back, George Male, a black eye. In the stands Stanley Rous declined an invitation from Umberto, the Crown Prince of Italy, to accompany him on to the pitch to advise the German referee the goal should be disallowed.

Matthews made a telling contribution despite struggling

to shake off the full-back Pietro Rava and suffering a chipped hip bone. He laid on the only goal of the first half for Tommy Lawton; then, with England 2-1 behind, broke clear in the seventy-seventh minute to cross a ball that Italy failed to deal with, allowing Willie Hall to score.

England received as warm a reception in Belgrade as they had in Milan. They travelled overnight, their train stopping in Venice, and arrived in the Yugoslav capital in the early hours. Not only was the platform crowded, the visitors were honoured with a full-blown civic welcome. Hapgood, without any warning, found himself pushed forward to reply to a long, scripted greeting delivered by a local dignitary. Matthews reckoned the reaction to Hapgood's unprepared response was the most enthusiastic he ever heard given to a speech. Even the England team joined in the applause, a mixture of relief and admiration that their captain had shown himself as steadfast when wearing blazer and trousers as he was in football kit.

The 2-1 defeat that followed provided yet another reminder that those who still regarded England as the foremost footballing nation, and there were many, were deluding themselves – even if the case that they were inferior to a good Yugoslavia side was not convincingly proven. Extenuating circumstances included a bumpy pitch, the damaged Matthews starting the game but being a passenger for most of it, Hapgood suffering an ankle injury and another questionable refereeing decision. This time Proseja's blatant manhandling of Broome went unpenalised when the England forward seemed certain to score.

Once again applying the laws was an issue. Frank Carruthers of the *Daily Mail* said in his report from Belgrade: 'I had thought that the Continental countries had at last accepted the British interpretation of the rules concerning obstruction, holding and pushing, but I cannot recall an occasion when such patent offences were committed and consistently permitted by the French referee.' Carruthers said it was not a matter of Britain being right and Europe wrong. What was needed, if countries were to continue playing each other, was a meeting 'to regularise the rules'.

The Yugoslavia defeat would be Matthews's last appearance in an official international for nearly eight years. His hip injury kept him out of the final tour game, a 2-0 win over Romania in Bucharest, and before England were due to play their next international normal life had been suspended. All but three of the current players – Matthews, Tommy Lawton and Raich Carter – had won their last England caps.

Chapter 7

'Remember the two million of our fellows
fighting for their lives and ours'

An airbrushed version of football history has Stanley Matthews playing only eleven club matches in the seven seasons between 1939 and 1946 – three League matches in 1939 and eight more in the 1945–6 season, all for Stoke City. This distortion was caused by the suspension of the Football League at the outbreak of hostilities and the fact that the fixtures that replaced them, although sanctioned by the Football Association, were not officially recorded despite the important remnant of normality they represented for the embattled nation. In fact, Matthews played at least two hundred times for clubs, country and other representative teams while serving in the RAF and the excitement provided during this period by an exceptional Blackpool team, of which Matthews became an integral part, has been available only to more assiduous students of the game.

Nor did wartime internationals, which attracted many hundreds of thousands of fans, receive the recognition they might have done. England players wore plain white shirts after the FA decided to remove their badge. The Wolves player Billy Wright said the absence of any sort of national emblem drained him of his confidence when he ran out for his England debut during the war. 'I felt as nervous as a kitten,' he said. The more experienced Raich Carter had another beef. He complained about playing seventeen times in some of the best teams England ever put out and not having even one cap to show for it.

On Saturday 2 September 1939 Stoke played their third match of the new season. The scoreline – Middlesbrough 2 Stoke City 2 – may have seemed a quintessentially English code for all is well with the world, but the reality was very different. German troops had crossed the border into Poland the day before and the British Prime Minister, Neville Chamberlain, set a deadline by which Germany must announce plans to withdraw or face a hostile response. At 11.15 a.m. on Sunday 3 September, Chamberlain broadcast, in tones as quintessentially English as the Stoke scoreline, a sombre message to the nation: 'I have to tell you now that no such undertaking has been received and consequently this country is at war with Germany.'

Few lives would not be seriously affected. Professional footballers learned very early on that theirs would not be among the exceptions. Play in the Football League was suspended almost straightaway. Not long afterwards, Stanley Matthews was conscripted into the Royal Air Force, adding the identity Matthews, Stanley Aircraftman No. 1361317 to that of Stanley Matthews, dashing England footballer. He would say that holding the lowest rank was a relief because it cleared him of having received preferential treatment.

Over the six years he served in the RAF, mostly stationed in the North-West close to Blackpool, he did make some progress through the ranks, but only, as he said self-mockingly, to the 'dizzy heights of corporal'. However modest this promotion, he still did not enjoy it. He said it was more difficult imposing discipline on others than on himself. He must have been, he reckoned, the mildest and most easygoing NCO the services had ever known.

His joining the RAF invited fairly obvious puns along the lines of 'the wingman who became a wingman', but he was an airman only in name. His role was that of a physical education instructor. The few times he did fly was as a passenger travelling to play in overseas football matches. The only bullets he fired at a foe he propelled with his leather football boots and the nearest he came to danger was after a match at Preston when the sirens sounded as the players were changing. He recalled that a teammate left his top set of false teeth in the dressing room and, as the players headed for the shelter, was shouted at for going back to retrieve them.

The government quickly took the view that anything more than a temporary suspension of the professional game at club and international level would be harmful to the nation's morale. Matthews recalled his commanding officer telling him that the War Office wanted footballers to help the war effort by continuing to play when circumstances allowed. He described this as music to his ears, while taking care to add that, if needed, he was more than willing to fight the enemy.

The two great wars of the twentieth century wrecked the playing careers of countless professional sportsmen. For the average footballer, the most precious years are those between the ages of twenty-four and thirty, precisely the span of Matthews's life disrupted by the second of the world conflicts. Arguably it was his greatest triumph that, as he himself once reflected having played on for twenty years after 1945, it did not affect his career as badly as it did others.

Hardly surprisingly, club football in the first year of the war proceeded like an unscripted play. No one was quite sure what was going to happen next despite the earnest efforts of officials. Restrictions on moving around the country were the biggest problem. Teams were forced to pull out of matches at short notice and there were comical last-minute attempts to drum up a full eleven. Allowing players to guest for other teams, which Matthews did a number of times, notably a prolonged spell with Blackpool, was a help. But it also gave the sense of a makeshift structure. This, at least, provided some excuse for club records not being kept as diligently as they might have been.

International football, which was essentially matches between the home nations, took a while to gain acceptance before spectator numbers picked up strongly. Key to this was the exceptional quality of the England team. In 1943 and 1944, England scored forty-five goals in ten unbeaten matches against Scotland and Wales. Matthews appeared in nine of them. England against Scotland excited the most interest. Thousands were locked out when England won 8-0 in front of 60,000 at Maine Road, Manchester, in October 1943 and in three matches in 1944, in which England scored fifteen times, more than 300,000 spectators passed through the turnstiles.

This was way above the turnout for club matches, although, in time, even some of these games started to attract gates that compared to pre-war figures. Blackpool, once Matthews became a regular on the wing, were especially popular. The team achieved a celebrity that has never really been recognised since. Attendances swelled wherever they played. A showdown between a Matthews-inspired Blackpool and Arsenal at Stamford Bridge in the spring of 1943 engaged the interest of the whole nation, drawing a vast gathering to west London.

Exactly a week after Chamberlain's declaration of war, it was decided to resume football in what were designated neutral and reception areas. A third category, evacuation areas, was rated at risk of heavy bombing and not suitable for large gatherings.

The Football League went to work establishing regional competitions. Initially they imposed a fifty-mile limit on how far teams could travel. This was lifted as certain clubs, particularly those on the south coast, were being excluded, but the basic concept of regionalisation remained. Longer-standing practices also stayed in place. Not surprisingly, given football's paranoia about how much players earned, these included a cap on match fees: professionals would receive no more than thirty shillings per game.

A story told by Stan Cullis, who captained England during the war, illustrated the resentment caused by this small amount. Tommy Lawton, sitting in the dressing room before one international match, waved a £1 note in one hand and a ten-shilling note in the other. 'There are seventy thousand here,' he said to his teammates, 'and this is all we are getting for turning out today.' Cullis also said, though, that he used to tell the players how lucky there were compared to the 'two million of our fellows fighting for their lives and ours. I wasn't going to ask for more.'

Friendly matches preceded the start of the regional format, which took time to organise. Two weeks after their 2-2 draw at Middlesbrough, Stoke were one of fifty-eight clubs which took part in what were billed as Football League friendly matches. Matthews was in the side that beat Coventry City 3-1 at the Victoria Ground. A crowd of fewer than 5,000 watched the game, the sort of figure that would persuade some Football League clubs that the wartime game wasn't worth it. Stoke's second friendly a week later attracted a much bigger crowd with Matthews again the main draw when Port Vale made the short trip to the Victoria Ground. The first meeting between the very adjacent neighbours for more than three years rewarded those who turned up with a red-blooded encounter that ended 3-2 to Stoke.

By late September, an emergency committee formed by the FA and Football League were ready with their plans. Clubs would be divided into eight areas – North-West, North-East, East Midland, Midland, West, South 'A' and 'B' and South-West

– with matches starting on Saturday 21 October. The teams grouped in the Western Division with Stoke were fellow First Division sides Everton, Liverpool and Manchester United, Manchester City of the Second Division, and Third Division North clubs Chester, Crewe Alexandra, New Brighton, Port Vale, Stockport County, Tranmere and Wrexham.

A flavour of how the abnormal circumstances affected these opening regional matches was vividly illustrated by the game between Arsenal and Charlton Athletic in the Southern 'A' Division.

For a start, the fixture took place at White Hart Lane, home of Tottenham Hotspur, who had taken in their traditional north London foe as lodgers. This was because Arsenal's Highbury ground was now the HQ of the Air Raid Precautions service and, in due course, was bombed. The scoreline was also a little weird, 8-4 to Arsenal, three of whose goals were penalties scored by Leslie Compton. The likely explanation for the high score was that Sam Bartram, the Charlton goalkeeper, went off injured to be replaced by Ralph Calland, whose usual role was playing left-back for Torquay United. At least the biggest crowd of the day, 8,931, had plenty of entertainment, even if it was more end of the pier than start of a new football season.

Things got dafter still. On Christmas Day 1940, for example, some teams played twice. Leicester City lost 5-2 away to Northampton in the morning, then in the afternoon exacted what almost makes sense of the phrase 'instant revenge'. With one team change, they beat the Cobblers 7-2 at their Filbert Street ground.

At Norwich's Carrow Road that day a match thrust wartime competition in Britain dangerously close to a charge of bringing the game into disrepute. Brighton turned up with five players, supplemented their ranks with two Norwich reserves and four soldiers from the terraces and lost by a pantomimic 18-0.

Even the football pools operators had to adapt to the times

with old adversaries forced to seek accommodations. To save money on paper and to release workers for the war effort, eight leading pools companies banded together to form Unity Pools. Littlewoods, one of the eight, had given their building to the government to use as a parachute factory.

Stoke City enjoyed certain advantages at the start of the war. One, they were not within an evacuation area, so the Victoria Ground could stage matches; and, two, they retained a number of their regular players because they lived locally. Registered Football League players who lived some distance from their clubs were permitted to represent a nearer one – and it hardly mattered if they switched loyalties to and fro, depending on where they were stationed, during the season.

On the debit side for Stoke, good players such as Frank Baker and Syd Peppitt, who were in the Territorial Army, were called up, and Matthews's availability went from good to patchy to non-existent. Constantly in demand, Matthews switched clubs as much as anyone.

Worst of all for the club, their prospects of becoming Football League champions for the first time, which had started to look so promising, evaporated with the suspension of the peacetime programme. Matthews's restlessness and Freddie Steele's wonky right knee might have scuppered the team's chances anyway, but Stoke had other fine players at the time, including Tommy Sale and Neil Franklin, an exceptional young centre-half.

It might be imagined that all clubs would have been enthusiastic about giving their players the chance to continue doing what they were good at, and to give fans an escape from the miseries of wartime. This was not the case. Derby County, for instance, became so discouraged by the limited public support when football restarted that they soon closed down, three seasons passing before they kicked off again. Aston Villa, Exeter,

Gateshead, Ipswich and Sunderland would all join Derby in spurning the launch of the regional leagues.*

Stoke City's directors took a more sanguine view of what the game had to offer at this time of danger and uncertainty. They figured, correctly, that attendances were bound to drop off given the initial shock of the nation being at war and the enforced dismantling of the old structures, but fans would soon recognise that the game played by professionals had not lost its entertainment value.

On a personal level, Matthews had a good war as far as football was concerned. He maintained a busy schedule for clubs and country. At club level he was soon two-timing. In December 1939, within weeks of the start of the regional leagues, he played his first game as a professional for a club other than Stoke. This was for Crewe Alexandra, who were just that little bit nearer his new base on the Fylde coast. By the time the season was out he had also gone north to play for Rangers against Greenock Morton in one of Scotland's wartime regional leagues and, in April, for Airdrieonians in a Scottish Cup semi-final replay against Dundee United, a match Dundee won 3-1.

He was allowed to play for Crewe even though the Third Division side had been placed in the same regional division as Stoke. Matthews's efforts failed to save Crewe from a 2-1 defeat by Manchester City, a result that moved City above Stoke at the top of the table. For once, though, Crewe fans did not care too much about the result. They regarded Matthews dressed in their colours at Gresty Road as ample compensation. England's right wing attracted more than three times the 1,500 or so fans who would normally turn out to watch the yeomen footballers of Crewe take on equally modest opposition.

---

* A number of players abandoned by their clubs at this time noticed that they were quickly re-engaged when it suited their former employers. This helped to build up resentment that came very close to causing a strike soon after the war ended in 1945.

Very early on, too, call-ups for a succession of international and representative matches robbed Stoke of Matthews's services. Stanley Rous, the FA secretary who effectively took over control of the England side during the war, understood the importance of picking Matthews whenever his military service permitted. Given the austere times, Rous appreciated fans wanted an hour and a half's distraction from their everyday anxieties. Choosing entertainers such as Matthews was soon given precedence over most other considerations. Accordingly, he came as near to being a constant in the England side as anyone.*

For obvious reasons, the vast majority of the international matches were against Scotland and Wales. This has encouraged a tendency to diminish England's achievement in winning such an impressively high percentage of their wartime matches. Some worthy judges have pressed a different view. Bill Shankly, the Scotland wing-half who was as forthright on the pitch as he was off it when he became a treasured manager of Liverpool, praised unconditionally the England team which beat the Scots 8-0 at Maine Road in October 1943.

Shankly said his country fielded their strongest possible eleven in that match, in which Matthews's first international goal for five years completed the rout. 'You cannot even argue about this – this was a great England team,' Shankly said. 'They had wonderful players in the side, and just as many waiting to get a game.' Brian James, an eminent football journalist at the time, wrote: 'The mere fact of the concurrent world conflict should not deprive them of their credit, for it did not disguise the evidence of their talent.'

Stoke did their best to serve the community throughout the disruption. Their chairman, Harry Booth, announced soon after

---

* What Rous did in fact was run England in a way that a manager would, in other words observing a principle of consistency when picking the team. Unfortunately, none of the panjandrums at the FA twigged that the resultant success might be trying to tell them something. After the war the selection committee, forever haggling, was reinstated.

the Football League suspended competition that the club aimed to form a team that could provide some attractive football. Attractive and effective, as it turned out. Their honours board records a successful first season in one of the regional tournaments: War League Western Division Champions 1939–40. This triumph, long forgotten by all but the most ardent Stoke fans, strengthens the argument that the Matthews-generation team might have won a First Division title if events had not intervened.

Matthews's new existence as a serviceman-footballer meant he missed Stoke City's opening match when competitive football resumed in mid-October. While Stoke secured a notable 4-4 draw at Everton after the reigning Football League champions led 4-1, Matthews was undergoing a new sort of training – and may even have been that rare RAF recruit who actually enjoyed an afternoon's square bashing as a way of topping up his fitness.

What he did not particularly enjoy were the orders bellowed at him on the parade ground by Sergeant Ivor Powell, the Wales international footballer. Powell, whose clubs included Queens Park Rangers and Aston Villa, knew Matthews well but, in the best traditions of those who drilled new recruits, treated him with brutal disdain. It did not last. Matthews would be best man at Powell's wedding.

By now the RAF had posted Matthews to a base near Blackpool, a place he already knew a little. He had taken a break there during one of his run-ins with Stoke. His partiality for fresh air meant he took straightaway to the resort on Lancashire's coast that looked out over the Irish Sea. Being stationed there was pure serendipity for Matthews. While other conscripts were being lewdly exhorted to get out of bed each morning, Matthews was on the beach by six for an hour's exercise before reporting for parade. Over the years this beach would become his Eden, a place to hone his fitness – and, in due course, a place to hide away. This was later, though. At the start of the war, it was a happy family unit – Matthews, Betty and their daughter – who completed the move from Stoke to what he called a comfortable billet in Blackpool.

No longer was it straightforward for Matthews to turn out regularly for Stoke. He faced a 130-mile round trip from his new home and, in time, growing demands to put national interest before that of a club. By early December 1939 Stoke were top of the Western Division despite suffering their first defeat, a 4-2 loss away to Crewe in their seventh match. Matthews had missed this fixture, against the side he would be playing for three weeks later, because it clashed with England's first wartime international against Scotland.

England beat the Scots 2-1 at St James' Park, Newcastle, in a match that was mainly distinguished by an improbable selection: a Scotsman picked for England. The Manchester City pair Sam Barkas and Eric Brook, driving to the game from Manchester, were hurt when their car crashed near Ripon. Brook was particularly badly injured. He suffered a fractured skull and never played again. England kicked off with nine men as frantic efforts were made to rustle up two replacements from the ranks of Newcastle United. Tommy Pearson, at the ground as a spectator, was one who stepped in even though he was a Scot from Edinburgh. The left winger would play two more internationals, both for Scotland, after the war.

The match at St James', together with the two England–Wales games, established before the end of 1939 that wartime internationals were viable, generating far greater interest than club matches. As well as these official fixtures, the FA soon established the popularity of representative games. Matthews, in particular, put numbers on gates and one of his command performances lifted morale just that little bit more. Also, these matches proved effective fundraisers for war-related causes.[*]

---

[*] Some leading players reacted against the miserly pay they received from the FA for these representative games. The unnamed plotters discussed forming their own all star team

The FA's growing fixation with arranging international matches meant that by Easter 1940 they had organised ten of them, far more than in peacetime. The clubs most affected by the loss of players started to grumble. Everton and Manchester City were the first to do so. Stoke joined in later than they might have done considering that, with Matthews picked for nine of the ten games, they suffered more than any other club. The response tended to be unsympathetic. A plea that Matthews be freed for a key home game in the Western Division against Port Vale received a flat rejection. The FA said Stoke could not go back on their earlier decision to release Matthews. The calls on star players did, though, become less frequent.

Matthews did play in Stoke's second match in the Western Division, a 4-2 win over Stockport County in which he scored, but the following weekend he turned out for the Football League against an All British eleven in a match at Goodison Park that attracted a crowd of 15,000, the permitted maximum attendance, and raised more than £1,200 for the Red Cross. Two weeks later he appeared in England's second wartime international, having missed the first the previous weekend. Both these matches were against Wales. Without Matthews, England drew 1-1 at Ninian Park; with him, they profited from one of his typically inventive performances to win 3-2 from 2-0 down in front of 17,000 at Wrexham. The fixture provided more funds for the Red Cross.

The fifty-mile journey to Wrexham was fairly easy compared to many Matthews had to make. Most of the time wartime rail travel in Britain failed dismally to match the precision time-keeping attributed to trains in Benito Mussolini's Italy. The

---

to stage fundraising fixtures against the top clubs. The takings would be split between themselves, the host club and the Red Cross. One of the movers behind the scheme gave a strong hint Matthews would be involved, telling a journalist: 'The names of the players I have in mind would assure us of capacity gates everywhere we went.' The rebels' main objective was 'to raise themselves out of the thirty-shillings-a-week class'. What would have been a difficult project to organise at the best of times never progressed further than being an interesting idea.

strictly enforced, nightly blackouts were among the several reasons. Matthews had any number of stories of train journeys that comfortably missed their scheduled arrival times. On one occasion, travelling to play for the RAF against the Army in Leeds, he was badly held up crossing the Pennines. Because it was Matthews who was delayed, the organisers put back the kick-off so the crowd would have their ninety minutes' worth of the man most of them had come to see.

Across the country teams and players showed great resourcefulness in getting to games. Walking long distances from railway stations to grounds was commonplace. Hitchhiking was not easy, although Tommy Olsen of Bury had rides in seven different lorries getting to a match against Oldham at Gigg Lane in 1941. He arrived just before kick-off and his two goals helped Bury to a 5-0 win.

Spectators, too, had their travel problems, even if they avoided the railway and drove to games. Driving at any time risked a 'misuse of petrol' charge, which led to some creative countermeasures. A Derby supporter, who lived in Belper, loaded up a piano whenever he made the return trip to the Baseball Ground. Apparently, 'Delivering a piano, officer' was a declaration of a far less profligate use of fuel than 'Going to a football match, guv'. Thomas Rennison, who rode his motorcycle from Chorley to Blackpool to watch Matthews play in April 1944, told a court he went to the game because not doing so would have been unpatriotic. It did not wash. Found guilty of wasting petrol, he was fined forty shillings.

A further problem for fans at the start of the war was a more severe winter than anyone could remember. One ice storm was so bad that encrusted branches fell from thousands of trees and birds dropped from the air in mid-flight, their wings iced up. Ready-frozen pheasant and rabbit could be picked up from the ground. The modest revenue being taken at the turnstiles gave the notoriously parsimonious Football League ample justification to reject a request by the players' union to raise match fees from thirty shillings to £2.

The relative unpopularity of club fixtures spread anxiety through boardrooms. Harry Booth of Stoke City was among the most vociferous chairmen in calling for the Football League to do something to persuade more people to attend matches. His was a powerful voice. If Stoke, with their conspicuous success and Matthews's box-office appeal, could not draw the crowds, what hope for the others.

Booth announced in the first week of 1940 that regional football had been a failure. He spoke out again in February, urging action to relieve the deep depression the game was suffering. He sent a letter to the management committee of the Football League suggesting three measures: the introduction of a cup competition, a system that made promotion and relegation possible even in a regional format, and summertime matches to offset the difficulties created by long winter blackouts.

The League responded to various ideas, not just those of Stoke, by announcing the season would be extended until 8 June, partly to accommodate a knockout competition but mainly to get through a huge backlog of fixtures caused by the harsh winter. Summertime matches on a regular basis were ruled out because they would compete for spectators with cricket and tennis, a considerate side of football that would not survive the century.

Stoke maintained the momentum built up at the start of the regional competition to win the Western Division. Matthews's appearances were more regular than in the early weeks of the season, his services not being required again by the FA until the last two internationals of the 1939–40 season.

The first wartime fixture at Wembley on 13 April was also the first time Wales had played at the ground. They celebrated their inaugural visit by defying Matthews's repeated thrusts down the wing to win 1-0 in front of 40,000. Cries of 'Give it to Matthews' when England were awarded a penalty five minutes from the end went unheeded. George Hall's fluffed attempt meant Bryn Jones's goal for Wales decided it.

A German propaganda broadcast warning of a Luftwaffe attack on Hampden Park failed to stop more than 70,000 turning out for Glasgow's introduction to wartime internationals on 11 May. Danger of a more mundane kind faced England when the RAF abruptly cancelled Sam Bartram's leave. This deprived the visitors of a goalkeeper against a side who were unlikely to be sympathetic. Eddie Hapgood, an outfield defender, prepared to take Bartram's place, psyching himself up to contend with Dave McCulloch, Scotland's imposing centre-forward. He was spared when Vic Woodley, the Chelsea keeper, arrived just in time for kick-off. The match, a 1-1 draw, was less exciting than the dramas that surrounded it.

The climax to the first wartime season saw Stoke fall short in the War Cup, the competition they had so vigorously supported, before winning the Western Division. Tommy Lawton's late penalty for Everton at Goodison Park put them out of the cup in the third round. The championship title they secured two weeks later was consolation only of sorts considering they, with all the rest, had started the season in pursuit of a far more prestigious prize. In any circumstances a deciding, top-of the-table game against Manchester United at the Victoria Ground would have been a momentous event. The result, 3-2 to Stoke with Matthews to the fore, suggests it did not disappoint. In fact noises off spoiled the show. These were the sounds of military recruiting officers calling a number of United players to national service. The Football League would not grant a postponement and the match kicked off late to allow the visitors to scrape together a team. Stoke's victory gave them the title with thirty-one points from their twenty-two games. United, the only team who could have caught them, still had a game to play but were now three points behind.

For that first season, 1939–40, Matthews played as often

for Stoke as FA call-ups and RAF duties permitted. It is likely, though, that his commitment to his hometown club was more tenuous than it had ever been. In the first instance his awkward relationship with Bob McGrory undermined it. His fondness for the salty fragrance of Blackpool put it under further pressure, as did the RAF's increasingly stringent travel restrictions. Then an ankle injury at the start of the next season, which caused his first prolonged absence from the team in nearly a decade, created further distance between him and his masters at the Victoria Ground.

He returned briefly, including for a 2-2 draw away to Tranmere Rovers. A little improbably, this first visit by Stoke to Prenton Park was for a Southern Regional League fixture, professional clubs having now been split into only two divisions, north and south. The occasion provided evidence of Matthews's imperishable appeal at a time when triumphant Battle of Britain pilots had overtaken footballers as national heroes. The host club's poster for the fixture left no doubt about why the visiting team were such an attraction: 'Tranmere v Stoke City (with Stanley Matthews, England's star right-winger)'. Soon afterwards, the ankle injury flared up again and this time Matthews's leg was placed in plaster.

Even a hobbling Matthews was hard to keep out of the news. The Stoke paper reported on its front page he was being sought by Scottish club Airdrieonians. It said this was because Matthews was working in Scotland, which must have been a temporary arrangement given there is no record he was ever posted there. Just possibly Matthews was actively seeking an alternative to playing for Stoke while awaiting his real preference – an arrangement to play for Blackpool, who were now his home club.

After recovering from his ankle injury he played hardly at all for Stoke in the second half of the 1940–1 season but was fit enough to be cleared to represent the Scottish FA against an Army eleven in Aberdeen in April. In May he returned to the England side for a 3-1 victory over Scotland, a match that attracted the biggest crowd yet for a wartime international with 78,000 descending on Hampden.

Without Matthews, Stoke, a championship-winning side the previous season, won only nine of their thirty-six matches in the Southern Regional League to finish well behind the title winners, Crystal Palace. At the annual meeting in June, the Stoke directors had to defend themselves against the charge that there was no incentive to watch the club now that most of the big names had gone, to be replaced by raw recruits signed on the cheap. Harry Booth excused the club's policy by saying that football generally had not 'held its competitive interest of pre-war days'. He expected Stoke to benefit in the long run from signing younger players.

Matthews's absence was highlighted by another charge: that Stoke had adopted a 'dog in the manger' attitude by refusing permission for him to play for Rangers, except in charity games. Booth denied that either the Glasgow club or Matthews had asked to release him for competitive games.

The outcome that Matthews almost certainly favoured, even if he never admitted it for fear of upsetting Stoke fans, came to pass just before the start of the 1941-2 season. In August Stoke consented to his playing as a guest for Blackpool FC.

Chapter 8

*'If the worst comes tae the worst ah'm the
wee boy tae stop Matthews'*

Blackpool's acquisition of the England forward was the club's greatest prize among a number of gains from having military bases in the area. Other clubs, notably Lincoln and Aldershot, also benefited from the sudden arrival in the vicinity of large gatherings of servicemen that included professional players. But none profited quite to the same extent as Blackpool. So great were the club's gains that the Blackpool Services team, attracting those conscripts who failed to qualify for Blackpool on the grounds of ability or for some technical reason, took to fielding sides of Football League strength.

Joe Smith, the Blackpool manager, acknowledged that Matthews's availability was on the understanding that he would be at Stoke's disposal whenever they needed him. The reality was that, although it was six more years before he signed for the Lancashire club, he was now more Blackpool than Stoke. The avuncular Smith, whose successful playing career had included five England caps, and the club's dynamic chairman, Colonel William Parkinson, were two more reasons Matthews favoured switching clubs.

Smith, shrewder than he liked to appear, was the only

manager throughout Matthews's long career who was happy for him to play as he wished – or, if you like, indulged him. Relaxed and unhectoring, Smith was certainly far more agreeable to Matthews than McGrory. One of Smith's favourite exhortations during his twenty-three years managing Blackpool was that the team should strive to be at least a goal up so that he could enjoy his half-time cigar. He was not particularly concerned how they achieved this lead so long as they did so by playing entertaining football.

Colonel Parkinson, too, was far more to Matthews's liking than Harry Booth ever was at Stoke. Affectionately known as Colonel Willie, he was a commanding presence around Blackpool as a businessman, pillar of the Baptist church, benefactor and champion of former servicemen. 'We became good friends and he did me many favours,' Matthews said.

The influx of so many good players meant that, in the words of the local paper, 'Blackpool will field nearly every week a forward line with a star in every position'. The line-up referred to, which epitomised the eclectic nature of many wartime teams, was Matthews (Stoke City), Jock Dodds (Blackpool), Ronnie Dix (Spurs), Alex Stevenson (Everton) and Eddie Burbanks (Sunderland).

This was the attack that Blackpool fielded for a pre-season friendly in which they beat a Blackpool Services team 4-1 on 23 August 1941. A week later Matthews appeared for Blackpool in a Northern League match against Preston North End at Deepdale, which was his first encounter with Tom Finney, nineteen at the time. Although Blackpool lost 3-1 in front of 12,000 spectators, they won the return 2-0 the following Saturday. A crowd of 20,000 watched this one, many of them holidaymakers drawn to witness Matthews's competitive debut at Bloomfield Road in the tangerine shirt. Preston were the team of the moment, having won the 1940–41 Northern Regional League and War Cup. A reporter characterised the matches as a contest between all the skills, notably the wizardry of Matthews, and a Preston side, driven by the demonically committed Bill Shankly at wing-half, who embodied a new style of teamwork.

Even against the sombre backdrop of war, Matthews's military service years playing for a dominant, attack-minded Blackpool side must have been hugely enjoyable. Towards the end of the war he referred to them as the best team he had ever played for. The admiration was mutual. A story surfaced in September 1945 that Blackpool wanted to buy him off Stoke for £10,000. The denial sounded more obligatory than convincing.

Nor were the football team and the beach the only things Matthews liked. He enjoyed everything about Blackpool, where he and his family eventually settled into a rented house on the South Shore, renowned for the Pleasure Beach amusement park. Matthews talked openly about setting up a business in the town, a small hotel possibly. 'I fell in love with it and so did Betty,' he said of the town and its shoreline. When Stoke reclaimed his services with peace about to break out, he preferred to commute to the Potteries rather than uproot Betty, Jean and Stanley Junior, the son who was born in November 1945. Maybe a pact – spoken or unspoken – between Matthews and Blackpool FC was already in place that the two of them would soon reunite.

Matthews could hardly have imagined that when he started playing regularly for Blackpool he would be paired with a target man who was the equal of Freddie Steele. But Jock Dodds was such a player, a predator who fed hungrily off nearly everything served him by Matthews.

After the opening defeat by Preston in late August 1941, Blackpool won their next seven matches in the Northern League with Matthews and Dodds prominent throughout. Matthews rarely scored himself but like a thief with a skeleton key could open up just about anything put in front of him. He was at his most canny when Blackpool, a week after beating Preston in the return match, swamped Southport 10-1. Dodds's hat-trick was just one of his many multiple-scoring feats as Blackpool ran up thiry-four goals against seven in their winning sequence. Dodds himself would reach twenty-nine goals by Christmas.

The regularity with which significant players such as Matthews were available – although there would be notable enforced absences – was a huge factor in Blackpool's success. Others struggled on a weekly basis to assemble even moderately adequate elevens. After Blackpool beat Blackburn 4-1 at Bloomfield Road in November 1941, the following appeared in print:

'A Blackburn official was wondering where their eleventh man would come from when up spoke a young aircraftsman who had been leaning against a wall close to the dressing-room door.

'"I can play football," he said. The agitated official halted in his tracks.

'"Who've you played for?"

'"Sheffield Wednesday and Aston Villa."

'"Where do you play?"

'"Inside forward."

'"Play centre-forward?"

'"I'll play anywhere."

'They gave him a jersey and less than five minutes later he was leading the Rovers' forward line.'

When Matthews and the rest of Blackpool's exalted forward line were playing, spectators suspended their cynicism about the competitive worth of what was placed in front of them. After Halifax lost 9-1 on their first visit to Bloomfield Road, a crowd of 10,000 turned out at Halifax to see their team duly go down to another defeat in the return fixture a week later. When Matthews represented the Football League against the Scottish League at Bloomfield Road in a match in aid of the RAF Benevolent Fund the crowd was 27,000.

The hotchpotch structure of football at this early stage of the war can only have reinforced feelings of public scepticism. In

1941–2, for example, the Northern League ran until Christmas and was followed by the War Cup, some of whose matches also counted towards a second League competition that ran until the end of the season. This caused all sorts of problems. In late spring the League announced the table was 'undergoing revision' with extra-time goals in those matches that doubled as cup ties being deleted from League results. In other words the score after ninety minutes represented the League score. For what must have been the only time in the history of organised football, a single match carried two different results.

Eventually, out of the disorder, the wartime seasons resolved themselves into a format – regional leagues taking place up until Christmas, followed by competitions that were part cup, part league – that fans had started to recognise by the time the old normality returned.

At least nothing could stop Blackpool going on to win the first half of the season's Northern League title on Christmas Day 1941. They maintained the momentum of their seven-match winning surge to be crowned champions despite finishing up with an unexpected home defeat against Rochdale. They won fourteen of their eighteen matches and, although they ended with the same number of points as Lincoln, twenty-nine, their four goals a game average was comfortably superior.*

Blackpool might well have won the cup competition that followed, but suffered what amounted to a farcical defeat by bureaucracy. After their League success, they established themselves as clear favourites by easing through the qualifying competition. Their successes included home and away victories

---

* Wartime football honours were a source of some celebration for clubs' supporters but the speed with which they were forgotten reflected their devalued status. Along with Matthews and his free-scoring fellow forwards, Allan Ure, Blackpool's veteran trainer, was briefly hailed as a local hero for his association with a third title by the club. Ure, son-in-law of the former manager Bill Norman, had been around when they won the Central League in 1919–20 and ten years later when they took the Second Division title to be promoted to the top division for the first time.

over a strong Liverpool side and a fifteen-goal spree against Tranmere. Dodds, prolific as ever, scored seven of these, the first three in under three minutes.

The cup run also featured the first time Matthews and Stan Mortensen, who was twenty and had been punishing defences in the Lancashire Combination, played together in what would become one of football's most destructive twosomes. The match against Wolves at Bloomfield Road on 10 January 1942 was described as Mortensen's 'baptism in big football'. He and Matthews both scored in a 6-1 win.

Blackpool started to contemplate completing a treble of the cup and the two League competitions either side of it. Cue the Whitehall farce. After excitement mounted over a home-and-away Easter-weekend cup tie against Manchester City, Blackpool had to withdraw from the competition because of an edict from London that military personnel must stay on their bases during the holiday. News of the ruling arrived too late for Blackpool to find suitable replacements. Telegrams whizzed to and fro before the Air Ministry ended the exchanges with a deadpan: 'Ministry regrets that no relaxation of ban on travelling is justified.' National security depended, apparently, on Aircraftsman Matthews, a physical training instructor, and his fellow servicemen being tied to their Blackpool camps over Easter.

Matthews was again refused permission to travel in May, this time on the weekend that England played Wales in Cardiff and Blackpool were away to Oldham. So it was that the great man, terror of the best defences in the world, added another club to his impressive collection when he played for Blackpool Services in a Lancashire Junior Cup match against Chorley. He scored a penalty and created a succession of chances in a 6-3 victory.

A season that had developed a life of its own ended with Matthews, restored to the Blackpool side, orchestrating a 7-1 victory over Blackburn Rovers in front of 10,000 fans at Bloomfield Road. By now very little was straightforward. The match was both the Lancashire Cup final and a League fixture. Despite the handsome win, Blackpool narrowly failed to collect their second League title of the season. The exact margin of their failure was 0.44 points of a complex bonus scheme.

Over the next two seasons, 1942–3 and 1943–4, Blackpool excelled as entertainers and achievers. They won two more Northern League titles, appeared in two Northern War Cup finals and in May 1943 beat Arsenal at Stamford Bridge in what was widely regarded as the greatest club match of the war. One writer referred to Blackpool as 'the wartime wonder team'. William Cuff, the Football League chairman, remarked in April 1944 that 'Blackpool have been the team of the season, the epitome of good football, a side who have maintained a fine football standard'. Many singled out Matthews for special mention. The *Daily Mirror* put the combined market price of the Blackpool team at £70,000, a huge amount for the time, with Matthews worth at least double the next man.

While others extolled the virtues of Blackpool and Matthews, the man himself made little of the pleasure they so obviously brought to thousands of fans. He even belittled the wartime game, saying the regional leagues produced a poor substitute for the football that had gone before. He described supporters as seeming listless and bored. While chronicling his international fortunes, he committed hardly any detail of Blackpool's accumulation of honours to his various memoirs. Maybe he felt that so many other teams being below strength debased Blackpool's success. More likely he was wary of dwelling on triumphs reaped at a time when many of his fellow professionals were fighting, some losing their lives. One who died was Bolton's admired captain Harry Goslin, a defender who played with Matthews for England against Scotland in the match at St James Park at the start of the war. Goslin, who had led his Bolton team to the local Territorial Army hall to sign up after a match in April 1939, was killed in action in Italy in 1943.

Blackpool won their first ten league matches of the 1942–3 season. Their remorseless form dipped only occasionally as they held on to the Northern League title, which was again decided on Christmas Day. Sixteen wins in eighteen matches and a total of ninety-three goals gave statistical ballast to their dominance.

They managed this success despite losing Mortensen, who had very rapidly established himself as an indispensable member of the team. One of life's incorrigible thrill-seekers, Mortensen volunteered to join an aircrew. His absence from the Blackpool team came perilously close to being permanent. He was lucky to survive when a Wellington bomber in which he was serving as a wireless operator crash-landed in Scotland. Two other members of the crew died and Mortensen was left with a bad head injury. This ended his career as a wireless operator, and also meant he was permanently grounded, because he could no longer take Morse code. Remarkably, though, after making a full recovery, he returned to playing for Blackpool sooner than he might have done had he still been flying. His ability as an explosive header of the ball was unimpaired.

Neither Mortensen's absence nor the wan-faced warriors of Whitehall could stop Blackpool adding the War Cup to their League success. Other potential problems did emerge, including a reminder by Stoke that Matthews was still officially their man. They refused to release him for the first leg of a cup tie against Everton in March 1943 because they wanted him to play for them. This proved meaningless when the RAF pulled rank by selecting him for a representative game on the same day. Initially Stoke again withdrew their permission for Matthews to appear in the return leg. They relented when told the RAF would not grant him the necessary travel facilities. 'In such circumstances to forbid another club fielding him would serve no purpose,' Stoke said.

Come the final against Sheffield Wednesday, the Football Association took the villain's role filled the year before by the Air

Ministry. The FA picked Matthews to play for England against Wales in Cardiff on the day Blackpool faced Wednesday in the second leg of the cup decider. Blackpool, held 2-2 at home in the first leg, pleaded unavailingly for his release. Their umbrage turned to celebration when they clinched the cup by winning 2-1 at Hillsborough in front of 47,657.

Not only did Matthews miss his club's notable success, he forfeited an interesting array of goodies. Each Blackpool player who took part in the return match received a five-unit War Savings Certificate and, given that the match was at the home of steel-making, a safety razor with packet of blades. Fish served at the post-match tea was a gift from Grimsby Town. On the train home the players mingled with the fans. No special carriage was laid on for them even though three extra ones were summoned to accommodate the throng wishing to travel back to Blackpool with the cup winners. The team celebrated by quaffing a dozen bottles of 'wartime ale' from the cup. The abstemious Matthews would probably have passed on this one.

A week later, 15 May 1943, Blackpool met Arsenal at Stamford Bridge in a match that momentarily propelled club football from the shadow of more serious conflict. Few opportunities existed for sides from the south to play those from the north. Here was one, though, of exceptional promise that repaid expectation with interest. It matched Arsenal, who had beaten Charlton 7-1 in the southern final of the War Cup, against Blackpool, the northern cup winners with a forward line that included the magnificent Matthews. A soldier who happened to be in London and went to the game wrote to his wife the next day: 'It says in the paper there were 55,000 there but I think they forgot to count another 20,000.' Matthews treated them to a performance full of sinuous trickery on which Blackpool built their 4-2 victory. The result confirmed reports of the audacious excellence of Joe Smith's team that had filtered south during the winter. 'Blackpool are not only Cock of the North, they are undisputed champions of England,' the *Daily Dispatch* told its readers.

A grimmer reality of these harsh times was contained in the soldier's letter about the size of the crowd: 'A lot of people got their pockets slashed open and had their pockets picked, but they know better than to pick on soldiers as they have no money.' Nor would the thieves have found much had they raided the coffers of the leading clubs. Even as Blackpool completed another highly successful season in 1943–4 evidence appeared that they were as strapped as everyone else. The club reacted enthusiastically to an announcement that football clubs would each receive a handout from an issue of 40,000 clothing coupons. 'We are just managing with our equipment,' a spokesman said, 'and we anticipate a coupon allotment to help us to renew that which is worn out.' Not long afterwards Smith appealed for someone to fill an important, recently vacated, unpaid post. A volunteer was needed to wash the players' jerseys and shorts.

If the game resembled an ailing cottage industry off the pitch, much of what happened on it was simply exhilarating. Five months after Blackpool's exciting win over Arsenal, England and Matthews reached the pinnacle of their wartime excellence in an 8-0 victory over Scotland at Maine Road. Frank Swift, England's goalkeeper who had a privileged view of the eight goals, said he had never seen 'such perfection in movement, unselfishness or team spirit'. He added that 'it was Stanley's match in particular', recalling that even some Scotland players clapped when Matthews scored the eighth goal.

Bill Shankly, who was so lavish in his praise for England's wartime team, did not feature for Scotland in the Maine Road massacre. He said that when he heard the teams announced he said two prayers: one of thanks to the selectors for leaving him out and the other to Adam Little, the Rangers player picked in his place.

The England display made it an 'I was there' occasion. There were 60,000 who could say this and many, many more who must have wished they could. Hundreds of those who were unable to get home after the match, including a large number of servicemen who hitchhiked to Manchester, were indebted to the local authority for opening up a large air-raid shelter, redundant since the blitz on the city ended, as temporary accommodation.

Some people went to extraordinary lengths to gain admission to the match. Tommy Lawton, the England centre-forward, reckoned there were plenty of dodgy tickets proffered at the turnstiles. He also reported seeing three small boys failing to fool officials when proffering forged press passes.

The personal satisfaction Matthews took from his performance at Maine Road must have been multiplied after what happened when he played in England's 8-3 victory over Wales at Wembley a month earlier. On that occasion he was effectively frozen out of the game by his teammates. The press latched on to this apparent snub. Some writers assumed it must be a retort to Matthews's insistence on playing the way he wanted even if this wasn't the way others wanted. The brouhaha became so strident that the FA issued a statement saying they had received letters from players insisting no slight against Matthews had been intended. Instead, they had implemented a plan, thought up by their captain, Stan Cullis – and made independently of Matthews – to attack down the left because Wales were known to have devised their defensive tactics around stopping England's right-winger.

This was certainly the case but the incident did not leave Matthews entirely unscathed. Why had he not been involved in hatching the plan or, at the very least, had it communicated to him? Also, the media's rush to surmise there had been a snub must have been informed by inside knowledge that Matthews, the centre of so much outside attention, was the subject of some resentment within the England camp.

The reason Matthews liked recalling the match, apart from the handsomeness of England's win, was because it amused him that his colleague Stan Mortensen had played – in a Wales shirt. Mortensen, who was twenty-two, had been picked as England's reserve and ended up playing for the opposition after Ivor Powell, the pitiless NCO who had drilled Matthews at the start of the war, broke a collarbone. Agreement was quickly reached that a replacement should be allowed and Mortensen was the only option. Matthews enjoyed recounting this incident and the fact that most of the 80,000 crowd thought when Mortensen came on that he was a patched-up Powell. Mortensen said later that a friend had bet him he would make his international debut that day but wasn't sure whether the unusual circumstances meant it counted.

Quite what a bow wave of interest Blackpool had built up with their attacking play was evident in that spring of 1944. After holding on to the Northern title at Christmas, they advanced to their second successive War Cup final, this time against Aston Villa. Their run included a quarter-final match at Bradford Park Avenue, who became the only club to set a ground record attendance during the war. On 8 April, 32,810 crammed into Horton Park Avenue to see Blackpool, with Matthews on the wing, complete a 4-3 aggregate victory in a two-leg tie.

It would be easy to overstate the force of Matthews's magnetism – and many have. Suffice it to say it is a matter of record that the five matches in which he played in April 1944 were watched by comfortably in excess of quarter of a million people – and this at a time when austerity and travel restrictions considerably complicated the simple task of going to a football match. The Scots were particularly partial to watching him perform, some compliment for a Sassenach who liked nothing more than harassing a Scotland defence. When Matthews played for the RAF against the Army in Edinburgh, 50,000 spectators saw the game; when, three weeks later, he was in Glasgow for the umpteenth Scotland–England wartime sideshow, 133,000 made it to Hampden. In the previous six months the Scots had lost 8-0 at Maine Road and 6-2 at Wembley, prompting a cartoonist in a Glasgow newspaper to draw a member of the home side dressed as a soldier in full kit, carrying a Lewis gun. He was telling a policeman: 'If the worst comes tae the worst ah'm the wee boy tae stop Matthews.' Unarmed, the Scots confined England to a 3-2 win.

At the end of the month a crowd of 26,800 at Bloomfield Road watched Blackpool score two late goals to win the first leg of the final against Villa 2-1. When the team then travelled to Birmingham the day before the return leg, hundreds of fans were waiting to hail them. Matthews was one of those feted thanks to the unfamiliar benevolence of the FA. This time they did Blackpool the favour of not selecting him for a clashing international against Wales. A report of the cup tie spoke of spectators storming Villa Park to see the wartime wonders. The whole pageant fell slightly flat when Villa won 4-2, the only blot on their performance being a handball dispute over one of their goals.

This match effectively marked the end of Matthews's first successful association with Blackpool – and a dip in the Lancashire club's fortunes. A spate of representative demands by England and the services limited Matthews's club appearances at the start of the 1944–5 season. Then, as his normally intransigent military employers became more accommodating as the threat of invasion receded, Stoke increasingly exercised their right to summon him home to the Potteries to play for them.

As early as September 1944 he was back playing for his old club when the RAF gave him leave to appear against Wolverhampton Wanderers. This particular dispensation did not simply reflect a lightening of the national mood. It was granted also because of a collection at the Wolves game in honour of Reginald Mitchell. A Staffordshire man who went to school in Hanley, Mitchell played a special part in what was now the impending defeat of Germany as designer of the talismanic Supermarine

Spitfire. Matthews not only put numbers on the gate to boost the collection, he reminded Stoke supporters what they had been missing when he laid on both goals in a 2-0 victory.

Later that year he started to turn out regularly for Stoke for the first time for four years. Again the RAF facilitated this by being more charitable than they might have been a year or two earlier. They also gave him extended leave when his father's stomach cancer required surgery at Christmastime, a deterioration closely followed by Jack Matthews's death in mid-January.*

Matthews was not the only one of Blackpool's guest players who found themselves recalled by their original clubs. More and more Joe Smith must have been chewing rather than smoking the cigars he so loved as he frantically cast around for last-minute replacements.

One of those who came into the Blackpool side, although not to fill Matthews's boots, was a promising wing-half called Bill Slater. He was still only seventeen when he made his debut for the club in the 1944–5 season. Slater, who would play alongside Matthews in the 1951 FA Cup final and make twelve appearances for England, was also a good cricketer. One wet afternoon before the end of the war Blackpool cricket club received a call from Bloomfield Road. 'You say the match is rained off,' the voice at the end of the phone said. 'Well, send Slater over here quickly. We're about to kick off against Preston North End and have only got ten men.'

Slater recalled his first experience of appearing in the same Blackpool side as Matthews: 'I preferred playing wing half but it so happened the vacancy Joe Smith had to fill was at inside-forward. I'd been taught at school that if the wing came back to

---

* A highly dramatised account of the deathbed scene at the hospital, with Stanley in attendance, appeared in Matthews's ghosted autobiography in 2000 and led to a lively disagreement between the ghost and David Miller, who wrote the authorised biography of Matthews eleven years earlier. What no one disputed was the depth of Matthews's sense of loss. (See also the footnote on page 243.)

collect the ball, which of course Stanley Matthews did, it was a useful tactic for the inside-forward to go up the wing ahead of him. After I'd done this a couple of times, Matthews came across – he didn't know my name – "Sonny," he said, "sonny, I would prefer it if you didn't run up the wing like that because you're just getting in the way." He was so polite about it but it was quite a shock. Can you imagine the star player telling you this?'

Matthews's wartime playing association with Blackpool petered out amid some confusion in the autumn of 1945. He had not played for them since early September when, two months later, after peace had been declared in Europe and the Far East, Blackpool said in a statement they had been notified by Stoke that the guesting arrangement was over. 'There are no differences between the clubs regarding the player and it has all been settled in a friendly spirit,' the statement added.

Bob McGrory, Stoke's manager, immediately denied they had put a total block on Matthews continuing to serve Blackpool. Rather, in view of the FA Cup being resumed, Stoke wanted him to play for them whenever possible so that they had a settled cup side. Matthews, who continued to serve in the RAF for another six months, could still play for Blackpool when it was not possible to do so for Stoke. As it turned out, he appeared as a guest only once more, an ill-starred return against Manchester United in March 1946.

The reason Blackpool had, by now, developed a relaxed attitude to letting go a player who had been such a boon to them may have been significant. The amicable tone of their statement almost certainly meant that the club and Smith understood they had won Matthews's heart over the preceding four years. Winning his signature was only a matter of time.

Matthews probably understood this, too. By staying in Blackpool once the RAF released him – 'I decided I preferred to live by the sea' – he gave what amounted to a statement of intent. Although he was playing full-time again for Stoke, he continued to do most of his training at Bloomfield Road. He would often turn up for Stoke's matches just in time for kick-off – or, in one case, just after. A crowd of 30,000 who gathered at Hillsborough, many of them just to see Matthews playing again for Stoke, were disappointed when he arrived too late to take part after a delayed start from Blackpool. His roots in the North-West went down still deeper when he and Betty set up there as the proprietors of the Romford, a small Promenade hotel.

With the war over, the football authorities had to settle a pay dispute during which the players threatened to strike. Members of the players' union who felt their clubs had used the war as an excuse to treat them perfunctorily were especially militant. In the end they settled for a maximum wage of £9 a week and a match fee of £5, which, being less than they wanted, meant resentment remained.

The agreement did, though, free up the top professionals to contribute fully to the post-war festivities without having to wrestle with their consciences about strike breaking. They were called on for a series of Victory internationals and other celebratory matches, for which caps were still not awarded despite such fixtures carrying on into 1947 when Britain played the Rest of Europe at Hampden.

Some months before the war was over, the authorities started to exploit football's propaganda potential. At the height of hostilities it was used as a domestic palliative for the game's principally working-class supporters. Late in September 1944, its brief changed significantly. Less than four months after the D-Day landings in Normandy and with the enemy still fighting back strongly, the Football Association resumed sending a team to the Continent. It was officially described as an FA Services team, but the strength of the party and the accompanying extras left no doubt that this was something more.

A squad made up of several well-known international foot-ballers, heading for Paris and Brussels, two of Europe's great capitals recently under the jackboot, delivered a powerful message about the Allies' confidence. Matthews and Raich Carter were among the players and the supporting cast included Raymond Glendenning, BBC Radio's foremost sports commentator of the day. His rich, untroubled tones coming back across the Channel from formerly occupied territories would provide great comfort to a nation still worried about the level of danger at the door.

In every respect the trip was a success, even if the travelling party itself was not entirely out of harm's way. The players and camp followers flew on to Brussels, after a 5-0 victory over a France eleven in front of 30,000 at the Parc des Princes, having barely had time for a bath. The reason for the rush was that only operational flights were permitted after dark. At the Stade du Daring Club, where the match against Belgium took place the following day, the terraces were swept for mines shortly before kick-off. RAF planes prowled the skies above, a reminder that fighting was going on barely fifty miles from the ground. The FA team's 3-0 victory was pleasing but almost incidental. Matt Busby, the FA's captain, received a whippet from the grateful hosts, a thoughtful if not entirely practical gesture.

Matthews, who played in both fixtures, was back in Belgium six months later. The FA party flew there in a Dakota, again for two matches on successive days: in Bruges against the Diables Rouge, the Belgian parachute regiment, and a return visit to the Daring club's stadium to play Belgium's national side.

Conveniently, this trip failed to make it into any of Matthews's memoirs, almost certainly for a reason that did not emerge for more than sixty years. During it the prodigiously disciplined player who never picked up a caution in his long career as a professional footballer was caught up in a scandal when he was accused of foul play off the field during this visit to the Belgian capital, leaving a small taint on his service record.

Documents released by the Ministry of Defence in 2009 showed that Matthews, together with fellow players Stan

Mortensen and Leslie Smith, faced what was a seemingly trivial but, potentially at least, quite serious charge. It concerned an incident in a shop, for which the charge read:

WHEN ON ACTIVE SERVICE:

> Conduct to the prejudice of good order and Air Force discipline, in that he [Stanley Matthews], when in BRUSSELS, between 24.3.45 and 26.3.45, improperly disposed of a quantity of coffee for personal gain.

'Active service' was an interesting classification of a football match, especially as it was the Football Association rather than the RAF or a combined services team the trio were representing. On the other hand, there was no disputing the charge. Mortensen admitted selling coffee and soap and Matthews owned up to selling just coffee.

When national newspapers latched on to the story, after the MoD's disclosure sixty-four years later, their sub-editors did not hold back. Headlines included: 'England Footie Legends in Black Market Scandal' and 'Never Booked – but Happy to Make a Fast Buck on the Black Market'. This, though, was as dramatic as it got. The final paragraph of the story under the first of these headlines, which had the subhead 'WW2 Shame of Sir Stan & Mortensen', was pure bathos: 'They admitted selling the goods and were given a dressing down by their commanding officers.'

A mix-up may explain why the punishment was no more severe than a dressing down. Unfortunately for the RAF's Special Investigation Branch, a tip-off that members of the FA party might be hawking contraband goods gave the right street but the wrong number of the shop in central Brussels where the offence would take place. By the time the mistake came to light it was too late to stake out the correct premises. This meant the case rested on the word of three shop assistants.

Mortensen and Matthews allegedly went to the shop, Bijouterie Assia, on Saturday 24 March and again two days later, which was when the Brentford player Smith appeared in the script. Of the three shop employees who gave witness statements to the SIB, Mme Marie Tumson, an Irish-born assistant, gave the most detailed:

I am employed at the BIJOUTERIE ASSIA, No.48b., rue Neuve, BRUSSELS. On Saturday, 24th. March, 1945, I was in the above shop in company with Mlle. MOSSELMANS, when two airmen entered. They both wore R.A.F. Uniforms. They informed me they wished to buy some bracelets. I have been shown some photographs and distinctly recognise the two airmen in question as being those on the photographs marked 'A' and 'C' which I have signed and dated. At this stage I did not know their names. Whilst discussing the bracelets these airmen asked me if I would buy some coffee and soap. They opened a suitcase in my presence and showed me some coffee and soap. As they were in a hurry, nothing was done in this connection and they told me they would return. On Monday 26/3/45, the same two airmen returned to the shop, Mlle. MOSSELMANS again being present. They brought with them some coffee and soap. I believe we paid 20 francs Belge for each cake of soap and about 1–2 (one to two) pounds of coffee at a price equivalent to 300 francs Belge a kilo. They did not purchase any bracelets or other items at this shop. On this latter occasion, they asked me – as I am Irish by birth and speak perfect English, if we were interested in buying English pounds (£). I informed them that it did not interest me but on rare occasions, and to help an Englishman out, I would change a pound or so at the official rate of 176 Fr. Belges per £1. No intimation was given by these airmen that they could get a better rate elsewhere but they did not change any money with me or the other shop assistants. On this occasion, the airman on photograph 'C', informed me that his name was 'MORTENSON' [sic] and his friend, who appears on photograph 'A' was STAN MATTHEWS. They both said they had played in an International Match that weekend, which they had won. I am quite sure that both airmen on photographs 'A' and 'C' were together in the shop on both occasions. I gave a business card of the BIJOUTERIE ASSIA to 'MORTENSON' who signed on the back of it in pencil, 'BEST WISHES STAN MORTENSON'. The card which you now show me appears to be the one in question that MORTENSON signed as the name 'STAN MATTHEWS' written thereon is in my own handwriting. I put his name on to remind me of it. I believe they left BRUSSELS that same Monday afternoon, as they came in again to say 'Good-bye'. On this last occasion there was another airman with them whose name I believe was SMITH, but who was in no way concerned with offering coffee, soap or English currency. I have not seen any of these three airmen again, nor had I seen any of them before prior to the occasions stated herein. I have read over the above statement and it is true.

BRUSSELS
MAY 16th. 1945.   Sgd. M. TUMSON . . .

The other assistants, Anne-Catherine Mosselmans and Jeanine S'Jongers, gave broadly similar accounts although Mosselmans added the detail that when the airmen came back to the shop on the Monday they had less to offer and she supposed they might have sold some of the goods elsewhere. In another interview, Tumson and S'Jongers said one of the players had hinted he knew other places where he could dispose of the goods, also implying he had done this on a previous visit.

Mortensen, whose name would be misspelled by investigators and witnesses throughout the evidence, and Smith gave written statements, something Matthews, for unspecified reasons, declined to do. Instead a member of the SIB team interviewed him in Blackpool on 12 April. He filed this report:

Under caution, he [Matthews] admitted selling 5 lbs. of coffee whilst in BRUSSELS. He stated that he sold 2 lbs on 24.3.45., in a small shop in BRUSSELS, the name and address of which he could not remember, and that he purchased presents with the money he received from this sale. The remaining 3lbs. he sold on 26.3.45., in a small café in BRUSSELS. He could not remember the name or address of this café. He denied entering any shop with MORTENSON and SMITH; introducing himself as, 'STANLEY MATTHEWS', the International Footballer and attempting to exchange sterling for Belgian francs. He also denied that the signature on the business card was his, and, from specimen signatures I obtained from him, it would appear that the signature 'STAN MATTHEWS' on the card is a forgery.

In their written statements, Mortensen and Smith also maintained they never went into a shop with a teammate. In line with Tumson's evidence, Smith denied he did any trading. Mortensen, on the other hand, admitted he had sold coffee and soap. He wrote that his brother-in-law, who was on the Continent, had reported that these items were scarce and he, Mortensen, had taken them over to give to him, only to find his relation was in hospital. Mortensen said he sold about four cakes of soap and some coffee to the shop, for about 300 francs, after going in there to buy a present for his wife. He denied trying to exchange English money for Belgium francs. He also said that if he felt he had done any wrong in the shop he would not have told them his name or signed the card.

It is possible to concoct any number of reasons why the investigation fizzled out. Perhaps the authorities felt it was a pretty minor offence not worth pursuing, particularly as the error over identifying the right address raised questions about the evidence. Conspiracy theorists might feel the charges were dropped because news of two highly respected footballers being arraigned for black-marketeering would be bad for national morale. The investigators themselves did not appear to support aborting the case. They even suggested that the evidence justified broadening the inquiry to take in the whole FA party.

One can only imagine the British authorities were mightily relieved that not only were the charges dropped, but also news that they were brought in the first place did not break at the time.

The story presented to the public of this second FA visit to the Continent was of a highly successful sortie into territory from which the Axis forces had recently been banished. The only incident beyond the football that made news was that some British troops, desperate to see the team play in Bruges on Saturday 24 March, had broken down a fence to gain entry. They were treated to four goals by Tommy Lawton in the 8-1 win over the Diables Rouge. The next day Lawton scored all his side's goals in a 3-2 win over Belgium.

Chapter 9

'McGrory's jealousy of Stan cost Stoke their
best chance of the title'

A series of headline-catching matches between the outbreak of
peace and the domestic game's return to pre-war normality in
1946–7 ensured no let-up in interest for football fans. The first
of three notable fixtures in which Matthews took part cast light
on what was a rapidly changing world.

In November 1945 Matthews played against the first club team
from the Soviet Union to visit the West – and did so wearing
Arsenal colours in what turned into a truly bizarre event.
Stanley Rous, the FA secretary, conceived Moscow Dynamo's
British tour after a conversation with the Soviet ambassador to
Britain, Ivan Maisky. Clementine Churchill, wife of Winston
and a friend of Maisky's, then played a lead role in hardening
the concept into reality during a trip to Moscow.

With the Iron Curtain starting to be drawn, the original idea
that Dynamo would be coming on a goodwill visit turned out
to be hopelessly optimistic. Relations between Britain and the
Soviet Union deteriorated in the weeks before the team left home,
a situation the tour itself did nothing to repair. The visiting party
proved endlessly disobliging to hosts who were on the lookout
to take offence at the slightest provocation. Robert Edelman,

the eminent American historian, identified it as the first case of the Soviet Union using sport for diplomatic and political ends. George Orwell wrote that Dynamo's visit reinforced the point that 'sport is an unfailing cause of ill-will, and if such a visit as this had any effect at all on Anglo-Soviet relations, it could only be to make them slightly worse than before'.

The politicking and peevishness that spilled over into the tour itself dogged the latter stages of planning to such an extent that Dynamo did not confirm their arrival time until the very last minute. As a result it was too late to find them a hotel. From landing at Croydon, they were taken to Army barracks for the night. The lodgings failed to impress the visitors, a member of their delegation describing them as feudal.

The tour's wider subplot was soon apparent and a British sportswriter's jest that the visitors might end up in the salt mines if they performed poorly would probably have been more accurate if presented as a fact. Lavrentiy Beria, one of Stalin's most brutal henchmen, who was closely associated with the Dynamo team, already had form trumping up charges to banish underachieving footballers into exile.

The pressure on them to perform well did not come only from their masters in Moscow. The great interest aroused in Britain by the visitors from what was then a strange land added to it, making for a particularly tense atmosphere when they played their first match against Chelsea on Tuesday 13 November. Matthews was merely a spectator on this occasion, one of those who entered Stamford Bridge legitimately. Several thousand got in unchecked through a broken gate, which was why the official attendance of 82,905 was reckoned to be some way short of the actual figure.

Two things struck Matthews about that day. First, the carefully stage-managed way in which the Dynamo players conducted themselves. This included presenting each of their opposite numbers with a bunch of flowers during the on-pitch ceremony before kick-off. The Chelsea players, standing there with their posies, would hardly have looked more embarrassed had they walked out in high heels.

Then there was the way Dynamo played. 'I don't think there was a dribbler in the side,' Matthews said, with feeling. In an observation that pointed the way to football as played in the twenty-first century, Matthews added: 'All the time the ball was being pushed along the ground – from back to half-back to inside-forward to winger to centre-forward, and at a speed that left Chelsea gasping.'

It was a style that partly accounts for Mikhail Yakushin, Dynamo's trainer, making this judgement on Matthews before the team left for home: 'His individual qualities are high, but we put collective football first and individualism second, so we do not favour his style as we think teamwork would suffer.' Matthews's British critics would have enjoyed this remark regardless of its political undertone.

A far more brazenly political comment that invoked Matthews's name, and may have been based on observations made during Dynamo's UK tour, appeared seven months later in the journal *Soviet Sport*. It referred to players in 'bourgeois countries ... who, after reaching the peak of glory, disappear into the gloom of a dark improvident, beggarly existence'. The article contrasted this fate with Matthews's and his business interests in a sports shop and hotel in Blackpool. 'But not a single bourgeois newspaper tries to tell how many former champions have disappeared and have not become possessors of restaurants and hotels,' it said. In this instance some former players might have found themselves identifying with this.

The businessman-footballer sitting in the stands at Chelsea saw the home team take a 2-0 lead and thought the build-up given to Dynamo had been overdone. His view changed as the visitors, fit and fast, rallied impressively to start their unbeaten tour with a 3-3 draw. Taken overall, the occasion was a triumph for Dynamo. Their carefully orchestrated behaviour during the preliminaries and their recovery to force a draw gained them the crowd's huge appreciation.

They won their next game 10-1 against Cardiff, which raised still further the sense of excitement when they returned to London to face Arsenal at White Hart Lane. Highbury was still out of commission and, much to the easily irritated Soviets' annoyance, Wembley, a possible alternative, was not prepared to postpone a greyhound meeting. This merely added to the grievance of having their request to play on Saturday afternoons, along with all the other best fixtures, rejected.

Matthews volunteered for the Arsenal match when he heard their manager, George Allison, was struggling to raise a strong side because some of his best players were still on active service. Matthews had wanted to test himself against the visitors after seeing them play at Chelsea. He asked Bob McGrory, the Stoke manager, to ring Allison, who was very happy to recruit the England winger for the day. Five guest players would eventually line up for Arsenal, including Matthews and Stan Mortensen.

Unsurprisingly, the Soviets, who had laid out conditions for their tour in a fourteen-point charter, including that they would not play national sides, had a good old moan. Arsenal, they reckoned, were starting to look suspiciously like a representative, rather than a club, team. They accepted it with poor grace, but with an excellent quip from Yakushin. 'To come to London,' he said, 'and not play Arsenal would be like visiting Cairo without seeing the Pyramids.'

The match, which took place eight days after the Chelsea game, was an anticlimax as far as the spectators were concerned but rich in evidence, for the many seeking it, that Dynamo were a bunch of mischievous foreigners. Dense fog, an early version of the famous London smogs or pea-soupers, made the conditions, at best, barely playable. The Russian referee, Nikolay Latyshev, a member of the Dynamo party, was one of the few officials who took the opposing view. Thousands of glowing cigarette ends were the most reliable evidence that the ground was packed with 54,000 people, the noise being turned right down because no one could see what was going on. A display of magnesium flashbulbs when photographers behind the goals could see enough to take pictures gave the only indication there was goalmouth activity.

Things were not much better for the players. Matthews reported that he could not see more than a yard or two in front of him, which made some wonder out loud how Yakushin had managed to gain enough knowledge of his playing style to so discredit it.

The result, 4-3 to Dynamo, was almost incidental, particularly when stories of all kinds of skulduggery emerged. Cliff Bastin, the Arsenal captain, claimed the referee was so biased he would have awarded the visitors a goal even if they had carried the ball into the net. Even before the kick-off the official raised suspicions when he asked the two English linesmen to run one touchline while he controlled the other. The main conspiracies, though, concerned the weather and the opportunities afforded by the lack of visibility.

Allowing substitutions had been one of the fourteen conditions and when Dynamo brought one on in the second half they apparently neglected to nominate who should come off. It was twenty minutes before Arsenal realised they had been playing against twelve men. On the other hand, Matthews told the story of the Arsenal forward George Drury not leaving the field after being ordered off. Drury was infuriated by the Dynamo goalkeeper's habit of lying on the ground and refusing to release the ball until surrounded by defenders. 'Are you a duck trying to hatch the thing,' Drury said scathingly and was sent off when he tried to hack the ball from his grasp. 'Quack, quack,' he said before wandering towards the tunnel. Some minutes later, Matthews spotted Drury still on the field. 'I reminded him he had been sent off,' Matthews said, "'I know, mate, but I couldn't find the way," he grinned – and disappeared back into the fog.'

Legend also has it that Wyn Griffiths, the Cardiff City goalkeeper who played for Arsenal after being injured during his club's match against Dynamo, knocked himself out by running into a goalpost towards the end and was replaced by a member of the crowd.

Dynamo completed their tour in Glasgow with a 2-2 draw against Rangers. The publicity the Russians generated south of the border ensured a big turnout of 92,000 at Ibrox. The occasion also stirred up at least as much bad feeling as the previous three matches. A Dynamo advance party, which arrived in Scotland twenty-four hours before the game, raised objections to some of Rangers' intended selections, including Jimmy Caskie, who they claimed was still an Everton player. Also, for the second time on the tour, the visitors played with an extra man for some of the time after a substituted player stayed on the field.

If the Russians did not have overwhelming success in terms of results, they did once again demonstrate that the football being played abroad, experimenting with new paradigms, was leaving the British game behind. The pity was that with so much else going on around the Dynamo visit very few in Britain chose to pay attention to how the visitors played.

Matthews next faced foreign opposition in January 1946 in the only Victory international played at Wembley. In contrast to the shenanigans of Dynamo's tour, the match against Belgium reflected the muted mood replacing the euphoria that immediately followed the war. A respectful crowd of 85,000, which included Clement Attlee, Prime Minister since July, watched England score an unremarkable 2-0 victory on a Wembley pitch not completely cleared of snow.

The match, played just weeks before Matthews's thirty-first birthday, took his appearances for England to forty-four, a record that, given not a great deal happened against Belgium, received even more attention than it might have done. Early in 1946 wartime internationals had still not lost the cachet that all but disappeared once players stationed abroad returned home, restoring the pool of eligible players to its full complement. Matthews, with one more appearance than Eddie Hapgood, was hailed for his achievement and, although he tried to dismiss the fuss being made of him, no one was listening.

The first hint of the fanfare celebrating the record was a letter in the Stoke evening paper five days before the game. It called for Matthews, whose 'like will never be seen again on a soccer field', to be given due recognition for surpassing the now retired Hapgood's total of England games. At the same time the FA, not renowned for their munificence, announced Matthews would receive £100 in Savings Certificates and an illuminated address.

Four days after the match, the city of Stoke came up with its own plans to honour Matthews. An organising committee, chaired by the pottery manufacturer Sir Ernest Johnson, promised him another illuminated address, which in time went on display in venues around Stoke, and a testimonial fund that would open at the start of February and run until the end of March. In an effusive speech, Sir Ernest said: 'No one has done more than Matthews to put Stoke-on-Trent in the forefront of the towns in this country . . . it is now up to the people of this district to show their practical appreciation of the player and the man.' The committee announced it would print subscription cards for people to donate to the fund. These would be available in public places, factories, collieries, business premises and clubs.

Events honouring Matthews lasted right into late summer. Dressed in RAF uniform, he received the first of his illuminated addresses at a meeting in late March of the Stoke-on-Trent City Council. He dreaded this occasion because of having to make a speech but found when the moment came he forgot his shyness. On 24 June, at a big lunch at the North Stafford Hotel in Stoke, the FA handed over their address and organisers of the testimonial fund passed on a cheque for £1,160 4s., made up from more than 5,500 donations.

Local support for paying tribute to Matthews was overwhelming, which raises the question of why he seemed so keen to underplay it? In none of his memoirs, for example, did he mention the thousands who gave to his testimonial fund. It can't simply have been his well-known modesty.

Maybe he felt it would have been inappropriate to do otherwise. Although the vast majority favoured honouring him, a very small but detectable undertow of resentment, not necessarily directed at him exclusively, did exist. Matthews was almost certainly aware of a letter that appeared in the local paper in which a female correspondent questioned the sporting public's homage to a footballer while they ignored others who had given so much in the war. She chided the 'sportsmen of Stoke-on-Trent' for not having 'shown gratitude in any substantial form to the women who gave their men, the mothers who gave their sons, the sporting ex-soldier who gave his limbs or eyes to keep Stoke from being blasted off the map'.

Such a letter would have affected Matthews, providing one more reason not to dwell on anything he might have done, particularly when more than half his England appearances had been in matches not thought deserving of international caps. He must also have had more than just an inkling that his time at Stoke City was drawing to a close and been embarrassed that the townspeople were being asked to contribute to a testimonial fund. Less than a year after he received the cheque he was playing for another club.

If he did have an inkling, he did not let on at the last of the ceremonies marking his record number of England matches. In mid-August, shortly before the 1946–7 season kicked off, Stoke City presented him with an inscribed silver tea service. 'There is no reason why we [Stoke City] shouldn't have a successful

(*Left*) Stanley's father, Jack Matthews, 'The Fighting Barber from Hanley', whose bout in London against George Mackness was described as 'the greatest fight ever'

(*Right*) Matthews (left) appeared in one schoolboy international. He was devastated when dropped after this game

(*Above*) Matthews supported Port Vale as a boy but, guided by his father, joined Stoke City
(*Right*) The famous 'lean' was soon in evidence

(*Above*) Nineteen-year-old Matthews (left, front row) played a part in both goals in the Football League's 2-1 win over the Scottish Football League at Stamford Bridge in October 1934

(*Right*) England players give the Nazi salute in Berlin in May 1938. No one wanted to take responsibility for doing this

(*Left*) The FA removed their badge from England's shirts during the war. Here Matthews plays against Scotland in 1944

(*Below*) Matthews (left, front row) before a United Services match in Belfast at the end of the war

(*Left*) A family mixed doubles in the garden at Blackpool. Stanley and Betty take on Jean and Stanley Junior, who went on to represent Britain in the Davis Cup

(*Right*) Stanley Matthews, Aircraftman No. 1361317, with daughter Jean in 1943

(*Left*) Matthews trains with his son, Stanley Junior, who was good at football but said he gave it up partly because the mentality of his opponents was, 'We're going to get Stanley Matthews's son'

(*Right*) Matthews plays against Blackburn at Ewood Park in his first season (1947–8) for Blackpool, the club he represented as a guest during the war

(*Above*) Matthews on his favourite training ground, Blackpool beach

(*Above*) Hungary's Magnificent Magyars before they humiliated England 6–3 at Wembley in November 1953

(*Right*) Matthews's look reflects the bemusement of his teammates during the defeat by Hungary

(*Above*) Stan Mortensen (right) shoots for Blackpool's first goal in the 1953 FA Cup final. He was eventually credited with the score although at the time commentators made it an own goal by Bolton's Harold Hassall

(*Above*) Matthews on one of the many runs that destroyed Bolton's defence in the latter stages of the 1953 FA Cup final. Here he confronts centre-half Malcolm Barrass

(*Left*) Matthews (middle row, second left) sits next to manager Joe Smith as Blackpool pose with the FA Cup

Matthews, carried on the shoulders of Jackie Mudie and Stan Mortensen,
holds up his medal after the 1953 FA Cup final

season,' Matthews told those gathered for the presentation, 'because certainly the team spirit exists right down from the boardroom to the players.' It was a harmony that would be tested to its foundations by Matthews's sundering his links with the club nine months later.

The third match of note in which Matthews played immediately after the war was an FA Cup tie at Bolton's Burnden Park ground that turned to tragedy. Its proximity to the Allies' victory was no coincidence. The country's most popular sporting competition had been sorely missed, which was why the authorities prioritised restoring it to the calendar. For many thousands, going to watch it was their way of celebrating the new peace.

The number of those who packed into the ground for the Bolton–Stoke quarter-final second-leg match on Saturday 9 March 1946 has been estimated from between 70,000 and more than 85,000. Sixty years later, an article in the *Bolton News* encapsulated what happened: 'Many thousands wanted to see Stoke star Stanley Matthews and had even climbed over the walls to get into the ground when the turnstiles were shut. The overcrowding at the Embankment end forced the barriers to collapse and bodies fell on top of each other and on to the pitch, suffocating many fans.'

Matthews's response to the tragedy changed markedly over time. One of his earliest reflections may seem slightly heartless: 'I am surprised the British public was so shocked coming so soon after the worst war in the world's history.' Put into the context of the time, though, it is more instructive than heartless, giving a powerful sense of just how deeply people felt about the lives lost during the war.

Matthews also recorded soon after the match that, with none of the players sure of the extent of the disaster until later – even though some of them did admit hearing a spectator call out, 'It is criminal to go on when people are dead' – his only thoughts in the second half were 'that we were still two goals down [from the first leg] and that something had to be done if Stoke were to survive in the Cup'. However, by the time he came to work on his 2000 autobiography his story had not only changed but it contained some highly emotional detail. He talked about tears welling up in his eyes towards the end, finding it hard not to be physically ill and seeing people in body bags at the side of the pitch.

What is clear is that immediately after the match he was deeply affected by what had happened. He joined in the fretting over whether the referee, George Dutton, who had ordered the players off the field in the first half, had been right to accede to the wishes of the police to allow play to continue. He decided Dutton had been correct. If he had called off the game, Matthews reasoned, before everyone knew how serious things were, 'thousands of Cup crazy fans might have stampeded' with more disastrous consequences.

Jack Matthews recalled visiting his brother in Blackpool two days later. He said the armour with which Stanley normally protected his emotions had, on this occasion, been penetrated. He found his brother still dazed and emotional. He had just written out a cheque for more than two weeks' wages for the Disaster Fund and asked Jack whether he thought it was enough.

It was almost incidental that the match had ended 0-0, putting Stoke out 2-0 on aggregate (two-leg ties were retained from the war for one season only). Two weeks later Bolton themselves went out of the competition, beaten by Charlton.

For Matthews, March 1946 got no better. Four days after playing against Blackpool in the Northern League, when he was a vibrant presence in Stoke's 6-3 victory at the Victoria Ground, he made one last guest appearance for the Lancashire club in a midweek home fixture against Manchester United.

It proved an unhappy afternoon. Not only did Blackpool lose 5-1, their enlisted outside-right injured his left knee, limped through until half-time and did not reappear after the interval. Matthews exacerbated the injury by applying too much liniment, which caused severe inflammation. As a result he was ruled out of England's match at Hampden Park in mid-April. Mortified, he went to the game anyway to sit among a crowd of nearly 140,000. The pervading mood of post-war good humour received a mighty lift as Scotland, having scored nine goals against thirty-six in seven straight defeats by England, won 1-0. Only England supporters regarded it remotely relevant that Matthews, present in each of the seven wins, was on this occasion in the stands.

As the country readjusted to being at peace, Matthews's own life entered a period of turbulence that led inexorably to his exit from Stoke in the spring of 1947. He would always say that before the start of the 1946–7 season he looked forward unreservedly to once again being a regular Stoke City player. But it is barely possible that his loyalty to the club had not been undermined by his happy experience playing for Blackpool and his setting up home – and hotel – in the town.

Then there was his relationship with Stoke, or, more specifically, with Bob McGrory. This had been riven with ever widening cracks since the Scot took over as manager in 1935 and if the war had not kept the two apart it is highly likely their coexistence at Stoke would have ended earlier than it did.

What would heighten the drama of Matthews's departure was the fact that Stoke's team in 1946–7, made up mostly of local players, was arguably the best they have ever had. 'Better than merely very good,' Matthews reckoned – and they might well have won the First Division championship had their much-feted outside-right not left them in the last few weeks when they were closing in on the prize.

Stoke took a while to establish the momentum that would carry them so close to winning the title. On Saturday 31 August

1946, when the Football League resumed after a seven-year interruption, they drew 2-2 at home with Charlton and then lost their next three games, including home and away defeats against Bolton. Matthews's own start was just as dismal. He suffered a muscle strain in the first of the Bolton fixtures and when he came back after missing four games was injured again in a 3-2 win over Manchester United at the Victoria Ground. His presence helped to boost the crowd to 40,000 but instead of wizardry the spectators were treated to the spectacle of Matthews hobbling for most of the match with a pulled thigh muscle. He faced another spell out of the side.

The result against Manchester United continued a revival by Stoke. It was their third win in a row, a sequence they extended to six victories when they beat Chelsea 5-2 in mid-October in front of 68,189 at Stamford Bridge. Matthews's contribution to this run of success had been one appearance cast mostly in the role of Long John Silver.

As he eased himself back to fitness, Matthews helped Betty and a small staff run the hotel in Blackpool. A press photo showed him in the hotel kitchen 'tasting soup at the stove before it goes into the guests'. What compounded his frustration was that his deputies for Stoke and England, George Mountford and Tom Finney, respectively were doing rather well.

The decision to give wartime football minimal recognition was what lay behind the seemingly remarkable statistic that Finney made his England debut less than a month after first appearing in the Football League. In fact, Finney broke through as a Preston player at the start of the war before being posted with the Royal Armoured Corps to Egypt where he served as a driver-mechanic in the desert campaign. When selected by England as Matthews's replacement on a visit to Ireland in September 1946, he was twenty-four and a war veteran as well as already being widely recognised as a footballer of exceptional promise.

Finney marked his arrival as an international with a goal in the 7-2 win over Northern Ireland in Belfast and he scored again two days later when England beat the Republic of Ireland 1-0 on their first visit to Dublin since 1912. Finney's good form meant he kept a fit-again Matthews out of the national team for the matches in November against Wales and Holland. The foundation of the debate over the relative merits of Mathews and Finney, which continues to this day, was firmly in place.

The debate has tended to concentrate on their playing styles, which Finney himself liked to underelaborate: 'The chief difference between Stanley's style and my own is that whereas he seems to prefer to carry the ball with the outside of his right foot, I use the inside of my left. Left, right . . . it's as simple as that.'

Other comparisons have looked more deeply at the two men. The cultural historian Joyce Woolridge analysed them in a 2002 essay on the development of football stardom. She referred to Matthews's increasing quirkiness and extreme self-discipline that added an ascetic gloss, while Finney's image was more that of an 'ordinary bloke' with an exceptional talent. Woolridge's essay took on a decidedly academic tone when she explored what the two had in common. She said they were representatives of a footballing subtype that might be termed 'the ghost' and suggested 'a vestige of nineteenth-century romanticism' existed in journalists' constant references to their pallor and delicacy. This made them appear too frail for a vigorous contact sport.

In November 1946 even the hugely popular *Picture Post*, not normally associated with scrutinising footballers, waded into the discussion of their different styles. The magazine described Finney as the more graceful mover but said that he 'was less spectacular [than Matthews], less of an individual, less of a one-man circus. Perhaps his greatest asset is that highly developed feeling for collective play that some critics miss in Matthews.'

Matthews could cope with another dig at his team ethic,

echoing those of Fleet Street critics such as Roy Peskett. What upset him was that a number of his detractors, factoring in that he would soon be thirty-two – while Finney was still in his mid-twenties – wasted no time in handing over his England place to the younger man. 'I was more than a little hurt when people who professed to be my friends turned around and began to say that I was out for good,' he said.

Still, the Matthews–Finney debate played out gently, over many years, compared to the eruption caused by George Mountford's form on the right wing for Stoke. Less eye-catchingly productive than Matthews, Mountford was dismissed as prosaic by some but was sufficiently effective to leave Bob McGrory facing a genuinely awkward decision once he had two outside-rights to choose from again. When this situation arose, after the big win at Chelsea, McGrory abandoned his usual forthright approach. Instead, he confronted the dilemma cautiously. He rang Matthews at his hotel in Blackpool only to be told by Betty that her husband was on the golf course with the Blackpool team. So he left a message in which he floated the idea that, rather than return straightaway to the first team for their game on Saturday at Arsenal, Matthews should have a run-out with the reserves the same day. He was careful not to couch this as a command and obviously hoped Matthews would go along with the idea of playing for the second team against Aston Villa.

Even if Matthews did pick up the nuance of McGrory's message he obviously felt that just mentioning his name in the same breath as the reserves, in the shape of a mere suggestion that he might play for them, was unacceptable.

Anyone who imagined that Matthews not only walked away from trouble on the pitch but did so whenever he encountered it elsewhere was about to be disabused. He showed he was perfectly capable of a good rant, apparently relishing the fact that McGrory was the target of his invective. He accused the manager of handling the matter very badly. 'What it amounts to is that I am dropped out of the team,' he said. 'It's no use the manager trying to pull wool over anyone's eyes.' In what was reportedly a stormy telephone call with McGrory he told him, unequivocally, that he would not countenance playing for the reserves – or the 'stiffs' as he referred to them.

'Frankly, and this is the truth,' Matthews said, 'if I had been told that the club preferred to continue fielding this winning team and had said, "You take another week's rest," I should have had no objection whatever. But I do object to being asked to play for the second team for it would serve no good purpose at all.'

As the row developed, Matthews stayed at home training with Blackpool. This led to accusations that he was avoiding a confrontation with McGrory. Matthews hit back: 'I have told him [McGrory] that I will not play for the reserves. Why go to Stoke to tell him again.'

'What hurt me most of all,' Matthews said, 'was a report that the Stoke players had sent a deputation to the management requesting I should not return in place of George Mountford.' He added that he was more than surprised at his colleagues for doing this and that it might be better if he left the club, which was something he was considering.

Transfer talk soon swirled around what was now a major national story. Chelsea, one of a number of clubs interested in Matthews, were reported to be prepared to shatter the British record by paying £20,000. The consensus was he would return to Blackpool, who, one pundit reckoned, 'would sell the Tower to get him'. Colonel William Parkinson, the Blackpool chairman, who followed the saga from his holiday hotel in Bournemouth, was more measured when asked about the club's intentions: 'I should like Matthews more than any other player in the world, but it will be a question of the price that Stoke will ask.'

Matthews was under siege. 'I was given little peace,' he said.

'The newshounds were chasing me for statements and the postman began delivering poison-pen letters, some of which accused me of poor sportsmanship.'

His latest reconciliation with Stoke, which may not have been what, deep down, he wanted, started with a denial by the players that the dressing room had turned against him. 'One or two of the boys are writing individual letters to Stan today to tell him what has been stated is not true,' Neil Franklin, the Stoke captain, said. 'We are all the best of friends with Stan.' Matthews said he was reassured to know the story of his isolation was unfounded. This still did not entirely resolve things, though, and instead of playing on the Saturday Matthews watched Blackpool beat Manchester United 3-1 at Bloomfield Road. Stoke's trip to London saw their run of victories end in a 1-0 defeat at Highbury.

Three days later he reported to the Victoria Ground to meet the Stoke board. A large press gathering was waiting when he arrived and knocked for admittance. The official word after an hour's discussion was that an amicable settlement had been reached. It included an assurance he could continue to train in Blackpool, allaying his great fear that he would be made to travel to the Victoria Ground to do this. He had said he would abide by such a decision, but refused to confirm he would have had to sell the hotel in Blackpool. 'It's my own private business and not for public discussion,' he said. It was also agreed he should take a week's holiday to recover from what he called the nightmare of the past week. For all the smiles and handshakes, those who fancied they caught a whiff of compromise about the deal would have been right to trust their imaginations.

Stoke's 3-0 home defeat by Wolves while Matthews was on holiday may not have entirely displeased the management. It meant that his recall for the match away to Sunderland on 2 November was a logical reaction. Matthews endorsed this by leaving his imprint on the 1-0 victory at Roker Park. His performance, in the words of one report, had 'the fans roaring with laughter at the ease with which he beat his man'.

After this the tension between Matthews and Stoke eased for a while. For four months all seemed well. The disappointment of a 1-0 home defeat by Sheffield United in the fifth round of the FA Cup, on an afternoon so cold that quite a number of seats at the Victoria Ground's first all-ticket match were left empty, was offset by consistent form in Football League matches. Matthews appeared regularly as Stoke positioned themselves to win the title.

Two League matches stood out for their interesting rivalries. First, Blackpool's visit to Stoke shortly before Christmas pitted Matthews against the players with whom he trained during the week. He was, he said, aware of rumours of his divided loyalties, which he was keen to discredit. This he felt he achieved. He was, in his own words, right on song as he laid on three goals and then finished with a party-piece solo effort, breaking from the halfway line to complete a 4-1 victory.

Then, on the Saturday before the Sheffield United defeat, he shone in a 5-0 home victory over a Preston side that included Finney. The match was billed as a showdown. The correspondent who reckoned Matthews 'settled the argument in his favour' probably spoke for the majority of the press box and maybe the country.

The harmony at Stoke even survived a potentially unsettling attempt by Arsenal to buy either Matthews or George Mountford. The Stoke board met and announced with sufficient firmness to discourage further inquiry that neither was for sale. The firmness impressed the local paper. It decided it was now more certain than ever that Matthews would 'conclude his great playing career where he started it – at Stoke'.

But quite how fragile the harmony was soon became evident. The cracks, irreparable fissures as it turned out, appeared over the Easter weekend in early April.

Matthews, saying he needed to conserve energy for his England recall against Scotland a week later, was excused from the first of the three holiday matches, a trip to Grimsby on Good Friday. Stoke won this 5-2 on a bitingly cold afternoon and McGrory opted to keep an unchanged side for the home games against Huddersfield on the Saturday and the return against Grimsby two days later, both of which Stoke won 3-0. Matthews said he accepted not being used at all over Easter although he confessed to being niggled by a summons from McGrory to appear at the Victoria Ground for the Huddersfield match only to be told he was not needed.

At least it meant he was fresh to face Scotland for the first post-war British championship match at Wembley. A buoyant atmosphere – and 98,250 spectators – filled the stadium, which made it disappointing for Matthews that he could not use the occasion to construct a compelling case to keep Finney out of the national side. Both he and England performed no more than moderately in a 1-1 draw.

In light of this, and the troubles that were brewing, Matthews might have reflected that he would have preferred to play for Stoke that day – and not simply because their match was just around the corner from his Blackpool hotel. Stoke's 2-0 win at Bloomfield Road not only completed a double over their rivals but again presented McGrory with a plausible reason for not tinkering with a side who were once more on a winning run.

An awkward situation seemed to have been resolved to Matthews's satisfaction when he returned to the Stoke side for the visit of Brentford on Saturday 19 April. His name had just appeared in the list of players retained by the club for the 1947–8 season and with a goal in the 3-1 win over Brentford he helped Stoke establish a club record forty-eight points in the First Division with five matches still to go. Stoke were keeping pace comfortably with all the challengers for the title.

Only later did Matthews have reason to revisit something

he had skated over at the time: McGrory's decision to name six forwards to choose from against Brentford. He picked up on a whisper that he would have been the one left out if Albert Mitchell had been passed fit. If this was the case, he felt the fact that he had not been told there was a possibility he would not play against Brentford was tantamount to deception on McGrory's part. The board denied he was merely on standby, but the programme provided fairly conclusive proof. The team printed the day before the match did not include Matthews at outside-right. George Mountford was down to play there before being switched to inside right to take over from Mitchell.

'I was fed up and unhappy with the way I was being treated,' Matthews said. He sought another meeting with the board and finally this time they agreed, grudgingly, to grant him what he had been waiting for – a deferred transfer to Blackpool. The decision would not be made public straightaway and Matthews would stay on to help Stoke maintain their push for the championship. Assuming the clubs could reach a deal the transfer would be wrapped up after the end of the season. A week after the Brentford match, Matthews, at peace with himself and Stoke City knowing he was now working out his time at the club, scored again in a 2-0 win at Blackburn.

Keeping a good football story secret for long was as unattainable then as it is today. In 1946–7 it was going to be doubly difficult to stop it leaking before the season was over. As a result of an exceptionally harsh winter and a government curb on midweek matches, so that absenteeism did not impede the industrial recovery, the Football League decided to extend its programme until mid-June.

In fact, it was only a matter of days before the secrecy surrounding the Matthews transfer was blown away. Reporters were waiting to interview him when he arrived to catch a boat for a match between the Football League and the League of Ireland in Dublin. Banner-headlined stories appeared in papers across the country, some of them spiced with what Matthews called speculations and exaggerations. Among them was one that he had threatened to quit football altogether if he wasn't allowed to leave Stoke, which he strongly denied. Once again he showed himself capable of being more ruffled off the field than he ever was on it. He issued a statement in which his irritation was plain: 'I have received many letters from Stoke and elsewhere criticising my action. To my correspondents I say: get your facts right before attacking one side.'

All sides now agreed the transfer should go ahead immediately, but the fact that, unusually, the player had nominated the club he wanted to join both simplified and complicated matters. It was an auction with only one bidder with Stoke City, the vendors, putting a reserve of £15,000 on their prize possession and Colonel Parkinson, the solitary bidder, professing to have only £10,000 in his wallet.

The negotiations took a while to get going but on 3 May 1947 Matthews played what would turn out to be his last match for Stoke for more than fourteen years: a 2-1 win over relegated Leeds United that was Stoke's seventh victory in a row, putting them second in the table.

One major consideration for Blackpool was Matthews's age. At thirty-two he was, by any normal reckoning, nearing the end of his playing days. As one national newspaper put it: 'Today Matthews's career is three parts run. Only a few seasons of first-class football remain.' Even Matthews could not have known that, incredibly, he had served less than half his time as a professional footballer. He himself said he expected to retire in three or four seasons, although this may have been a device to do Colonel Parkinson a favour at the negotiating table. At around the same time he had told people he felt as fit now as he had ever done.

Blackpool's wily manager, Joe Smith, also worked the line about the time fast approaching when Matthews would be clapped out. 'We'll get a couple of seasons out of him,' Smith said, 'that's all. Then he'll be put out to grass.' As Matthews said: 'I might have been a racehorse to listen to him.'

Smith, who conducted negotiations in close consultation with Colonel Parkinson, reckoned he produced his real master-stroke, a bottle of whisky, during the haggling that closed the deal exactly a week after the Leeds game. This took place in Glasgow where all the principals in the transfer talks had gathered for a fundraising match between a Great Britain side, featuring Matthews, against the Rest of Europe. The fixture was widely referred to as the 'Match of the Century' – promotional hyperbole is more ancient than some people imagine – and generated over £30,000 to help relaunch the International Football Federation.

All along Colonel Parkinson's message had been: 'We are paying no fancy fee for Matthews. A reasonable fee, yes, for a player of his reputation – but no record £20,000 or £15,000.' Just as things were threatening to stall, with Stoke having come down to £12,000 and Blackpool still offering only £10,000, Smith broke the deadlock. Knowing McGrory's penchant for a wee dram, he opened the whisky, served him 'a couple of snorters' and 'in no time both sides had agreed to split the difference and the world's greatest footballer came to Blackpool for £11,000'.

'It was the cheapest bottle of whisky I ever bought,' Smith said. 'Saved me at least a thousand on the transfer fee.' On another occasion he said: 'We didn't buy Stanley Matthews, we pinched him.'

McGrory, nursing a head-throbbing hangover, confirmed the transfer had been agreed on the morning of the match. 'We are very reluctant to part with Stanley,' he said. 'He has rendered fine services to the club but the directors have considered his own interests in reaching their decision.' Matthews was told the news as he entered the dressing rooms at Hampden. 'I'm very glad to hear it,' he said. Buoyed, perhaps, by the knowledge that he was now a Blackpool player he then gave an entertaining performance in a 6-1 victory that, for once, because Scotland were not the ones suffering, the Hampden crowd of 134,000 thoroughly appreciated.

The actual signing took place after the match, shortly before midnight, in Matthews's hotel room, the player standing at the dresser to write his name on the form. The most eagerly followed transfer negotiations in British football were finally over and Colonel Parkinson, having pursued Matthews with quiet purpose, had got his way. Smith's whisky-bottle gambit had helped trim the price, which was good business at the time, and exceptionally good business as things worked out.

Matthews had already helped to reduce Blackpool's pre-1939 debt of £34,000 with his wartime performances that made the club such an attraction. The government provided additional vital funds after requisitioning Bloomfield Road from July 1940 until the fighting was over. Although Blackpool continued to play at the ground they received £700 a year from the War Office plus compensation for damage to the stands.

The deal with the government and the capture of Matthews were just two examples of Colonel Parkinson's business nous, which explained how Blackpool managed to be so successful with one of the smallest grounds in the First Division. They did not explain it completely, though, and precise details of how the club overcame their relatively slim takings at the gate were not something the chairman was going to divulge. 'Too many people in the game want to know this,' he told the club's annual meeting in August 1947. 'Why should we tell them?'

In the same address, Colonel Parkinson told his audience: 'What we want – and what may one day be built – is a new stand not far from the present site, a ground that will hold 60,000 spectators.' Perhaps if the club's visionary leader had not died suddenly of a heart attack soon afterwards it might have happened. As it was Blackpool fans had to wait more than fifty years for the ground to be significantly improved.

For Stoke fans, the sense of theft was instant. Matthews was now a Blackpool player and Stoke City must press for the laurels of First Division champions without the player who for years had embodied their reputation for attacking football.

And in the end Stoke came within just a few moments of Matthewsian sorcery and claiming the title. They gathered three points out of four in the two matches straight after he left – a 0-0 home draw against Sunderland and 1-0 win at Aston Villa – which meant victory over Sheffield United at Bramall Lane on Saturday 14 June would make them champions. Liverpool, top of the table with fifty-seven points, Wolves and Manchester United were all ahead of them but had completed their forty-two matches. A win for Stoke, by whatever margin, would take them past Liverpool on goal average.

An estimated 12,000 Stoke fans travelled to Sheffield that day to experience the anguish of seeing their team lose 2-1 and stay in fourth place. Instead of a thirty-two-year-old outside-right acting out an heroic script, a Sheffield United veteran came up with a painfully anticlimactic plot for the Stoke faithful. Jack Pickering, thirty-eight, playing his only League game of the season as stand-in for injured inside-left Jimmy Hagan, scored after three minutes and laid on the home team's winner for Walter Rickett, soon to join Matthews at Blackpool, in the second half.

The frustration of the Stoke players was best expressed by the goalkeeper Dennis Herod in an interview he gave years later. He left no doubt where he reckoned the blame lay for Matthews having departed when so much was at stake. 'Bob McGrory's jealousy of Stan's fame cost Stoke their best chance of the First Division title,' Herod said. The decision 'to sell the best forward in the world to Blackpool was sheer stupidity'.

Matthews was more hotelier than footballer on the day he might have been lifting the First Division trophy wearing a

Stoke shirt. He was back with his family in the Romford on Blackpool's South Promenade, having played four matches in three European countries in less than a fortnight towards the end of May. Such an intense schedule, made possible by the growing use of air travel, offered a glimpse of the professional footballer's future.

Within days of switching clubs, Matthews flew with England to matches in Switzerland and Portugal and then he and Mortensen travelled on to Denmark where Blackpool, having finished their League matches much earlier than Stoke, were midway through a summer tour.

Some commentators expressed surprise that Matthews and Finney were both included in England's sixteen-man party to go to Europe. Finney had been preferred for the 3-0 win over France at Highbury on the day Matthews played his last match for Stoke against Leeds. One explanation put forward for both wingers being selected by England was that Matthews was recalled simply as cover for Finney.

In fact, he played in both matches, despite annoying his critics in England's 1-0 defeat by the amateurs of Switzerland in Zurich. Roy Peskett, of the *Daily Mail*, never shy to express his reservations about Matthews, said he held the ball far too long, allowing 'the Swiss scissors defensive formation' to block the middle of the field.

Billy Wright, playing at right-half behind Matthews, gave an interesting reason why the outside-right might not have been quite himself. 'The small ground was so packed,' Wright said, 'that they put seats alongside the touchline to cater for an overflow of spectators. This meant it was so cramped on the wings that we could not play to the strength of Stanley Matthews and Bobby Langton.'

Just as they did in 1938, when they lost 2-1 in Switzerland, England stubbornly overlooked the fact that, among the leading foreign national teams, football by shirt numbers resided in the local museum. For example, Switzerland's No. 9 operated from a deep-lying position, alien territory for an English centre-forward. Other continental teams were doing this but England, to their future embarrassment, still regarded it as some pointless foreign eccentricity.

One apparently compelling reason for England deciding the defeat in Zurich could be dismissed as 'one of those things' was what happened in the next match, a first international against Portugal. A dispute over the size of ball to be used that delayed the start in Lisbon threatened to sour the occasion. By the time England had won 10-0 it had lost any meaning.

England played well enough but really the result reflected a hopelessly inadequate performance by opponents who felt so humiliated that they skipped an official banquet that evening and were later suspended by their association. What was note-worthy from an England perspective was that Matthews and Finney were both successfully accommodated, with the naturally left-footed Finney playing on the left wing. Peskett, inevitably perhaps, reckoned Finney outshone his fellow winger. Another plus for England was that Mortensen, brought in at inside-forward to partner Matthews on the right, showed a speed and incisiveness that ended any doubt that he was good enough to play the international game.

If Matthews gained anything significant from the visit to Portugal it had less to do with the football than the setting. He was awakened to the possibilities offered by European resorts and living in the sunshine. Professional footballers of that era, before foreign travel was commonplace, tended to be home birds. Matthews, for all his cloistered upbringing, was destined to spend several years leading the life of a wanderer, partly through inclination and partly as a result of the gradual deterioration of his domestic circumstances.

His time in Portugal in the spring of 1947 left an indelible impression. After arriving in Lisbon, England travelled to Estoril, where, Matthews noted, the locals were understandably proud of their town with its white buildings and the finest gardens he had ever seen set against the blue sea and sky. He even liked what he saw when he looked in at the Casino. He remarked on the 'poker-faced gamblers', recognising in them a trait of his own. He was less enamoured by officious police who enforced quirky rules. A ban existed on the public use of cigarette lighters, to protect the local manufacture of matches, and woe betide pedestrians who ignored designated street crossings.

From Lisbon, Matthews and Mortensen moved on to another historic European port city, Copenhagen. Here, for the first time, Matthews wore the club's tangerine shirt as a fully signed-up Blackpool player rather than a wartime guest. He and Mortensen went straight to work developing their reputation as the most destructive attacking combination the club have ever known. Without a win after some decidedly lacklustre performances, Blackpool were geed to a 6-1 victory over a Copenhagen XI by their England duo who each scored a goal. Two days later Matthews laid on the first three goals for Mortensen in a 5-0 win over another Copenhagen selection.

Because of the timing of his transfer, Matthews had been a late inclusion in the Blackpool party that toured Denmark. His separate travel arrangements included flying home alone while the others returned by train and boat. Finally, nearly ten months after the 1946–7 season kicked off, he had time to sit back and quietly contemplate what had been a tumultuous period in his life.

It cannot have been easy ordering his thoughts. He had left Stoke but had a real sense of loyalty to his hometown fans. They had been the sounding board for his talent. Their enthusiastic response had been the first public validation of what he had to offer. He knew what a betrayal it would have been had he exulted in any way about his departure to Blackpool even though his desire to leave the club had been barely concealed for some time.

On the fans' side, Stoke's success during the 1946–7 season despite Matthews's frequent absences – he missed nineteen of the forty-two matches – helped to soothe away any bitterness there might have been about his leaving. And when the moment came there was no great outcry around the Potteries, as there had been nearly a decade before, even though he left with the First Division championship so tantalisingly within reach. The season after Matthews departed, when Stoke slumped to fifteenth place in the First Division, the club's average attendances actually rose by nearly 1,000 a game.

As far as his feelings about Bob McGrory were concerned, Matthews said very little at the end. A diplomatic silence, most probably, although maybe it showed he did harbour some admiration for his arch rival.

For his part McGrory, who, along with other managers, saw an unacceptable solipsism in the older Matthews, succeeded in suppressing his inner thoughts about his England star until an unguarded moment nearly two years after Matthews had left the club.

Matthews's friend Peter Buxton, the *Evening Sentinel* journalist, told the story: 'Blackpool came to Stoke for a Cup tie [in January 1949] and tickets were at a premium. I asked Bob for a couple as I shared a taxi home with him and Stoke's Bill Williams from a boxing show in Hanley. "Get them off bighead," said Bob. I protested that Stan was certainly not bigheaded and I still got the tickets off Bob, but clearly he was no longer a Stan fan.'

Chapter 10

'Twelve months ago I was not considered good
enough to make the Stoke team'

Family man, hotelier, footballer: Stanley Matthews had much
to occupy him by the time he joined Blackpool in 1947. Too
much, as it turned out, and it would not be long before he and
Betty dispensed with the hotel business. Even with a small
staff and Matthews's brother Arthur to help run their seafront
establishment they found it increasingly difficult to cope.

Matthews did what he could when he was around. Shopping
for supplies was one of his duties. He was also, a guest remembered, a very attentive host, making it his duty to talk to
everyone staying. He himself said little, though, about his brief
contribution to this aspect of Blackpool's holiday trade. Maybe
he preferred to brush over what he saw as a failure, particularly
as a story told by a family friend suggests he was the prime
mover in buying the hotel. Elsie Ashley, once the Mayor of
Newcastle under Lyme, became a friend when she stayed at the
Romford with her husband, Danny. 'Stan bought the hotel [in
1945] when Stanley Junior was two weeks old and Betty was
still in the nursing home after having him,' she said. 'It came as
something of a shock to her that he'd bought it.'

The way things turned out, Betty was right to be shocked. As she probably suspected, her husband was not, temperamentally, an hotelier given that he was, heart and head, a footballer. Another guest, Terry Hulme, who was a Stoke City fan, remembered Matthews's far greater commitment to being a professional sportsman: 'It was very exciting for me to see him, early mornings, turning out with ten or so garden canes, going on to the beach opposite the hotel, pushing the canes into the sand at regular intervals ready for him to do his swerves round the canes. This was his private training before going to the Bloomfield Road ground for official training.'

This dedication to practising and staying fit was always going to undermine the hotel venture, even if he had enjoyed it and had stayed happily married to Betty. His exceptional fitness kept him going as a player and coach for so long that there was really no need to embark on a retirement business, which was what he saw it as at the time. He bought the hotel, he said, because 'I had passed thirty and I didn't think I had too many years left in football'.

Daughter Jean was delighted when her parents eventually decided to sell the Romford. She described life in the hotel as horrible: 'We had no family life, never had a meal together. It was all too hectic for my parents. And the winters, when the twenty-eight bedrooms were empty and the wind was howling on the front and I had to go upstairs to my bedroom on the first landing . . . I can remember that.'

When they did sell up they moved into The Grange, St Annes Road, Blackpool, which was a good decision for the family as a whole. The fact it was here that the relationship between Stanley and Betty was tested to destruction was irrelevant. Venue had little to do with their falling-apart, which they worked at keeping from the outside world. They tried, too, not to involve their children. Doing their best for them was the one thing that truly united them.

Jean had happy memories of her childhood, particularly when

the family were installed in their new surroundings: the large house with the big garden, where playing games was a major part of family life. 'Pop decided to cut down the orchard at the bottom of the garden – sacrilege wasn't it! – and make a tennis court so he could keep fit during the summer when there was no football. That's how we all started playing tennis.'

She also loved the outings with her parents, particularly her father, made possible by abandoning the responsibilities of the hotel. 'When we went out it was often on Friday nights to the cinema. Cowboy films were a favourite. We didn't go in until the lights were out and we used to sit in the back row so no one would see us and then we would slip out at the end before the national anthem. Other times we would go for walks on the Prom and Pop would always wear a hat and dark glasses so that no one would recognise him. It never worked. They wanted to chat mostly and he'd always oblige them, but he didn't want to be recognised. He was very modest really.'

Others testified to his being a doting father to Jean, whose own recollection was of 'a fantastic father – very kind, very good, who could be quite strict at times. When I was twenty-two he was still picking me up at ten o'clock from the local tennis club dance. Perhaps my brother got away with a little more than I did, being the younger one. Or rather I paved the way for him to do whatever he wanted, which he didn't do. Like Pop, he had a very disciplined life.'

Elsie Ashley said that Matthews was a loving family man who went to great lengths to help the children with their careers. She also recalled visits to the house in St Annes Road: 'It was always exciting to visit them there because celebrities appearing at Blackpool Opera House would make a beeline for his house. Charlie Chester [the comedian] was a great friend of Stan's, so was the bandleader Ted Heath.' She described Betty as a wonderful mother and housewife.

What was striking about Ashley's insights, delivered in the

immediate aftermath of Matthews's death in 2000, was that they were such a rare glimpse by an outsider into his family life during his first marriage, rarer still for containing an observation of any description of Betty. Very few of Matthews's playing contemporaries had any recollection at all of Betty. One close friend recalled that after Matthews remarried in 1975 he quite often saw him shopping in the supermarket with his new wife. 'I never saw him doing that with Betty,' the friend said.

All of which chimes with what Matthews confessed much later, that the breakdown of his marriage to Betty took place progressively over a number of years. He was not the sort to share problems and one family member speculated that his determined internalising of this very personal sadness might have affected his playing form.

For the moment, though, he had the excitement of preparing for his first Football League season as a Blackpool player to distract him. The club's investment in the English game's most recognised figure was already paying off. At the start of the previous season hundreds of the 750 season tickets were still unsold. A year on and with the arrival of the Wizard, the club chanced printing two thousand season tickets – and all of them had gone.

After the Burnden Park disaster, the Home Office imposed a maximum attendance of 29,500 on Bloomfield Road. With so much interest, the local football scribe wrote that the ground 'has become the famous pint pot into which a gallon cannot be poured'.

On Saturday 23 August 1947 they flowed in their thousands to watch Matthews, sniffling with hay fever, appear in his first Football League match for Blackpool. Chelsea were the visitors – not the Chelsea of the days of plenty provided by their twenty-first-century benefactor Roman Abramovic, but a team who under their Scottish manager Billy Birrell specialised in mid-table finishes. They were beaten 3-0 with Matthews making a relatively subdued contribution to the home team's success, because, in the view of Spectator, the *West Lancashire Evening Gazette*'s correspondent, he was placed 'on an austerity ration of passes'.

This particular bee became firmly lodged in Spectator's trilby for the opening weeks of the season. He even wrote a footnote on it after a home win over Blackburn in early September. The game's only goal was Matthews's first for the club, but in his main report Spectator described the goalscoring pass to the outside-right as 'an event in itself'. The footnote added: 'By my watch there was a period near the end of the game when the ball was never within 20 yards of Matthews for fifteen minutes. This is equivalent to engaging a star and giving him a walking-on part.'

On another occasion, after a home defeat by Newcastle, he wrote: 'The only difference between Stanley Matthews and the 30,000 spectators was that the 30,000 had paid to go in and he had entered for nothing.'

Deliberately starving Matthews, using him as a decoy in other words, was not new. What had never happened was the ruse being deployed systematically, which the consistency of Spectator's disgruntlement – he groaned at one point that he was tired of reporting it – suggested might now be the case. More probably he was a lone voice. Matthews never griped about it, which he would have done had he been wantonly overlooked. If it did happen more likely it was the result of Joe Smith's policy of letting the players get on with it: if Matthews wanted more of the ball he should go looking for it.

Certainly Matthews, an advocate of non-interventionism from the touchline, preferred this style of management to the parade-ground intolerance of McGrory at Stoke. Even Matthews, though, felt Smith overdid this at times. While never complaining that he suffered as an individual, he did say the team might have benefited from a little pre-planning. This might have 'made the difference between us being nearlies and landing the silverware I felt our overall talent deserved'.

Smith's relaxed approach may explain why Blackpool had more success under him in the FA Cup than they did in the League. The knockout format was far more suited to a side who were better at occasional pyrotechnics than sustaining the long, slow burn needed to win the First Division. The FA Cup and the international stage were where Matthews gave his most vivid performances.

Thirteen days after his 'walking-on part' against Blackburn, Matthews hogged the spotlight with the audacity of an Olivier when England won 5-2 in Brussels. The match was the one in which, in Finney's words, Matthews put 'the fear of God up the Belgians' as he turned the Heysel Stadium into his personal fiefdom. George Hardwick, playing in the England defence that day, touched on the old hypothesis that Matthews may on occasion have placed himself rather than the team at the centre of the piece. 'I'm sure Stan did it just to show us,' Hardwick said of the fourth goal that was greeted with such rapture.

And Matthews shone again a month later in England's 3-0 win over Wales in Cardiff. Walley Barnes of Arsenal, who would captain Wales, was deputed to mark Matthews in this his first international. Before the match Matthews signed autographs for Barnes's friends while the two players chatted, which Barnes remembered 'was the nearest I was to get to him during our stay in South Wales'. He said he even expected Matthews to send him the wrong way when he went to shake hands with him after the game.

Blackpool's stuttering League form yielded just one victory in October 1947 when Portsmouth, lodging at the Matthews hotel, failed to profit from the proprietor's absence – he was away giving Barnes a torrid time in Cardiff – and lost 1-0 at Bloomfield Road.

On the credit side for Blackpool, their inconsistency did little to affect their growing popularity. The biggest of a number of large crowds that watched them assembled for their visit to Highbury in early November when, in addition to nearly 70,000 inside the ground, 20,000 were locked out. This, though, was the only cheery news as far as this particular match was concerned. For Matthews, especially, it proved an unhappy occasion. A match in the capital he had keenly awaited as a chance to showcase his talents in a Blackpool shirt marked the start of a sorry end to 1947.

He suffered a bad thigh strain in the first half of the 2-1 defeat by Arsenal, which meant he missed the following weekend's home fixture against Sheffield United – a match overshadowed by the death of Matthews's great ally at Bloomfield Road, Colonel Parkinson, who was seventy-one. Immediately after the game, Parkinson was reported to have collapsed while in lively conversation with a Sheffield director in a passageway leading to the club offices. A depressed Matthews then went down with tonsillitis.

Finally, Stoke played a Scrooge-like role in ruining Matthews's Christmas. First, the town appeared as if a ghost from his past when a rumour circulated that he was being lured back to Stoke City. He was supposed to have sold the Romford, still in his possession at this point, and was to take up residence in a small manor house in Stoke, from where he would manage a big hotel in the town. The story ignited one of Matthews's rare flashes of public annoyance. He said he objected to the fabrication that he had sold his hotel because it 'might be prejudicial to my livelihood in Blackpool'. Also, he had no intention of leaving the town as he was happier than he had ever been in football.

If this was intended as an indirect swipe at the place of his birth, he may have regretted it. Stoke City retaliated by bringing him further woe over the holiday period. Freddie Steele's deadliness in front of goal, once so admired by Matthews, was now a source of irritation as the centre-forward scored both goals in Stoke's 2-1 win at Bloomfield Road on Christmas Day. Matthews did all he knew to prevent this. One account of the match said that he had bored through his old club's defence with ease and combined with Andy McCall for the best goal of the game. Two days later Matthews returned to the Victoria Ground – 10,000 locked out this time – where he suffered more frustration. Stoke scraped a 1-1 draw they barely deserved.

A good run in the FA Cup was now desperately needed to give some meat to what was in danger of turning into a lean season for Blackpool. These were the high days of the cup, which in the inter-war years had joined a select group of sporting contests – the Grand National was another – as national events. One sociologist has noted that their rise in popularity, with radio and later television boosting media coverage, coincided with a drop in church attendances. He described them as the 'new sacred'.

The FA Cup final was as much about fans venturing beyond their straitened horizons as it was about the game itself. The prize of a glamorous trip to Wembley gave the whole of the competition an allure way beyond what the Football League offered each week. In the 1930s, 1940s and 1950s, several clubs, large and small, established record attendances for FA Cup ties, the most striking being the massive 84,569 for the Manchester City–Stoke quarter-final in March 1934.

In 1947–8 Blackpool, with Matthews on the wing and helped by a favourable draw, set out on the cup run that their fans longed for – not just to compensate for the unfulfilled promise of a title-challenging League season but to end years of anonymity in the cup. Blackpool had not reached the last eight for nearly a quarter of a century.

Drawn at home in the first three rounds against Leeds, who were in the Second Division, Third Division North side Chester and then Colchester of the Southern League, who had upset Huddersfield of the First Division in an earlier round, Blackpool scored thirteen goals without reply. Next they travelled to

London to play Fulham, another Second Division team. A 2-0 win put them in the semi-finals.

Matthews did not disappoint in any of these matches. Even the vanquished relished the experience. They felt complimented by the fact that the country's most eminent player had bestowed his best form upon them. After Colchester lost 5-0, their star-struck players gathered around Matthews while he signed their programmes. Colchester's thousands of travelling supporters also went home happy, having witnessed the minor miracle of Stanley Matthews playing against their club. Neither the result nor the great difficulty they had reaching the Victoria Ground diminished their enjoyment. Fifty-two coaches had been booked to make the round trip, of which forty had to be cancelled at the last minute when the government reinforced petrol restrictions. The fans happily switched to going by train, a hurried rearrangement that meant travelling overnight and arriving in Blackpool in the early morning.

A theatre visit during Blackpool's trip to London for the quarter-final against Fulham emphasised Matthews's position as the team's main attraction. The whole party went to the Victoria Palace to watch the Crazy Gang, who every few minutes kept calling out for Matthews. A member of the audience said: 'One of the Gang paraded up and down the aisles paging him, while the England forward crouched low in his seat seeking to make himself invisible.'

Blackpool's other Stanley, Mortensen, whose contribution to Blackpool's cup exploits of these years vied for recognition with Matthews's, had what was indisputably 'Mortensen's match' in the semi-final against Tottenham Hotspur at Villa Park.

All week the story had been whether Spurs' redoubtable Welsh half-back Ronnie Burgess, yet another former miner, would be fit to mark Matthews. One paper carried a preposterously staged photograph of Burgess supposedly having a fitness test. It showed the player being tackled by his manager, Joe

Hulme, who was wearing a suit and trilby as he played the role, according to the caption, of Stanley Matthews. Passed fit to face the real Matthews, Burgess and Vic Buckingham clamped the winger in 'remorseless shackles', as one commentator put it. This would have been fine if Blackpool had not had a player capable of punishing teams who stretched their defensive resources to contain Matthews. Mortensen's strength and zest produced one of his greatest cup goals – and he scored thirty at a rate of more than one a match – as he burst through Spurs' overburdened central defence to strike a brilliant equaliser four minutes from the end of normal time.

Matthews's part in this goal was not simply the indirect one of having tied up two Spurs players for most of the match. As Mortensen explained, he and Matthews had worked on a variation whereby the winger moved inside a few paces and then paused rather than head off on a run. The pause was Mortensen's cue to start a run towards goal and Matthews would roll a through ball into his path. It worked perfectly on this occasion (and again a month later when the pair played for England against Italy in Turin).

Mortensen's two further goals in extra time, to secure a 3-1 victory, completed an outstanding hat-trick, but the storming first goal was the one the sports editor of the *West Lancashire Evening Gazette* wanted to show his readers the next day. The paper's photographer at the match hung his head. He explained that the national and news agency photographers, assuming a Spurs win, had packed up and gone by then, 'and when I saw Mortensen streaking for goal I was just too excited to take pictures'.

For the next six weeks Blackpool's focus was on the trip to Wembley to play Manchester United in the final. For manager Joe Smith it would revive memories of 1923 when he had been Bolton's winning captain in the first Cup Final held at Wembley. For just about everyone else it would be a fresh experience.

Around town tickets for the match were the gold standard by which the prices of all other things were measured. Matthews received hundreds of letters, many of them containing cheques or even cash.*

The team performed indifferently during these busy six weeks, which for Matthews and Mortensen included travelling to Glasgow where they helped England win the British championship with a 2-0 victory. In their Blackpool shirts, the two Stanleys had a lean time of it with every member of the team mindful of staying fit to be available for Wembley selection. They did manage one notable success, a 3-0 victory over Arsenal, who were on their way to winning the championship by seven points. Many in the crowd of 32,678, a record for Bloomfield Road, suspended their admiration for Arsenal's popular England Test cricketer Denis Compton, booing him for a number of fouls on Matthews. This was no time for one national treasure to damage another.

The Arsenal win came amid six defeats in League games. But the nation's clubbable football scribes, who had recently formed the Football Writers' Association, had seen enough during the preceding months to place Matthews and Mortensen first and second, with five votes separating them, in the ballot for the inaugural Footballer of the Year award. Matthews would win it a second time, in 1963, and came to regard this double recognition as among his most precious achievements, a rebuff to those critics who doubted his true worth. He always displayed prominently the original bronze statue he received.

After the heightened anticipation, Blackpool might easily have faltered on the club's first appearance in an FA Cup final on 24 April 1948. Instead they contributed fully to as good a final

---

* This left him with the chore and expense of returning the money, the one compensation being the letter writers' fabulous tales. He recalled one along the lines: 'The ticket is not for me but for a good friend who has done me many favours. I would not ask but this friend is an avid Blackpool supporter . . .'

as anyone could remember. The big disappointment was that they lost, 4-2, when a victory would not have flattered them.

An accumulation of things undid Blackpool, two of which were Matthews-related: the effective job done on him by the Manchester United full-back Johnny Aston and, in the view of some observers, Joe Smith's decision to play Mortensen at centre-forward, to exploit Allenby Chilton's lack of pace at centre-half, rather than keep him at inside-right where he had been such an effective partner to Matthews. This was just about the only specific measure Smith took to counter United, which led to further criticism of the manager's passive approach to how his teams played. On the other hand he could have argued that he was not passive enough. It was only because he tinkered at all that Blackpool did not win.

Aston was so diffident about his ability when he joined United after he was demobbed from the Marines that he asked to be put in the third team. His promotion to the first team by Matt Busby was swift and he rarely played poorly against Matthews, starting with the 1948 final. 'I think in our personal clashes in that final I came out first,' he said. He was upset that a newsreel of the final showed him on his hands and knees. 'I think that was the only time he [Matthews] beat me.' Aston was in the Finney camp when it came to comparing the two wingers, rating him more highly because of his willingness to graft. Matthews, he said, was the better entertainer, who 'sometimes played to the gallery a wee bit'.

Blackpool twice went ahead against United. Matthews insti-gated their second goal with a clever free-kick to Hughie Kelly who headed it on for Mortensen to maintain his record of scoring in every round. United's second provided the game's debating point. Johnny Morris took a free-kick while Blackpool were still wondering which way it had been given. Jack Rowley, poorly marked for a dangerous player, punished the distracted defence with a strong header. Matthews described this incident as pivotal, although another such moment was when Jack Crompton's reflex save kept out a shot by Mortensen that looked certain to restore Blackpool's lead. United produced by far the stronger finish during which first Stan Pearson and then John Anderson, from thirty yards and with the help of Kelly's deflection, scored goals.

Matthews was in a chirpy mood despite the defeat and a valedictory tone to some of the writing that suggested his hurrahs were fast running out. Geoffrey Green, *The Times*'s courtly football correspondent, seemed to be reviewing a career when he wrote: 'Nothing remains to be said of Matthews's supreme artistry and countless thousands will remember with gratitude the immeasurable entertainment this man has provided over the years.' Another writer applauded Green's words 'in these days when Matthews is to so many people a god no longer'.

The man himself felt differently about the time he had left. He confessed to having been lonely and disheartened when England ignored him straight after the war, and demoralised by headlines such as 'The King Is Dead, Long Live the King' when Finney replaced him. And although he was happy to move to Blackpool, he was hurt by the fact that Stoke had sold him because the club, or rather McGrory, had lost faith in him as a player. 'Twelve months ago I was not considered good enough to make the Stoke team,' Matthews said, in effect conceding what he had been unable to at the time.

Now, after a season in which Blackpool finished ninth in the First Division and had reached the FA Cup final, he said he was a better player than he had ever been. For the first time, at the age of thirty-three, he spoke with conviction about going on beyond the prescribed upper-age limit for playing football professionally.

His performances for England in 1947 had re-established him as an international player and he was in an optimistic mood when he again flew off in mid-May with the national team to Europe. This time the destination was Turin for another of those matches against Italy, classified as a friendly, that showed how intrinsically dramatic sport is and does not need the endorsement of a World Cup or Olympic flag fluttering over it.* Even the flight out had its dramas with the BBC's Raymond Glendenning needing oxygen during the short final hop in a Dakota over the Alps from Zurich.

In his ghosted autobiography, Matthews paid himself the compliment, not something he did often, of proposing that the forward line who played in Turin 'was the greatest ever to represent England'. For those of a certain age, particularly, it does have a ring about it: Stanley Matthews, Stan Mortensen, Tommy Lawton, Wilf Mannion and Tom Finney. Their collective contribution to a momentous 4-0 victory was undeniable.

The five were one of the reasons the match attracted interest way beyond the two countries involved. It was reported that the organisers received 400,000 ticket applications from all across Europe. Italians greeted the England party as if they were royalty – or, as Geoffrey Green recalled much later, 'as though we were Beatles of another era, showered with flowers, surrounded by television cameras – absolute chaos at all times'.

Although Matthews's part in the match was not one of his major works, he did provide the pass from which Mortensen

---

* Two footnotes to the match – one desperately sad, the other entirely trivial – are worth mentioning. By a grisly coincidence, Swift and Valentino Mazzola, the two captains in Turin, would both die in plane crashes – Swift in the Munich air crash in 1958, Mazzola in 1949 with Torino when their plane flew into a hillside while descending into Turin.

The trivial postscript involves an improbable moment of personal grooming. Some years later, when Matthews was living in Malta, a shopkeeper asked him about an incident towards the end of the game when he casually ran a comb through his hair. Matthews presumed what must have happened was that, in the extreme heat, he had dried a hand on his shorts and then wiped the sweat from his face, giving the impression of slicking back his hair. The story gradually took root. Thirty years later it cropped up in South Africa in a conversation with an Italian player of Matthews's vintage, who now worked as a chef near Johannesburg. On this occasion Matthews himself brought it up because, he said, he had started to believe the story himself. The Italian chef gave him a curious look and said: 'It never happened, Stan.'

fired in a goal that shone out even among his many gems. Scored after four minutes, it also had the important effect of undermining Italy, who were still World Cup holders from the 1938 competition, before their confidence reached those danger levels at which they become unbeatable.

In time, Billy Wright, still a relative newcomer to the England team, was one of the few who shared a dressing room with Matthews who was prepared to criticise him publicly as a team player. He would describe him as 'a pain in the neck to his colleagues who waited in vain for the pass that never came'. For the match in Turin, though, the synergy between Wright and Matthews was a feature that at least one correspondent commented on: 'England function so much better with Wright playing at right-half. He links so well with Stanley Matthews, who feeds off his passes that are always so accurately and intelligently placed.'

From a pass by Wright, Matthews set off down the wing. He jinked and feinted before, spotting Mortensen's angled run to the right, he found his inside-forward with a pass of maybe forty yards. Carlo Parola shepherded Mortensen wide and towards the goal-line and imagined he had finished the job with a tackle that toppled the Englishman. As he fell, Mortensen responded to his goalscorer's instinct by letting go a shot that dipped at speed just inside the near post. Green asked Mortensen in the bar whether the goal was a fluke. 'You've got to have a bit of luck sometimes,' Mortensen said. This did not detract from Green's enjoyment of the goal. He wrote in his book *Great Moments in Sport*: 'I can still see it, still hear the astonished, painful grunt of that 75,000 crowd, like some huge animal stopped in its tracks by a hunter's bullet.'

Lawton and Finney, with two goals, were England's other scorers, while Frank Swift, the goalkeeper and captain, also deserved great credit for a number of stops as Italy tried desperately to repair their damaged pride. Stanley Rous, the FA secretary, had greeted Swift on the day of the match with the words, 'Good morning, skipper', which was the first he knew he had been handed the captaincy. An even bigger surprise, Swift said, was when Matthews, never a vigorous player, made a hefty shoulder charge in the first minute. 'Then I knew there could be only one result,' he said. Finney reckoned the whole team performed with distinction. 'Only those who played for England in Turin, or the few supporters who were there, will ever properly appreciate the true merit of the performance,' he said.

Chapter 11

'He did seem to have an eye for financial benefit'

After another tour of Scandinavia with Blackpool, Matthews returned to a Britain still firmly in the clasp of post-war austerity. Blackpool FC was one of the few things that could be described as booming. The club office staff received so many requests for season tickets that by as early as the first week in June they were returning as much as £200 a day to applicants. But a Blackpool footballer's lot, even one of Matthews's magnetism, was hardly one of opulence.

In 1948, most footballers were earning less than £10 a week and would still have to wait until 1961 before the maximum wage was scrapped, by which time it was £20. Expenses were so tightly scrutinised that there was no chance here of skimming off a little extra. Few players bothered even to claim them and those who did soon learned not to be greedy.

This applied equally to club and country. On top of a paltry match fee, which did not rise above £10 until after the war, England players were granted second-class rail fares and 'reasonable' reimbursement for other costs. Matthews said the Football Association once docked his claim for sixpence, the amount he paid for having tea at a station buffet on the way to playing against Scotland. On another occasion, Matthews was one of a group of England players waiting in the foyer of a London hotel for a taxi to take them to the cinema. Walter Winterbottom spotted them. He ushered them outside where he pointed out a bus stop across the road. 'And I want you back by ten o'clock,' he added.

Nor did Matthews benefit by one penny from the transfer fee paid for him by Blackpool. The idea of players receiving a percentage of the transfer money or a signing-on fee was merely being debated at this point by, among many others, Matthews himself. He was against such payments. 'Certain players would be continually moving from club to club,' he said.

Players explored various ways of supplementing what they earned, or, in some cases, replacing their domestic incomes with those promised by foreign clubs. The best-known player to go in search of what proved to be an end-of-the-rainbow fortune was Matthews's old Stoke teammate Neil Franklin, an outstanding defender who had seemed destined for a long international career. He joined an exodus of players to Colombia, setting off with his pregnant wife to play for Santa Fe of Bogota in return for a salary way beyond what he was making in England. It was no more than a scam. None of what he was promised materialised. He returned home to find himself ostracised for leaving without telling the FA and for breaking his contract with Stoke.

Matthews said he never thought seriously about signing a long-term deal with a foreign team. On the other hand he liked, increasingly, to travel. This was partly to do with money and partly with his domestic situation. Out-of-season trips to coach and appear in exhibition and some competitive games became integral to his life. At home, he was almost certainly better placed than any other player to boost his bank balance from endorsements. His name was the first to flash up when commercial interests started seriously to exploit players' popularity. Very early on Matthews was even persuaded to convert himself into a limited company – Stanley Matthews, Ltd

– to try to profit from his reputation. It was floated with a capital of five hundred £1 shares, with his wife, Betty, a co-director. What became of this venture is not clear.

Matthews's growing reputation for making a little extra on the side is supported by a number of anecdotes. Bill Slater recalled an episode when Blackpool spent the night at a hotel in Birmingham before a match against Aston Villa. On the morning of the game Matthews set off on his own, not even telling Joe Smith where he was going. 'One or two of us went to stretch our legs,' Slater said, 'and there was Stanley in a bookshop signing books.' Slater added there was no sense of 'him being greedy or mean or anything like that, but he did seem to have an eye for financial benefit from various things that he was involved with'.

If Matthews needed reassuring of his worth he had only to consider the increasing regularity with which he received requests to appear in benefit matches. He took to charging for doing this but even handing over £100, which was not an unusual amount for him to ask, was a sound investment for the beneficiary.

Too injured to play, he ran the line in an overcoat at a testimonial match for Ben Collins, the former Northampton Town full-back, in April 1954. The several hundred he put on the gate comfortably covered the outlay on Matthews's fee. The spectators were happy too, particularly the many Matthews obliged with his autograph as he patrolled the touchline during the game.

It was not uncommon for the beneficiary to make Matthews an offer. Josh McCosh, who managed the Dublin club Drum-condra, undertook to fly Matthews from Blackpool and back in a day with £500 in cash for appearing in a benefit match. His presence filled most of the 46,000-capacity Dalymount Park. After paying Matthews and other expenses, McCosh reckoned he still had £2,500 left over.

Some of the extra-curricular money-making schemes that

Matthews signed up to are familiar today. He endorsed a range of products, including the health food Bio-Strath, did a boot deal with the Co-op and contributed a column to the *Sunday Express*, the first by an active footballer although it was entirely ghosted for him by the paper's northern sports editor. Less obviously this life-long abstainer appeared in cigarette advertising and overcame his preference for privacy by going on stage in a vaudeville act.

A family member once confronted Matthews after being amazed when he stumbled across a magazine advertisement of him extolling Craven "A" cigarettes. One version of this ad included an action shot of Matthews playing for Blackpool plus a second image of him in an England shirt smiling and apparently holding a cigarette, although this looks like a mock-up. 'It wasn't till I changed to Craven "A" that I learnt what smooth smoking meant,' Matthews was credited with saying. When confronted Matthews said he was appalled. In other words it had appeared without his knowledge. He said he sought an apology from the manufacturers, which duly arrived – together with a gift of several packs of the offending cigarette.

All this would be fair enough if there were not more or less conclusive evidence that Matthews knowingly took part in cigarette advertising. In 1946 he appeared in what was described as the first 'in a famous screen advertising series for Player's cigarettes'. The film, complete with a British Board of Film Censors certificate, which indicates it was shown in cinemas, featured Matthews demonstrating his skills to the BBC football commentator Raymond Glendenning. At the end Glendenning, a pack of Player's Navy Cut in hand, said, 'It's always a real pleasure to meet great players like you', before the film closed with a shot of a hand, supposedly Matthews's, reaching out to take a cigarette.

A little expediency seems to have been going on here. Naivety, too. Accepting the financial benefits of appearing in cigarette advertising while hoping no one would notice was a shimmy too many, even for him. However, if it were the case he collaborated in making tobacco ads it would not have been the pact with the devil it would be seen as today. The full, harmful effects of cigarette smoking were only just emerging. When the Player's film appeared in the UK, a promotion in the US was proclaiming 'More Doctors smoke Camels than any other cigarette!'

The vaudeville act was the idea of his show-business friends, including Charlie Chester, who persuaded Matthews to turn his footballing skills into a stage routine. Chester stayed at the Romford hotel when he appeared at the Blackpool Opera House. He helped to push forward the stage proposal by introducing Matthews to his contacts in the entertainment world.

Tom Moss, a local comedian and revue producer, engaged Matthews and his Blackpool teammate Harry Johnston in June 1948 to appear in *Holiday Showboat* on St Annes Pier in Blackpool doing a football tennis act. Matthews said that when he and Johnston saw themselves in greasepaint for the first time they nearly collapsed. A friendly reviewer for the local paper was complimentary. 'I am beginning to think this net football act which two Blackpool and England players are presenting may set a fashion on the contemporary stage,' he said. 'It has an unexpected excitement in it. In the end it had one of those prim, hypercritical audiences for which St Annes is almost notorious making mob noises.'

Maybe he misunderstood the nature of the mob noises. Although the show was resurrected for the Moss Empire circuit in 1949, this time with Matthews partnered by his brother Ron – topping a bill that also included the Tower Circusettes – there is no evidence that it set pulses racing any more than it established the act as a fashion on the contemporary stage. If there was a high point, for the Matthews brothers that is, it was when they took part in a charity show at the Victoria Palace in London and shared a dressing room with the comedian Norman Wisdom.

One other thing it led to, before it was quietly shelved – 'It was something I was talked into and didn't much enjoy,' Matthews said – was an unusual instance of Matthews being replaced by Tom Finney. Blackpool occasionally gave Matthews permission to do the show during the football season, including in Preston in February 1949 after Blackpool played Preston. Matthews hurt his left ankle quite badly in the match, an injury that would seriously affect his season, not to mention the game itself. Blackpool 'took reprisals . . . and at times the match was nearly a street brawl', a report said. The heavy strapping on Matthews's ankle made it impossible for him to go on stage with Ron that evening. Instead he compered the show with Finney standing in for him.

From Matthews's point of view, the best consequence of his brief life in the footlights was that through Tom Moss he met Arthur Millwood, an osteopath from Bury. Millwood, a leading figure in establishing osteopathy in Britain in the 1920s, was an interesting character, at once a showman and health guru. One of his students in the 1960s, John O'Brien, who became an authority and writer on the practice that had been developed in the United States, recalled Millwood arriving at the British School of Osteopathy in London in a big, expensive car, which he parked ostentatiously outside the building. He then appeared upstairs in the main lecture room wearing the best suit his Manchester tailor could create and a flashy bow tie. Moss recommended Millwood as someone who could fix Matthews's ankle. So started an association that would have a profound influence on the rest of Matthews's life. Matthews described Millwood as a marvel. He credited him with seeing him through a number of injuries – persistent knee trouble was one – and helping other family members. When Matthews's son became a successful tennis player, he suffered elbow and wrist problems that Millwood treated successfully.

The flamboyant Millwood was much more than a manipulator

of bones and massager of muscles. A vegetarian, he had firm views on diet and he found in Matthews, already a fastidious eater, as susceptible a disciple as he could have hoped for. One of Matthews's most treasured possessions was a letter, closely typed on two sides of foolscap, sent to him by Millwood. It contained instructions on what to eat – although he never converted Matthews to vegetarianism – what not to eat and when to eat those things that were allowed. The letter passed to Ron Matthews who protected its contents as if they were a sacred text.

Millwood, who was awarded the OBE in 1973, also directed Matthews to a naturopathic clinic in Bristol, Towerleaze, where he was introduced to fasting as a health benefit. Matthews said he visited this clinic every six weeks, driving down from Blackpool on a Sunday morning and staying until Thursday. He would not eat a thing on the first two days and have a light salad on the Wednesday. But it wasn't just the diet, he said. 'There would be steam baths and enemas, exercises and long walks along the beach at Weston-super-Mare.'

Even when he moved to live abroad Matthews would return to the UK to see Millwood. An obituary of the osteopath, who died in 1986 aged eighty-four, referred to Matthews having visited him recently about his knee. Millwood also treated Denis Law, the Scotland and Manchester United centre-forward.

While Millwood was his main source of ideas, Matthews evolved his own strategy for staying healthy. In his playing days this focused on being in peak condition for the Saturday game. 'Even a fit body can be that little bit fitter on different days,' Matthews said, showing an attention to micro-management of his food intake that seems extreme even by today's health-conscious standards. He continued the habit of fasting, although only on Mondays, when, his daughter said, 'you tended to keep out of his way, because he would be a bit short-tempered'. Beyond this he restricted himself mainly to eating salads and drinking fresh juices, carrot being his favourite. If he ate bread, it was only the crusts after painstakingly removing the dough.

He took supplements, too. Charlie Chester described the smell of malt wafting from cupboards in his home that were also packed with phials of vitamins. England teammate George Hardwick said Matthews took pills by the score. 'He was a near hypochondriac,' Hardwick said. 'We would share a room and the bathroom shelf would be crowded with boxes. I would say, "Stan, leave me enough room for my toothbrush".'

But not all Matthews's fellow players rejected his ideas on healthy eating. Dennis Viollet changed his diet after joining Matthews at Stoke in the 1960s. Viollet's wife, Helen, said her husband started breakfasting on the supplement Complan, raw eggs and honey 'because that's what Stan did'.

Grainy film footage of Matthews in FA Cup action, lean and impassive, effortlessly rolling the big, brown, leather ball past defenders, is as evocative of the 1950s as images from silent movies are of an earlier era. Matthews's contributions to the FA Cup were what ultimately defined his time at Blackpool, obscuring the part he played in the club's impressive form in the Football League during his fourteen full seasons there. Blackpool ended up outside the top ten on only four occasions and had second- third- and fourth-place finishes.

Evidence of the galvanising effect this consistency had around the club was plentiful. The supporters negotiated an arrangement to fly to matches in the south at a cost for the longest trip, to Portsmouth, of £9 5s., while the issue of a bigger ground to satisfy the ticket demand for home games kept cropping up. At a lunch given by supporters to celebrate the 1948 Cup Final appearance, Peter Fairhurst, Blackpool's deputy mayor, said: 'The club is giving a real service to the town. Its present ground is utterly inadequate. You deserve as a club, and can command, the cooperation of the municipal authority and the whole bag of tricks.'

And it was not just Blackpool supporters who wanted to watch their team. A crowd of 77,696 filled Stamford Bridge in October 1948, the biggest attendance ever to watch Blackpool in a League game.

Joe Smith deserved great credit for the success of a club with none of the cachet or resources of names such as Arsenal, Liverpool and Manchester United that resonated then as they do today. Affable and at the same time shrewd, Smith was an arch-recruiter of players who might have regarded Blackpool as a holiday destination but not somewhere to go to make a living. Matthews was his master signing, strengthening the side and also acting as a recruiting agent simply by being there.

Smith was aware that, despite the near miss in the Cup Final, his team was a work in progress. 'Joe was always planning improvements,' Matthews said, 'and I suppose you could say that first Blackpool team I played in was in a transient stage.' If the manager needed confirmation that more still needed to be done, the results in the 1948–9 season provided it: sixteenth in the League and, particularly hard for Matthews to bear, a fourth-round defeat by Stoke City in the cup after drawing at the Victoria Ground.

Part – a major part very probably – of Blackpool's problem was that Matthews missed seventeen League matches because of injury. A tweaked muscle in his groin was followed by the ankle injury in the roughhouse match against Preston that led to Finney taking the stage as Matthews's understudy.

Two matches he did not miss were that FA Cup fourth-round tie and replay against Stoke. In contrast to Smith, McGrory, having had his fill of wilful star players, was not interested in expensive imports. He was building a side in his own image, one that a commentator referred to as 'the famous £110 team, the team that cost a mere £10 signing-on fee for every man in it – and ranks among the best in the land'.

Matthews played well in the match at Stoke that ended 1-1, a result that apparently prepared the way for Blackpool's progress to the next round. It was not to be and, to make matters even more irritating for Matthews, George Mountford scored the only goal of the replay a week later. The man whose steady performances on the right wing were a big factor in Matthews's departure from Stoke finished neatly after winning the chase to connect with Freddie Steele's header downfield. Gate receipts of £4,266, a record for Bloomfield Road, provided Blackpool with a morsel of comfort.

Three weeks later Matthews suffered the quite serious ankle injury. It would affect him for the rest of the season and was aggravated when he came back too early through his eagerness to play for England against Scotland at Wembley in early April, a match the Scots won 3-1.

His overhasty return proved particularly ill advised with regard to his international career. He had been playing well for his country towards the end of 1948, notably in a 6-2 win over Northern Ireland, in which his fortunate goal direct from an intended cross was one of only three he scored in thirty-seven post-war internationals, and in a 6-0 victory against Switzerland. Although the selection committee decided against risking him for the summer tour to Sweden, Norway and France, the FA primed a London reporter to scotch rumours that there was more than the ankle injury to his omission. 'You can discount any stories that the maestro has been dropped,' he wrote. Another report from London was more interesting for disclosing the sort of company Matthews kept these days than for revealing anything fresh about his fitness: 'He was run to earth in the company of Danny Kaye [the American entertainer] and repeated that the ankle he hurt in the Preston match at Blackpool in late February was still not completely healed.'

As it turned out, Matthews would not only miss the three matches in Europe but the next nine after that. He did not return until England's ill-starred first appearance in the World Cup in

1950. If the intention had been to bring him back once his ankle was better, it did not happen for two reasons: the haphazard way the selection process worked and Walter Winterbottom's ambivalence about Matthews as a player. Matthews said that under Winterbottom, even when he did return to the England team, 'I always had the feeling my inclusion was tenuous'. This, he added, remained the case until the end of his international career.

Interestingly, though, despite Winterbottom's misgivings about him being real enough, Matthews would make well over a third of his England appearances, playing in twenty-one out of thirty-one matches, between October 1953 and May 1957, a period that covered his fortieth birthday.

Still, for the moment Matthews was primarily a club player, a former international. In the four seasons between 1949 and 1953 he gained just three caps. He was remembered more for being left out of the World Cup match against the United States in Brazil in June 1950 than for any of the three fixtures in which he appeared.

When Matthews made the news now, it was often simply because he was a national figure and had little to do with his football. In 1949, for example, he acquired a four-year-old racehorse, Parbleu. His first visit, with Betty, to see the horse at stables in Beverley, Yorkshire, was a photo opportunity the papers could not resist.

This led to the idea that Matthews was a bit of a racing man. Matthews himself apparently grew to believe this. By the time he came to tell the story of his life he informed his autobiographer that he always fancied being an owner to give him added interest when attending meetings and this was why he decided to buy Parbleu.

This is very different from what he said at the time: that the colt had been given to him by a friend whose details he was not prepared to reveal, except that he was definitely not a Blackpool man. Which could, just conceivably, have been an elaborate hoax to dispel the idea that he was being profligate by splashing out on a horse. This supposedly keen racing man also commented when he acquired Parbleu: 'I go to the races very infrequently and am not particularly interested.' He had not given a thought yet to what his racing colours would be.

Parbleu had failed to live up to his heritage. The son of the 1939 Derby winner, Blue Peter, he had won a couple of modest handicaps at northern tracks and had recently been sold at the Newmarket sales for 710 guineas (£745 10s.). He managed four wins for his new owner with the jockey decked out in tangerine, red and white hoops, a kaleidoscope of Matthews's club colours. The prize money was less fancy and Parbleu was sold for 1,000 guineas (£1,050) in 1951.

One thing Parbleu did do was supply Matthews with material for two favourite stories. One was how ownership of a racehorse provided his friend Charlie Chester with some good gags. The best of them related to Matthews's thrift, which, Chester said, led to Parbleu being placed with a dubious trainer who charged less than three quid a week. Asked by Matthews to let him have the manure for the roses at his hotel, the trainer said: 'At less than three quid a week, Stanley, there won't be any manure.'

The other tale concerned the day Parbleu's trainer tipped off Matthews that his horse was certain to win a handicap at Beverley. The same afternoon Blackpool were playing Newcastle away and by the time the match kicked off the players of both sides, including Matthews, had invested in the colt.

The way Matthews told it was that Parbleu duly skated home, winning by six lengths, information that was relayed to him during the match by a spectator. Matthews ran to where the shout of 'Eh, Stan Matthews – your 'orse won' had come from and asked the price. He then ran all over the field telling everyone, teammates and opposition: 'It won at hundred-to-eight, it won at a hundred-to-eight.' Matthews finished the anecdote by saying a confused radio commentator informed his listeners that Matthews was playing like a man possessed. He was criss-crossing the field and even dropping back in defence.

As Matthews himself said, he wasn't really a betting man. On one of the few other occasions he did break this rule he filled all the requirements of being a mug punter. He and his Blackpool teammate Ernie Taylor were in Dublin after the 1953 FA Cup final to play as guests at £100 a time, plus expenses. 'Not to be sneezed at when Blackpool were paying me about twenty pounds a week,' Matthews said.

At their Dublin hotel they met the jockey Duggie Page, a friend of Matthews's. Page put them on to a 'sure thing', Sea Lion, that was running at the Curragh. They had each been paid £400 in notes for four appearances and Matthews, for perhaps the only time in his life, was knowingly reckless with money. He persuaded Taylor that they lump the lot on Page's tip.

Making his way to place the bet with £800 in his pocket, Matthews bumped into another acquaintance. This one assured him that there was an even surer thing, King of Tudors. This put Matthews in a dither. He was still undecided until the very last moment when he forsook Sea Lion simply because King of Tudors' name came over the public address.

What compounded Matthews's misery – Taylor, he said, was far more relaxed that Sea Lion had won at generous odds – was that he had resolved to place half his winnings on another Page tip in the next race. This also won. 'Ernie and I played our four games for nothing,' Matthews said, with feeling.

Chapter 12

'The FA have had to send a soccer
SOS to Old Man Matthews'

Proof of the respect Stanley Matthews commanded during his later years as a player is that the disrespect that did occur seemed improper and, in some cases, shocking. According to Ray Wilson, the full-back who was a member of England's 1966 World Cup-winning team, even referees treated him deferentially. 'I never gave many fouls away,' Wilson said. 'The most was when I played for Huddersfield against Stanley Matthews in his comeback game for Stoke City. I coughed twice and the referee blew.'

Obviously, though, given Matthews's quirkiness and the unsparing ridicule that has always flown around football dressing rooms, he was not immune from gentle mocking, although much of it was behind his back. One teammate recalled that when Matthews grew a little picky about which games he played in – the word was to avoid muscular full-backs such as Bolton's Tommy Banks whose 'hit-and-miss tackling', as one newspaper put it, Matthews did not relish – his teammates would wonder: 'Which leg do you think Stanley's going to notice a slight tear in this morning?'

As a player Matthews was never a great mixer, which was one

reason much of the banter took place in his absence. He was bathed, dressed and away long before the others were ready to go. Some responded to his solitariness better than others. 'He never went to pubs, didn't mix a lot, seldom went anywhere, always dashed off home,' Jackie Mudie, a long-time friend and teammate at Blackpool and Stoke, said. He also set himself apart by using a side door rather than the players' entrance, behaviour that engendered a certain amount of jealousy. Mudie felt not even Mortensen was immune from this.

One group who did not feel constrained about voicing criticism of Matthews in his presence were spectators. This was hardly surprising. Wags and barrackers have always enjoyed debunking really good players and pillorying really bad ones and Matthews fell comfortably into the former category. Even his own supporters could pick on him during home games. Derek Hodgson said: 'Stanley liked to hold the ball and that's when the crowd used to say, "Get on with it Matthews, get on with it." I found it amazing when I went to Bloomfield Road that there was an element there who used to get at him.' If Matthews was hurt by it he never showed it.

Examples of something much harsher being directed his way were rare, which made them all the more startling.

Johnny Haynes, the Fulham and England forward, went to Denmark with Matthews with an invitation side in the early 1960s. When Matthews came across Haynes having a beer on the morning of a match, he said head-waggingly to him, 'Oh Johnny, Johnny, Johnny . . .' In front of several players Haynes responded by swearing industrially at Matthews and carried on drinking. The player who recounted this fifty years later was still so shocked that anyone could address Matthews in this way he would say only that the second and third words of the rebuke were 'off' and 'Stan'.

Like Haynes, Danny Blanchflower, the great Tottenham cap-tain, had iconoclastic tendencies. He once answered a reporter's question about when he thought Matthews would retire by saying: 'Oh, it's a matter of brains . . . Stan doesn't have enough brains to quit.' The insult was gratuitous and said more about Blanchflower than it did about Matthews. It was also misguided because it contained the implicit criticism that by playing right through the 1950s and into the 1960s Matthews went on far longer than he should have done. This overlooked the fact that two of Matthews's performances in the fifties – in the 1953 FA Cup final and for England against Brazil in 1956 – were among his most memorable, regardless of his age. And even in the 1962–3 season, during which he had his forty-eighth birthday, he played in thirty-one of Stoke's League matches when they secured promotion back to the First Division as Second Division champions.

Matthews's determination to carry on did make things awkward for managers and the national selectors. Such longevity was unique for an outfield player and those prepared to take him on needed to be convinced they were not confusing his current worth with what it had been ten years before. The England selectors found it particularly hard to divine whether what Matthews did on a football field in his late thirties and early forties had substance or was the work of an illusionist.

An example of the FA's uncertainty occurred in the autumn of 1949. The selectors had been at pains to make clear Matthews had not been dropped from the summer tour of Europe, that his ankle injury had been the reason. They then inexplicably did not bring him back for the match against the Republic of Ireland when he was fit again and playing well for his club.

His consistently high form for Blackpool in a run of ten unbeaten matches in the closing weeks of 1949 was one of the main reasons that, for the first time in the club's history, they were well placed to challenge for the First Division title at the end of the Christmas programme. They were a little unfortunate not to finish this programme in first place rather than third. The additional points that would have put them top had eluded them when at West Bromwich Albion in November they led 2-1 with twenty minutes to go only for play to be abandoned because of fog. By a mischievous twist their hopes of winning the title survived until they lost the replayed match at West Brom 1-0 in late April.

The FA again acted irrationally towards Matthews when, in January 1950, they invited him to go on a goodwill tour of Canada in May and June. Quite why they asked him this so early, when the tour overlapped with England's first participation in the World Cup, was hard to fathom. Matthews accepted the invitation to Canada, regardless of the clash of dates with the world tournament in Brazil. Soon afterwards a newspaper columnist came close to predicting correctly what would happen: 'The prospects are that if Matthews is still playing at the end of the season, or even only for another few weeks, the brand of football that is giving even new glamour to his name at the present time, he will be invited to South America instead of to Canada.'

As it turned out he went to Canada *and* South America, despite a disappointing second half to the 1949–50 season for Blackpool. He missed thirteen matches, including a quarter-final defeat in the FA Cup at Liverpool, because of a damaged muscle in his left leg.

Once again Blackpool had done well without winning anything, but there were positive signs for the future. Season ticket sales for 1950–51 were buoyant and a shrewd piece of business by Joe Smith in October 1949 had already started to accumulate benefits for the club.

Managers were not yet the celebrity figures they were to become and Smith's presence on the dockside at Southampton on a morning in the early weeks of winter would have meant something only to the keenest football fan. He was there to welcome a nineteen-year-old South African signing, Bill Perry, arriving on the *Edinburgh Castle*.

Perry, whose father had emigrated from London, had received a glowing recommendation from Billy Butler, an old teammate of Smith's at Bolton who now lived in South Africa where he managed Johannesburg Rangers. Perry made an immediate impact on the English game. Playing on the left wing, he repeatedly outfoxed Johnny Carey, Manchester United's experienced defender, in his first Football League match in March 1950 as Blackpool won 2-1 away. His most famous contribution to footballing history would come three years later, on the end of a Matthews cross.

Matthews left for Canada straight after the English season. He sailed with the FA party on the *Empress of Scotland* on a record-breaking crossing from Liverpool to Quebec. The newly refitted liner introduced the players to the grander end of sea travel. Some gentle banter with stewards who were mostly Liverpool or Everton supporters, supplemented the advertised entertainment.

It was Matthews's first trip outside Europe. He liked what he saw of Canada when he arrived and his affinity with the country would grow steadily. In time, it was somewhere he would go regularly to play football for decent money and also to take refuge, both before and after the break-up of his marriage.

As much as Matthews was fascinated by Canada on his first trip there, Canadians were fascinated by Matthews – to the point where it became an issue within the FA party. The focus on the thirty-five-year-old winger was so great at one reception in Montreal, every speech dominated by the speaker extolling his genius, that a number of players went to Reg Flewin, the captain, to ask for something to be done about it. 'We are sorry for Stanley himself much more than ourselves,' Tim Ward, the Derby County player, said. The deputation's intervention did, apparently, have some effect.

One thing in particular intrigued the local media: how could a professional as skilled and celebrated as Matthews, who played in football's most prestigious league, earn so little compared to their own ice hockey and baseball players? It did not take long for the topic to fascinate Matthews, too, and a story filtered back home that he was open to offers from Canadian football clubs. This was almost certainly something inferred by reporters from an unguarded comment by Matthews – and may well have been what he was thinking – but Blackpool quickly stamped on the idea that it would happen in the immediate future.

The locals had read about Matthews's skill as a footballer and were instantly smitten when they saw him play. Over a period of nearly four weeks he appeared in most of the eleven fixtures as the team travelled across to the west coast and back again. A 4-4 draw in British Columbia against an All Stars team was the only game they did not win. When injury kept Matthews out of a fixture in Saskatoon, for which tickets had been snapped up on the understanding that he would play, the disappointment threatened to turn nasty. The farcical nature of the match helped to defuse the situation. Saskatoon, having borrowed two FA players to make up their numbers, were swamped 19-1.

Matthews received news early on in the visit that he had been included in the twenty-one-man England squad to play in the World Cup finals. Walter Winterbottom, who had told him this was a distinct possibility, detailed two FA councillors, Harry Hughes and Joe Richards, who were touring with the FA party in Canada, to report back on the player's form and fitness. Their favourable assessment meant that he and Fulham's Jim Taylor were selected ahead of candidates from the England B team, who had been playing – disappointingly – in Europe, to fill the final World Cup places. As one national newspaper put it: 'The FA have had to send a soccer SOS to Old Man Matthews'.

Matthews and Taylor would stay in Canada before travelling directly to South America in mid-June to join the main England expedition that was flying from London to Rio, via Paris, Lisbon and Recife.

The last match Matthews played in Canada was on 14 June, a 4-2 win over Manchester United in Toronto. He performed well in the floodlit game in front of 24,809 spectators, Canada's biggest sporting crowd for any event other than horseracing, but picked up a minor injury. This ruled out any possibility that he would turn out against the United States in New York four days later – a match of special interest given that the US would be taking on England in the World Cup in Brazil in less than a fortnight.

The FA team arrived in New York only three hours before kick-off after a fourteen-hour train journey. Matthews was in the crowd of 8,000 to hear them boo and chant 'We want Matthews' when it was announced he was not playing. They booed again during a sterile game won 1-0 by the FA XI. Offside tactics continually frustrated a home side containing ten of the players who in 11 days' time would achieve a result that reverberated around the footballing world. Johnny Hancocks, the diminutive Wolves forward who wore size three boots, which made Matthews's six and a halves appear enormous, scored the goal. An FA official reportedly told his American audience at the post-match dinner: 'Wait until you meet the real England team in Brazil.'

After the match, Matthews and Taylor linked up with the Manchester United pair Johnny Aston and Harry Cockburn and the four of them flew on via Trinidad to Rio. When their flight was delayed a Brazilian newspaper, eagerly awaiting Matthews's arrival, rushed out a story that he had disappeared.

In fact, the players were late by only a matter of hours and were soon installed in the team hotel, the Luxor, on the highway that skirts Copacabana Beach. 'It wasn't a good hotel,' Matthews said. The cooking was a particular problem. Few trusted the dishes on offer, which included fried eggs floating in black oil for breakfast. It improved a little after Winterbottom donned an apron and gave the kitchen a lesson in English cooking. This was too late for several players who had resorted to bananas as their staple. A daily player allowance of £1 10s provided only limited scope to finance a supplementary diet.

A far greater disappointment for Matthews was that he was left out of the opening World Cup match against Chile in the newly built Maracanã Stadium on Sunday 25 June. The niggling injury he picked up in Canada may have been the reason but the official line was that he had arrived too late to acclimatise. Aston, who had flown with him, was included, though. This suggested that Arthur Drewry, a Grimsby fish merchant who was the one FA selector on the trip, had decided to stick with the majority of the players, including Tom Finney on the right wing, who five weeks earlier had beaten Belgium 4-1 in Brussels.

The players gained a flavour of what it would be like to play in the mighty Maracanã, under construction until the very last moment, when they went there for the opening match of the tournament, Brazil against Mexico, the day before they played Chile. The official attendance of 82,000 was a gross underestimation if you consider that the ground, which for the final between Brazil and Uruguay would hold nearly 200,000 spectators, looked crammed. Vernon Morgan of Reuters, a wonderful, excitable character, wrote the deathless line when covering the final: 'The stadium is so full even the toilets are overflowing.' The more understated Matthews said: 'You've never seen scenes quite like it . . . It was our first experience of seeing fans behave with such fervour.'

England beat Chile 2-0, unconvincingly. George Robledo, the Newcastle inside-forward who had been raised in England and spoke no Spanish, only broad Yorkshire, played for the land of his Chilean father and smacked an England upright with a free kick from thirty yards. Chile had other near misses and Billy Wright, England's captain, said: 'There was no elation in our dressing room after this victory . . . After our poor start, we were determined to show the United States just how well we could play.'

This determination dissolved into one of the most frustrating performances, and abject results, in England's international history.

Drewry again stuck to the dictum about not changing a winning side for the match against the United States. This meant still no place for Matthews despite a rising clamour for his inclusion after he had proved his fitness beyond doubt. Stanley Rous was reportedly among those advocating a role for his distinctive method of opening up defences. 'Why transport the greatest of them all, Stanley Matthews, from Canada and keep him here as a reserve?' was typical of the press comment.

Matthews flew with the team – an hour's bronco ride in a small plane – to Belo Horizonte, the state capital of Minas Gerais. He said the match was agony to watch, but counted himself lucky not to have been on the field. 'We could have played for twenty-four hours and not scored,' he said. 'It was a bad ground and the Americans fought and chased.'

The game remains a classic entry in the rubric of sporting upsets. A Haitian, a Belgian and a Scotsman, Eddie McIlvenny at wing-half, had all been drafted into the US squad not long before the New York match and it was the Haitian, Joe Gaetjens, on an accounting scholarship at Columbia University in the city of New York, who scored the match's only goal shortly before halftime.* Beyond the fact that England dominated territorially, the story of the game differed according to who was telling it. Predictably, Winterbottom thought England unfortunate. He called it 'a silly match in many ways' on an awkward pitch with clusters of tall grass on an otherwise hard, bare surface. He reckoned England hit the woodwork eleven times while the US's goal was lucky, a shot by Bahr going in off the back

---

* The goal must have been the high point of Gaetjens's tragic life. He would fall victim to the political turmoil in his own country, where his family opposed the dictator François 'Papa Doc' Duvalier. After being arrested, Gaetjens was never heard of again.

of Gaetjens's head as he tried to duck out of the way.* John Macadam dismissed the idea that the result was a fluke. He said in the *Daily Express* that England were 'beaten and outplayed by American amateurs and semi-pros'. Others said the goal was an intentional deflection that wrong-footed goalkeeper Bert Williams, who had Bahr's shot covered. Film of the match missed what happened, cutting from open play to a shot of the ball nestling in a corner of the net. Bill Jeffrey, the Americans' Edinburgh-born coach, attached huge significance to it: 'This is what we need to make the game go in the States.' So he would have been disappointed by the immediate impact at least. Only one US newspaper, the *St Louis Post-Dispatch*, carried a match report. Walter Bahr, a key player in the American victory, said his wife was the only person to meet him at the airport when he arrived home. 'Nobody made anything of it,' Bahr said, 'but we didn't expect them to.'

Matthews, after fifteen months out of the side, was restored to the right wing for the final group match back in the Maracanã against Spain. Finney reverted to the left wing and in the first half, with Matthews prominent, England put together some fluent passages without managing to score. They conceded a goal soon after half-time when a mix-up involving right-back Alf Ramsey laid on a goal for Zarra. Once again they tried in vain to break down a massed defence. The 1-0 defeat meant it was Spain who went through to the four-team final group, from which Uruguay would emerge as champions.

The whole Brazil experience placed English football in a truly world context for the first time. Still the lessons did not sink in immediately, and the FA provided little evidence that they

---

* Back in England Winterbottom would seek to justify England's failure to equalise by devising a training exercise. He staged it at the FA's youth academy at Lilleshall. One side had a goalkeeper and five defenders, none of them allowed to leave the penalty area; the other had ten outfield players. 'It was a revelation,' Winterbottom said. 'Nobody believed how difficult it was to score when you packed your defence the way the Americans did.'

thought there was much worth learning. They started losing quite serious money on the trip once England were eliminated and the whole party flew home almost immediately, leaving no one behind to study how the best national teams were changing the game. More shock treatment, notably on an afternoon at Wembley in 1953, would be needed before this happened.

Winterbottom understood that foreign teams were moving the game on, which meant the hasty retreat from Brazil, denying him the chance to find out more, represented an opportunity missed. Just as relevantly, Ramsey, destined to be Winterbottom's successor, also registered football's developing mode. To an extent, Matthews did, too. But club managers and FA officials, who paid little attention to what had happened in Brazil, partly because media coverage was so threadbare, stood doggedly by the well-tried conventions of the English game. Most obvious was the continued adherence to the so-called WM formation: the W represented by the positioning of the five defensive and midfield players and the M formed by the five forwards. Introduced in the 1920s by the Arsenal manager Herbert Chapman, this was still rigidly observed.

The England party looked a little sheepish, guilty even, as they posed for a photograph on the steps of their plane after touching down in London a week after losing to Spain. Matthews and Mortensen made their separate ways back to Blackpool, where, on arrival, Mortensen demonstrated that English footballers were no different then from today. 'Rio's all right,' he said, 'but the best sight I'd seen for three weeks was Blackpool Tower from the train.'

Matthews returned home determined to include in his repertoire some of the skills he had picked up from the South Americans. More significantly probably for him, and maybe even for the English game, he also brought back with him a pair of fitted lightweight boots as worn by the Brazilians.

Unlike the clodhoppers with bulbous toecaps that English

players laced on before kick-off – one writer compared them to Victorian shepherd's boots – this new footwear was so supple, Matthews said, it could be bent in half like a bedroom slipper. He took a pair of the boots to the Co-operative Wholesale Society in Manchester who agreed to copy them. This proved harder than seemed likely. The problem of securing the paper-thin leather uppers and lightweight soles was eventually solved by the manufacture of special nails.

The finished product featured in a popular advert that said Matthews had helped the Co-op 'design a football boot that will cause a sensation in British football circles . . . lighter, more flexible than any other you've seen'. In time Matthews took to wearing weighted shoes to games, so heavy he could hardly walk, to create the sensation of his new boots feeling even lighter.

Matthews received £20 a week for the product that bore his name and was the hottest selling boot of its day. At least this was more than the new top-rate weekly wage of £14 that Blackpool would be paying him in the coming season, but was a puny amount compared to what equipment endorsements would come to be worth. Into the bargain – a bargain for the Co-op, that is – Matthews agreed to make Saturday morning promotional appearances in whichever town Blackpool were playing.

On one occasion Matthews argued he made nothing at all out of his association with the Co-op. This was when Blackpool stopped paying him the unofficial boot allowance of £2 10s., which the other players received, because of his sponsorship from the Co-op. Aggrieved, Matthews pointed out to Joe Smith that by the time he had paid for his travel to have the boots fitted and bought cigarettes and alcohol to keep the fitters happy he was out of pocket. The club restored his boot money.

What may have helped to inspire Matthews to make the boot deal, however modest, was his growing appreciation of how British footballers were being short-changed. He had been struck by the incredulousness of the Canadian press at how little he earned; then at the World Cup he encountered much discussion of the riches being bestowed on some of the foreign players, particularly the Brazilians.

While the FA had been campaigning with the fervour of a mean-minded Dickens villain to peg match fees at £20, other countries were far less inhibited. Brazil were on £200 a man for each of their three matches in the final group. They beat Sweden 7-1 and Spain 6-1 and then surprisingly slipped up 2-1 against Uruguay when each member of the team stood to gain an estimated £10,000 from winning the tournament. They are figures that may help to explain why Brazil had so much more success in those early World Cup years than England.

Evidence of Matthews's renown showed itself in various ways, some of them surprising. Leonard Gribble, a successful crime writer, made Matthews the central character in one of his novels in 1950. Gribble, who in 1939 had published *The Arsenal Stadium Mystery*, returned to a football theme with *They Kidnapped Stanley Matthews*. The book started with a synopsis of the story that said it had been written 'with the cooperation of the great player himself, and the reader is introduced to his family and taken into the hotel he owns in Blackpool'.

Early on Gribble described Stanley and Betty Matthews together at their hotel on a Saturday evening. They were in their private room at the Romford 'where photographs of Charlie Chester, the comedian, and Fred Ferrari, the tenor, stared back at them from their places beside the white-faced clock on the mantelpiece'. During the football season 'Saturday nights with her husband came only once a fortnight', but Betty Matthews 'had been brought up in an atmosphere of League football . . . [and] knew what the game demanded of its players and their wives'.

The story ended happily with the kidnapped Matthews reunited with his family at the Romford. The children, Jean and

Stanley, 'knew only that their father had been away and that his absence had meant that their mother had been very much upset, and even Uncle Arthur [Stanley's brother] and Chef had been very subdued'.

Even more bizarre than Matthews being featured in a crime novel, he was the subject of a political cartoon in a Danish newspaper that, improbably, entered a very British debate over Matthews's absence from the 1949 honours' list. Some felt it wrong that the Australian cricketer Donald Bradman rather than England's outstanding footballer should be the first person knighted for sporting achievement (only administrators among sporting folk had previously received the honour).

The cartoonist lampooned this decision by drawing a monocled Matthews wearing a morning coat and talking to a small boy on a stool. He alludes to the quote by William Gladstone, 'You cannot fight against the future. Time is on our side', by telling the boy that 'time is on our side if only we remember that neither half lasts more than 45 minutes'.

Most surprising of all, perhaps, was that Matthews in his mid-thirties was himself still able to add to his lustrous reputation as a player. A book, *Soccer from the Press Box*, by journalists Archie Ladbrooke and Edgar Turner, appeared in 1950 giving this present-tense assessment of Matthews: 'An enigmatic winger able to kill the ball stone dead whether it reaches him fast or slow; who can head a ball beautifully but hates doing it; who can baffle a man by wriggling his hips; who has speed so that no one in the four home countries can live with him.'

The book was published around the time that Matthews's club performances emphatically repudiated any idea of a marked decline in his powers – even if the FA selectors were not convinced. They picked him for the first post-World Cup international, in which England beat Northern Ireland 4-1 in Belfast, but then dropped him.

Matthews's response was to produce something special for

his club on the first day of the 1950–1 season. Blackpool were at White Hart Lane to take on the newly promoted Tottenham side who were expected to win playing the so-called push-and-run football with which they would secure the title. Rex Adams, a travelling reserve that day, recalled the Spurs forward Eddie Baily, so cockney he might have been recruited by Central Casting, greeting Matthews in the car park with a loud cry of: 'What 'o, maestro.' They were prophetic words. Matthews dazzled – 'absolutely unplayable', Adams said – as he laid on all the goals in a 4-1 win and left full-back Charlie Withers wondering whether he was in the right job.

A hint of Matthews's continued high level of fitness was contained in an aside in a match report in November. It speculated that he had probably been quicker in the mud than his horse, Parbleu, had been in finishing unplaced in that afternoon's Manchester Handicap. Then two electrifying performances in early December 1950, in a 3-2 home win over Sheffield Wednesday and a 4-4 draw at Arsenal, in front of 57,000, had journalists dipping into the purple ink. 'Stanley Matthews blasted Arsenal with his brilliance,' one wrote.

In the new year, after Blackpool won 3-0 at Aston Villa, the other players stepped aside so that Matthews was on his own to receive the crowd's standing ovation.

The recently arrived Perry's consistent performances on the left wing undoubtedly helped Matthews, placing defences under threat from both flanks of a dangerously balanced attack. A run of nineteen unbeaten matches that started on Boxing Day and ended in April with a 2-1 defeat at Huddersfield – even in this game Matthews shone with his 'firefly magic' – put Blackpool in contention for the First Division title and the FA Cup.

The FA acknowledged Matthews's fine form by recalling him, for one match only, against Scotland at Wembley. Inside-right Wilf Mannion suffered a fractured cheekbone early on in this game after which Winterbottom took the surprising decision for a manager to accompany Mannion to hospital. Captain Billy Wright assumed responsibility for switching the team around and moved Finney from the left wing to partner Matthews on the right. They blended well but not quite well enough to overcome the numerical advantage of a determined Scotland, who won 3-2.

A far greater disappointment for Matthews than the defeat by Scotland and his subsequent rejection by the national selectors, after he initially lost his place when injury kept him out of the match against Argentina in May, was Blackpool's failure to land either of the two ultimate domestic prizes. They finished third in the league and were runners up in the FA Cup for the second time in four years.

Tottenham, driven on by the tireless play of their future manager Bill Nicholson and without the distraction of a Cup run, romped clear in the closing weeks of the race for the League title. They ended four points ahead of Manchester United and ten in front of Blackpool. In the Cup Final, in which lucky breaks so often have a role, particularly when two good sides are involved, fortune favoured Newcastle.

One piece of misfortune struck Blackpool before the final. Injuries deprived them first of their good centre-forward, Allan Brown, and then of his chosen replacement, George McKnight. So Smith decided to shuffle the forward line and pick Bill Slater, whose best position was wing-half, at inside-left. Slater was a twenty-four-year-old student, having first done national service in the Army, and was still an amateur, the last to appear in a Cup Final. Nine years later he would play a key part as skipper in Wolves' FA Cup final win over Blackburn, but on this particular afternoon his role was as a willing but probably ill-advised stand-in forward.

Newcastle won the final 2-0, the match turning on a passage of play early in the second half that led to the opening goal. Matthews had been orchestrating a series of Blackpool attacks and it was after one of these foundered that Robledo, who had played for Chile against England the previous summer, lunged for possession in midfield. The ball could have broken anywhere. It was pure chance that it turned into a perfect pass for the athletic Jackie Milburn to beat Blackpool's offside tactic. The Newcastle centre-forward, released into open space, galloped forward to score a goal that inspired Newcastle to take control of the game. His second goal five minutes later threatened to free the net from its moorings.

History would have taken a very different course after Blackpool's 1951 Cup Final defeat if pressure on Matthews to end his time at the club had succeeded. Other clubs sensed a loosening of the bond between Blackpool and their illustrious winger, which they decided to test. Matthews might be receptive to approaches after the disappointment of a second defeat in a Wembley final.

If he was flattered that, well into his thirty-seventh year, a club as big as Arsenal showed an interest in him he was entitled to be. Rumours acquired substance when in July the Arsenal manager, Tom Whittaker, and a scout, Joe Shaw, dropped in at Bloomfield Road because they 'happened' to be in the area. At this point, within days of the midnight deadline on 31 July 1951, Matthews still had not re-signed for Blackpool. Arsenal were prepared to pay £20,000 based on their belief, a club official said, that Matthews was still such box office that they would recoup this amount in a season.

His reward for staying at Blackpool was a disappointing 1951-2 campaign. A knee injury meant he made fewer League appearances in a season, eighteen, than he had since he was still a teenager at Stoke. A candidate for his finest moment of the season must have been switching on the Blackpool Illuminations in September. He was only the eighth person to be granted this honour – Lord Derby, the Duke of Kent and the actress Anna Neagle were among his predecessors – and a big crowd gathered to watch the ceremony on the steps of the Town Hall. Some of them shouted 'Bad luck, Stanley' when he mentioned he had stood on the steps twice before 'without that beautiful English Cup', a reference to the homecoming after two FA Cup final defeats.

The illuminations included an animated tableau of lights that showed Matthews scoring a goal. The irony was almost certainly unintended – Matthews had not scored for Blackpool for nearly three years. Maybe it was meant to be an incentive, in which case it worked. Two days later he scored in Blackpool's 3-1 win at Sunderland.

A run of disappointing results followed this victory before Matthews's season took a sharp downward dip when he badly twisted his knee in mid-November in the first encouraging result for weeks, a 6-3 win over Newcastle.

He was out for two months and when he returned in January for a third-round FA Cup tie at West Ham he spread 'alarm and despondency' on the occasions he got the ball but failed to prevent a 2-1 defeat. The result gave clear evidence of the importance of a good cup run. This one defeat was blamed for Blackpool's loss of £967 on the season compared to a profit of £4,036 when they reached Wembley a year earlier.

Worse still, as far as Matthews was concerned, his injury flared up again after the West Ham match. This led to another long spell of recuperation and when he returned he promptly suffered further knee damage playing in a practice game. His last appearance of the season was for the reserves in a Central League match, a crowd of 13,000 turning out to remind themselves what they had been missing.

Blackpool's ninth-place finish in the League was quite a feat in the circumstances. In addition to Matthews's problems, a contagion of cartilage injuries struck the club. Five players were affected with Mortensen and Perry ending the season in the same Manchester nursing home.

Chapter 13

'I had the honour of being taken to
the cleaners by Matthews'

Like all good factual dramas, the story of Matthews's season of
seasons – 1952–3 – resembled an overloaded work of fiction.

After Matthews was involved in some extraordinary League
results early on, he was struck down by a new injury. The long
absence from the game that ensued very nearly ended with him
heading back to Stoke, once more an option since his antagonist
there, Bob McGrory, had resigned in May for health reasons. And
then there was the FA Cup run played amid the anticipation of
an impending Coronation that gave the sense of a nation finally
shaking off the monochrome grimness of the post-war years.

Having recovered well over the summer from his knee injury,
Matthews scored four League goals in a month at the start of
the season, as many as his total in the previous four seasons,
as Blackpool put five past Aston Villa and Wolves and buried
Charlton 8-4, having led 8-1, at Bloomfield Road. This was
the first time twelve or more goals had been scored in a First
Division match since 3 February 1937.[*]

---

[*] Matthews had been in scintillating form on that occasion, too. The day after turning
twenty-two, he had undone West Brom in Stoke's 10-3 win at the Victoria Ground.

Matthews was showing the sort of form that resurrected the debate over whether, aged thirty-seven, he should be recalled by England. And it so happened that Walter Winterbottom, the England manager, was in Blackpool at this time to make a personal contribution to the discussion. Speaking at the Jubilee Theatre as a guest of the Blackpool and District Referees Association, Winterbottom reacted with characteristic vigour when his assertion, in answer to a question, that 'Matthews has never been dropped' drew sceptical noises from the audience. 'Some of you people are very prejudiced,' he barked. He then elaborated that Matthews had been left out in the first instance because he was injured and then England's good results, notably a 3-2 win in Austria in May, had made it hard for the selectors to change the side. 'I've seen Stanley today,' Winterbottom said, 'and he tells me that he's feeling fitter than he has done for two or three years. Today he's enjoying his football. He is, in common with a few other men, under consideration for a cap whether it's his first or his eighty-first.'

Matthews had not been entirely straight with Winterbottom, however. Two days before he spoke to him he had been performing brilliantly in front of a crowd of 66,682 at Arsenal, in a game Blackpool eventually lost, when he started to limp. The problem was a thigh injury that would prove annoyingly persistent. His appearance on 11 October in a 4-2 home win over Burnley, in which he did well in bursts, would be the last time he played until January.

This period of inactivity proved a fertile time for all sorts of stories about Matthews's future and the state of his mind now that a succession of injuries had made him so painfully aware of his footballing mortality. One was that he had lost his appetite for the game and this most recent setback, not as bad as he was making out, was simply an excuse not to play. Another was that he was looking to leave Blackpool, which was the real reason he had sold the Romford hotel.

The transfer talk became a reality on 14 December when a Sunday newspaper broke the story that Stoke wanted to buy him back. The previous day Blackpool had lost 4-0 at Stoke and, after the match, board members of the two clubs discussed the possibility of a return to his hometown. The new manager at the Victoria Ground, Frank Taylor, presumably felt, given that he shared Matthews's fixation with physical fitness, they would work well together once the player had recovered from his latest injury.

Stoke's interest in re-signing Matthews and Blackpool's readiness to encourage the possibility agitated him. He said, at first, that he wanted to stay: 'I'm happy in Blackpool, always have been, am settled here.' A story also circulated that he was behind the report in the Sunday newspaper and by now he was aware of the rumour that he could have played during the past two months if he had wanted to. 'Wanted to,' he said, testily. 'My life is football, why shouldn't I want to play?'

The transfer saga dragged on for nine days, taking two sharp, dramatic turns before being resolved. With Blackpool pressing Stoke to name the price they were prepared to pay, all of a sudden Matthews changed his mind. He told the Blackpool board that for sentimental and business reasons he would now like to return to Stoke. But there was a final twist: a sudden announcement by Blackpool on 23 December that Matthews was no longer for sale.

In his autobiography Matthews recalled that it was during the 1952 close season that Stoke made their bid to reclaim him, which was incorrect, and that Joe Smith was responsible for his staying put. Smith, Matthews said, put his foot down once he heard about Stoke's interest and convinced the Blackpool board 'I still had years in me'. Interestingly, Matthews added that Smith then had to convince him that this was the case.

Smith almost certainly did put his foot down but, with the board unpersuaded that selling Matthews would not be good business, had to do so more than once. It was well over a week after the story broke that Blackpool finally decided to keep Matthews. It was probably a combination of Smith making a case for him to stay and Stoke deciding they could not afford him. Blackpool wanted more than they had paid for him in 1947, which was the price Stoke were thought to be sticking at in their bid to get him back.

Who knows what might have happened had Matthews moved back to the Victoria Ground at that point? What history does relate is that four months later Stoke were relegated, having spent two decades in the First Division, and a week after that Blackpool had their greatest day.

Any slight doubts Smith might have had over keeping Matthews would have been understandable. He must have been concerned about Matthews's ability to stay fit long enough to play more than a few games at a stretch. Also, he had built up a squad at Blackpool that had strength in depth, reducing his dependence on any one player. He had introduced players of quality such as the goalkeeper George Farm and forwards Allan Brown and Ernie Taylor, who had been inveigled into leaving Newcastle not long after laying on Milburn's second goal in the 1951 Cup Final.

Still, though, Smith almost certainly did fancy that Matthews's talent, undoubtedly special, was protected by an exterior that had been fired granite hard by his desire to flaunt it for as long as he could. The manager's strongly expressed faith in this hunch may well have been what persuaded the Blackpool board to hold on to Matthews at least until the end of the season.

As had happened twelve months earlier, Matthews returned from a long injury break just in time for the third round of the FA Cup. This suggests that while the muscle damage might have been real enough, Smith had advised Matthews, in 1952 and now twelve months later, not to hurry back before Blackpool's entry into the competition. Winning the cup was the fulfilment both men sought above all others. In those days, Matthews would reflect with feeling many years later, 'the FA Cup had real status'. Perhaps the outburst 'Why shouldn't I want to play?' was more about frustration at having to bide his time than indignation.

Three days before the tie at Sheffield Wednesday on 10 January 1953, Joe Smith received a breakfast-time call at the Palace Hotel, Buxton, where the team were resting before the visit to Hillsborough. The call was to report on the fitness of Matthews and Mortensen, who were in the same Manchester nursing home. Smith came off the phone to say that, later that day, Mortensen was to have a second cartilage operation in the space of a year, but Matthews had responded well to manipulative treatment on his thigh and would be fit for Saturday.*

On an afternoon so bleak the referee insisted on a white ball being used, Matthews did not only play well enough to justify the gamble of recalling him for such an important match, but he made one major contribution. His lobbed shot from a punched clearance by Ron Capewell flew back over the keeper's head to become the first goal of Blackpool's historic Cup run.

Matthews would claim one reason his comeback was a success was what he called 'a diabolical stroke' of kidology. He primed Harry Johnston, who knew several of the Wednesday players, to inform their dressing room that he was still some way short of full fitness. 'Really lay it on thick,' Matthews said he told Johnston. 'Say you and the rest of the boys are fed up with Matthews being big-headed enough to insist on playing – even when he's not fully fit.' Apparently Wednesday fell for it completely, particularly after Matthews started off by limping. Left-back Norman Curtis, who was used to following Blackpool's winger like a dance partner, for once allowed him generous amounts of room.

---

* This might have sounded as though someone with healing hands had magically cleared up Matthews's long-term injury. In fact, his trip to Manchester was precautionary, one last bout of treatment to ensure he would be able to play.

In the second half Blackpool surrendered the lead Matthews had given them and only two minutes remained when Ernie Taylor scored the winner with a volley on the turn after Matthews, Allan Brown and Bill Perry created the opening. The Blackpool players danced a jig of joy at taking the spoils from a tight match away from home against a strong team.*

However, the spoils were more laurels than lucre. Although the cup was important to a club's financial wellbeing, the figures reveal why, in the days before the wealthy middle classes submitted to football's attractions, clubs could not afford to pay hefty wages. The big gate of 60,199 at Hillsborough yielded takings of just £7,700. By the time the taxman and the FA had exacted their dues, Blackpool's share boiled down to barely £1,500.

With Matthews's return, Blackpool also put on a spurt in the League during which they briefly glimpsed the possibility of a League and FA Cup double, last achieved in 1897 by Aston Villa. Matthews, with Taylor's unflagging help on the right, schemed the outstanding result of this surge, a 3-2 win over the eventual title winners, Arsenal, at Bloomfield Road. In the end, though, Smith's preference to make the cup a priority, which included resting Matthews at key moments, compromised any chance of winning the First Division. After a miserable 5-0 defeat at Manchester City on the last League Saturday of the season, Blackpool finished seventh in the table.

The win over Sheffield Wednesday in the third round was an appropriate start to Blackpool's cup run, which would be epic in conclusion but often more music hall than Cecil B. DeMille in execution. It would develop the knockout format's potential for

---

* Not everyone was delighted to have Matthews back in the team. His long-time understudy, Albert Hobson, who had grown used to the limelight during Matthews's recent convalescences, asked for a transfer. 'I realised there wouldn't be a first-team position for me for a year or two,' he said, quite understandably underestimating how long it would be before he was first-choice outside-right. He did last one more season at Bloomfield Road before moving on to Huddersfield.

excitement like none other. In all but one of the six rounds they secured their victories with goals in the last eight minutes – and in the 1-0 fourth-round win at Huddersfield the goal was not only late but a complete fluke.

Defender Tommy Garrett, yet another footballer taken from the coal-mining conveyor belt, was a few steps inside the Huddersfield half when he lifted a ball goalwards. It was not a shot, he said, 'but as soon as I saw the wind take it away I knew it was going to finish in the net'. He scored only two other goals in his fifteen years at the club.

Southampton of Division Two in the next round was the only tie that Blackpool won without the late-goal tactic. Instead, Southampton co-opted the tactic for themselves when their cricketer-footballer Henry Horton headed an equaliser just before the end in a 1-1 draw at Bloomfield Road. Blackpool won the replay 2-1 at The Dell with the turning point another equalising goal by Horton. This time, though, Horton sliced the ball into his own net and Allan Brown gave meaning to his nickname 'Bomber' with the explosive power of his winner two minutes later.

Poor Brown was doomed to be the tragic hero of Blackpool's cup triumph. Injury had kept him out of the 1951 Cup Final and now he suffered a more devastating setback in the act of winning the toughest assignment of his team's cup run.

A week after their win over Arsenal in the League, Blackpool once again faced the team who were widely regarded as the best in the land, this time in a quarter-final of the cup away from home. Highbury heaved with the excitement of it all. Matthews's presence in the capital, as ever, gave the occasion an added frisson.

Determined not to make the same mistake as Sheffield Wednesday, who had given Matthews too much room, and mindful of how just one man marking him had not been enough for them the previous Saturday, Arsenal did what others had done before. Matthews reckoned three, sometimes four, players closed him down whenever he received the ball. Johnston, Blackpool's estimable captain, reported that at half-time Matthews said he intended staying close to the touchline in the second half because 'they seem to be liking my company out there'. With Matthews as a decoy, Johnston added, Brown became the match-winner.

Blackpool scored first in the seventy-seventh minute through Ernie Taylor's shot on the run from Brown's rolled pass, a lead that Arsenal cancelled out when Jimmy Logie knocked in a ball freed from goalkeeper George Farm's grasp by what was then a legal challenge by Doug Lishman.

With less than three minutes left, Blackpool attacked from the kick-off and Brown, bursting through on to a loose ball, just got his boot to it as Jack Kelsey, the Arsenal goalkeeper, crashed into him. One assessment from the press box was that Blackpool had deserved their 2-1 win because they had outwitted and outplayed Arsenal largely thanks to Brown. But the centre-forward was in no condition to celebrate.

Jackie Mudie, the first player to reach Brown after he scored the winning goal, had intended to haul him triumphantly to his feet. Instead Brown told him: 'Leave me, Jackie, my leg's broken.' It was his left leg, shattered just below the knee. His season had been brought to a harrowing end.

At least there was some good news for Blackpool. Mortensen, who had made an excellent recovery from his cartilage operation, told his teammates when he joined them at their training head-quarters in St Annes just before the Arsenal tie that the specialist had said he could play again soon. Joe Smith was so delighted that he surprised the players with a rare sighting of his wallet. According to Matthews, the manager bought half-shandies all round.

With Brown's injury, Smith was intent on hurrying Mortensen back for the semi-final against Tottenham at Villa Park. He did

not risk him in the next League game, which provided Blackpool
with the psychological lift of beating Spurs ahead of the Cup
tie.* Instead Mortensen returned a week later, seven days before
the semi-final, in a match against Sheffield Wednesday at
Hillsborough. The immediate benefit of this was a huge boost to
Blackpool's morale, effectively removing any sense that the team
had been weakened by Brown's misfortune. In the 2-0 defeat by
Wednesday and in the semi-final itself, Mortensen the talisman
outperformed Mortensen the goal-scoring demon he once was
and would, very soon, become again.

Blackpool complained that overzealous watering of the Villa
Park pitch affected their performance in the semi-final. Even
so, they played their part in a thunderous contest won 2-1 by
Jackie Mudie's goal in the final minute. Ramsey's response to
Blackpool's performance, so curmudgeonly a fortnight earlier,
was very different when he reflected on the semi-final some
years later. He describe it as the finest match he ever played in –
a superlative indeed, considering his blunder decided it. 'I had
the honour of being taken to the cleaners by Matthews,' he said,
although Matthews himself pointed out that for most of the
match Ramsey was up against Bill Perry.

A Matthews corner, headed in by Perry, had given Blackpool
a lead that Tottenham cancelled out when Eddie Baily stepped
over Les Bennett's cross to allow Len Duquemin to convert
from short range. This was how the score stayed until the final
moments when Ramsey, who had had a good game, appeared
to have averted danger when he beat Mudie and Perry to an
awkwardly bouncing loose ball. He chested it down but instead
of the traditional hoof into the stands that was required at such
moments, he tried to guide the ball back to his goalkeeper, Ted

---

* Not only did Blackpool win 2–0 at Bloomfield Road, they managed to irritate Alf Ramsey,
the Spurs and England full-back. He grumbled that Blackpool were no more than a one-
man band: 'It's just Matthews, Matthews, Matthews . . .' He would soon have far greater
reason to be rueful.

Ditchburn. Mudie was on to it in an instant and slipped the ball under Ditchburn's body.

As Blackpool celebrated, Ditchburn rose to his knees and shot Ramsey a stare the full-back must not only have seen but felt.

Chapter 14

'That is nothing like good enough . . . there should be
some national recognition of his prowess'

The excellence of Joe Smith's freewheeling team was not the
only thing that differentiated Blackpool FC at this time. No
other club had a group of supporters quite like the Atomic Boys.
They, too, would have their finest hour on Saturday 2 May 1953,
Cup Final day.

Nearly half a century before the Barmy Army started following England cricket teams around the world, a small core of
Blackpool supporters trailed their football team wherever they
played. They may well have been the first organised band of sports
fans who placed harmless ostentation and good humour above
the sinister intent normally associated with such groupings.

The Atomic Boys were formed in the late 1940s by Syd Bevers,
a dedicated Blackpool fan whose intention was 'to brighten up
spirits generally' after the war. Loudly dressed and taking with
them a live duck as a mascot, the group were not immediately
admired by the vast army of flat-capped, Woodbine-puffing
supporters who dominated the terraces.*

_____

* At a match at Huddersfield in December 1949, home team officials banned the Atomic
Boys from parading before kick-off. The sequence of events that followed reached a

In time, though – and just as the Barmy Army have done – the Atomic Boys achieved a degree of acceptance for their innovative antics. On Cup Final day, just before noon, Bevers led them down Whitehall before turning in to Downing Street. He wore a flowing tangerine cloak and tall silver headdress; his face was stained coffee-brown and he had a cheroot gripped between his teeth and clutched a seven-pound stick of Blackpool rock

In those days the road to the Prime Minister's front door was open to public access. Bevers strode up to No. 10 and, to everyone's surprise, when he knocked on the door it opened. Ushered inside, Bevers did not emerge for nearly ten minutes. A secretary told him that Sir Winston Churchill was out for an hour but gave an assurance that the stick of rock, with, as Bevers proudly pointed out, the PM's name stamped right through it, would be presented to him.

Bevers and his troupe then headed for Wembley. Matthews, who was well-acquainted with the group, warned Bevers not to take the mascot with him because it would land him in trouble. Naturally Bevers ignored this and managed to get it into the stadium in a carpetbag. The duck treated the crowd to a brief pitch-side waddle before kick-off.

The days of luxury coaches with tinted windows and as much interior space as the average 1950s footballer's house were still beyond the horizon. Accordingly, Central Station, Blackpool, became the focus of the first ritual of the 1953 Cup Final

---

pre-Monty Python level of farce. In protest at the ban, one of the Atomic Boys, 'Flash' Dawson, ran on to the pitch before kick-off carrying under his arm the duck, which he deposited in the centre circle before running back into the crowd. A policeman strode forward, solemnly tucked the bird under his cape and, spotting a coal bunker just beyond the touchline, dropped it in there, where it remained throughout the match. Bevers then retrieved the mascot, its white feathers discoloured by rain and coal dust, but was not allowed to take it away before signing a slip of paper headed, 'Lost property restored to owner'.

weekend, a crowd of at least 2,000 gathering there on Friday morning to see off the team.

Cyril Robinson was the big surprise among the players who posed for the regulation departure shot on the London-bound platform. Just as Bill Slater had gained an unexpected summons for the 1951 final, so this time the twenty-four-year-old Robinson was the long-shot Wembley selection, also given his chance because of injury. He had played fewer than a dozen first-team games and up until recently had not even been certain of a place in the Central League side.

Mortensen's recovery meant Allan Brown was more than adequately replaced. Unfortunately for Joe Smith he had no such back-up when, two weeks before the final, left-half Hughie Kelly chipped a bone in his right ankle against Liverpool. Kelly had played in the 1948 and 1951 finals as the third member of a redoubtable half-back line that also included Harry Johnston and Eric Hayward. Hayward had retired to be replaced by Ewan Fenton but Kelly was still the best left-half with no obvious cover. Smith's selection of the unproven Robinson was a gamble.

Full-back Tommy Garrett might also have missed the match had he been the delicate type rather than an ex-miner made of the right stuff. His nose was badly broken in the defeat by Manchester City a week before the final. Barely able to see out through the plaster covering his face, Garrett announced there was absolutely no chance of his not going to Wembley.

What did not emerge until after the match was that Matthews himself went into the final injured. Less than a week beforehand, he had hurt his thigh in a five-a-side kickabout in Stanley Park, Blackpool. When the team arrived at Wembley from their hotel in Elstree on match day a doctor injected him with a painkiller. Matthews would cite the injury for declining an invitation to join England's tour of South America that followed the final. Given Matthews's age this might have put an end to his international career. Such an outcome was about to become unimaginable.

On other occasions the injury would have been bad enough
for Matthews to tell Joe Smith he would sit this one out. Not
this time, though. And herein lies the reason why the debate
that continues today over calling it 'The Matthews Final' when
Mortensen scored a hat-trick (or did he?) misses the wider point
– even if Matthews apparently missed it himself by naming the
relevant chapter in his autobiography 'The Mortensen Final'. The
point is that Matthews's participation drove the narrative from
the moment Blackpool qualified for Wembley and continued to
drive it during and after the match. Dropping out was simply
not an option.

The story of the final was straight from la-la land: a thirty-eight-
year-old with a name as recognisable as any in the country comes
to the sanctum of his profession to seek its most ancient prize
having lost two earlier finals. He receives thousands of letters
from well-wishers in the build-up to the match, which he calls
his ultimate challenge. Shortly before kick-off, Queen Elizabeth
II, whose Coronation will be held in a month's time, takes her
place in the royal box as Britain's first reigning monarch to watch
a football match. And this is the dull part of the drama. If ever
the play was the thing it was now, a match pumped to exploding
point with excitement until its last few moments. Never was
an eponym more correctly bestowed on a sporting event than
giving Matthews's name to the 1953 final.

What is more, that day captured the essence of the FA Cup
final's most evocative years when football was the preserve of
the working man and Wembley Stadium's capacity was 100,000.
With rain having given way to piercing sunshine and with no
shadow cast by an encircling roof – it was not added until 1963
– the arena from the air must have looked like a giant marigold
with the tangerine scarves, rosettes and other paraphernalia of
Blackpool fans spread around the unsegregated stadium.

Matthews complained about the distribution of tickets, with

only 24,000 of them allocated to the clubs taking part. This meant that, in theory, 76,000 went elsewhere, although Matthews did also note that many of these ended up where they belonged. It was reckoned Blackpool fans accounted for close to a third of the spectators.

And it was still overwhelmingly a fan's, rather than a corporate, occasion. Entry to club matches in England was available for less than two shillings, keeping the game within reach of the lowliest paid. The record receipts of £49,900 for the 1953 final represented less than £2 a spectator.*

Matthews said he slept fitfully the night before the final. It might have eased his worries had he known that others were just as fretful. For Nat Lofthouse, the outstanding Bolton forward, it was Matthews who filled his waking moments. The Wizard of the Dribble he might have been but the asset that Lofthouse feared most was the precision with which Matthews placed his centres. 'I was thinking beforehand whether our defence could cope with Stanley's accuracy,' Lofthouse said, 'You never saw him place a cross inside the six-yard box, where the goalkeeper might reach it. It was always half a yard outside, tempting.'

Small, inconsequential things stick in the memory when a scene is too congested to absorb in its entirety. Lining up in the tunnel before being led out on to the Wembley pitch by Joe Smith, Matthews remembered being struck by Bolton's shorts, which, he said, seemed to be made of black satin. They also caught the eye

---

* Blackpool and Bolton would receive a mere £7,000 each for staging one of English sport's greatest contests. On the other hand, the clubs' wage bills were still not much higher than any everyday business. Maximum weekly pay was pegged at £14 (soon to go up to £15) regardless of whether in that particular week a match was abandoned because of bad weather or a player was entertaining vast numbers watching the Cup Final. In 1953 the viewing figure was raised considerably by what has been described as the first mass television audience. It was left to the players themselves to leverage what extras they could from reaching the final. In Blackpool's case, a players' organising committee chaired by Harry Johnston threw a celebration dance at the Tower Ballroom in mid-April. Around three thousand turned up, each paying four shillings, to mingle with the players. Matthews, known for his early-to-bed routine, surprised everyone by staying up until 2 a. m.

of the Duke of Edinburgh. Introduced to the players before kick-off, the duke set the tone for a career in carefree asides. 'You all look like a bunch of pansies,' he told the Bolton team.

The new queen's consort hardly had time to settle into his seat before Lofthouse, more panzer than pansy, put Bolton in front, although he needed none of his defence-busting power to complete scoring in every round of that season's cup. His shot from outside the area in the second minute lacked venom but did bounce awkwardly and George Farm, who would have a poor match, made a complete nonsense of it. The ball slithered through the keeper's grasp into the net.

Farm's charge off the line did stop Lofthouse adding a second. The centre-forward shot off balance against the foot of a post and Kenneth Wolstensholme, the BBC's television commentator, thought he saw a Blackpool hand touch the ball in the frenetic action to win control of the rebound.

Spared falling two goals behind, Blackpool had their best spell so far and ten minutes before half-time equalised with a goal that featured another defensive mishap. Mortensen cut to his left after running strongly with the ball into the penalty area. With a clear sight of goal he failed to connect cleanly with his left foot and his shot rolled into the path of the fast-arriving Harold Hassall who diverted it past his keeper, Stan Hanson. It was later attributed to Mortensen as the first goal of his hat-trick – the only hat-trick in an FA Cup final in the twentieth century.

That Hassall was in place to assist in the goal was the result of an earlier misfortune suffered by Bolton, which would be a key factor later in the afternoon. Eric Bell, who operated on the left side of Bolton's strong half-back line, had switched to the wing after tearing a muscle in his left thigh. Bobby Langton had moved from the left wing to inside-forward in place of Hassall, who fell back into Bell's position – hence his being on the scene to deflect home the shot Mortensen had aimed across the goal from the left.

Quite possibly, under today's ruling, Hassall would have been assigned the own goal because without his stumbling intervention the ball might well have gone wide. Mortensen said: 'I aimed for the far post and thought the ball might have gone in. But Hassall ran into the line of flight and diverted it into the near corner.' Hanson had indeed moved to protect his left-hand post and the ball ended up in the opposite corner of the net, having passed him on the right. In the television commentary box, Kenneth Wolstenhome called it like this: 'It's a goal! Hassall! Hassall has scored!' Soon after Blackpool's second goal Wolstenholme did refer to Mortensen having scored twice. He then corrected himself, saying that the Blackpool opener had been an own goal by Hassall. The commentary made no mention of a hat-trick either when Blackpool's third goal went in or when the Queen handed out the medals.

Clifford Greenwood, of the *West Lancashire Evening Gazette*, seems to have been one of the few in the press box preparing to award the goal to Mortensen. He scribbled in his notebook: 'Mortensen equalised, in off Hassall.' The overwhelming consensus, though, in evening newspapers published on the day of the final and in the Sunday and Monday morning papers on the next two days, was to give it to Hassall. None did this more confidently than the *Yorkshire Sports and Evening Argus* whose second deck of headline read: 'Hassall "Own Goal" Victim'. Alan Hoby in the *Sunday Express* said Mortensen's shot 'was going well wide when Hassall diverted it into the net. He held his head in horror when he saw what he had done.' The *Daily Mail*, published two days after the final, recorded that Hassall's was the first 'wrong end' goal in a Cup Final since 1946 when Bert Turner of Charlton scored for both teams in Derby's 4-1 win.

Nothing definitive appears to have been passed down by the FA in the match's immediate aftermath. The FA Challenge Cup Committee minutes and their Annual Report gave only the result. Not until July, with the publication of the *FA Yearbook*, did the organisers attribute the goal to Mortensen, siding with those who felt his shot was destined for the corner of the net before Hassall intervened. This did not end the uncertainty, though. As late as 1962 the author Alan Davis said in a portrait of Matthews that Hassall's intervention 'caught Hanson going the wrong way' and resulted in the Bolton player scoring against his own team.

The flaw in how Bolton rearranged their line-up was that there was now an invalid opposing Matthews on the wing. Bell had no chance of tracking back in the way that was known to frustrate Matthews. Mortensen said Matthews would occasionally chide wingers who helped out their defences for operating outside their job description.

For the moment, Matthews was subdued, as if sensing he would be needed in the final scenes of the briskly developing drama, which at this stage was relying heavily on human error to maintain the tension. Bolton, who had finished fourteenth in the League, seven places below Blackpool, pushed forward with greater purpose in the minutes before the interval and regained the lead when Farm erred once more. He reacted late and with no real conviction to Langton's hopefully floated ball into the six-yard box. In this instance Wolstenholme confirmed Billy Moir as the scorer only after half-time – 'He must have touched Langton's cross with his head' – as a result of information passed on from the dressing room.*

As was his way, Joe Smith offered little beyond generalities during half-time. Keep playing your normal game was his message down the seasons and now, he reasoned, was no time to change it, even if Blackpool fans felt something different needed to happen if they were not to leave Wembley disappointed for

---

* This may have some relevance to who scored Blackpool's first goal. Clearly the commentator was in touch with the teams but received no intelligence that crediting Hassall with an own goal was incorrect.

the third time since the war. Two people Smith did have a word with were Matthews, telling him not to drop so deep, and Ernie Taylor, who needed to work harder to get the ball to Matthews.

Blackpool's foreboding deepened to something close to despair ten minutes after half-time when Bell, of all people, extended Bolton's lead. As Doug Holden's looped cross from the right dropped into the penalty area it seemed to be heading for an unequal contest between the able defender Eddie Shimwell and Bell, who had hobbled into the goalmouth. Improbably, Bell rose the higher, off only one leg, to slant a header downwards into the net.

Faced with a 3-1 deficit and thirty-five minutes to go, Blackpool had to respond to the game's dramatic possibilities if it was not to descend into anticlimax. In his autobiography, Matthews said not only did he decide to 'give it a real go' but was pleased to see as he looked around that all his teammates 'were still buzzing'.

Ralph Banks, Bolton's thirty-three-year-old left-back, said Matthews was phenomenal in harassing the Bolton defence, which grew steadily more frail as tiredness exacerbated the destabilising effect of Bell's injury. Matthews's pace over ten yards, Banks said, became almost impossible to resist.

Banks, whose younger brother Tommy was noted as one of Matthews's sternest adversaries, also felt frustrated that those around him were slow to react to the mounting threat. He was struggling himself with cramp from the effort of trying to contain Matthews. As he looked around he could see that Hassall, playing out of position, was confused about his responsibilities, while the forwards Langton and Moir were not falling back to help out as they should. 'We were in a right state,' Banks said.

With just over twenty minutes left, Matthews ran back to collect Taylor's short pass. Confronted by Banks defending a large open space, Matthews merely pushed the ball past him. By the time Banks had turned and started to run back Matthews was ready, with his next touch, to lift a cross towards the far post. Banks said he shouted at Hanson to let the ball go, reckoning, if left alone, it would have gone out. Instead the Bolton goalkeeper reached it with his fingertips from where it fell for Mortensen, despite the close attention of two defenders, to hook the ball just inside the upright. Up in the stands it was too much for Matthews's mother-in-law, Mrs Vallance, who fainted from the excitement. The score was 3-2.

Matthews now exhorted all those around him to feed him the ball whenever possible. Signs that the Bolton defence was in trouble were not even subtle. Players stumbled and dragged themselves about as if affected by the percussion from a bomb blast. For twenty minutes they somehow denied Blackpool the equalising goal as Matthews played, in his own words, the game of his life. An exhausted Lofthouse watched Matthews in amazement: 'He stood there, toes turned inwards, looking like a little old man – until he moved.'

Jackie Mudie would say his main contribution to Blackpool's victory was being tripped just outside the penalty area and slightly to the left of the goal with three minutes left. Mortensen, who appeared to have hurt his left thigh quite badly when scoring Blackpool's second, was moving freely again as he strolled over to pick the ball up. He placed it without pause or ceremony and walked casually back. He spent no time at all lining up his shot. He took five easy paces towards the ball.

The slow-motion build-up was what made the next split second so stunning, bringing the stadium to the boil in an instant. The speed of Mortensen's shot was such that the first anyone knew – a motionless Hanson included – that the scores were level was the ball dropping from high in the net behind the Bolton goalkeeper. Mortensen said that at the last moment a small gap appeared inside Hanson's right-hand post. Even a guided missile might not have found its target with quite such precision.

The goal that secured what subsequently would be deemed a hat-trick by Mortensen was as much a thing of pristine beauty as his first two had been untidy. Even Matthews looked in danger, fleetingly, of losing his composure among the knot of players congratulating Mortensen as they hurried back to the centre circle. Mrs Vallance fainted for a second time. 'We were all crying,' Jean, Matthews's daughter, said.

If Bolton were to save the match, they knew what they had to do: stop Matthews. But the knowing and the doing were now held apart by iron rods of fatigue. Another break by Matthews and this time Malcolm Barrass, a formidable barrier who had been so dominant early on, moved across to cover him, only to be turned north then south. When he turned again it was to see Matthews's centre arcing over Hanson. The ball dropped tantalisingly on to Mudie's left boot at the far post, too steeply, though, for the inside-forward to control the ball. All he could do was shuffle it out for a goal kick.

Moments later, in time added on for injury, Matthews was advancing again having gathered the ball in his own half. The background noise, biblical in its intensity, matched the drama as perfectly as any soundtrack ever did an epic movie. Matthews stuttered forward on tiptoe. He tapped a pass to Fenton, who cut infield only to lose possession in a tackle by Johnny Wheeler. Fortunately for Blackpool the ball broke to Taylor. He pushed it straight back out to Matthews, who was just outside the penalty area and about ten yards from the goal line.

Matthews looked up and there was Banks between him and the goal. It might just as well have been a well-oiled revolving door for the ease with which Matthews spun past the left-back to within two paces of the edge of the six-yard box. For a moment it seemed Matthews might shoot, a clear possibility that, fatefully, drew Hanson towards his left-hand post. If Matthews did entertain thoughts of scoring the winner himself, he changed his mind and, although he slipped, he had enough purchase on the turf with his left boot to hit a controlled centre with his right.

As Lofthouse feared and foretold, Matthews kept the ball away from the rapidly filling area immediately in front of goal. Instead he dragged it back at an angle of some thirty degrees. Matthews said his heart and hopes fell when he noticed Mortensen had made a run to the far post. Mortensen said this was a deliberate ploy to drag defenders with him and he shouted to Bill Perry to fill the space behind him.

This Perry did, having already guessed, he said, what Matthews would do. He raced forward to meet the winger's cross in the precise spot Lofthouse knew Matthews would aim it: just outside the six-yard box. Now Matthews's fear was that Perry would go for the power and the glory when, with Hanson having been teased out of position, accuracy was what mattered.

It probably helped that Perry's body position when Matthews's pass reached him meant that not only did he have to strike the ball with his weaker right foot but also, as he said, 'had to hook it a bit'. In other words, he was in no position to blast the ball and had little choice but to concentrate on precision. His execution was faultless and for the second time in a few minutes Hanson was helpless to stop the ball spearing the gap between him and his right-hand post. At least he saw it coming this time, even if he was on all fours having stumbled in his desperate attempt to get back to block Perry's shot. 'I nearly wept for joy when I saw the ball in the net,' Perry said.

The Blackpool players were torn between whether to hail Perry or Matthews. Only momentarily. Soon Matthews was wrapped from view by teammates who reeled him along in a crablike dance before dispersing reluctantly, Perry and Mudie the last to leave him. Matthews, dazed, smoothed back his hair with his left hand. The spectators were in ferment. A confused scoreboard operator gave a fourth goal to Bolton as well as Blackpool. Mrs Vallance swooned, again.

Wolstenholme, whose unscripted words at the climax of another famous Wembley final in thirteen years' time would become a familiar jingle, struggled in vain for the telling phrase, before extinguishing Matthews's career more than a decade ahead of time. What he did register, unequivocally, was whose final this had been, and the surname had only two syllables. 'There it is [the final whistle] . . . and where's Stanley Matthews . . .'. Wolstenholme said, '. . . there's Joe Smith running on to . . . there's Stanley, at long last he's done it . . . and everybody cheering him . . . what an end to a great career . . .'. In the coming years, many a defender – a certain Brazil left-back in particular – would have cause to reflect despondently on this greatly exaggerated termination.

Such a tumultuous conclusion left, inevitably, a sense of anti-climax. A pounding, ripping yarn had suddenly been quelled by the peep of a whistle. Matthews wandered a little aimlessly, wearing his familiar look, a mixture of diffidence and self-containment, as players of both sides shook his hand, slapped his back. After being the fourth Blackpool player to receive a winner's medal from the Queen – could he really hold his lifetime's ambition so easily in one hand? – he winked a slightly awkward, chummy wink at the TV camera.

Back on the pitch Johnston called for three cheers for the Queen, a nice sense of occasion whether or not it was scripted, before he and Matthews – and the Cup – were hoisted on high by their teammates. The first quotes from Matthews were self-effacing, as they would remain on the countless future occasions when he was asked about the match. 'We were on top for most of the game,' he said, 'and finished much fresher and stronger than Bolton, who tired very quickly. Nobody knows how pleased I am that I've at last got that medal, but I'm glad we've won too, if only for George Farm's sake.' Once he had changed, Matthews headed for a pre-arranged meeting before going on to the official celebrations at the Café Royal in Regent Street. He had told his brother Ron that, if Blackpool won, he should take their mother to a certain hotel. He wanted Ada to be one of the first to see his medal before she and the family returned to Stoke.

The 1953 final was the start of a trail that continues to this day, the match still alluded to and reminisced over with great frequency. Matthews's own celebrity, already assured, was gilded with another coat. His first summons was from BBC Television to appear the next day on the popular panel show *What's My Line?* He was to be the mystery personality. Panellist Gilbert Harding got him in two guesses.

The team returned to Blackpool on the Monday. The crowds lining the route grew deeper the further north their train got. At Crewe, well-wishers slowed the train's progress as the cup was held out of the window; at Warrington, factory whistles drowned out the cheering crowds and an announcement of 'Congratulations to Blackpool' over the station's loudspeaker; and big turnouts at Wigan and Preston confirmed that this was as much a northern triumph as it was Blackpool's. Overwhelmed by it all, Matthews was reported to have locked himself in the train's toilet, 'his only refuge from the crowd of schoolboys, porters, women, soldiers and reporters'.

In Blackpool itself 'over 300,000 excited, almost hysterical, people' greeted the team's return. Matthews was the cynosure of all eyes when the team paraded through the streets in a single-decker bus with an open roof. On the steps of the Town Hall, Matthews addressed the crowd in a flat Stoke accent: 'I am told by one or two people that I was the match-winner. As a matter of fact I don't believe that for the simple reason that we have here eleven match-winners.' A big bash followed in the vaulted splendour of the Spanish Hall at the Winter Gardens.

When the excitement started to subside a clamour rose for him to be honoured. At a council meeting in the week following the final, Alderman Jacob Parkinson said: 'It has been suggested the honorary freedom of the borough should be conferred on Stanley Matthews. To me that is nothing like good enough ... there should be some national recognition of his prowess.' Mayor-elect Edwin Smith, citing Don Bradman's knighthood, said: 'I think Stanley Matthews ranks as high as the Australian cricketer.'*

The trail also led to the mystery of whatever happened to Matthews's nine-carat-gold medal. At some point, this precious symbol of his most feted achievement went missing. In 1965, the BBC produced a programme to mark Matthews's fiftieth birthday. On it he appealed for the medal to be returned. 'For years I have been lending it out to exhibitions and charity shows,' he said, 'and the last person I lent it to hasn't returned it.' He then held out the empty medal case to the camera and said: 'Whoever has it please let me have it back.'

He never did get it back. In due course the FA gave him a replica but it was only after he died that the medal was found – at his first wife's home. Stanley Matthews Junior said: 'The medal was discovered in a large box containing other family mementoes in a cupboard at my mother's home. She had not recognised its significance.' Nick Hancock, the comedian and an ardent Stoke City fan, bought it for £23,500 at an auction in 2001. He then loaned it to the Stanley Matthews museum at the Britannia Stadium, where it is a popular exhibit even though it was won in a match that didn't actually involve Stoke.

---

* In 2000, the trail led to a spat between Les Scott, the ghost of the Matthews autobiography, *The Way It Was*, and David Miller, whose authorised biography had been published in 1989. Miller, who knew Matthews well, reviewing the autobiography for the *Daily Telegraph* wrote: 'The book is lengthy, informative, sometimes puzzling, occasionally offensive and uncharacteristic of the man – and too often inaccurate.' He concluded: 'Perhaps it should be *The Way It Wasn't*.' Miller referred to embarrassing moments in the book, including that Matthews had made a deathbed promise to his father to win the FA Cup for him one day. Miller pointed out that when Jack Matthews died in 1945, the romance surrounding his son and the FA Cup was non-existent. He added that, having talked to Matthews intimately over four years, 'I find it hard to accept the sentimentality of this anecdote'. Scott responded, in print. He said he had worked on the autobiography with Matthews almost every day for eighteen months. Matthews's daughter, Jean, and her husband, Bob, had helped in the endeavour. 'One thing they gave me,' Scott wrote, 'was an account written by Stan in 1959 and sent from South Africa of how he had made a promise to his father on his deathbed to win an FA Cup medal. Miller's assumptions and accusations would have hurt him deeply.'

Chapter 15

'We saw a different Matthews,
a forager and a fighter'

The idea that Stanley Matthews would walk out of Wembley after the 1953 FA Cup final into the honeyed hue of the sun setting on his career was a seductive one, but sentimental schlock was not something he understood. What he did understand was that football was, increasingly, the one area of his life he could depend on to deliver contentment.

He did titillate those who hoped the match-winning pass to Bill Perry might go down in history as a glorious parting shot when he turned down the Football Association's invitation to tour South America followed by a fixture against the United States in New York. He excused himself on the grounds the thigh injury that needed treating before the Cup Final was still a problem. In early July he and Betty joined Charlie Chester and his wife on holiday in San Remo. Surely here was a thirty-eight-year-old trying out life's gentler rhythms.

Matthews himself was surprised by quite how thoroughly he buried this possibility. In the twelve more years before his last match he relentlessly heaped statistics on the idea that amid the eulogising that followed the 1953 cup final would have been the right time to retire. He made a further 275 League appearances,

28 in the FA Cup, 21 for England and 2 for the Football League, and scored 15 goals.

The most eye-catching of these figures is the number of England caps he added to his collection before he played his last international. This was in May 1957 when he was 42 years and 103 days – a record for seniority that still stands and seems in no immediate danger of being threatened by an outfield player (although, with forecasts of greater longevity, who is to say it will never be broken).

Had Matthews accepted the belated offer to go on the summer tour – the FA asked him only when the clamour for his inclusion rose after his Wembley triumph against Bolton – he would have been in line for four more caps. In South America, England drew with Argentina in a match cut short by rain, beat Chile 2-1 and lost by the same score to Uruguay, the world champions in 1930 and 1950.

The match in Yankee Stadium, New York, on 8 June was the first floodlit international played by England. The English press hailed the 6-3 win, but neither as a revenge for the World Cup humiliation three years before, nor in its billing as a celebration of the Coronation six days earlier, was it entirely convincing. Hardly anyone in New York noticed it was going on, devaluing it as a reprisal for Belo Horizonte and as an observance of the royal pageant in Westminster Abbey.

Tom Finney had been England's regular selection on the right wing for some time, including for all four matches overseas in the summer and the first home international of the 1953–4 season against Wales in Cardiff in early October. Although Finney was thought to have had a poor game in the 4-1 victory over Wales, it was still a shock when, ten days later, he was left out of the FA's ninetieth anniversary match against a Fifa team expansively subtitled the Rest of the World (all the players came from Western Europe).

Matthews replaced Finney, making him at thirty-eight and

nearly nine months the oldest player other than a goalkeeper to play for England. His recall after two and a half years by fickle selectors may well have been influenced by the special circumstances of the match. It was, after all, a birthday party that needed an entertainer. Also it was Wembley's first showpiece since the Cup Final and the possibility of a Matthews encore would ensure a full house of 100,000.

In fairness, Matthews had also made a strong case for his inclusion regardless of the Wembley party needing a good juggler. His form had been winding up nicely with a stand-out display in an otherwise disappointing performance by Blackpool in the Charity Shield game at Arsenal. Highbury was always a favourite Matthews venue and the fact that it was Blackpool's first domestic game under lights and 40,000 turned out to watch seemed to inspire him even more. Not enough, though, to trump the collective excellence of Arsenal, who won 3-1.

Tom Reid, the Scotland manager, provided further testimony to Matthews's good form. Four days before the Rest of the World game, Reid was at Bloomfield Road to watch Blackpool lose 2-1 to Sheffield Wednesday. His comment that 'Stanley Matthews is the greatest player I've ever seen', based on his performance against Wednesday, was given added force by the fact that the team overall played poorly.

The 4-4 draw with the Rest of the World left everyone happy, not least Matthews because he did more than enough to justify his selection both as light entertainer and serious contributor.

Just as important, in the scheme of Matthews's later life, was the presence at Wembley that day of a South African called Lubbe Snoyman. He was a goalkeeper for Johannesburg Rangers, who were touring the British Isles. He was so determined to watch the man touted as the world's greatest footballer that he trekked down to London from Inverness in the Scottish Highlands, where Rangers were playing.

At half-time Snoyman was annoyed. It had been a pointless expedition. Matthews, closely marked, had hardly touched the ball. By the end, though, he wondered whether he was imagining what he thought he had seen in the second half. 'Long after everyone had left the ground I remained in my seat near the royal box, wondering whether I had dreamed it,' he said. 'It was incredible. Matthews laid on a one-man show . . . I had never seen anything like it.'

Snoyman resolved to bring Matthews to South Africa, where the roots of football's popularity were burrowing deep, particularly in the black community. He rang Bill Perry, a friend from when they played together in Johannesburg, to ask if he would sound out Matthews about making the trip. A day or two later Perry rang back to say Matthews was interested.

The England selectors, sharing Snoyman's view of how Matthews had performed, retained him for the World Cup qualifying match against Northern Ireland at Goodison Park in November. Matthews received excellent reviews for his part in the 3-1 win: 'Take Matthews out of our forward line and Ireland must have won'; 'We saw a different Matthews, a forager and a fighter.' And so it was that he was kept for Hungary's visit to Wembley on 25 November 1953, a match that the visitors would win 6-3 – and finally convince even the dinosaurs that the traditional English way of playing was in need of revision.

The story of Hungarian football is one of a vertiginous rise and plummet. World Cup runners up in 1938 and 1954 and Olympic champions in 1952, 1964 and 1968, these brilliant and formidable opponents were unbeaten for more than four years. Very different from today when the might of the Magnificent Magyars can be glimpsed only by watching flickering film footage.

Having scouted the way ahead for football, Hungary were

bowled over by others rushing past them in pursuit of the game's
major prizes. In the first twenty years of the world rankings that
Fifa introduced in 1992 Hungary failed to break into the top
thirty nations.

But when Hungary came to Wembley in 1953 they were
in the process of compiling their record sequence of thirty-
one matches without defeat. Still, the mood in England was
generally bullish. Hungary had just been held 2-2 in Budapest
by Sweden, their refulgent star Ferenc Puskás missing a penalty,
and had arrived in London after a long train journey that took
in a practice match in Paris. Also, England felt protected by
their record of never having lost at home against a team from
outside the British Isles. Surely Hungary, none of whose players
had been to England before or had seen an English team play,
were not going to change this.

Even astute observers of the game, such as Charles Buchan,
wrote loftily about the match without feeling the need to
underpin their confidence with reasoned analysis. 'The clever
ball-control and close passing of the Hungarians do not alarm
me in any way,' Buchan said with an Olympian flourish. The
one Hungarian journalist who travelled with the team said the
visitors would be lucky to draw.

One of the few voices that cautioned against overconfidence
– or confidence of any type – belonged to Geoffrey Green of
The Times. He had seen enough of continental teams and their
new playing models to say with startling prescience in a radio
discussion: 'One of these days we shall wake up and find six
goals in the back of our net.'

Even though the prevailing view was that England would
win, Hungary's visit stirred greater interest than any home
international had for some time. Touts outside Wembley were
soon trading steeply upwards. The priciest tickets, £2 10s.,
fetched a tenner while the 3s. 6d. cheap seats went for 30s.

Among the spectators was a young English professional

(*Right*) Matthews gives one of his greatest international performances at the age of 41, dominating Brazil's highly rated full-back Nilton Santos (seen here) in the 4–2 win at Wembley in May 1956

(*Left*) Matthews, a day after his forty-second birthday in 1957, gives a superb performance in Blackpool's 4-0 win at Charlton Athletic

(*Right*) Matthews, Duncan Edwards and Billy Wright train at Highbury before England's 2-1 win over Scotland at Wembley in April 1957. Matthews played only twice more for England

(*Above*) Stoke supporters welcome Matthews back to the Victoria Ground
after he rejoined the club, aged 46, in October 1961

(*Below*) Matthews, aged 50 and recently awarded a knighthood in the New Year Honours,
plays his last Football League game, a 3-1 home win for Stoke over Fulham on 6 February
1965. The crowd of 28,585 would almost certainly have been bigger had it been known
at the time he would not play again

(*Above*) Autograph hunters surround Matthews after his first match since being re-signed by Stoke in 1961 ends in a 3-0 win over Huddersfield Town

(*Right*) Fitness fanatic Matthews appeared in cigarette advertising. The extent to which he colluded in this particular campaign is unclear

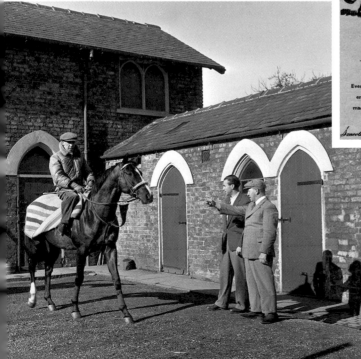

(*Left*) Matthews (second right) runs his eye over the racehorse Parbleu that briefly carried his colours

(*Above*) Lev Yashin (left) an
Ferenc Puskás carry Matthew
after his testimonial match
Stoke on 28 April 196

(*Left*) Matthews after the
testimonial match with
his wife, Betty, and Lev Yashin

(*Above*) Matthews with his wife, Betty, and children,
Jean and Stanley, after receiving his knighthood in 1965

(*Right*) Matthews
(front right) with the
board of Port Vale,
where he learnt
the perils of being
a manager

(*Above*) In retirement in Malta, where Matthews played for a post office side in Paoloa

(*Below*) Matthews with Mila Winterova, who became his second wife

(*Right*) Matthews became a frequent visitor to South Africa, where, in later life, he found fulfilment coaching in Soweto until the UN placed him on its blacklist

(*Left*) Matthews with Tom Finney – the two wingers were endlessly compared – at Stanley's eightieth birthday celebrations in 1995

(*Above*) Matthews's coffin is driven past a full stand at the Britannia Stadium, which replaced the Victoria Ground, on 3 March 2000

(*Above*) These 9-foot figures of Matthews, representing his three ages as a footballer, stand outside Stoke City's Britannia Stadium. Three local craftsmen sculpted them

player, Malcolm Allison, who would become a brashly successful coach, notably of Manchester City, after his playing career was ended by tuberculosis. He was with a friend and their banter before the game was probably typical of what was being said around the stadium.

'I went to the game with a player called Jimmy Andrews, a Scottish boy,' Allison said. 'As we were walking into the ground, the Hungarian team were warming up and Jimmy said to me: "We'll murder these, Mal." I said: "Why's that, Jim?" He pointed to Puskás and said: "Look at that No. 10 over there, he's about a stone overweight".' Allison remembered that Puskás 'did have a little tummy on him'.

'We completely underestimated the advances Hungary had made,' Billy Wright, the England captain, said. And he confessed that he too poked fun at the Hungarians before kick-off. 'We should be all right here, Stan,' he said to Mortensen when he first saw the visitors' lightweight, cutaway boots. 'They haven't got the proper kit.'

David Godblatt, in his *Global History of Football*, also mentioned the Hungarians' kit while contrasting the teams' general appearance. His observation was very different from Wright's: 'To a man the England players look as though they have just rolled up their sleeves for another hard shift at the factory. Their kit is baggy; the Hungarians' is fitted. On their feet are heavy, high-cut leather clodhoppers; the Hungarians wear lighter, low-cut modern boots. Their frames are like oxen; the Hungarians look sinewy.'

Wright said he first sensed he was wrong to have belittled Hungary when he walked towards the centre circle for the coin toss. Puskás, who had arrived there before him, was doing tricks with the ball on his left foot. Wright's eyes widened as Hungary's captain finished his routine by flipping the ball on to his thigh before letting it run down his shin and on to the centre spot. Wright, who had never met or even seen Puskás before, said that the Hungarian captain then smiled at him as if to say that was only the start.

Puskás was true to his mischievous grin. Allison and Jimmy Andrews, in common with all around them, watched in wonder as the team from the Soviet empire unmasked English clubs' continued allegiance to the WM formation as fidelity of the blindest kind. 'They played with a deep centre-forward and destroyed England,' Allison said.

The England players were not the only people confused by Hungary's tactics. A range of different formations used by coach Gustáv Sebes has appeared in print since. It was 4-2-4 – but not quite; maybe 3-1-2-4 or even 2-3-3-2. The point this confusion makes is that it was a fluid system, a forerunner of what became known as Total Football. Matthews said not only did Hungary outwit England with their field positions, they mixed the high-tempo British game with the South American ingredient of short, quick passes.

Walter Winterbottom, the England manager, who was well aware of the shifting patterns of the game outside Britain, said that he was virtually powerless to adapt the national team's style of play if it jarred with the way clubs were playing. 'I could not just get a team of players and say, "Look, lads, this is the way you're going to play." The clubs had to get it so the players were used to it.' The clubs, he said, were run by strong-minded men who 'were just cheque-book managers, they weren't coaches'.*

It frustrated Winterbottom that the club managers were not 'getting it' despite the evidence being set before their eyes. Surely, for example, they had registered that the Swede Gunnar Nordahl, notionally centre-forward for the Rest of the World

---

* More enlightened managers such as Ron Greenwood and Jimmy Hill came through with the next generation.

when they played England at Wembley a month before, had roamed far and wide, particularly wide.

'Nordahl was a centre-forward but he stood out on the right wing, which left our centre-half with nothing to do,' Winterbottom said. 'The players asked me what they should do about this. I said, "Leave him and wait for someone else who's going to fill his place and latch on to him." I told them that they shouldn't pay any attention to shirt numbers otherwise if the opposition put the No. 9 on their left-back the centre-half would follow him out there, which would be silly.'

This was precisely the kind of thing Winterbottom felt club managers should be addressing. Their failure to do so was one of the reasons England were caught out so badly by Hungary. Nándor Hidegkuti, their centre-forward, played in a deep position, from where he distributed the ball or made attacking runs. Hidegkuti scored after fifty seconds of slick play that were enough to warn England of impending ignominy. He went on to complete a hat-trick and killed off the game with Puskás with three goals in under ten minutes midway through the first half.

Winterbottom may have felt frustration, but it was not all one way. After such a disastrous result, the recriminations were booted back and forth even more keenly than the ball had been in the match itself. There were those, players included, who reckoned the result was as much an indictment of the manager as anyone.

One version of events from inside the England camp was that Harry Johnston complained right from the kick-off that it was impossible for him to mark Hidegkuti because the No. 9 kept retreating behind his own lines. Wright responded by saying, 'Leave it to half-time, Walter will sort it out then.' This proved wishful. Winterbottom, the story went, never mentioned it and nothing was put in place to make it harder for the Hungarians. Matthews said Winterbottom spent much of the interval talking to George Robb, England's left wing.

Nowhere in England was the sense of damaged pride more acute than in Blackpool, where before the match the selection of four of their players – Matthews, Johnston, Mortensen and new cap Ernie Taylor – was a source of civic celebration. One national newspaper had greeted the announcement of the England team by saying: 'It's almost Blackpool v Hungary next week. If Taylor and Matthews produce no more than their normal club form, the merry Magyars from Budapest are in for the shock of a Soccer lifetime.'

As it happened poor Taylor was the one left dazed and disorientated. The five-foot-four former submariner, unfortunate to be blooded in this of all internationals, never appeared for England again. The other three Blackpool players received reasonable notices, Matthews despite the unanimous agreement that his partnership with Taylor on the right side of attack had been a failure. Geoffrey Green, so accurate with his prediction before kick-off, sought comfort in the fact that 'we have our Matthews and Finney', even though Finney did not play.

Maybe the Hungary defeat and its effect on the morale of the Blackpool players who took part – possibly, too, on those around them at Bloomfield Road who had been so buoyed by their selection – accounted for an arid two months for the club. Between mid-November and mid-January they failed to win a match, scuppering any chance they might have had of finishing top of the League. Given this poor run, sixth place in the final table, fewer than ten points behind champions Wolves, was a reasonable outcome.

What uplifted Blackpool's season was another run in the FA Cup, not this time all the way to Wembley – not even as far as the quarter-finals – but involving as many matches in the competition as they played a year earlier. Once again Matthews appeared in all seven.

More than 100,000 people watched the four matches,

lasting seven hours, it took Blackpool to beat Luton in the third round.*

Blackpool then needed two goes to beat West Ham in the fourth round before relinquishing their grasp on the cup in the fifth. Their exit was particularly galling for Matthews as it took place at Port Vale, the club he supported as a young boy. Roy Sproson, who played for Port Vale that day, recalled the 2-0 upset some years later: 'I was marking Ernie Taylor. No disrespect but he was arrogant, jibing at me all through. When we looked like winning I started getting back at him, "Come and watch me in the next round, Mr Taylor." I was only a cocky kid then. At the end, Taylor just walked off, wouldn't shake hands. Stanley took it very well though, but I bet he was mad inside.'

By the time of England's next match after the Hungary defeat, against Scotland at Hampden in April 1954, Matthews was thirty-nine. Although the selectors had no reason to impute the failures of the Hungarian debacle to their right wing, they were in a dither, again, over whether an outfield player of his age had the legs, lungs and heart for the international game.

They dropped him for the Scotland fixture, to which Matthews responded with a brilliant rebuke. At the precise time he could have been playing at Hampden, he gave such a performance for Blackpool in a 2-2 draw away to Spurs that the 40,000 crowd at White Hart Lane gave him a standing ovation. Many spectators, one report said, were left gaping in admiration. Not so the selectors, although neither were they ready to abandon him. They left him out of the early summer tour that included a

---

* The tie assumed a soap-opera feel with one episode involving a wedding drama. After the first replay, Jackie Mudie had to ring his bride, Brenda Rushforth, to say their wedding was off as it coincided with the second replay. Fortunately, the priest at St Cuthbert's Roman Catholic Church in Blackpool and the proprietor of the hotel staging the reception were able to put it back by just twenty-four hours. This at least meant the hotel did not have to dismantle an elaborate set, which would not have disgraced the much later TV programme *Footballers' Wives*. A wedding arch made of goalposts greeted guests at the hotel's front entrance. Inside the floor of the main reception room was marked with the white lines of a football pitch with a white football on the centre spot. The FA Cup stood alongside the wedding cake.

return against Hungary in Budapest, only to include him hours later among the forty possibles for the World Cup finals in Switzerland in June.

When Puskás heard England's selection for Budapest he said that the omission of 'your great, so great footballer Stanley Matthews – that I cannot understand at all'. He understood it even less after Hungary won the return 7-1. He dismissed the England team on this occasion as much weaker than the one he played against at Wembley.

Overlooked by England, Matthews went on tour with Blackpool to Germany. Once again he embarrassed the national selectors who had doubted him with some fine performances, especially in a 4-0 win over Strasbourg.

After this he received a cable from Winterbottom calling him home to train with the England players, a summons that still did not amount to the selectors having made up their minds about taking him to the World Cup. In an echo of the tortured process that surrounded his selection for the 1950 finals, he was not in the reduced squad of twenty-five players but was told he would be considered later. Not until two weeks before England's opening World Cup match against Belgium was he eventually confirmed as a member of the squad.

The 1954 world event was a source of pride and disappointment for Matthews. Halfway through his fortieth year, he played as well as anyone. Kenneth Wolstenholme, commentating on the tournament for the BBC, said after the group matches that Matthews was the only England player who was regarded as world class, none of the others being able to control the ball by continental standards. The great sadness for Matthews was that England's elimination in the quarter-finals ended his ambition of winning a competition whose legitimacy even the Football Association now deigned to recognise.

England opened with a draw against Belgium in the St Jakob Stadium in Basle. Under the obscure rules of the competition, extra time was played despite the groups being decided on a league basis. This resulted in the 3-3 score after ninety minutes becoming 4-4 after added time. England's attack functioned well but the defence, unchanged from the 7-1 defeat in Budapest, was fragile throughout with Gil Merrick's lapses in goal particularly damaging. Louis Carré, Belgium's centre-half, said containing Matthews had been the chief problem. On occasions, after England's outside-right had done a party piece, the crowd chanted 'Wunderbar! Wunderbar!'

Despite this, Matthews's absence from the next match against Switzerland, with a thigh strain and skinned toe, would prove less significant than Syd Owen's leg injury that kept him out of the game. Billy Wright switched to Owen's place, his first appearance at centre-half for England, and the defence was far sturdier as a result. England beat the Swiss 2-0 and so won their preliminary section courtesy of another puzzling regulation that meant the seeded teams – England and Italy in group 4 – did not meet.

After their sound start to the tournament, England's quarter-final against Uruguay was a great disappointment. They lost 4-2, undone by another substandard performance by Merrick. The goalkeeper, who conceded fifteen goals in his first thirteen internationals, had now let in thirty in ten games and never played for England again. Matthews, on the other hand, had a stormer. Wright said he was the undisputed man of the match having been given a free-ranging role, which at least showed England were starting to relax their rigid observance of field positions. According to one report, Uruguay's defence 'never really knew where to expect the next pinprick from the English master'. He created numerous openings for others and had chances of his own, one of which resulted in a shot against a post. 'We should have beaten those Uruguayans,' he said. 'Let's be fair – we'd none of the breaks. They pulled no punches. I've never played against a team that pulled as few.'

If Uruguay did practise the dark arts, as Matthews's remark suggested, they were not as ambitious or blatant in this respect as their continental neighbours. Brazil, who also lost 4-2 in their quarter-final against Hungary, were the main aggressors in a match that is remembered as the Battle of Berne.

The Brazilians, as if trying something diametrically different from Pele's beautiful game before deciding it was the better option, went down fighting – literally – on the pitch and off it. Joined by officials and journalists, they carried their thuggery into extra time by invading Hungary's dressing room after the final whistle. Matthews was shocked, saying that if England's game was violent you could only call Brazil's murder. He sympathised with the English referee, Arthur Ellis: 'He could not see tackles that were utterly malicious, tackles that could have maimed. He could not have seen the private feuds that were raging everywhere towards the end. It was a disgrace to football.'*

Hungary went on to reach the final but, with Puskás not fully fit, they lost 3-2 to West Germany, their first defeat since a friendly in Austria in 1950.

Matthews returned home washed out. He was among the first to suggest there was 'too much football', something that would grow into a familiar refrain. 'Once upon a time a professional was assured of at least three months' holiday from the game in the summer,' he said. 'Now some of us are getting about three weeks.

'I've to report for training at Blackpool on July 26 – and I'll be there, too, for I must be fit for the new season – but some time before then I must go somewhere for a holiday with the family, somewhere in the sun, I hope.'

---

* Brazilians saw it rather differently. They blamed the referee. A front-page editorial in *Diario da Noite* said that Ellis should never set foot on Brazilian soil unless he wanted to leave behind a widow. Fifa dipped their hands in water. They did nothing beyond leaving the question of discipline to the national associations – and that was that.

Here again he was in the vanguard of what would become a staple of the professional footballers' life: going abroad to work on the tan during the close season. Only on this occasion he was thwarted when Stanley Junior, went down with measles. A planned trip to Madeira had to be abandoned. Instead the family went to Yorkshire.

Chapter 16

'We had no idea this would be Stanley's final England game,
otherwise we would have carried him off shoulder high'

The notices extolling Matthews's performances during the 1954
World Cup did not quite represent the wider press coverage
he was now receiving. It had never been wholly uncritical and
some newspapers increasingly moderated their admiration.

Matthews himself said as much. He recorded that he became
embroiled in what he called an unspoken battle with certain
journalists who would generalise those occasions he played
poorly into proof that he was too old for professional football. A
typical example of the censure he attracted appeared in a report
on the Football League's 6-0 win over the League of Ireland in
Dublin in September 1954: 'Matthews, bubbling over with all his
clever tricks, entertained the crowd . . . but his style of slowing
up the attack set the inside forwards a rare puzzle at times.'

He described the idea that physical decline was affecting how
well he played as balderdash, although he conceded that getting
over injuries took a little longer than it used to. What mattered,
he said, was that he was still very fit. He pointed out he was
absent from only eight League matches in 1954–5, the season of
his fortieth birthday. This was fewer than a number of the much
younger Blackpool players missed.

He might have added that on top of the thirty-four League matches, he played seven times for England, including in their three matches on a European tour in May 1955. And less than forty-eight hours after returning from this tour, he flew to South Africa for his first experience of playing in a country that, just as Canada did, would become a retreat during the dramatic events that shaped his later life.

For the moment, a host of different theories about how to adapt to the game's new age flew around the room during selection meetings. Billy Wright said the selectors were acting like headless chickens after he and Matthews were two of only four players – Roger Byrne and Nat Lofthouse were the others – who, having played in what was a good if unavailing England performance against Uruguay, were kept for the next match against Northern Ireland in October 1954.

Don Revie was a victim of the disconnected thinking. He was picked out as the player to fill Nándor Hidegkuti's deep-lying role. But, without the coherence that coach Gustáv Sebes brought to Hungary's deployment of this new way of playing, England performed like an orchestra without a conductor.

Having given first caps to Revie and Johnny Haynes against Northern Ireland, a match England won 2-0, the selectors promptly ditched them. For his part, Matthews, aware that he was now the target of a sceptical press, assisted in both goals against the Irish as he gave more reasons for those who had it in for him to swallow their bile.

He was England's best forward in the 3-2 win over Wales at Wembley, although according to one anguished scribe this was as much to do with the others' incompetence as the brilliance of England's ancient winger. His excellence in England's next match was undisputed. He drew universal paeans for his performance in a 3-1 win over the new world champions West Germany, also at Wembley, on 1 December 1954. One headline said simply, 'Stan the Superman'; another said, guilelessly, 'Matthews Strafes the Fatherland'. Werner Liebrich, the centre-half in a much-changed German side from the World Cup-winning version, said in his memoirs that Matthews's performance that day 'put him at the very peak of international players, someone like Maradona or Beckenbauer'.

By the time of England's first international of 1955, against Scotland in April, Matthews had passed forty. His birthday on Tuesday 1 February was three days after Blackpool played a friendly against Leeds at Elland Road. Joe Smith originally gave Matthews the day off. He changed his mind at Leeds's request after news that Matthews would not be playing produced a stampede for refunds from the Yorkshire club's fans.

Very probably Matthews was happy about his late call-up. Leaving him out looked like a concession to a man about to reach what most people regard as a milestone birthday, a final adieu to youth. With his age now an issue, Matthews would not have favoured being indulged because of his seniority, nor having a fuss of any sort made of him. 'If I was 45 or, let's say, 50, there'd be something to make a fuss about,' he said. 'But 40 – why, for goodness sake, there's no reason why a footballer should not be playing at forty.'

There was a reason, of course. Most outfield players simply did not have the sinew, puff or desire as they set out on their fifth decade still to be playing. Matthews, who, according to one account, charmed the Leeds crowd after his late summons, gave one of the better performances by a Blackpool player in his first match as a forty-year-old, a dull, goalless game at Bloomfield Road against Sunderland.

Soon after this he celebrated being the first man in his forties to play for England since goalkeeper Alec Morten in 1873. He did this by being a major irritant to Scotland's defence in a 7-2 victory at Wembley. In the same match, the left-half Duncan Edwards, the eighteen-year-old Manchester United marvel, became England's youngest player of the twentieth century. The old and the new were simply too much for the Scots, who had not lost at Wembley for twenty-one years.

Before the match, teammates reminded Harry Haddock, Scotland's left-back, that Matthews had no left foot and he should work on this weakness. Haddock said afterwards that the first time he tried to do this, Matthews beat him on the inside and shivered the crossbar with his left boot. Haddock prided himself on being quick and thought he had the speed to deal with Matthews if he could stay on his inside and force him down the line. 'But he kept losing me,' he said. Afterwards Matthews said the press had built up the threat posed to him by Haddock to such an extent that he had been even more rigorous than usual in his preparation. He starved himself for three days, apart from drinking lime juice. On the morning of the game he went for a walk in weighted shoes.

Given a steady supply of passes by the reinstated Revie, Matthews had a part in all seven goals, four of which were scored by Dennis Wilshaw, the first time an England player had managed a hat-trick against Scotland.

No one much enjoyed the trip to Europe that followed. It confirmed the English game's deepening struggle to keep up with what was happening on the Continent. Over eight days, England played in Paris, Madrid and Porto in northern Portugal, Matthews appearing in all three games. If anything the 1-0 and 3-1 defeats by France and Portugal provided light relief either side of a 1-1 draw against Spain darkened by violence. Even Matthews suffered rare moments of discomposure. Billy Wright said the England players were astonished to see him drawn into the roughhouse. 'He conceded a free-kick with a tackle,' Wright said, 'the first time anybody could recall him committing a foul.' According to Nat Lofthouse, Matthews was so incensed by the play of full-back Campanais that he was heard to mutter: 'I could spit at you.'

The European season completed, Matthews returned to

Blackpool for just long enough to renew his club contract before taking up the invitation to South Africa instigated by Lubbe Snoyman. His projected two-week stay to make guest appearances would end up being nearly a month.

With the attractions of staying at home diminishing, Matthews did not take long to adapt to life in South Africa. He enjoyed the climate and appreciated the chance to bolster his bank balance during the previously unremunerative summer months. The money issue went deeper than simply grasping every opportunity that came his way. His decision to carry on playing through those years when most of his fellow professionals were establishing themselves in new jobs with long-term guarantees, or setting up businesses, had implications for his future. It was now reasonable to assume that football would be the only livelihood he ever had, the only source of income to sustain him in old age.

Once he did achieve security in later life, the stories of his generosity flowed almost as freely in the opposite direction from those that damned him as the owner of a tight fist.

The financially fruitful visit to South Africa was the consequence of Snoyman's trip to Wembley eighteen months earlier, although it did not happen as Snoyman had intended.

One of eleven siblings – ten of them boys – Lubbe Snoyman was building a successful motor dealership in Johannesburg. He was a persuasive character but, after returning to South Africa from his visit to Britain with Johannesburg Rangers in 1953, he had failed to convince the Southern Transvaal FA that flying Matthews to South Africa was economically viable. Upset by this, Snoyman leaked what he regarded as the association's lack of ambition to the local press. This had the desired effect of getting public opinion behind a visit by Matthews, and the undesired one of alerting a rival association to the idea of sending out the invitation.

Snoyman was mortified when news reached him that

officials in Natal had signed up Matthews. He had agreed to play for an Invitation XI in an exhibition game in Durban on Saturday 28 May 1955, which was just six days after England's match in Portugal. Snoyman was even more annoyed when the Englishman's visit caused a rush to the box office. Tickets sold in their thousands while Matthews was still risking injury on England's European tour.

'You see what's happened,' Snoyman, who was now manager of Johannesburg Rangers, railed at the Transvaal FA. 'At least some people know a good idea when they hear one.' He then summoned his friend Eric Litchfield, the sports editor of the *Rand Daily Mail*, and together they drove the four hundred miles to Durban to try to persuade Matthews to play in Johannesburg.

'It was a bit like the first time I saw him play – disappointing to begin with,' Snoyman said. 'He was damned awkward about granting Eric and me an interview, and even when we met he greeted us with a good deal of reserve.' During the course of the discussion Snoyman said he thought Matthews could make a small fortune in South Africa as a one-man entertainer, which helped to melt the frostiness. By the end, Snoyman said he was still not too taken with Matthews's personality but he had agreed to play in Johannesburg's Rand Stadium in three days' time, which was Union Day. Hardly surprisingly, given the awkwardness of the meeting, neither man knew at the time that they had just embarked on an association that would grow into a fast and lasting friendship.

Snoyman was just one of a number of football officials eager to invest in Matthews to promote the game in southern Africa and raise money themselves. Back in Blackpool, the local paper reported: 'Matthews intended to tour South Africa for a fortnight. The people have swarmed to watch him in such numbers that he will have been there nearly a month when he takes a plane home.'

One small side issue over appearance money did arise, but

seems to have been quickly forgotten. The problem involved Matthews's Blackpool teammate Bill Perry, who scored two goals in the Invitation XI's 3-2 win over Natal at the Kingsmead Stadium in Durban. Perry then refused to play in the match in Johannesburg, the one Snoyman had persuaded Matthews to take part in, when the Southern Transvaal FA turned down his request for a £50 appearance fee.

'Stan Matthews is paid for his tour,' Perry said, 'and quite right, too – he's a great artist. But I'm also a professional footballer. I didn't want £400 or £500. But I did ask for £50. The match wasn't for charity but for the Southern Transvaal FA, who made a good profit out of it.' It is possible only to speculate that the higher figures Perry mentioned were based on knowledge he had of amounts Matthews was receiving.

In the match in Johannesburg, Matthews represented a team made up mostly of visiting professionals against a Southern Transvaal XI. The hastily printed programme was unequivocal about the headline act. The cover carried a large drawn picture of Matthews running with a ball at his feet. This was set against an illustration of a full grandstand and the words:

RAND STADIUM
UNION DAY
Tuesday, 31st May
STANLEY
MATTHEWS
OFFICIAL SOUVENIR PROGRAMME

The capacity crowd of 36,000, who kept calling out 'Give it to Stanley', were treated to a 5-5 draw with Matthews leading the way back after the local team led 5-1 at half-time. He scored a penalty after being tripped and laid on three of the other goals. Snoyman remembered the match for Matthews's tussle with the very good Johannesburg Rangers left-back, Morrie Jacobson.

In 1953, when Snoyman and Jacobson toured the UK together, they met Joe Harvey, the former Newcastle United player. On that occasion Snoyman mentioned Matthews's name, having just watched him play at Wembley. He was surprised when Harvey said he would be happier when Matthews retired. He said Matthews was a menace who spent his time ruining young full-backs. 'The man is merciless,' Harvey said. 'He humiliates them.'

When it came to his turn to face Matthews in the Rand Stadium, Jacobson ridiculed the idea that he would be humiliated by the forty-year-old in a match played at altitude – and for the first half an hour he did have the better of their exchanges. Snoyman said he squirmed in his seat as the crowd whistled in derision at Matthews. 'I had staked my football reputation on the man,' he said.

Everything changed suddenly when Matthews swept past Jacobson as if, Snoyman said, 'the tough little full-back wasn't there'. This was the moment the complexion of the match changed. Matthews used the next hour to authenticate all the reports of his wizardry. He transformed the crowd's doubts into a respect that would make him a welcome guest to South Africa whenever he chose to visit. Poor Jacobson suffered the fate foretold by Harvey. 'The flair and attack that are the hallmarks of a truly exceptional player never returned,' Snoyman said.

Now everyone in South Africa wanted to watch the Englishman. In the hectic days that followed Matthews was driven and flown thousands of miles. He played in Lourenço Marques, which is now Maputo, the capital of Mozambique; another match in Johannesburg; made an appearance for Southern Rhodesia in a 4-2 win over Portuguese East Africa in Salisbury, which became Harare; and went to the mining settlement of Rhokana in Northern Rhodesia, later renamed Zambia, where he played a half for each side in a match between local teams.

He could also have played in Kenya, where 'the authorities implored me to go but I had to say no. I can't play football twelve months in a year.'

Snoyman gave some idea of the rewards Matthews received with a story about the trip in Eric Litchfield's car to Mozambique. When they returned to Johannesburg the boot was stuffed with escudos.

Matthews arrived back in Blackpool in late June excited by his month away. 'Wherever I went they were reporting ground records,' he said. He then added, slightly overdoing the altruism: 'I am so glad about this because apart from everything else it meant that South African football was making good money for itself and it needs every penny it can make if it is to establish itself on a big scale.' He was excited, too, about the prospect of going back. 'I've been invited to return on an all-expenses-paid trip with my family,' he said.

The date of Matthews's return to Blackpool rather undermines a story told years later that he made a smiling return from Africa on the eve of the 1955–6 season, just hours before the opening match against Arsenal.* In fact, he had time to go on a family holiday to Yorkshire before the season started, and play for Britain against the Rest of Europe in a match in Belfast. Europe won 4-1 with Matthews and the Wales international John Charles reckoned to be the only British players who 'measured up to the Europeans'.

A rather better, little-told story than the one that wasn't even true was an unfortunate first attempt to feature Matthews on *This Is Your Life*, the TV programme that had just been imported from the United States. Matthews was to be the first to appear on the British version in July 1955, most of the arrangements having been done while he was away in South Africa. At the

---

* What did happen, but not for another five years, was that he came back late from a trip to Canada – and the friction this caused was a factor in his leaving the club.

last moment the programme was postponed after a national newspaper leaked the news. This broke a code of secrecy that was considered sacrosanct. Elaborate plans that included flying the 1953 FA Cup-winning team to London had to be scrapped.

The programme's producers waited only a few months before successfully snaring the nation's favourite footballer at the second attempt. This time Matthews himself nearly rumbled what was going on. He said he noticed knowing winks between members of the family and then was surprised to see his mother with her hair permed: "'What's all that about,' I asked her and quick as a flash she replied, "I won it in a raffle". Guests on the programme, screened in February 1956, included his immediate family, his father-in-law Jimmy Vallance, footballers Stan Cullis, Tommy Lawton and Eddie Hapgood and a schoolteacher and newspaper vendor from Stoke.

Blackpool had experienced a dreadful season in 1954–5, the worst during Matthews's time at the club. They were humiliated 2-0 at home by York City of the Third Division North in the third round of the FA Cup and finished nineteenth in the League. They secured First Division survival only after Matthews raised them to a 6-1 win at Manchester City on the penultimate Saturday.

Coming so close to being dashed on the rocks of relegation produced a reaction from Joe Smith that demolished any idea he might have a liquid centre. The avuncular one displayed managerial ruthlessness of the highest order to end the Blackpool playing careers of two of the club's most popular figures: Harry Johnston, captain for the nine post-war seasons, and Stanley Mortensen. Both had complained to Smith about being left out of the first team. The immediate effect was a lecture about the incompatibility of sentimentality and success. Then, within hours of each other in November 1955, they were on the way out.

Johnston, who was nearly five years younger than Matthews,

went off to manage Reading; Mortensen, six years Matthews's junior, left to resume his playing career at Hull. If they harboured any animosity they overcame it. In 1967 they returned to Bloomfield Road, Mortensen as manager with Johnston as his assistant.

The important thing for Blackpool was that Smith's decisive action worked. In 1955–6 the club had what remains their most successful season in the First Division. They did not lose a match until late September when Matthews was injured in the early minutes against Manchester City. Although they faded over Christmas and beyond, they finished runners up to the out-of-sight champions, Manchester United's ill-starred Busby Babes.

Smith rebuilt Blackpool around young players such as the athletic Jimmy Armfield, a full-back who made 569 appearances for Blackpool between 1954 and 1971, centre-half Roy Gratrix and forward Dave Durie. The manager resisted any temptation to include Matthews in the clear-out, judging he was still needed even with his forty-first birthday approaching. He was correct. His outside-right confounded critics not only with his unflagging form but by his physical resilience. He appeared in thirty-six of the forty-two First Division matches, equalling his record for the club.

The legend of Matthews was now such that, wherever Blackpool played, parents would take their children to watch so that their CVs included: 'I saw Stanley Matthews play football.' Once again, in 1955–6 Blackpool were the most popular visiting team. Their relatively modest home attendances contrasted with a table-topping average of nearly 43,000 spectators for away games – 6,600 more than Wolves in second place. After Blackpool routed Newcastle 5-1 at Bloomfield Road in March 1956, a Newcastle director at the game ridiculed the 23,000 attendance. 'With this team,' he said, referring to Blackpool, 'we'd have fifty to sixty thousand every week at St James' Park.'

The England selectors' stolid singularity produced a very

different response to the excitement Matthews still generated. They dropped him for the match against Northern Ireland in November 1955, sloshing Blackpool seawater on the wound by picking his club teammate Bill Perry for the first of his three caps. Johannesburg-born Perry's Londoner father made him eligible and he came in on the left wing with Finney switching to fill Matthews's place on the right.

As the selectors went on ignoring Matthews, newspapers enlightened them as to the national mood. Their message grew particularly strident when he was overlooked for the trip to Hampden, a year after he had so demoralised the Scots in the 7-2 rout at Wembley. The word blunder appeared on most back pages, while a whimsical essay in one national newspaper looked at the decision through the eyes of a Scottish fan. His view after the 1955 thrashing was: 'Aw canne see a glimmer o' hope till Stanley's deid.' Now, he went on, 'Stanley is deid in a football sense. Stone deid, killed by his own selectors.'

Even George Young, Scotland's captain, joined the criticism. 'As captain maybe I should be glad [that Matthews has been dropped],' he said. 'But I am not – no more than the disappointed spectators who love to see him play.'

So it was, after Johnny Haynes's last-minute goal gave England a barely deserved 1-1 draw at Hampden, that the selectors recalled Matthews for what would be an immense display in a 4-2 victory over Brazil at Wembley in May 1956. Even those critics who held to the view that Matthews was simply a solo cabaret act had to concede that on this occasion he deployed his showstopper, the soft-shoe shuffle segueing effortlessly into a quickstep, for the greater good. This despite supposedly being so nervous beforehand that when Haynes asked him for his autograph in the dressing room he was unable to oblige because his hand was shaking so much. He told Haynes he would do it after the game.

Matthews was worried because he was up against Brazil's

captain Nilton Santos, who was ten years younger than him and touted as the best left-back in the world. The Brazilians, shaping up for what would be an outstanding triumph in the 1958 World Cup, had helped to bring on Matthews's jitters by proclaiming Santos's invincibility. This might have been the case – against anyone other than England's outside-right on this particular day.

Didi, Brazil's flawless midfielder who also played at Wembley, said the reason the unequal contest was not quite as predicted had nothing to do with Santos playing badly. It was, he said, because of 'Stanley Matthews, who gave a complete exhibition of his genius . . . He did not score any goals but he was the creator of almost all of them.' The British press endorsed Didi's verdict. Frank Coles wrote in the *Daily Telegraph*: 'Matthews played one of his greatest games to remind the selectors who had recalled him so grudgingly that it is he, not they, who must decide the time to retire.'

At the banquet in London after the game, Sylvio Pacheco, president of the Brazilian Football Confederation, presented Matthews with a silver cup, twelve inches high, as a measure of the esteem in which his country held a player regarded by Didi as being in the same class as Garrincha or Julinho. As an endorsement by a Brazilian, it could not have been more generous.

European football writers added their own endorsement in the spring of 1956. They voted Matthews first winner of the Ballon d'Or, an award for the Continent's best player, just ahead of the Real Madrid pair Alfredo Di Stéfano and Raymond Kopa.

Nine days after playing at a jammed Wembley against Brazil, Matthews was in East Africa having a kickabout 'with a horde of wildly excited Arab and African children in the island of Zanzibar'.

He said he accepted the invitation to go to East Africa at a time when it seemed the national selectors had abandoned him. No pressure was put on him to change his plans so that he was available for England's tour of Europe. His visit to Zanzibar took place two days after England had drawn 0-0 with Sweden in Stockholm, a result that was followed by wins in Finland and West Germany.

A pattern in Matthews's life of going abroad on his own each summer was starting to emerge. He obviously enjoyed travel and welcomed the fact that his overseas excursions to coach and play football supplemented his income. How significant it was that he travelled without his family, despite his devotion to his children and the family's offers to accompany him is hard to say. Looking back, though, a possible clue is that when in the late 1960s he formed a relationship with the woman who would become his second wife, he had her by his side wherever he went.

Any number of factors has turned men and women into missionaries. Through an accumulated set of circumstances, Matthews seemed to slip into a role as a wandering evangelist for football, albeit one whose calling was strongly linked to his worldly needs. The American news agency's report of his visit to Zanzibar in the summer of 1956 conveys a sense of this. 'No game had been arranged for him in the island,' it said, 'but when the barefooted Arab and African children mobbed his car, he got out, led the way to a bare patch of ground and said, "Let's have a game".' It quoted Matthews as saying: 'I never dreamed that football – and my name – were so familiar in such a remote corner of the world.'

He had a point. Right from his first visit to Africa in 1955 Matthews attracted a public response that a twenty-first-century celebrity with a reputation forged by the white heat of mass-media coverage and worked on by a team of agents might have envied. Matthews did not even have an agent – they did not really arrive on the scene until the 1960s – unless you count the imaginary one to which he was said to have alluded to stall those making persistent demands on his time.

Zanzibar and a match in Dar es Salaam, in the former Tanganyika (now Tanzania), were diversions from Matthews's main destination. This was Kenya, where he spent most of the three-week trip. Here he played in a number of exhibition matches, one of them for the Kenyan FA in the African Stadium in Nairobi (since renamed the Nairobi City Stadium). Two other Englishmen, who were doing national service in Kenya – John Hurst, who came from Blackpool, and Tom Kelly – played on the same side as Matthews.

An incident recalled by Kelly showed that even in these early days of Matthews's African travels he was, like any good missionary, adapting to the conditions. Matthews was sitting in the changing room before the match in a well-worn, creamy-white raincoat that went right down to the ground. A young reporter came in and asked to see his boots. 'Certainly,' Matthews said. He pulled up the raincoat just enough to show off footwear so old and scruffy it almost matched his raincoat. Kelly said he exchanged smiles with Matthews when the reporter's inquisitive look turned to one of astonishment. 'We both knew what he expected to see – a new pair of football boots. But Stan was wearing a very well-worn pair, perfect on the hard ground of Africa,' Kelly said.

After the match, which ended 2-1 to the Kenya FA eleven, Kelly said a reception in honour of Matthews took place at a posh country club 'for us to be personally introduced to the great man'.

This time Matthews did not linger beyond his original departure date and was back in Blackpool before the end of May. Restless as ever, he went to work on his tennis in the garden of The Grange, the family home in St Annes Road. Even in that year's poor summer, the court he had installed was in constant use. His son, Stanley Junior, had happy memories of playing there, with the family dog, Boobie, chasing balls over the large lawn that separated the court from the house. He recalled his father and Charlie Chester, who was appearing in a summer show in Blackpool, hauling a television on to the lawn so that they could watch horseracing, enjoy what sun there was and not miss the children playing tennis. 'It was pretty pointless. So they could see anything at all in the glare they had to barricade themselves in behind this TV,' he said, 'which meant they couldn't see the tennis or enjoy the sun.'

Stanley Junior remembered his father as an extremely competitive tennis player. Surprisingly, given how even-tempered he was on the football field, he could be demonstrably very upset when he lost at any pastime – chess, tennis, table tennis, bowls – other than football. 'He was putting himself on a hiding to nothing,' his son said, 'because later on when I was able to beat him at tennis and table tennis he was always up against it.' He liked his children to be competitive, too. He would play a game with them when they were very young that started with him suddenly asking: 'Who's the boss?' The winner was the first to touch together their thumb and middle finger and say: 'I am.' He also took gleeful pleasure in encouraging their competitiveness when they were old enough to play each other at tennis. 'Early on my sister would give me points and beat me because she was reasonably good,' Stanley Junior said. 'But when I started to win she got mad and our father loved that. It was all good fun.'

Jean and Stanley Junior were both promising players at this stage: Jean had already entered Junior Wimbledon and in time young Stanley would win the boys' title there. Now, in the summer of 1956, it was father's turn to demonstrate he was no chump with a racket. Years later Stanley Junior would describe his father as a good club player, who 'didn't have any strokes per se, but was fit and could run everything down, get everything back'. This was helped by his hand-eye coordination that rivalled its highly developed foot-eye counterpart. He reached a men's semi-final of the South Shore open tournament after beating Eric Claff, the champion for the past five years, in the first round.

A month later he shared in an impressive family haul at the South Shore club's closed event by winning the men's handicap singles and doubles. Jean, seventeen years old, won the women's doubles and was runner up in the singles and Stanley Junior, who was ten, won the under-fifteen and under-eighteen singles titles. In a photograph of the presentation ceremony, Matthews, with his two children, looks the model of a tennis player, lean and tanned in pristine white shorts and one of the new Fred Perry sports tops. He exudes the benefits of an unblemished lifestyle predicated on abstinence.

His self-discipline led, soon afterwards, to a brief skirmish with the forces of temperance. He attended a black-tie dinner at the National Sporting Club in London to celebrate his twenty-five years 'in first-class football'. After the meal the comedian Tommy Trinder, a board member of Fulham Football Club where he would later become chairman, toasted the guest of honour's skill and sportsmanship. Matthews's deadpan response – 'I feel as out of place as Fulham would be if they were in the First Division' – was well received. But the talking point of the evening was the presentation to Matthews of a drinks cabinet stuffed with booze.

Some of the reaction was as unexpected as the Danish cartoon questioning Matthews's omission from the 1949 honours' list. A Scottish priest, the Reverend Samuel Ballantyne, even waded into the debate over the cabinet – while addressing the Synod of Aberdeen. Like the cartoon, this probably said more about Matthews's fame than anything else. 'Why should a clean-living man be encouraged to poison his friends with a deadly narcotic drug to which he himself is not addicted,' Ballantyne rhetorically asked his audience.

Matthews sided with his friends. He said he was upset by the reverend's remarks. He did not regard drink as poison and he liked to offer guests to his house what they wanted.

A quarter of a century after starting to make an impact at Stoke City, not only was Matthews still a valued and regular member of a First Division team, he was attracting spectators in greater numbers than any individual in the English game had done before or has done since. He was, too, a current England player, although not for much longer. Opinion was divided when the selectors finally stopped picking him: had they lost their nerve over the unreality of including a forty-two-year-old or were they genuinely convinced he was not worth his place.

The match against Northern Ireland in Belfast in October 1956 started a run of seven appearances in successive England matches that would be Matthews's international finale. The background noise of well-rehearsed objections to his style of play remained and there did seem to be a decline in his form towards the end of these seven matches. A long season may well have taken its toll because, before his farewell sequence, he excelled in fixtures against the Irish, Wales and, in late November, Yugoslavia. His play may also have suffered from distractions that a player today would leave to an agent. These included an increasing number of invitations, mainly from Africa, to play abroad during the summer.

Against Northern Ireland in October, Matthews scored after only two minutes of the 1-1 draw. At 41 years 248 days he remains England's oldest goalscorer. Jackie Blanchflower, a member of the Northern Ireland team, asked Matthews afterwards: 'Why are you always picking on us?' This was a reference to Matthews's previous England goal having been against the Irish eight years earlier. Matthews, as deadpan in his humour as he was in his play, said that before he scored again Blanchflower would have a long beard.

Matthews never did score another. This was his eleventh and

last, but his ability to contribute the occasional goal was only one of the advantages he offered England against good opponents who would reach the quarter-finals of the 1958 World Cup. 'In the second half Matthews practically took on Northern Ireland on his own,' one report said.

By Christmas, Matthews had played three more times for the national team. He played well in the 3-1 win over Wales at Wembley – well enough, in fact, for Frank Coles to note, misguidedly, that 'while Finney's international career is probably at an end, there is no sign yet, thank goodness, that Matthews has passed his peak'. But it was two weeks later in the 3-0 win over Yugoslavia, also at Wembley, that he produced what would be the last of his soaring performances for his country.

'He is better now than he was against us seventeen years ago – and he was the greatest in the world then,' Yugoslavia's coach, Moša Marjanović, said after Matthews had driven the visitors' defence to a range of illegal interventions in their failed attempts to stop him. Matthews wondered wryly whether staging the match at Twickenham would have been more appropriate. He was alluding to a very passable imitation of a rugby tackle performed on him by Branko Stanković, Yugoslavia's left-back and captain. The centre-half Ivan Horvat said: 'England were a one-man team – Matthews.'

The match against Denmark on 5 December at Wolves's Molineux ground was the first of England's four qualifying matches for the 1958 World Cup finals – and the first time they had played one against a country other than a British Isles team. In the authorised biography of Matthews's life, it says that intestinal problems that troubled him for years flared up before this match and may have been why he played an unusually peripheral part in it. It was the reason he spent the night before the match staying with his mother rather than with the team in Wolverhampton.

By the time of England's next match against Scotland in early

March, Matthews was a Commander of the Order of the British Empire (CBE), having been recognised in the 1957 New Year Honours. He was now a heartbeat away from a knighthood, which failed to inspire an elevated performance in a 2-1 win against the Scots. He did, though, lay on the title-winning goal in this his final appearance in the British championship.

With six minutes to go, Matthews found himself in a familiar position: hemmed in by defenders on one side and the Wembley touchline on the other and a match to be won. His response was typically deft. He stood two defenders on their heels, squared the ball into the goalmouth and, on this occasion, watched Duncan Edwards thunder a first-time shot into Scotland's net.

What with his modest performance against Scotland and suffering ankle and thigh injuries that kept him out of the Blackpool team while they finished a creditable fourth in the table, Matthews had a disappointing end to the 1956–7 season. Given this, he may have reflected it was only to be expected that a customs officer took him aside at Manchester airport. He was returning from a club friendly against Anderlecht. The officer wanted £12 10s. off him for the tape recorder he had received as a tribute gift from the Belgian club.

The England selectors chose not to continue his run of misfortune, although their faith in his powers survived for only two more matches. Both were World Cup games that England won comfortably to ease towards qualification for the 1958 finals.

Of the forwards who played against Scotland, Matthews was the only one to keep his place against the Republic of Ireland for his final Wembley appearance on Wednesday 8 May 1957. John Atyeo's restoration to the side, apparently at inside-right, was the key selection. In fact, Walter Winterbottom deployed the Bristol City player as a second centre-forward alongside Manchester United's Tommy Taylor, which was a success in that they shared the goals in a 5-1 victory. But Winterbottom's experimental arrangement meant that Matthews was stranded without an inside-forward. Geoffrey Green reported that 'he got little from Atyeo'.

It was much the same against Denmark in Copenhagen a week later. Matthews's selection for his eighty-fourth England appearance, twenty-three years after the first, had caused a stir in the Danish capital. The headline 'Matthews Playing – Box Office Besieged' told its own story. Little did they know that it would be his last appearance for his national side. Once again, though, with Winterbottom retaining the Atyeo–Taylor partnership, the notional star of the show ended up with a bit part in the 4-1 victory. George Dick, the former Blackpool player who was now a coach in Denmark, watched the game. He said Matthews received just six passes in the second half. 'Time and again I heard him call for the ball, but he was ignored,' Dick said.

Not everyone saw this as an excuse, though. Desmond Hackett, making a name for himself in the press box, wrote a line in the *Daily Express* that may well have tallied with the selectors' thinking: 'It was sad to observe that the old master, Stanley Matthews, looked a very old master indeed.'

'We had no idea this would be Stanley's final England game, otherwise we would have carried him off shoulder high,' Billy Wright, the captain in Copenhagen, said years later, by which time he had suspended the misgivings he once had about Matthews's style of play. He added that such a gesture 'would have been only right for one of the greatest footballers of any time'.

Wright went further, adding his support to those who felt England erred by not taking Matthews to the 1958 World Cup finals. He recalled that only a year before the Copenhagen match he had played at left-back for Wolves against Blackpool, having been switched from centre-half by his manager, Stan Cullis, specifically to take care of Matthews. Instead, he said, he was made to look foolish and flat-footed.

After flying back from Copenhagen to London, Matthews ruled himself out of England's next match four days later against the Republic of Ireland. He told his wife in a telephone conversation that he had aggravated an ankle injury that he first suffered playing tennis the previous summer. He tested it with what he called 'a hard run', after which he said: 'I can walk and dribble the ball but I cannot get off the mark quickly enough.'

For the fixture in Dublin, in what turned out to be England's first match of the post-Matthews era, Finney moved to the right wing and David Pegg, another of the tragic Busby Babes, made his one England appearance, on the left wing, in a fortunate 1-1 draw.*

Matthews said he could have no complaints about losing his place. He did add, though, that he was very disappointed not to go to the World Cup in Sweden – and, with a substantial body of others, thought the selectors were wrong not to take him.

---

* Finney's cross in the last minute, headed home by Atyeo, saved England – but not Atyeo's international career. Like Matthews, Atyeo would not be chosen when the selectors picked their next team the following October, and neither man played for England again. If anything, dispensing with Matthews made more sense than discarding the twenty-five-year-old Atyeo, who had scored five goals in six internationals. In time, Atyeo became a maths teacher, opting for a more exact science than trying to fathom the England selectors.

Chapter 17

'I'm not going back as a peep-show or a gimmick'

Now heading for his forty-third birthday, and an England player no longer, Matthews played on for eight seasons, until the age of fifty, adding more than 160 Football League and FA Cup appearances. To an extent it was the longest curtain call in sporting history, but to regard it simply as this would be to underplay Matthews's continuing worth. His stout service for Stoke in 1962–3 when, in his late forties, he helped them to the Second Division title by playing in three-quarters of their matches was among the finest achievements of his career.

Unmistakably, though, these years were suffused with a sense of an astonishing life as a professional footballer being honoured.

One of the more bizarre celebrations took place eight days after Matthews played his last game for England in Copenhagen in May 1957. He had planned his latest African trip, taking in Ghana, South Africa and Nigeria, during the winter. He knew it would involve another quick turnaround at the end of the European season, but could not have foreseen what awaited him within hours of arriving in Accra.

Kwame Nkrumah, Ghana's Prime Minister, a man who understood the value of harnessing football's popular appeal, was determined to include the game's most renowned player in the celebrations marking his country's independence. Hence Matthews found himself, seated on a throne carved from a block of wood and ivory in the shape of an elephant, being crowned 'Soccerthone', the King of Soccer.

As well he might, in a news film of him, Matthews looked slightly bemused, swathed in a kente cloth, a sacred garment worn only on occasions of great importance, and crowned with a headdress of plaited fabric. At some point he had an ivory sword of office placed in his hand. Gin spirit was poured on the ground before the throne and two new footballs were placed at his feet. A witch doctor spat on the balls, having first danced around him chanting wildly. 'It was the greatest thrill of my life,' Matthews said. 'I wonder what they will say in Blackpool when they hear about it.'

Newsreel also exists of Matthews making one of his five appearances in Ghana. A voiceover, in what now sounds comically enunciated English, described the scene: 'Stanley Matthews, the ageless wizard, takes the field again but in case you hadn't noticed it's not Blackpool he's playing for this time. The scene is Accra stadium and his teammates are the Hearts of Oak, Ghana's leading side . . . over the bar, but never mind in a few minutes Stanley's back again as slippery as ever . . . all the spectators are cheering for Stanley, the uncrowned king of soccer.'

After Ghana, Matthews flew to Johannesburg for two matches. On the way home he stopped off in Nigeria, where he made one more exhibition appearance. In the South African games, between teams made up mostly of Transvaal players, Matthews showed off the stunts the crowd had come to see. Len Leisching, his marker in the first of the matches, said: 'I tried three slide tackles against Matthews. Each time I was badly beaten. I then made up my mind to keep on both feet. What happened? He came up to me with the ball seemingly glued to his feet and forced me to lose my balance. Then he was off like a flash.' Matthews's side won 7-3.

Two of Matthews's teammates in the Johannesburg matches, Johnny Hubbard and Don Kitchenbrand, South Africans who were on the books of Glasgow Rangers in Scotland, had memories of something different. In an incident related by Hubbard, he asked Matthews whether he would play for him in a benefit match in his hometown of Pretoria, to which Matthews replied: 'Tell you what, I'll take the gate takings and pay you.' Kitchenbrand said: 'Money was his game. Matthews was very shrewd, very tight with his money.'

It is impossible to know the spirit in which Matthews delivered his apparent rebuff to Hubbard or whether he had been inundated to breaking point with demands on his time. The incident does, though, have companion anecdotes about Matthews's impatience at unsolicited approaches, of which there were many.

Matthews's own recall of the trip was an understandably positive one. He talked about the excitement generated by the matches in which he played, a queue for one game forming at seven in the morning for a 4.15 p.m. kick-off. He returned home slightly early because of what he said was a minor muscle pull, but was soon back in action on the family tennis court.

Eleven-year-old Stanley Junior was making good progress. He won the Northern under-sixteen title and was the youngest of six boys recommended by the Lawn Tennis Association for a 'national sifting' programme. Twelve months on he would retain the Northern title and become Lancashire's youngest junior champion. Still only twelve, Stanley Junior moved to London to live with the Chesters in Finchley and continue his tennis development.

The feeling that the end of Matthews's career was nigh kept being discussed by commentators even though the man himself continually made it clear that it would not happen imminently.

When Matthews featured on BBC Television's *Hall of Fame*, he told the interviewer: 'I'm in pretty good shape still. I give myself another two years.' And yet when Blackpool visited Sheffield Wednesday the biggest crowd of the season turned up after a rumour circulated that this would be his last appearance at Hillsborough. Blackpool won 3-0 as 'Matthews pulverised the home defence with his devastating bursts of speed'.

In Nottingham, for Matthews's first appearance against Forest at the City Ground for twenty-five years, news that he would be playing sent 'everybody crazy with excitement', partly on the basis that he might not pass that way again. A crowd of nearly 42,000 watched him give 'an international-class performance'.

Blackpool were due to be the first English team to travel by air since eight Manchester United players lost their lives in the Munich air disaster that February. But their trip to Belgium in March 1958 to play a friendly against Standard Liège was cancelled – not for safety reasons, but because Matthews was injured. Liège told Blackpool not to travel. They had advertised Matthews would be playing and the club said it would be unfair to spectators to stage the match without him.

Belgians were not alone among overseas audiences who wanted to watch Matthews before he retired and worried that the last chance to do this might be rapidly approaching.

Matthews's presence was the main stipulation when Australia invited an English team to go there in the summer of 1958. In the first instance he was to be part of a Football Association party. Then Blackpool were to provide all the players. When a row broke out over first-class travel, Newcastle said they would go tourist class in Blackpool's place. The Australian organisers accepted this counter-offer, described by Blackpool as being 'in shocking taste', provided Matthews was in the Newcastle team. Finally, Blackpool undertook the trip after reaching a compromise that involved playing two extra matches.

Blackpool left for Australia a few hours after losing 2-1 at Tottenham, a result that meant they finished the 1957–8 season seventh in the table. Add this to a 5-1 third-round defeat in the FA Cup, during which the West Ham crowd sang 'Bye, Bye Blackpool', and the season was no more than so-so by the club's recent standards.

Matthews's worth to the side as a player and commercial presence was still unarguable even if his truly outstanding performances, as opposed to those when he acted his age, were no longer delivered as regularly as of old. He reserved one of his finest for Stamford Bridge in March 1958 when he visited thirty years' experience of humiliating full-backs on Chelsea's Ian McFarlane.

The young Chelsea side, occasionally referred to as Drake's Ducklings after their manager Ted Drake, scored early through Jimmy Greaves. Blackpool's cause looked lost not long afterwards when McFarlane crocked Matthews through what one writer described as a haphazard tackle. The injury to his right knee would keep Matthews out for most of the rest of the season, but not for the rest of the match. Bandaged up, he returned 'to exact revenge in the best and only way he knows'. Skimming this way and that over the squelching mud, he picked pitilessly on McFarlane in retribution for his earlier clumsiness. And by laying on three goals in Blackpool's 4-1 win he made the full-back's teammates suffer, too.

The preoccupation with when Matthews might retire meant the exit plans of another Blackpool veteran, manager Joe Smith, escaped the same sort of scrutiny. When the announcement came early in 1958 it took nearly everyone by surprise – not least Joe Smith.

In his autobiography, Matthews said it was still not clear, nearly half a century later, whether Smith left of his own accord or was pushed. In fact it was perfectly clear at the time: Smith, Blackpool's manager for twenty-three years – and the man responsible for bringing Matthews to Bloomfield Road – received a great big shove. Without any warning, the board offered him the chance to retire. When he refused it, he was told he would have to go at the end of the season. In a statement, the club said the time had come for a younger man to be appointed. Smith said: 'I never wanted anything like this to happen. I wanted to go out of the game quietly and sweetly. I think the way this thing has been done is lousy.'

Matthews may have forgotten all this because his birthday fell on the same day the Smith story broke. This anniversary was becoming a far greater distraction than he would have liked. The date 1 February was now heavily ringed in newsroom diaries all over the land to remind editors that Matthews was a year further into his forties. The year being 1958, he was forty-three. Being a Saturday made it an even better news item. Blackpool were playing at Aston Villa. Wally Hazelden, who at sixteen was Villa's youngest player, made a presentation. A crowd of 45,000 watched a 1-1 draw in which Matthews 'played as if it was his twenty-first birthday'.

In the end, Smith accepted his fate. On the day of his last home match in charge, against Everton, he stepped forward with good grace to receive a cheque for £1,000 presented to him in front of the directors' box by Albert Hindley, the club chairman. Ronnie Suart, a former Blackpool player who had shown managerial promise at Scunthorpe, was already in place to succeed him.

Blackpool's 1958 tour of Australia could have been subtitled the Stanley Matthews Roadshow, the hosts having said, in effect, they didn't mind who came just as long as Matthews was one of them. He was the player people wanted to meet and watch. He even took his family with him, paid for by the organisers in their eagerness to ensure his participation. With his keen eye for exacting benefit of any kind, Matthews did not miss the opportunity to secure superior tennis tuition for his son while in Australia. He arranged for young Stanley to spend time in the care of Harry Hopman, an outstanding coach who was involved with sixteen winning Australia Davis Cup teams.

The tour in fact began in the United States, where the team arrived having been pampered in first class on a flight aboard a Boeing Stratocruiser.* They had a comfortable ride, too, in the one match they played in America, the Los Angeles All Stars being dispatched 13-2.

The standard of football in Australia, where they played twelve matches, was rising but was still not particularly high. An FA team who went there in 1951 had won their 20 matches, scoring 153 goals against 14. This time, Blackpool scored 73 and conceded nine. The closest result was a 1-0 win over an Australia XI in Adelaide. A week later, again against an Australia XI, Matthews scored in a 7-0 win in Melbourne watched by a crowd of 30,000.

In Hong Kong on the way home, Blackpool played twice and maintained their unbeaten record. Thousands turned out to greet Matthews, an extraordinary response given that there had been no television to promote the tour. 'The Matthews adulation reached fever pitch,' Armfield said. 'The fans went absolutely crazy.' He remembered thinking that Matthews was truly a world figure, a comparative rarity for that time. As elsewhere, everyone in Hong Kong wanted to know how much longer Matthews would keep playing. When a reporter asked him the inevitable question, he said: 'Two more years and then I will reconsider my plans.'

A more critical audience awaited him in England. At the start of the new season journalists were not alone in giving Matthews more uneven reviews than at any time since his earliest days

---

* Jimmy Armfield said that none of the players had experienced anything like the treatment aboard the Stratocruiser that flew them to America. The plane was the ultimate in luxury with the team sitting on the upper of two decks. They were served a three-course dinner with a liveried steward carving roast beef from a silver trolley. Downstairs a bar provided space for passengers to drink and chat.

as a professional. A letter to the local paper after Blackpool drew at home against Everton in October 1958 complained that he received too many passes in view of the fact that when in possession 'he held the ball until the opposition's defence massed'. Matthews answered back with vintage performances at Leicester, where he 'completely disorganised the stumbling City defence' in a 3-0 win, and at Highbury where he 'wrecked the Arsenal defence' in a 4-1 upset watched by 54,792. On the other hand he was good but mostly average in Blackpool's last decent cup run while he was still there, in 1958–9, when they lost in a quarter-final replay at Leicester.

Saddest of all that season was the League match at Old Trafford, watched by nearly 62,000, where a section of the crowd booed Matthews whenever he touched the ball. The spectators who heckled thought he had dived when tackled by full-back Joe Carolan, resulting in a penalty that produced Blackpool's only goal against United's three. 'Why pick on me?' Matthews said. 'I didn't make the decision.'

Carolan absolved Matthews of blame, saying: 'I did not tackle Stanley very cleanly.' He also said: 'When you think of all the pleasure that Matthews has given to fans for so many years it seems little short of heresy that some of them should have turned on him in this spiteful way.' Maybe the heresy was a sign that spectators, once prepared to forgive him his trespasses, felt that as a declining star he no longer qualified for the reverence of old.*

To compound Matthews's unhappy afternoon he emerged from the match with an injury to his right knee, whether from Carolan's tackle is unclear. He played just a handful more matches that season and missed the first two months of 1959–60.

---

* Albert Hindley reckoned something else tinged the booing at Old Trafford. The Blackpool chairman thought it was 'an aftermath of Munich. United have been given such adulation – and deservedly given it after a magnificent comeback – that too many of their supporters seem to think that their team can do no wrong.'

While the injury was a message to many clubs that Matthews was now too old and crocked to be a sound investment, Stoke City and Port Vale saw value in trying to bring him back to the Potteries. Blackpool rebuffed the approaches of both. Hindley said: 'Matthews has always said that he wanted to finish his career at Blackpool and it is at Blackpool that he will finish it. When the end comes we will show again that we know how to treat our long-service players . . . But the end has not come yet and it would be absurd to say that it had.'

Hindley's words were almost certainly more tactical than accurate. Even in 1959 a football chairman being deliberately misleading over an important asset was hardly novel. In twelve years Matthews may have seen off four would-be successors to play on Blackpool's right wing – Albert Hobson, Rex Adams, Sandy Harris and Johnny McKenna – but reckoning that a forty-four-year-old's playing days were running out was clearly not absurd.*

His recurring knee trouble meant that 1959–60 was the first season, outside the war years, in which Matthews did not appear in an FA Cup tie since 1932–3. Also, he missed twenty-seven Football League matches. The knee was mostly to blame, but he was unavailable for the visit to Newcastle because of an attack of lumbago, the sort of ailment more associated with an old people's home than a professional football club. A letter to the Blackpool local paper suggested Newcastle's Irish left-back, Alf McMichael, was the real reason Matthews did not go to the North-East. Maybe, and the fact he had been absent from seven of Blackpool's twelve visits to St James' Park since the war gave some credibility to the theory. But it seems unlikely lumbago would have been cited had there been no truth in it.

---

* Tom Finney announced in April 1960 that he would retire at the end of the season – and he was seven years younger than Matthews. 'Tom's decision won't influence me,' Matthews said, a pronouncement that seemed particularly defiant in view of his physical condition at the time.

Unmistakably, Matthews's professional career was winding down, even if this process would take time – as proportionately long as the exceptional span of years when he was at his brilliant, burnished best.

There were still times when he could be mistaken for the gleaming model of the forties and fifties. In March 1960, during his one prolonged run in the team that season, Matthews featured in a sequence of five successive wins that steered Blackpool clear of relegation bother. It included gaining maximum points at Leeds, Manchester City and Chelsea with Matthews's performance in the 3-2 victory at Stamford Bridge summed up thus in one report: 'The crowd was enthralled; the Chelsea defence nonplussed.'

Also, when free of injury, he demonstrated the stamina of a much younger player. In 1960–1, his last full season at Blackpool, he appeared in well over half their League and FA Cup matches – twenty-eight out of forty-three – and would go on to make more than sixty appearances during his short second stint at Stoke.

If the adulation at home was less intense, when Matthews went overseas he still enjoyed a level of uncritical acclaim that surpassed even that which he had been used to when creating his own legend in England. In the summer of 1960 he was warmly received in South Africa, and afterwards on a short coaching trip to Australia. He arrived for his third visit to South Africa in May. His old friends Lubbe Snoyman and Syd Chaitowitz, the owner of Johannesburg Rangers FC, met him at Jan Smuts airport and hyped up his return to Johannesburg by driving him into the city in a pink Cadillac convertible. They kept having to slow down so that Matthews could acknowledge groups of bystanders who waved and cheered.

Matthews stayed for nine weeks and played fourteen matches, invariably turning the ultimate team sport into one-man exhibitions. He was less popular with Fifa, football's international governing body, for playing some of these games as a guest for Rangers in South Africa's National Football League. The ad hoc arrangement was seen as an unwanted precedent that could undermine the character of the NFL, and spread to other national leagues. Fifa took steps to prevent this happening.

One other controversy provided insight into Matthews's position on a subject of mounting international concern, South African politics, and his reasons for coaching in the black townships, of which much has been made.

Just before he left England, an article in a South African newspaper accused Matthews of being a signatory to a letter condemning the white-ruled country's policy of racial segregation, known as apartheid. Matthews denounced this as 'a pack of lies', while an English newspaper, which reported the stir the episode caused, said: 'Matthews has always said that politics are politics and football is football and there is no sensible reason why the twain should ever meet.'

Also relevant was Matthews's request to pay 'a courtesy call' on a member of South Africa's cabinet. This resulted in his meeting Ben Schoeman, the Minister of Transport, who was described as a keen sportsman.

Matthews's denunciation of the letter and his visit to Schoeman support the idea that he was, at the very least, indifferent to South Africa's internal politics and it was circumstances rather than an abhorrence of apartheid that, in the first instance, led him to coach in the townships. This would tie in with a life hitherto uncluttered by the call of messianic impulses. But once engaged in the townships Matthews would almost certainly have related emotionally to youngsters who, like him, had enjoyed few privileges at an early age.

He returned from South Africa for his final season with Blackpool, when the club narrowly avoided relegation. By mid-October they had won only one of their thirteen League matches and were bottom of the table. Matthews had a leg injury and missed the one win, a 5-3 victory over Aston Villa, that attracted fewer than 20,000 to Bloomfield Road. No one could remember when a match in August had stimulated such apathy.

The arrival of inside-forward Ray Parry, bought for £25,000 from Bolton, marked the start of a brief rally before another spell of poor results. These included a 6-2 defeat at Second Division Scunthorpe in what was Matthews's forty-ninth FA Cup appearance for the club out of a possible fifty-four – and, as it turned out, his last for them, too. Occasional unforeseen wins – 5-2 and 2-0 over Wolves and Manchester United respectively – and a 2-1 victory against another team in trouble, Newcastle, in which Matthews, after passing a late fitness test, laid on the winner, heaved them out of last place in mid-April.

They ended up one position above the relegated clubs – Newcastle and the now Finney-less Preston North End – having made sure they would not go down on the second to last Saturday with a 2-0 win at Birmingham. Even the abstemious Matthews, having contributed fully to this success, sipped the champagne delivered to Blackpool's dressing room by the Birmingham chairman, David Wiseman, after the game. He was left out of the final fixture against Manchester City because 'he was feeling the strain of recent matches'. This at least gave him time to pause before flying to North America, having been signed to play for Toronto City in the newly formed, four-team Eastern Canada Professional Soccer League.

One factor that may account for Blackpool's poor season was difficulties that arose over manager Ron Suart's efforts to join the rush to dismantle, finally, the antique WM system. More specifically, Stanley Matthews may have been the problem that undermined Suart's efforts.

This supposedly more flexible age in terms of field positions still required players to follow a script. Matthews, indulged by Joe Smith, had never been good at this, even when there was general acceptance of the old, more rigid system. Suart's experiment in deploying Matthews in different positions was soon frustrated by the player's wanderings. Matthews said he fell out with the manager over the latter's insistence that when picked on the wing Matthews stayed on the wing. No manager he had played under, at club or international level, had ever done this before, Matthews said. 'Were they wrong?' he asked.

In a match at West Ham in September 1960, with Matthews this time deployed as a deep-lying centre-forward, the home team were also experimenting, with a 4-2-4 line-up. The result was a lively 3-3 draw, but neither players nor spectators quite knew what was happening. 'The game was so bizarre at times that it was difficult to judge the playing merits of either side,' a match report said.

Matthews again started off in a central role in Blackpool's next match, a visit to Bloomfield Road by Chelsea, but repaired to the wing after the visitors took an early lead. This caused further confusion and Chelsea won 4-1. For the remainder of the season Suart found Matthews an unstable presence. His availability was unreliable because of fitness problems and, when he did play, he tended to give greater priority to his own concerns – such as how he was coping with his full-back – than to Suart's carefully laid plans.

Matthews said that with things deteriorating between him and Suart during the 1960–61 season they both figured the time had come for him to leave the club.

But as the sporting career of one Matthews ebbed, that of another flowed with youthful promise. On 10 September 1960, Matthews went to London to see Stanley Junior beat Keith Wooldridge 6-2, 6-4 in the final of the British junior championships on the hard courts at Wimbledon. At fourteen years and nine months, he was the youngest winner of one of the country's most prized titles for emerging stars.

As with his own triumphs, Matthews refused to make a fuss of his offspring's successes – nor of his role in enabling them. In addition to his support and encouragement, he was a faithful practice partner. Even on harsh winter days, father and son would hit together on a public cement court in a converted hangar at Blackpool's old Stanley Park Aerodrome. The cramped court had only a two-yard run-back behind the baseline. Stanley Junior recalled that at times it was so cold they would heat the balls on a stove 'so they would be a little livelier'.*

The year 1961 saw one highly significant development towards an improvement in pay. Led by the Fulham player Jimmy Hill, a personable and persuasive character who would later be an innovative manager at Coventry and then a trenchant media pundit, the Professional Footballers' Association won their battle to end the maximum wage, then £20.

Throughout the dispute Matthews was closely involved. Early on he spoke out against strike action, which he said he opposed on principle, but changed to supporting it, because, he said, his Blackpool teammates were in favour and his loyalty to them was paramount. His greatest contribution, though, was at a PFA meeting at Belle Vue, Manchester, by the effortless device of having his name invoked during the main debate.

Several versions have been recorded of what many regarded as the pivotal exchange in the discussion. This one is what Jimmy Armfield, Blackpool's union delegate who was sitting next to Matthews, remembered:

'My dad's a miner, earning £10 a week,' a young player said. 'I play in the lower divisions and I earn twice as much. I train in

---

* Matthews's support for young Stanley was, quite possibly, partly responsible for the failure of the first attempt by television to screen Football League matches live on a regular basis. ITV struck a £150,000 deal with the League in 1960 and chose as their first match a fixture at Bloomfield Road between Blackpool and Bolton – on the same September Saturday as the junior final at Wimbledon. ITV executives presumably had Matthews in mind when they picked Blackpool. This backfired when he did not play, on the pretext of being injured, and went instead to watch his son. The injury that Matthews cited for withdrawing had not stopped him turning out the previous Monday nor would it a week later. Further disappointments followed for ITV, when Tottenham and Arsenal barred cameras from their grounds. In November they abandoned the deal.

the open air and play football on Saturday – he's down the pit for eight hours at a time, five days a week. That can't be right. We earn quite enough as it is.'

'I'll answer that, Mr Chairman,' Tommy Banks, the Bolton and England full-back, who had risen quickly to his feet, said. 'Now then, son, thee tell thi father from me, I can do his job. In fact, I've done it. And so can any one of these lads in this hall, including thee. But if thi father wants to know why we want more brass, tell them to come and play against Brother Matthews in front of 30,000 fans. That's why we want more money.'

What made Banks's impromptu speech all the more powerful was his reputation as one of the few full-backs who relished playing against Matthews, while Matthews was known to be correspondingly wary of the Bolton hard man. As Banks sat down, laughter and cheers rang around Belle Vue, no one laughing louder than Brother Matthews. 'I believe that moment turned the meeting,' Armfield said.

Not long afterwards, at the end of the 1960–61 season, Blackpool announced they had offered contracts to thirty-four of their players under the new, unrestricted wage agreement. Matthews, despite, as he put it, no longer seeing eye to eye with Suart, was one of them. Speculation about how much he would earn ranged from £25 a week to 'about £100', the latter figure reported by a national newspaper. Matthews, in Canada by now, denied the £100 claim. All the club would say was that only one player had been offered more than the forty-six-year-old winger, the figure being more than £25 and less than three figures.

The issue, if it was one at all, soon became irrelevant. Matthews's time as a Blackpool player was about to come to an end after his trip to Canada helped to strain further his relations with Suart. This was not because he went abroad but because he spent much longer away than Suart – and Betty Matthews – expected.

It is not hard to work out what the big attraction was for

Matthews in Canada. Steve Stavro, the Canadian grocery-store magnate who would remain an influential figure in Matthews's life, was responsible for Toronto City signing him up in 1961. Stavro, seven years old when his family arrived in Toronto from Greece in 1927, was a big ideas man. These ideas had brought him massive wealth in the retail business. When the Eastern Canada Professional Soccer League launched he decided the key to success would be signing foreign players even Canadians knew about. In discussions the name Stanley Matthews recurred more than any other. Stavro duly dispatched George Gross, a journalist who was Toronto City's general manager, to England to get their man, money no great object. Gross sealed a deal with Matthews while the pair sat in the stands watching Stanley Junior play tennis in Bournemouth.

Doing very nicely in Canada, Matthews evidently did not find it hard to push the new English season to the back of his mind. The club started to worry and sent a letter telling him to be back for training by 19 July 1961. Two weeks before this deadline Betty said that there had been no suggestion in his letters home that his return would be later than this. Then, with two days to go, a cable arrived from Matthews asking Blackpool for an extension so that he could stay in Canada to continue treatment for an old internal complaint. The club agreed. They put back the date they wanted him to report to Bloomfield Road to 5 August, in time for a practice game three days later and fixtures in Northern Ireland on 11 and 12 August.

There was still no sign of Matthews on the day of the practice match and there were barely twenty-four hours to go before the first fixture in Ireland when he rang the club to say he would be back imminently. So it was that he touched down in London on the morning of the match against Distillery and straightaway boarded a flight to Belfast, where Suart met him in the foyer of the team's hotel. Suart's public greeting was friendly enough: 'It's a pleasure to see you here.' He then ushered Matthews away and spent the next twenty minutes talking to him in private. He emerged to say: 'Matthews and I have discussed the position and I shall be reporting to the directors.'

Matthews said, mistakenly, in his 2000 autobiography that he had been in South Africa immediately before flying back for the matches in Northern Ireland. In fact, he expunged from his several memoirs nearly all reference to the controversial trip to Canada. At the time he hedged around the reasons for his overdue return. 'I know that I am six days late,' he said, 'but I did promise Blackpool I would be back in time for the start of the League season [on 19 August] . . . I did not realise until this week that my presence in Ireland was so essential.'

Was he dissembling here? It seems highly likely in light of what Canadian newspapers had reported. Clearly Matthews had given serious thought to staying on until after the start of the League season in England. Stavro's wealth meant he was being rewarded well beyond what he earned for playing in England. He received $500 Canadian (£180) a match plus expenses for his fifteen appearances for Toronto City and had indicated he would play in an exhibition match for Toronto against Real Madrid in Vancouver on 25 August, presumably having been promised further remuneration. Frank Bain, secretary of the British Columbia Soccer Commission, told the *Vancouver Sun* that Matthews had informed him he was looking forward to playing in the game against Real Madrid.

Right the way through Matthews seems to have been pushing his luck, encouraged to do so no doubt because he knew Suart was not particularly keen to keep him at Bloomfield Road. He may have been feeling a little guilty, though, about his late return from Canada because he made himself available for both matches in Northern Ireland, a risky thing to do straight after his twenty-two-hour journey from North America.

And so it proved when he broke down in the second of the matches. He gave a performance that excited the crowd in

Blackpool's 5-1 win over Distillery in Belfast. But the next day against Portadown he lasted less than twenty minutes before suffering a recurrence of the knee injury that had been troubling him for two years. He had been in too much of a hurry to make amends and would now miss the start of the new season.

After hearing what Suart had to say, Albert Hindley, the Blackpool chairman, called a full board meeting to discuss Matthews's tardy return from Canada. This took place in Blackpool three days after the Portadown match. The statement that followed read: 'The matter has been considered and no further comment is to be made at all.' In other words, Matthews had received a rollicking.

The story that Matthews would leave Blackpool, after fourteen years and 428 League and FA Cup appearances, and return to Stoke broke on Monday 16 October 1961. Journalists knew something was afoot before the transfer was officially announced – and not all of them approved. Desmond Hackett, well paid by the *Daily Express* for his trenchant opinions, said Matthews was wrong to carry on playing. His comments appeared under the headline: 'Don't Do It, Stan. Retire with Pride – now'. Which may be why, when the deal was sealed, Matthews was keen to stress he was not going back as 'a peep-show or a gimmick. I have too much respect for myself and football for that.'

Stoke had never really given up on re-signing Matthews. As one paper put it, they had popped the question almost annually in recent seasons. Then Tony Waddington, the Stoke manager, took up the chase with enthusiasm. He had arrived at the Victoria Ground as youth team coach in 1953 after injury ended his playing career at Crewe. He was made first-team manager, aged only thirty-five, in 1960 and was soon on Matthews's trail, encouraged by Jackie Mudie, Matthews's great friend and former Blackpool teammate who had been at Stoke for six months.

The enthusiasm with which Waddington pursued Matthews was in contrast to the strained relationship that would exist between the two men during much of the time they were together at Stoke. Matthews's considerable seniority, an unusual position for a player in respect to his manager, and his much higher profile did not help and he would never really succumb to Waddington's control. On one occasion, when Matthews expected to be playing at the Victoria Ground, he found out that Waddington had not picked him only when he arrived in Stoke the night before the match and read it in the local paper as he booked into his hotel. He was soon driving back to his Blackpool home.

Very little became public, but almost as much grit built up in Matthews's relationship with the club during his second spell at the Victoria Ground as had accumulated by the time he first left in 1947. The idea that this was personal, between Waddington and his star signing, was evident from an exchange Matthews had, some years later, with a player who was with him at Stoke second time around. Matthews reacted with incredulity when his friend Dennis Viollet wrote to him from the United States casting a benevolent light on Waddington in comparison to a manager he had played under in America. 'I cannot believe Waddo was "an angel" compared to your manager,' Matthews wrote back.

Despite this, Matthews's second coming to Stoke would work to the considerable benefit of both player and manager – and the club – and they did the best they could to rub along while he was still playing. Matthews's wife, Betty, was the one person who was against his going back to the Victoria Ground. She was not happy about him playing in the Second Division and, although she was glad they were staying put in Blackpool, the arrangement, as far as she was concerned, had an additional downside. It meant her husband spending extra nights away, even for home games when he would book into a Stoke hotel the night before. It can only be supposed that Matthews was not as upset about this as she was.

Waddington had tried to sign him nearly a month earlier than he did when he heard Matthews, having recovered from the knee injury, had been selected for Blackpool reserves. Waddington wanted him for Stoke's match against Norwich City on 23 September. Blackpool did not dismiss the possibility but told Waddington that 'because of circumstances it could not be pursued for a fortnight or so'.

After Matthews played two games in the reserves, he regained his first-team place at Blackpool for the next two fixtures. The second of these, at Arsenal on 7 October, would be his last appearance for the club. Although no one realised its significance at the time, the match proved a fitting send-off with 41,166 descending on Highbury. The result was less appropriate – a 3-0 win for Arsenal.

Stoke were playing in the capital the same day and Waddington – by chance, apparently – met Matthews in a central London hotel. This gave him the opportunity to check for himself that they both wanted the transfer when the time was right. They parted not knowing that this would be in just over a week, after Ron Suart dropped Matthews for the visit of Bolton to Bloomfield Road on Saturday 14 October.

Again by chance, apparently, Albert Henshall, the Stoke chairman, was staying in Blackpool on the weekend of the Bolton game. He was watching the Ryder Cup golf match at Royal Lytham & St Annes, a course just to the south of the town. Matthews had helped him find a hotel room and Henshall said he planned to go to Bloomfield Road as a spectator on the Saturday. When news reached him that Matthews would not be playing he contacted Blackpool. 'I knew he might be thinking of a transfer,' Henshall said.

On the following Tuesday the Blackpool board summoned Matthews to a meeting, at which Waddington was also present. Matthews came out less than fifteen minutes later, having agreed to the move on the understanding he could continue to live and train in Blackpool. 'Stan wouldn't discuss the terms of his contract,' Waddington said, 'he just signed the forms and said, "You fill in the details".' A public signing took place on the BBC Television programme *Sportsview*, an idea of Waddington's that Matthews said he agreed to reluctantly.

Matthews recalled years later that there had been some nastiness at the board meeting over the question of a transfer fee. He said the figure was £3,500, while newspapers put it at less than £3,000. The clubs described it as nominal. 'There is no question of a transfer fee in itself,' Waddington said, confusing things further, 'but certain other things have to be settled.'

What sparked the unpleasantness, Matthews said, was a board member telling him that Blackpool had made him as a player, which was why the club wanted and deserved a fee. Matthews reacted furiously to this because, he said, he was already upset about a fee being asked for at all. '"You – made – ME?" I said, totally flabbergasted.' He wanted the fee to be waived in recognition of his fourteen years' service and given that an impoverished Stoke could barely afford it.

At the time, nothing was made of this, not publicly any-way. Albert Henshall said: 'Frankly it would have been an embarrassment to haggle over Stanley at this stage of his career. No fee could represent what football feels about him.' An indication a transfer fee was involved was an idea that circulated in Stoke, and was reported in the press, that local traders should be asked to pay it. This would be as a thank-you for the increased takings they could expect every time Matthews played at home in front of hugely inflated attendances.

The 'other things' Waddington referred to included a £1,000 long-service benefit due shortly to Matthews, a £300 payment for his signing for another club not having sought the transfer, and what to do about the testimonial match that Blackpool had promised him when it looked as though he would end his career there. All this seems to have been settled amicably, including the testimonial question. Hindley said Stoke should 'be assured we [Blackpool] shall make a substantial contribution to it'.

Stoke were struggling when Matthews rejoined them. They had finished eighteenth in the Second Division the previous season and now, after thirteen games of 1961–2, were in nineteenth place with ten points. Matthews could have played at Plymouth Argyle, Stoke's first match after his transfer. Waddington reasoned a more effective way of using his return to re-engage disaffected fans would be if his comeback appearance was at the Victoria Ground. This meant putting it back until the home game against Huddersfield a week later.

The 3-1 defeat at Plymouth meant Stoke had slipped even further down the table when, on 28 October, Matthews stepped out in the colours of his original club for the first time since 19 April 1947. He spent the night before the match at the North Stafford Hotel. He was as nervous as he had ever been before a game. Peter Buxton said that Matthews lay in his room for hours under a towel, like a boxer before a big fight. When Betty came to see him on the day of the match he asked her to leave.

Betty was one of several family members who went to the match. The others were Matthews's brothers, Jack, Arthur and Ron, his children, Jean and Stanley Junior, and his seventy-five-year-old mother, Ada, whose presence underlined what a special occasion it was. She had not watched him play since the 1953 FA Cup final. 'Mother only decided to come an hour or so before kick-off,' Ron said. 'The family thought that as her heart was not too strong the excitement might be too much for her – but she made up her mind to go.'

As was his custom, whether he had stayed in a hotel or arrived on match day by train, Matthews walked to the ground, mingling with the many thousands drawn as never before to an event in Stoke. At some point after his arrival he presented each of his teammates with 'a snappy new trilby', a curious choice of gift although it was in keeping with his preoccupation with things sartorial.

The long build-up and rituals over, the first, vital test of whether his homecoming would be a success was at hand. His presence had already had an effect on the players. Geoff Hickson, Stoke's reserve goalkeeper, said the day after the signing was announced 'there was a buzz in the dressing room. Suddenly the room became silent. Tony Waddington had quietly opened the door and walked in, unannounced, with Stanley Matthews. I have never felt such a powerful presence. The hair on the back of my neck stood up and I shivered. We were in the presence of greatness.'

Would the fans' reaction reflect a similar sense of wonder? 'It exceeded everything you could have hoped for,' Buxton said. A crowd of 8,409 had watched Stoke's last home game against Preston North End. Now there were 35,974 paying £6,545, another indication of how cheap it still was to go to football. A headline in Stoke's evening paper said: 'Eager Fans Cause Miles-Long Jams on Way to Ground'. And, on top of it all, Stoke won 3-0.

Matthews, with Ray Wilson, the England left-back, marking him, had a quiet but effective game. This was the occasion when Wilson said he only had to cough with Matthews nearby and he was penalised. There may have been a sliver of truth in it. Without being particularly conspicuous, Matthews contributed fully and, aided by a referee who did, perhaps, feel a duty of care, 'had a passing hand in all Stoke's goals'. At the end many of the crowd and some of the directors were in tears, Buxton said.

Stoke's next match at Swansea, watched by a season's best for the Vetch Field of 12,127, was lost 1-0, which meant they were now just one position above the two relegation places – and made it all the more improbable that by the end of the year the talk was of promotion to the First Division. They won six of their next eight League matches, Matthews scoring in two of them, and drew the other two. The fourteen points meant they were up to seventh in the table when they won 2-0 at Bury on Boxing Day, nine points behind leaders Liverpool.

The rest of the season did not go quite so well, even after Waddington had 'exploited Stan to the maximum' by using him to lure Dennis Viollet, one of Manchester United's Munich survivors, to the club for £23,000. Disappointments included a 1-0 FA Cup defeat by Blackburn in front of 49,486 at the Victoria Ground, a turnout that yielded unprecedented receipts of £9,204. Such was the anguish at the match-deciding penalty that one Stoke fan filed a lawsuit against the referee for damages. In the League, with Matthews in and out of the side with his old knee trouble, results were uneven. It did not matter. Eighth place in the final table was more than could have been hoped for before the Wizard came along to sprinkle his stardust.

In terms of financial benefit, Matthews wiped out several times over whatever fee Stoke had paid for him. Average gates for home League matches in 1961–2, including the ones before Matthews arrived, were up by 6,181, making an aggregate increase of nearly 130,000. Then there were the takings from the FA Cup tie against Blackburn and, before that, a money-minting third-round replay against Leicester, when 38,315 saw Matthews score his first cup goal since 1953 as Stoke beat the First Division visitors 5-2. With total gate receipts up by more than 60 per cent to £80,680, an overall loss of £7,108 the previous year became a profit of £16,577.

At the annual meeting Waddington was congratulated on 'a stroke of genius' in bringing back Matthews. Henshall said: 'Stan's return was undoubtedly the highlight of the season. Apart from pulling the crowds in he had an almost magical effect on his teammates and supporters alike.'

Chapter 18

'Kick the old devil. He's been killing us and
you're waving him past'

Matthews's travels of the previous year, and their repercussions, did nothing to discourage him from taking off again in the summer of 1962. His compulsion to climb aboard an aeroplane whenever possible was as strong as ever, maybe even stronger now that his two children, to whom he had been such a devoted parent, were starting to make their own lives.

He had already been briefly to Toronto in February, a three-day trip that coincided with his forty-seventh birthday and took in a guest appearance at a sportswriters' dinner. What he was unable to do now was return to Canada to play for Toronto City – or fulfil an agreement to play eight games for the Australian club Moreland. The Football League had banned players from summer commitments to overseas teams, a measure that may have had something to do with Matthews's late return the previous August. Announcing the ban, Alan Hardaker, the League secretary, complained that players had come back stale and overworked. South Africa, too, was no longer somewhere Matthews could turn up and play regularly. In September 1961, Fifa had suspended the country's membership over its policy of racial segregation that had already landed Matthews in one minor controversy.

Instead, Matthews went to Israel to appear in exhibition matches. From there he joined his Stoke teammates on a tour of Turkey and then flew to South Africa on what amounted to a social visit. He was back in time to watch, with Betty and Jean, his son achieve the greatest of his tennis successes when he won Junior Wimbledon.*

Of the forty-one Football League games Matthews Senior had left in legs that had already covered thousands of playing miles – many of them while manoeuvring a heavy leather ball over the badly churned surfaces that were taken for granted throughout his career – all but ten were as his heroic contribution to Stoke's centenary season, 1962–3.

Mudie, Matthews and Viollet had brought flair to the attack, which Waddington would add to by once again using Matthews as bait, this time to sign Jimmy McIlroy from Burnley in early March. The manager also beefed up the squad by acquiring Eddie Stuart, a South African who had been at Wolves for more than a decade, and Eddie Clamp, an expensive import from Arsenal who took on the role of Matthews's unofficial minder. Matthews said that Clamp was the only player he knew to be tougher than Stuart. 'Stoke now had the two hardest players in the Football League,' he said.

Artist and artisan did not blend straightaway. After a 0-0 draw at Luton on 8 September 1962, Stoke were seventeenth in the Second Division with a record of played six, won none, lost two, drawn four. The Luton result was, though, the third draw in a row and the successful fusion of the disparate talents was

---

* The tournament, against a field of some of the world's best young players, was a proper examination of his ability. He reached the final by beating players from Switzerland, Poland, West Germany and Austria for the loss of one set, and then defeated the Soviet player Alex Metreveli, who, eleven years later, would reach the Wimbledon men's final, to take the title.

under way. With Matthews husbanding his physical resources to combine dangerously with Mudie on the right, and Stuart and Clamp buttressing a defence known as the Waddington Wall, Stoke remained unbeaten for a further fifteen matches, eight of which were won. By Christmas they were poised just behind the leaders.

Snow and arctic temperatures that set in just before the new year brought a halt, not just to Stoke's progress, but to most outdoor sports and many other activities in the British Isles for the next several months. Having won 2-1 at Rotherham on Boxing Day, Stoke did not play another competitive match until 2 March 1963 when they beat Walsall 3-0 to go fifth in the table. Four days later they lost 3-1 at Leeds in the FA Cup, the third-round tie scheduled for 5 January having been postponed eleven times.

Matthews spoke of his boredom during the long periods of inactivity although there were compensations. It meant his daughter's marriage to Bob Gough, a bank employee, took place without any playing distractions, and he had time to rest his still troublesome knee. There was also his forty-eighth birthday, but this hardly qualified as a compensation.

If ever Stoke needed a reinvigorated Matthews as a vital source of inspiration, now was the time. Even with a three-week extension to the season, a fixture list that should have unwound over four months was concertinaed into less than three. And Stoke had the added burden of a club centenary match when the great Real Madrid side visited in April. Matthews's contribution would be far greater than simply being a talisman.

Soon after the season resumed, Stoke went top during a sequence of six wins and one draw. Two of these matches were against title contenders Sunderland. A goalless draw in front of 62,138 at Roker Park on Good Friday preceded Stoke's 2-1 victory on Easter Monday when 42,366 were at the Victoria Ground. They then stumbled at the end of April/beginning of

May, losing three times in a row. After the third of these defeats, it was Matthews who rallied the team. Voted Footballer of the Year for the second time by the Football Writers' Association, he gave two superb performances in a top-of-the-table encounter at Chelsea and a home match against Luton. The wins not only helped to settle Stoke's promotion, they sent them up as Second Division champions.

The 1-0 win at Chelsea on Saturday 11 May, watched by 66,199, had echoes of Matthews's visit to Stamford Bridge with Blackpool in March 1958. Then, full-back Ian McFarlane, with his 'haphazard tackle', set Matthews's competitive fires ablaze; now, half-back Ron Harris, whose nickname Chopper told its own story, rekindled them.

In his autobiography, Matthews devoted eight pages to the 1963 Chelsea match, mostly colourful stuff about how Harris set about him. If none of the newspaper reports made quite so much of this confrontation, they did agree that Harris had opened with a brutal tackle in the first minute that ignored the ball and propelled Matthews into touch at high speed. Harris kept this up, Matthews said, for twenty minutes before the referee finally intervened after another late tackle that ripped a large hole in his stocking. 'A bit late, son,' the ref said. 'Got there as quick as I could, ref,' Harris answered from his stock of quips.

Having simply been admonished, Harris kept up his barrage, prompting the first of two interventions by Eddie Clamp. As Matthews told it, Clamp took hold of Harris's shirt, called him a little sod and said he would take him out of the game if he clobbered Stanley again. After the referee separated them, Clamp came out with what Matthews described as one of the best lines ever uttered on a football pitch: 'That's the trouble with you referees, you don't care which side wins.' Clamp carried out his threat when Harris did clobber Matthews again just before half-time, subjecting him to a tackle the like of which, Matthews said, he had not seen in thirty years of football. 'I never had a spot of bother from Chopper Harris for the remainder of the match,' Matthews added.

The Chelsea player John Hollins, who missed the match through injury and watched from the stands, recalled that even the home fans disapproved of the treatment meted out to Matthews that day. 'It was very strange,' he said, referring to the first of Harris's heavy tackles. 'One moment our supporters were right behind the team, willing our players on, then went silent. It was as though they felt the promotion didn't amount to very much if we had to foul Stan Matthews to get it.'

Matthews made two telling ripostes to the roughing-up he received from Harris. The first was to play a big part with Mudie in the build-up to Jimmy McIlroy's deciding goal; the second was to help out in defence so willingly it might have been his normal practice.

Stoke, with three matches left, were now division leaders with a game in hand over Sunderland, who were a point behind, and Chelsea, a further two points back. Matthews was too bruised to play three days later at Bury, a match Stoke lost 2-1. This result meant that, come Saturday 18 May, Sunderland, who had won in midweek, topped the table by a point from Stoke. With a home match that day against Chelsea, they looked to have promotion within their grasp even if it was their final fixture while Stoke and Chelsea had two to play.

The outcomes that Saturday could not have turned out better for Waddington's team. Their 2-0 win over Luton and Chelsea's 1-0 success at Roker Park gave Stoke the title regardless of what happened in their final match. The crowd stood and applauded for two minutes after Matthews scored Stoke's second. Running on to McIlroy's through pass, he veered to his left past Luton's goalkeeper Ron Baynham and, with his left foot, passed the ball into the net for his seventy-first and last goal in the Football League. Thirty years after his key role in returning Stoke to the First Division the old dazzler in the No. 7 shirt had done it again.

The national press lauded Matthews's contribution, including Peter Wilson, the *Daily Mirror*'s 'Man They Couldn't Gag', who had been vociferous for some years in advising Matthews to retire. Reminded of this by Matthews, Wilson told him he had abandoned counselling this eight months before.

Stoke's successful season translated into home gate receipts of £83,224 – up by more than 40 per cent – but a slightly reduced overall profit of £12,046 as a result of transfer deals. Their sense of achievement contrasted with Sunderland's utter misery when Chelsea followed up beating them by trouncing Portsmouth 7-0. The result gave the London club the second promotion place on goal difference.

An even more striking contrast existed within the Stoke City community. It emerged that the mood of elation, particularly among the fans, was not universally shared by the dressing room. While Matthews's relationship with Waddington had long been edgy, Mudie's, it turned out, was no better. He said that the team weren't looked after as they should have been when they won promotion. The players had to pay for attending the celebration dinner and the promise of an overseas tour, with wives included, never happened. Mudie also said that Waddington wasn't straight with him over how much he earned compared to the others. The manager told him they were all paid the same, but Mudie found out his £40 a week was £10 less than Dennis Viollet and Jimmy McIlroy received.

Matthews said the greatest satisfaction Stoke's promotion gave him was that it legitimised his regular inclusion in the side. This was why he resolved to carry on playing when the team returned to the First Division. What he had not reckoned on was that an injury he picked up in the gentle surrounds of his back garden in Blackpool, rather than courtesy of some heavy-footed defender on the football field, would hasten the end of his career.

Hasten may sound an inappropriate verb, given that the end

had been nigh for some time, but Matthews might have gone on longer even than he did had he not strained his back playing tennis at home in late July. He said at the time: 'It is worrying because nothing like this has happened before.' It was the main reason he managed only nine League and four FA Cup games in 1963–4.

The 1963 close season had begun with Stoke playing four exhibition matches on a tour of Israel, one of them an additional fixture that brought Matthews a golden windfall. Albert Henshall, who was with the team, told how the organisers of the fixture were prepared to pay Stoke handsomely so long as Matthews played. At first Matthews refused. He had been suffering from heat exhaustion and said he wanted to put his feet up. When Waddington pressed him, Matthews made what he thought was such an unreasonable demand that the game would be called off. He asked for two hundred gold sovereigns – and was as surprised as everyone else when the next morning at breakfast a dishevelled Waddington appeared, took a leather bag from his pocket and spilled the glistening coins on the table. No one ever found out how Waddington had done it.

On his return from Israel, Matthews re-signed for another season at the Victoria Ground, which put an end to any thoughts of going to play either in South Africa or Canada. With restrictions still in place, only as a free agent could he have done this. Staying at home did, though, have its rewards.

He went to Buckingham Palace for one of the occasional lunches held by the Queen and Duke of Edinburgh for small groups of 'distinguished people', and he was feted in his birthplace when made the twenty-seventh Freeman of the City of Stoke-on-Trent. 'At 48,' the local newspaper noted, 'Matthews is only five years younger than the federated borough of Stoke-on-Trent.' He received his freedom a few days before hurting his back and arrived at the council chamber having played a 'blinder' in a Stoke City practice match in the morning.

Still, the highlight of his summer was probably a trip to Wimbledon with Betty to watch their son, now seventeen, play in the men's singles for the first time. Stanley Junior won his opening match easily against the Italian player Sergio Tacchini, now more famous for designing sportswear than his tennis. In the next round, on Court No. 2 – two heartbeats from Centre Court – he assumed what even then was a familiar British persona, that of the plucky tennis loser. He performed doughtily but unavailingly in going down 7-5, 4-6, 8-6, 6-2 to Rafael Osuna, the Mexican who by the end of the year would be a grand-slam champion, having won the US title. 'I've never seen Stanley play better,' said his father. 'On this showing all he needs is experience.'

As it turned out he needed more than that. Stanley Junior never quite realised the high expectations created by his Junior Wimbledon success. He would say many years later that having such a famous father did have an effect. It was one reason he chose tennis. He had been a very good young footballer but the opposition 'kicked the shit out of me . . . the mentality was, "We're going to get Stanley Matthews's son".' Then, as a tennis player, memory of his father meant success was expected while failure was seen as an act of treachery to his sporting genes.[*]

Stoke's first match back in the First Division since 1953 took place on 24 August 1963. It was too big an occasion for Matthews

---

[*] His one really memorable win as a senior was in the first round of the 1969 French Open when he beat Ilie Nastase four years before the Romanian won the game's major clay-court title. He beat Nastase by a curious scoreline 6-3, 0-6, 0-6, 6-4, 8-6 that may reflect his own steadiness and the Romanian's more mercurial nature. Matthews remembered that his one great moment of inspiration came in the fifth set when at break point down he went to the net after hitting a second serve to Nastase's strength, his forehand. 'I won the point,' he said, 'which I think I'd have done only once if I tried the same thing a hundred times.' At the end of his playing career Matthews moved to the United States where, faithful to his heritage, he coached until he was sixty. 'Would I have liked to have done better as a senior player? Sure,' Matthews said. 'But I played in the Davis Cup for Britain, was on the circuit for ten years and life has turned out great since I stopped playing in 1974.'

to miss, particularly as Tottenham Hotspur, championship runners-up the previous season, were visitors to the Victoria Ground. He did well on a placid afternoon in front of 40,000, laying on the first of Jimmy McIlroy's two goals in an encouraging 2-1 win, but his decision to play was ill-judged.

His back was not ready for ninety minutes' football and would be a recurring problem for the less than two years he remained a Football League player. He played his ninth and final League match of 1963–4 on 11 January, a 2-1 defeat at Leicester in which he saw little of the ball as Stoke dropped to nineteenth in the table with just Blackpool, Ipswich and Bolton below them. A chill removed the possibility of his playing in a home League match against Blackburn on his forty-ninth birthday, 1 February 1964, and it was on this day that, effectively and quite unexpectedly, he announced his retirement – or, more accurately, had it announced for him in curiously Delphic terms that lacked any input from the man himself.

The Stoke paper the *Evening Sentinel* reported on its front page: 'Stan Matthews has virtually retired from football after speculation dating back many years.

'On his forty-ninth birthday today the news was made known that Stan would only make enough appearances in the future to enable him to beat the Billy Meredith record before disappearing from the soccer scene he has graced since he made his League debut at Bury on March 19th, 1932 . . . He will probably make occasional appearances for Stoke City as required, but has given up the idea of being a regular member of the first team.'

The story was unsatisfactory. It went on to say that the decision 'has been made by Stan alone', but Waddington was the only one who spoke publicly about it. He said: 'Stan has been considering what would be the appropriate time for him to retire and we discussed the matter after the [FA Cup] match on Wednesday. There has been no disagreement, and the decision has nothing to do with Stan not playing on his birthday.'

If this were the case then surely Matthews could – and would – have said so. He had friends in the press whom he usually sought out on occasions such as this. Did his omission from the match on his birthday upset him and precipitate the announcement? Did he collude in the story, that his chill made it impossible for him to play, in return for certain favours, including a testimonial match? After all, he had driven down from Stoke the day before the Blackburn game wanting to play – and news that the club had granted him a testimonial broke a full year before it took place in April 1965, rather than a matter of weeks beforehand, as he wrote later.

Then there was the curious line about making enough appearances to beat Meredith's record. Matthews had already played more matches than the outstanding Wales international winger, so the record referred to must have been the age at which Meredith played his final game for Manchester City. This was 49 years 245 days in an FA Cup tie in 1924. But Matthews had addressed this: 'I'm not all that interested in that sort of record; not, in fact, interested in birth certificates at all.' Perhaps, even if Matthews did not mind whether he broke Meredith's age record, Stoke did not want to be seen to be denying him the chance to do so, which is why they offered the prospect of occasional appearances.

They proved to be very occasional indeed. After the announcement that he had 'virtually retired', he played only two more competitive matches, both at the Victoria Ground: an FA Cup fifth-round tie against Swansea on 15 February 1964 and his farewell League appearance, against Fulham, on 6 February 1965, by which time he was Sir Stanley Matthews and fifty years old.

He had already played three FA Cup ties in the early weeks of 1964, including a replay against Ipswich in the fourth round, when a 40,000 crowd saw him score Stoke's first against Swansea in a 2-2 draw. The goal, with a precise, left-footed shot from near the edge of the penalty area, made him the oldest scorer in the cup's history and was his last in any competition. His modest aggregate for such a long career was 9 FA Cup goals, 71 in the League, 11 for England and 2 for the Football League.

He hurt his right knee against Swansea and missed not only the replay, which Stoke lost 2-0, but the remainder of the season. Even without the injury he might not have played. Waddington admitted to a policy of 'use and discard' and, with Matthews now working out his days, the manager almost certainly regarded him as dispensable. By mid-April, Matthews was fit again but there was still no place for him in the club's first appearance in their 101-year history in the final of a national competition. Wise decision or not, Stoke lost the two-leg decider of the League Cup against Leicester 4-3 on aggregate.

What with this disappointment and a seventeenth-place finish in the League, Stoke's return to the First Division was frustrating, and made even less satisfactory by some Stoke fans demonstrating that hooliganism among football supporters did not arrive, along with rising affluence, in the final quarter of the twentieth century. The checklist of damage done to a train bringing fans back from a match at Blackpool included eight seats slashed and seven dining tables 'presumed to have been thrown through a window'. After a similar incident soon afterwards, British Rail banned all Stoke supporters from travelling on their trains to away matches.

Matthews's mood hardly helped to raise spirits. The distinct whiff of a mouldering relationship with the club, or maybe it was just with Waddington, hung over those exhibition and other matches he graced as he wound down his time at the Victoria Ground. In late March 1964, he turned out in a benefit game for Port Vale veterans Roy Sproson and Selwyn Whalley on the same day that the Supporters Club played Stoke City Old Stars, a side Matthews seemed uniquely qualified to represent – certainly more so than Waddington, who scored a hat-trick. And in May he was absent from Stoke's tour of South America, pursuing instead his own, more lucrative schedule. This comprised a visit to Jamaica, a trip to Scandinavia with an Old England team, which ended just in time for him to watch Stanley Junior lose in the first round at Wimbledon, and then a return to Canada. The restrictions imposed by Hardaker no longer applied to the retirement-bound Matthews.

In Canada he played a handful of games in the west. One of these was in Calgary for a team called Atco. The opposition was supposed to be an all-star XI from Edmonton, but they failed to show up. Local players were recruited from the stands and lost only 5-4. If this was a poor advertisement for the state of Canadian football, Matthews's popularity seemed to be unaffected. Journalists hustled for an audience. 'He is courteous and quiet,' one wrote, 'and his grey hair is going away. He resembles the classic specifications of an accountant or a home-appliance salesman. He isn't cut to the image of an athletic notable, but fate has a way of picking unlikely material.'

The same author also quoted Matthews as saying, 'Soccer has been good to me . . . a football to kick and a cup of tea now and then' – a nice, whimsical aside, and fateful, too. When he returned to his Blackpool home the simple pleasure of kicking a ball turned into a source of discomfort with a recurrence of his back injury. The stiffness became so bad that there was a possibility he might not play again. In September 1964 he was admitted to a Stoke hospital for a manipulative operation. The procedure, no longer practised, involved his back muscles being stretched.

If he also needed psychological balm, this was soon being prepared in Whitehall in London. Harold Wilson, who entered 10 Downing Street in October 1964, was the first Prime Minister who recognised football's political potential. One of his earliest tasks in office was to make recommendations for the 1965 New Year Honours. The story goes that Wilson floated the idea of Matthews receiving a knighthood, an honour never previously bestowed on a current professional player. A civil service mandarin responded sniffily, pointing out that Mr Matthews already had a CBE. The implication was that this was quite enough for a footballer. 'Who has the final decision?' Wilson asked. 'You do', he was told. 'In that case, he receives it,' the Huddersfield Town-supporting PM said.

The honour, described by Matthews as 'the greatest that can be bestowed on any British person', meant another visit to Buckingham Palace for the investiture on 23 February and a further encounter with the royal family whose acquaintance with Matthews was by now considerably deeper than it was with football. There is a good story that illustrates this point. A car Matthews was travelling in was held up in London one day. He had climbed out to find out why when the reason, a car carrying the Duke of Edinburgh, passed close to him. So close that the Duke wound down his window and called to Matthews to stop being a nuisance. They had a brief chat, which included a royal summons to tea. Within the hour Matthews was sipping from bone china at the end of The Mall.

By the time his knighthood was announced Matthews's back was much better. By late January he was fit enough to play in a reserves fixture in the Central League against Manchester United. His performance on a clinging pitch excited speculation that he would play in the FA Cup fourth-round tie against Manchester United on Saturday 30 January, the day of Sir Winston Churchill's state funeral, which was two days before Matthews was fifty. Waddington did not decide to leave him out until shortly before kick-off, which must have been a factor in nearly 50,000 turning up at the Victoria Ground. The manager said he based his decision on the frozen pitch being too hard. Matthews had preferred surfaces with a bit of give in them since his knee became chronically painful. On occasion a visit from the Stoke fire brigade was needed to ensure a slightly soggy 'Matthews pitch'.

Fulham were the visitors to the Victoria Ground a week later, Saturday 6 February 1965, for what would prove to be Matthews's 697th and final League game. Stoke beat the west London club 3-1 in front of a crowd of 28,585, a modest attendance given the circumstances. The local paper attributed this partly to disenchantment among fans after Stoke's poor cup showing against United, held 0-0 at home and beaten 1-0 four days later in the replay at Old Trafford. What must also have affected the gate was that, contrary to what has often been written about the Fulham fixture – including by Matthews himself – no one knew this was his competitive farewell. It was seven weeks before a report appeared saying that he was unlikely to play another League match because his back was again giving him pain.

Still, Fulham's visit brought Fleet Street out in strength to celebrate the longevity of Stoke's furrowed-brow knight. 'Without Stanley Matthews,' John Moynihan wrote in the *Observer*, 'this game would have been merely another average, unsatisfying romp between two undistinguished teams. But, as often on countless occasions since 1932, Matthews's personality shone through the disorder, majestically transforming the occasion.

'Fifty by five days, a Knight, and playing in his six-hundred-and-ninety-ninth [sic] League game, watched by 21 photographers perched beside the Fulham goal like starlings, the man in the familiar red and white shirt padded and spurted through 90 minutes of grandeur.'

They were comments that gave some credibility to Matthews's claim, made years later, that at heart he felt he was retiring too early and could have gone on for another two years. On the other hand, the Fulham defence gave Matthews, who laid on Stoke's second goal for John Ritchie, a well-sprung ride. Jimmy Langley, the full-back marking Matthews, might have been hand-picked for the occasion. One day short of his thirty-sixth birthday, Langley had brought his wife and two children to the game and considered this an occasion to confront Matthews with nothing more threatening than deference. Graham Leggat, a member of the Fulham forward line, was reduced to tears of laughter as he recalled the following: 'Stoke had a full-back who was kicking me all over the ground. Jimmy Langley was our left-back and as Stan goes at him Jimmy waves him past. "Go on, Sir Stan," he says, "go on." "Kick the old devil," I say. "He's been killing us and you're waving him past".'

Matthews might have played again had his fitness allowed. There was also the distraction of working on his testimonial match, scheduled for Wednesday 28 April. This would prove a grand occasion despite the extraordinary politicking that complicated the build-up. It became so bad that Peter Buxton, one of the twelve-strong organising committee, threatened to go to the International Court of Justice in The Hague.

The most bizarre episode would deepen further the antipathy between Matthews and Waddington. Buxton, whose fellow organisers included Ron Matthews and Charlie Chester, said Waddington tried to hijack the match when he realised the biggest names in world football were being assembled to take part. 'Waddington pretended to have Fifa president Sir Stanley Rous on the phone line, giving instructions that overseas players were not allowed and that Stoke City had to take the event over,' Buxton said. 'In the end a phone call to the Fifa president by accountant Bill Green revealed that no such conversation had taken place and the magnificent occasion went ahead. But it also ensured that, once again, Stan was not wanted at Stoke.'

Rous's involvement in another Fifa-related problem concerning the testimonial was genuine. Through his intervention as a behind-the-scenes fixer a difficulty over gate money was ironed out. Receipts from non-competitive fixtures held under the aegis of the game's world governing body had to go to charity, an irritating detail that only came to light a few days before the match but the kind that Rous specialised in sorting.

However much it was Matthews received – he said the match

grossed 'some thirty thousand pounds', but neither the public, nor the taxman, was exposed to too much detail – it must have been a substantial amount. In addition to money taken at the turnstiles, a post-match ball proved popular. And on top of this, Stoke City promised Matthews an undisclosed sum. 'The club will not be mean in showing their appreciation,' Gordon Taylor, the chairman, said.

The match itself was relentlessly promoted with Matthews himself doing his bit, up to and including Stoke's last home match on the preceding Saturday. He announced over the loudspeaker: 'I want to thank you all for your wonderful support – and I hope to see you on Wednesday night for what will be the greatest occasion of my life.' Everyone pitched in, even the Duke of Edinburgh, who said in a message that Matthews 'has become a legend in his own time, which is a distinction reserved for only really great men'.

A crowd of 34,450 – and a press box of more than 150 from around the world – turned up to see the match on a mudbath pitch that ended, incidentally, 6-4 to an International XI over a Sir Stanley XI. Josef Masopust, Europe's Footballer of the Year in 1962, captured the essence of what made the game a success: 'Nobody felt the necessity to gain points, nobody's legs were hampered by defensive tactics. We played only for the joy of the game, for the beauty of football. And Stanley proved he deserved all the honour given to him. His run had not lost its speed, his technique was still the best.'

The quality of the cast, a tribute to Matthews, meant it was never likely to be a dud. The International XI consisted of Lev Yashin (Soviet Union); Helmuth Johannsen (Denmark), Karl-Heinz Schnellinger (West Germany); Svatopluk Pluskal (Czechoslovakia), Ján Popluhár (Czechoslovakia), Josef Masopust (Czechoslovakia); Willie Henderson (Scotland), Ladislav Kubala (Hungary), Alfredo Di Stéfano (Spain), Ferenc Puskás (Hungary) and Frits Vanden Boer (Belgium), with Jørn

Sørensen (Denmark) and John Ritchie (Stoke City) used as second-half substitutes. On Matthews's side were Tony Waiters (Blackpool/England), George Cohen (Fulham/England), Bobby Thompson (Birmingham); Johnny Haynes (Fulham/England), Ron Flowers (Wolves/England), Jim Baxter (Rangers/Scotland); Stanley Matthews (Stoke/England), Jimmy Greaves (Tottenham/England), Alan Gilzean (Tottenham/Scotland), Bryan Douglas (Blackburn/England) and Cliff Jones (Tottenham/Wales).

It was an evening for reminiscence and romantic musings, which no one did better than Geoffrey Green writing in *The Times*. In his report, he told a story that was enhanced by typically inventive speculation. 'Once, in the Plaza del Toros in Madrid, when other English players had left the arena feeling green at their first bull fight,' Green wrote, 'Matthews remained, imperturbably capturing the footwork, turns and balance of the toreadors in his movie camera. Later, no doubt, he spent many an analytical evening at home with that film.'

Within weeks of Matthews's emotional valediction at the Vic – and a post-season tour when he played for the club in friendlies in Copenhagen and Stockholm – he had signed up as general manager of Port Vale. 'Those of us who wanted Stan to have a seat on the Stoke board and act as a roving ambassador for the club and the pottery industry went unheard,' Peter Buxton said. 'Stan went instead to Port Vale and again the rawest of deals.'

Matthews's association with Stoke City had been such a long one that isolating any one reason for his defection to Vale Park would be an oversimplification. Also, a case could be made, as it was, that it had nothing to do with any goings-on at the Victoria Ground. It was the result of nothing more elaborate than his great friendship with Jackie Mudie, now the player-manager at Port Vale.

Possibly, but probably not. So many of the conspiracy theories had Waddington's name attached to them that to an unknowable extent he surely influenced Matthews's decision. Just by being who he was, Matthews had not, for some years, been the easiest of men to work with, unless the other party was prepared to make concessions. This was not Waddington's way – he even reduced Matthews's wages by nearly a half to £25 – and the pair's continued coexistence at Stoke would have been, at best, fraught.

A story told by Derek Hodgson bears this out. 'The adulation at the Potteries was unbelievable when Stanley came back,' Hodgson said, 'but what happened then was the business of Stanley always wanting that little bit extra and Tony trying to catch up with him, as it were.

'Tony was absolutely furious when Stanley went to Port Vale because that was a direct challenge to Stoke City and Tony Waddington. I can remember one night after Port Vale signed a player that Stoke wanted, or something like that, having a couple of hours with Tony in his office when he said he was sorely tempted to go to the *People* and say: "I'll tell you the story about the real Stanley Matthews." He was referring to all the back payments the club had had to make for him to play in certain matches and that kind of thing. I remember telling Tony it would be an error because he would lose. Attacking Stanley Matthews would be like trying to attack Winston Churchill. Stanley was too big for that, regardless of his faults and foibles.'*

Waddington took heed but still seethed. When Matthews asked for complimentary seats at a match at the Victoria Ground, Waddington said: 'Sorry, the directors don't want you here.'

---

* The high regard in which Matthews was held locally meant he largely escaped open criticism from Stoke City and their fans for his move so soon after his generous send-off. Matthews, who denied a report he had been offered either a coaching or administrative post at Stoke, said he wanted to stress his decision was 'in no way a reflection of my relationship with the club who have always treated me with great consideration'. Gordon Taylor, the Stoke chairman, responded in his annual report. It referred only to the fact that Matthews had moved on. He did not bother to say where to: 'The board wish to express their congratulations to Sir Stanley Matthews on his knighthood and, although regretting the loss of his services, extend their best wishes for a long and happy retirement.'

What no one knew then was the extent to which Matthews would mellow once sprung from the vice-like emotional hold of being a professional footballer who was never satisfied unless meeting the lofty demands he made on himself. The sudden, unaccustomed freedom might have proved psychologically devastating. Matthews, helped by a dramatic change in his personal circumstances, coped with this far more successfully than might have been expected.

Looking back on Matthews's life, Jackie Mudie remarked on the different stages he went through. Early on, Mudie said, 'he was a bit of a private person and seldom accepted social invitations', towards the end of his playing career 'he mixed more and would join in with the laughs', and after he retired he was 'different again, much more sociable and relaxed'. Peter Buxton, another of Matthews's friends, also noted these changes, which, he said, included 'a new zest for enjoyment' and a greater warmth in his relationships, particularly when he returned to live in Stoke in 1989.

He even managed a brief rapprochement with Waddington at a dinner in his hometown. Matthews was at the top table sitting close to his friend Huston Spratt, a local press photographer. Towards the end of the evening, Waddington, who was at another table, came over to Matthews. Spratt recognised immediately what a good picture the two former protagonists shaking hands would be. 'I asked Stan if he minded,' Spratt said. 'He was quite kind and said, "No, not at all." So I posed up the picture for one of my photographers. It was the only time, I think, they spoke to one another over the rift.'

Chapter 19

'She is especially interested in establishing a
personal friendship with English footballer
Sir Stanley Matthews'

Matthews set himself a labour of Herculean grimness when
he committed himself to reviving Port Vale, the just-relegated
Fourth Division club. All along it looked to be no more than
a job interview to join the long list of great players who have
failed as managers.

Attaching himself to the club with what must qualify as
imprudent haste seemed to be at odds even with his own better
judgement. Shortly before he accepted the post at Vale Park he
had been to Canada for another playing stint with Toronto City.
While there a reporter asked him about going into management.
'I've never really thought about it . . . There are too many
headaches,' he said. If he had thought about it he might have
given Jackie Mudie a thanks-but-no-thanks when his former
teammate came to him shortly after his return from Canada.
Instead, over a weekend, he was persuaded by allegiance rather
than logic to take on a task for which his suitability was, to
say the least, unproven. The local evening paper described his
decision as 'as dramatic and unexpected' as when he rejoined
Stoke City in 1961.

Up until Mudie's approach, Matthews looked destined to take on a task for which his credentials were far more impressive: a knight of the road answering the many lucrative offers from around the world to coach and appear in exhibition and friendly games. Charlie Chester, his comedian friend, even offered to suspend his stage career to assist him in this. Matthews's second mistake, after the initial one of saying yes to Mudie, was to not entirely abandon this roving brief. He spent nearly as much time in aeroplanes as he did in his Port Vale office.

He did cancel going to Iceland in order to conduct his brief negotiations with Mudie and Tom Talbot, the Port Vale chairman. But quite unrealistically, given that he was put 'in full control of the playing side of Vale's affairs', he was soon dashing to the airport. Trips to Egypt, Kuwait, Berlin, Switzerland and Singapore remained in his diary and many more followed. The club commented that these excursions would take him away from the club for only a short time, which would still have been too long even if they had not underestimated the frequency of his absences. On top of this, Matthews put more pressure on his time by deciding to continue to live in Blackpool and make round trips 'practically every day' to Vale Park.

The tax office disabused Matthews of any thoughts he might have had of turning out himself for Port Vale. They told his accountant that if he did play they would go after what Matthews called 'the nest-egg generated by my farewell match'.

So he decided to look instead at the other end of the age spectrum with a big idea that many managers, particularly of hard-up clubs, had had before and many more have had since: save money and create future assets for the transfer market by nurturing young players. 'I want every parent to know that if their boy has his eyes on a soccer career, Port Vale will do their best to help him and look after him,' he told the press, naively. Letters offering sons, grandsons, friend's sons, nobody's sons for tuition by Sir Stanley Matthews arrived in great numbers. This the club trumpeted as a positive result. In reality it meant having to spend time and money sorting through an awful lot of dross. If there was an upside it was that Waddington had to defend himself against not having instituted a similar policy at Stoke. To which Matthews's old adversary responded by inviting his critics to name one player from the area whom Stoke had missed and had gone on to achieve success elsewhere.

Matthews found out for himself what Waddington meant. He said he combed North Staffordshire and South Cheshire for young talent – and ended up recruiting from as far away as Canada, flying over two teenagers he had spotted on his recent visit, and from what he called those hotbeds of football, the north-east of England and central Scotland. And to his great regret, the one player of true quality he took on, Ray Kennedy, from Seaton Delaval in Northumberland, was allowed to go. Kennedy, who went on to play for Arsenal, Liverpool and England, said later that Matthews had not recognised his ability. Matthews's line was that Kennedy was clearly a good player, but slow and overweight. The club's unavailing efforts to address this lack of mobility included tying his bootlaces together to make him quicker by shortening his stride. Matthews said that holding on to him became untenable when a rule came in stipulating that players must receive a £500 signing-on fee on their sixteenth birthdays. This was a punitive amount for a club of Vale's means. Releasing Kennedy was, Matthews said, the correct thing to do at the time.

Port Vale did win their first match under Matthews, a 1-0 home success against Colchester. One observer at that game posed and answered his own question: Matthews's chances of success, he decided, 'seem to be fairly good'. A case of damning with faint enthusiasm that Port Vale answered by finishing no higher than thirteenth in the Fourth Division during Matthews's three seasons at the club. They did have one modest run in the

FA Cup, winning through two rounds in 1965–6 before losing 2-1 at Cardiff City of the Second Division.

The first ripple of the trouble that would engulf the club, and taint Matthews's tenure as general manager, occurred before 1965 was out. Bo'ness United, a Scottish junior side, complained that Vale had broken the rules in poaching their seventeen-year-old forward Roddy Georgeson. The complaint failed to gain momentum, in any case Georgeson did not stay long at the club. Nor did it have any immediate effect on Vale's northward-looking ambitions. In April 1966 Mudie hailed as 'a terrific breakthrough' the news that another Scottish junior team, Broxburn, were to become a nursery side for Vale.

The optimism this story generated meant Matthews set off in a buoyant mood for a close-season visit to South Africa, this time accompanied by Betty. Reports arrived back in the UK of Matthews's high level of fitness, notably in front of 27,000 in an exhibition game at Johannesburg's Wanderers Stadium. But his luck was to turn. Soon after his return Matthews was involved in a car crash in the Staffordshire village of Brown Edge. Mudie was driving Matthews and three Vale teenagers to a training session at Leek Town's ground when the car skidded on a bend and hit a National Coal Board lorry. That evening Matthews, the most badly injured, was operated on at North Staffordshire Royal Infirmary to repair a rupture of the small intestine. He also fractured three ribs. A deep gash over his right eyebrow was among several cuts and grazes he received.

As it turned out, the incident's more lasting effect was not so much the injuries as heightening the sense that Matthews's time at Port Vale was a doomed exercise. This grew right at the end of the 1966–7 season with Mudie's resignation as player-manager. Mudie resorted to the old standby, personal reasons, for going. Almost certainly the real problem was the well-rehearsed one of a football club trying to be successful while deeply in debt. Matthews blithely soldiered on. He remained defiantly upbeat through the simple expedient of not bothering to find out how it was that others kept the club going in such straitened circumstances.

One of the ways they did it was by infringing a number of rules. This came to light through the behaviour of a Matthews signing from the North-East who was proving a handful for his landlady. She told Matthews the boy was not a bad person but had 'unsociable' habits. The crimes she listed included bed-wetting, being generally untidy and making long-distance telephone calls. Eventually the landlady kicked him out. As a result the club provided the player with a small weekly sum to cover his living expenses. The boy told his headmaster who, in turn, told the football authorities about the payments. In Matthews's quaint phrase, such remuneration was 'deemed illegal by the Football League'.

The League and Football Association launched an investigation driven on by Alan Hardaker. The League secretary had little time for Matthews. He considered him to be always out for himself and, rumour had it, envied his knighthood. Also he compared Matthews unfavourably to the less buttoned-up Finney, who once did a plumbing job at Hardaker's Lancashire home. The investigation into Port Vale led to the club facing six charges. Five of them involved irregular payments, including bonuses, to a number of young recruits. In February 1968, after Port Vale admitted all the charges, a joint commission of inquiry fined them £2,000 on behalf of the FA. It also recommended the club be expelled from the League and censored the board, Matthews and the club secretary for gross negligence.

If one of the commission's objectives was to discredit those regarded as miscreants, it must have been disappointed – particularly in respect of Matthews. He and the club received a generally sympathetic press. The Stoke evening paper attacked football's system of justice in a front-page editorial. It questioned casting the FA and League as judge and jury and denying the accused parties the right to legal representation. Arthur Hopcraft, one of the most eloquent observers of the game, wrote in the *Guardian*: 'It will never console Sir Stanley Matthews and the directors of Port Vale to know that the offences which brought them public disgrace last week are only distinguishable from those of other clubs by their want of expertise in covering up.' He added that Matthews had been humiliated 'for lacking sufficient stealth in a common improbity'.

Two weeks later, the Football League did indeed expel Port Vale and handed out a second fine of £2,000. With the club nursing an overdraft of £82,373, neither punishment was particularly helpful. At least, though, the expulsion came with the get-out for the board of being allowed to apply for readmission. This they did.

Matthews said that for the first time in his life he used his name and reputation for gain. It was after he contacted every club chairman that Port Vale were voted back into the Fourth Division, by forty votes to nine, at the June annual meeting.

Matthews, who stayed on for a short while as general manager – operating alongside Mudie's successor, Gordon Lee, who was appointed in May – said the saga left a sour taste in his mouth. No doubt it was made more bitter by the amount of money the club never paid him. In three years he had not drawn a penny of his £75 weekly wage, which, with expenses added in, totted up to close to £9,000. In due course, with a new chairman in place, he did receive a cheque for £3,000 but that was it. He would have created a fuss, he said, if he hadn't hated unpleasantness.

Matthews would have considered his three managerial years an exercise in futility had it not been for a trip to Czechoslovakia with the Port Vale team two weeks before the 1967–8 season. For reasons he could never have foreseen, the excursion would have a resounding effect on the rest of his life.

By the time the football authorities decided to investigate Port Vale, Matthews had begun a relationship with Mila Winterova, a married woman eight years younger than him. They had met in Prague the year before when he toured Czechoslovakia with the Port Vale team.

Irving Toorchen, a New Yorker who at the time worked for the advertising agency Central News Ltd in London, was the person indirectly responsible for Matthews's introduction to Mila. Matthews could not put an exact date on when he met Toorchen. All he could remember was that it was shortly before his farewell match at the Victoria Ground. Matthews recalled thinking as his playing career ended that he was better off than most who had given their young lives to professional football: he was healthy, had money in the bank, a house in Blackpool, owned two cars and 'I even had something else. I had Irving Toorchen.'

Erica, the oldest of Toorchen's three daughters, remembered her father as 'a very, very good networker and businessman'. She said also her mother sometimes called him 'Irving the Unnerving' because you never knew what surprising idea he would come up with next.

Soon after the testimonial game, Toorchen, Matthews and the television commentator Kenneth Wolstenholme formed what Toorchen called a sports-orientated agency. One of its first ventures was an abortive attempt to can and market Matthews's favourite tipple, carrot juice. They talked about it with a director of Express Dairy over lunch at the Savoy Grill. The mood was buoyant and Matthews's excitement at the prospect of receiving a royalty on sales was understandable. Then came the Del Boy moment. The first cans arrived and the carrot juice came out dark brown with what looked like a film of scum on the top. The project died soon afterwards, partly because Toorchen had a new scheme.

The agency's next project involved the Czechoslovak boot-

and-shoe company that had been known as Bata before being nationalised in 1945. Toorchen had established contacts in the Communist state through his advertising work. Now the idea was to link with this company to promote their football boots, using Matthews's name. Step one would be a visit to the works in the late summer of 1967. But not just the two of them. Toorchen told Matthews to bring his boots along and the Port Vale team. They would play a couple of friendly matches, all expenses paid by the state-owned boot-makers. On 24 July, Matthews wrote to Toorchen on Port Vale FC notepaper saying he was sending off the team's visa applications that day. He said also: 'In regard to the football boots, I am free to enter under contract, and if the business materialises, I agree to pay the Agency 25 per cent of the revenue received.'

This arrangement had to be revised a few weeks later as the football authorities' investigation into Port Vale hotted up. Matthews wrote again to 'Dear Irving' on club notepaper. This time he mentioned the FA giving the directors of Port Vale a rough time and expressed concern that, in the circumstances, his pursuit of a boot deal might attract adverse publicity. His letter also indicated that the agency had ended its involvement in the deal but he, Matthews, wished to keep it going with Toorchen as a private project. 'If you are successful, your fee will be ⅓ of the revenue earned,' Matthews said.

Ahead of the visit to Prague, Toorchen wrote to his friend Jiří Winter, a prominent and eccentric artist also known in Czechoslovakia by the nickname Neprakta, meaning Imprac-tical.* Winter, whose drawings and cartoons were exhibited around the world, was married to Mila Winterova, a fluent English speaker who worked at the US Embassy in Prague.

---

* Winter's English friends called him George. One possible explanation for the nickname 'Neprakta' was the collection of wholly impractical items with which he cluttered his large house. These ranged from anthropological objects, mostly from far away, to some unlikely pets, such as a live scorpion.

In his letter, Toorchen asked George and Mila to meet them at Prague's Ruzne airport. He added that he would have a football team with him, including their manager, Sir Stanley Matthews.

On the way to the airport Mila said she rummaged in her handbag to find Toorchen's letter giving the name of the manager. This amused her husband because, as he told her, she had only forgotten the most famous name in football. An indignant Mila pointed out she had never seen a football match in her life.

Matthews recalled being introduced to the Winters in the airport's VIP lounge. He noted that Mila was blonde, well-dressed and attractive. Erica Toorchen, only a child when introduced to the Winters on one of their visits to England, recalled Mila's immaculately styled bouffant hairdo. Just as striking to Matthews on the day he first met Mila in Prague was how impeccable her English was, even for an interpreter. This paid off that evening when the Czechoslovak Chamber of Commerce gave a dinner in Matthews's honour. Mila's fluent translation kept the table-talk flowing on what might have been an awkward occasion. Mila also remembered this moment and not just because the press interest in Matthews bore out what her husband had said about his fame. She said she was struck by how closely Matthews resembled her father, which might have been why she liked him from the moment they met. He was polite but appeared nervous and 'would have escaped altogether given the slightest opportunity'.

The next day Toorchen and Matthews headed for Zlin, temporarily renamed Gottwaldov by the Communists. Here they held talks about the boot project at the company's head-quarters and Port Vale won the first of their matches 2-0 against the local team. Matthews played, which helped to attract a crowd of more than 7,000. 'Stan was treated like a god,' Mick Cullerton, a Port Vale player, said. 'Everywhere we went, huge crowds would follow. They hadn't come to see Port Vale, that's for sure.' The schedule then switched back to Prague and a reception given by the British Cultural Attaché, after which a group of guests went on to dinner at an old hunting lodge. Matthews and Mila were among them. They went for a walk in the grounds and were so deep in conversation that they accidentally stepped into the shallow end of a swimming pool, which caused an embarrassing commotion. Overshadowing the embarrassment was Matthews's reflection on the flight home that Mila was one of the most remarkable people he had met. He would describe this visit to Czechoslovakia as 'the best tour I've been on'.

Matthews did not have to wait long for a reunion. Soon after the start of the 1967–8 English football season he received a letter from Czechoslovakia suggesting he pay another visit to the boot factory. He wrote straight back accepting the offer – quite apart from anything else, he said, a deal worth £72,000 was difficult to ignore – and addressed a second letter to Mila asking her to be his interpreter.

By the end of this trip, which included Mila taking him to the ballet, an experience he honoured by falling asleep, Matthews's feelings for his recent acquaintance had risen to something approaching infatuation. This time he said he travelled back to England marvelling at how, aged fifty-two, he was behaving like a teenager. Or maybe he was simply being himself rather than the introspective footballer who felt constricted by the intense public scrutiny forever intruding on his life.

In fact, Mila was notable – notorious, even – for reasons Matthews would never know, although he did once challenge her about a rumour she was a Communist spy. Adopting an attitude of shock and anger, she managed to steer him away from the truth, which anyway he would not have wanted to believe, that this 'most remarkable' person had indeed been an agent working for Czechoslovakia's secret police at the time she met Matthews. She had done her most productive work while employed at the US Embassy.*

Mila Winterova was born Gertruda Leonore Schwabova on 5 April 1923. Although her birthplace was the Czechoslovak town of České Budějovice and her father, Karl Schwab, was an officer in the Czechoslovak army, the family were German nationals. Her mother, Anna, whose maiden name was Metzlova, was Jewish. Schwab's postings, one of them to Prešov in Slovakia, meant Gertruda, an only daughter, went to at least three different schools, where she was taught in both German and Czech. After she left school in 1942 she attended a language course in Prague, where she learned the basics that would make her an excellent English speaker, before finding a job as an industrial worker for a company called Klement.**

One of the few episodes from her past she did divulge after starting her relationship with Matthews was that she had been abused and arrested by a German officer towards the end of the Second World War. The StB file gives her arrest date as January 1945, but with a very different version of why it happened from the one she would tell Matthews.

A flaw in the story she gave Matthews – and that is repeated in a notice that hangs in the church of St Peter ad Vincula in Stoke alongside a crucifix*** – was that she was arrested for failing

---

* Matthews was not the only one unaware of this dark side of Mila's life. At the time Jiří Winter married her, he knew just as little as Matthews about the second of his four wives, who herself had had three previous spouses.

** This information about Gertruda's life before she became an agent, and after it was decided in 1955 that she was 'suitable for collaboration', is publicly available from The Institute for the Study of Totalitarian Regimes in Prague. It appears there in the files of the StB, the plainclothes, state-security force set up by Czechoslovakia's Communist party in 1945, the year the Red Army and US forces liberated the country.

*** The crucifix belonged to Mila's family. She brought it with her when she moved to Stoke with Matthews in 1989. The notice that hangs with it in the church reads in part: 'Many icons and relics were put into hiding during the Second World War and this crucifix was protected by the family of Lady Mila [Matthews]. She herself was imprisoned for refusing to become an informer on fellow University students. She later escaped and the crucifix then stayed in her possession.'

to inform on fellow university students, which overlooked the fact that all universities in Czechoslovakia were closed during the war. Mila never went to one. The version in her StB file says she alleged that Gestapo interrogators told her the reason she was arrested and transported to Terezín, the concentration camp north-west of Prague, was for failing to register she was living with a blackmarketeer, Jaromír Balcar, who was wanted for forging vouchers to buy iron.

Balcar was clearly a bit of an operator who also became known to Czechoslovakia's Communist regime for his intelligence work on behalf of the Americans at home and abroad. Gertruda's former friendship with him was probably what first brought her to the attention of the StB who then persuaded her to monitor what Balcar was doing for the Americans. She appeared to take on the role wholeheartedly. An extract from her file stated: 'She noted that she thought it was right to fight against persons such as Balcar because she had long ago decided to work in favour of the current socialist order with all her might.' But, as other entries in her file indicate, the StB were never entirely convinced by these flights of leftist zeal. They were hard to reconcile with her liberal lifestyle. For all this, Gertruda's collaboration promised to be helpful.

Gertruda's behaviour after the Red Army freed Terezín's inmates in May 1945 was more sybaritic socialite than serious socialist. Despite having been locked up by the Germans her notes reported that 'she often met with German officers after her release and there were rumours that she sympathised with the Germans'. She also liked to fraternise with Americans and gained a job as 'an interpreter and representative of the US Army'. This was courtesy of a Lieutenant Williams, with whom she had an affair; a more senior US officer, Lieutenant Colonel Zeizer, was also described as a lover at about this time; and in 1946 she was engaged to Dr René Jaeger, an attaché at the Swiss Embassy in Prague. Jaeger's parents disapproved and had their son transferred to Stockholm. Gertruda followed him there in 1947 but gave up the pursuit and settled briefly with an office clerk, Mikuláš Zbožínek.

Very briefly, in fact. The marriage lasted barely a year as Gertruda entered, even by her standards, a turbulent period of her life. During the early 1950s she would take out Czech citizenship, marry twice more and become an agent in the pay of the Communist regime. A reappraisal of her character in the 1960s described her as very calculating, which could be seen from the fact that 'she always considerably improved her economic status after every fresh marriage. This is most evident concerning her latest marriage to an artist [Jiří Winter], who is able to financially fulfil almost her every wish (car, furs each worth 20,000 crowns, etc).'*

In March 1955, when she was first cleared to work with 'the bodies of the Ministry of the Interior', Mila had reverted to her first married name, Gertruda Zbožínková. At this stage she was assessed as 'a flighty woman who generally sought contacts with foreigners [and] was used to living a comfortable and carefree life . . . She is also very clever and purposeful.' Politically, she had been 'totally reactionary' but this had improved 'and thanks to the influence of her co-workers it appears that she now has a correct attitude towards the current peoples' democratic regime. It is, however, possible that she merely pretends to do so.' Her personal file also recorded that during interrogation she had given no information about her liaisons with US army personnel, which was noted as something that could be used to blackmail her.

Despite this failure to disclose 'compromising facts' and the caveat about the validity of her correct attitude, she was made an agent with the code name Gréta (agents were a step up from

---

* This later appraisal made the lurid claim that in her younger days she demonstrated her determination as a person by keeping a human skull on her bedside table. It also depicted her as a racist who disliked 'Jews and coloured persons'. Her file said she did not speak to her Jewish mother for several years.

informers and eligible to be more generously rewarded) and had a registration number, 2769. A handwritten promise of her collaboration, dated Prague 12 March 1955, was placed in her StB file:

> For honourable and patriotic reasons I am willing to collaborate with members of the Ministry of the Interior to secure the safety of our peoples' democratic republic. With my collaboration I wish to contribute to the construction of socialism and the preservation of peace. I swear that I shall not speak to anybody about these things and I am aware that if I were to break this silence I would be guilty of revealing state secrets.

> Zbožínková

Agent Gréta was far from being some exotic figure from the pages of fiction or even a latter-day Mata Hari. She was one of many agents and informers in the Czech state after the Second World War doing relatively untaxing duties. On the other hand she did play a significant role for the StB when she started work at the US Embassy, where she stayed for thirteen years. She claimed later she was a cultural assistant, but her police file says she was an office worker in the press department.

Her controllers made the point that along with most locals working for the Americans in Czechoslovakia she was viewed with suspicion by her employers. The StB assessed her work as an agent inside the embassy as generally good although her moody character was a weakness. She was pronounced trustworthy despite 'her past contacts with Germans and Americans'. When she decided to stop working at the embassy after meeting Matthews a note inserted in her file said: 'In view of the fact that Gréta's handwritten reports contained topical events at the US embassy I propose that the file of personal notes be destroyed.'

Her departure did not mark a clean break from the secret

police. The last known date on her control sheet was not until 5 April 1982, by which time she had been Lady Mila Matthews for seven years. But no evidence exists that she was actively involved as an agent after 1968 or that she was put under pressure to combine her life with Matthews, which involved a great deal of travel, with undercover work.

By the time she met Matthews in 1967 she had married and divorced her third husband, Milos Látal, and had been the second wife of Jiří Winter since 1961 when she replaced the first, Zdeňka. Right from the start theirs seems to have been an unconventional marriage. The Winter ménage was now made up of Jiří, his mother, to whom he was utterly devoted – a friend remembered there was 'hell to pay' for anyone who did not behave well to her – his new wife Gertruda and Zdeňka who stayed on in the house for another two months.*

A female cousin of Winter's, who emigrated to Australia, remembered meeting Gertruda shortly before she married Jiří. 'The three of us went to a boxing tournament, which Gertruda thoroughly enjoyed,' she said. 'And after that we had coffee and cognac at her place. It was a one-bedroom flat, which I thought was fantastic. It was not common to have a place of your own in a Communist country.' The cousin said Gertruda was a good hostess who was always beautifully dressed. 'But I remember thinking there was something hard about her and there were a lot of things about her that no one knew. I do not think anyone knew that she had been a German citizen. Her collaboration with the Communists does not surprise me.'

---

* Family members say that Winter's distress was genuine when told, fifty years later, about Gertruda's background. Given that he was Jewish and had lost many of his immediate family in the Holocaust, he would almost certainly have recoiled from someone with her heritage had he known about it. She would not have found it hard to disguise her German roots, particularly as she spoke perfect Czech, having been born and brought up in the country. Maybe she even invoked her mother to present herself as a Jew, suspending her alleged anti-Semitism, to find favour with Winter. He may have been the one who started using the nickname Mila because he objected to calling her Gertruda or Leonore, which were both German names. Trude was another of his names for her.

Whether Mila was also behaving like a teenager or playing the more sinister role of an enemy agent when, at this very early point of their relationship, she started regularly exchanging letters and flowers with Matthews is impossible to say. What is likely is that she was experiencing as much emotional turmoil as he was, possibly even more. Whereas Matthews had his own life, his family's and his new friend to ponder, she had all these plus having to consider her Communist paymasters. And in her case the new friendship was not so straightforward. Not only was there her clandestine role, she had to make up her mind whether the rather gauche English footballer represented a passport to a superior life in the West or a potential love conquest or both. After all, she had form when it came to men and seeking personal betterment.

On the face of it, at least, the exchange of endearments on a regular basis meant their relationship was on the threshold of something less coy. It needed a set of circumstances to push it beyond this. Irving Toorchen was there once again to oblige. He asked George Winter to come to London in November 1967 to work on a magazine cover. Naturally, Mila would come, too. She rang Stanley and during their conversation she agreed to visit him in Stoke, without her husband. Again a question hovers over her motives for so readily agreeing to a tryst with someone she had met just a handful of times.

Matthews would fret for months over telling Betty about Mila. Mila, on the other hand, acted nearly straightaway – her task, she would suggest in a misty-eyed book she co-wrote with Stanley about their romance, *Back in Touch*, made easier by the nature of her relationship with Jiří. She claimed that after six years their marriage remained unconsummated and as far as she was concerned never would be. She said although she loved Jiří she was not *in love* (her italics and her dubious distinction). They shared the same house but not the same bed. Their separate rooms were foreign territory.

Much of this is almost certainly self-serving. A close relation of Winter's told me: 'Jiří had separate rooms with all his wives. The reason was because he was a hard-worker. He used to work in the nights until two or four in the morning. He didn't want to wake up his wives when he came back to the room.' The same relation was just as vehement on the specific matter of Jiří's relationship with Mila: 'Jiří was a normal, young and healthy man. Even younger by fifteen months than Gertruda. If she says they had no sex, she has to have had some reason for that, but no, it's not true.'

Maybe the reason was to do with her being unable to have children. A young cousin of Jiří's remembered a group of his female relations being told this by Mila soon after they married. Mila's StB file also referred to it, saying it was the result of a surgical operation because of health problems when she was young. The file's author speculated that this might have caused her mood swings. Maybe it also contributed to her failed marriages and her denial about having sex with Jiří.

Mila said she spent an hour rehearsing what she would say before going to Jiří's studio, where she told him she thought she was in love with Matthews. As she related it, his startled reaction was not because she had fallen for another man. His grievance was that someone as sophisticated, cultured and cosmopolitan as she was could not possibly associate either with a provincial Englishman or with a footballer – or, worse still, with someone who was both. He agreed, though, to sanction her going off to a dull, industrial town to spend time with a vulgar sportsman on the grounds that it might expedite the end of the affair.

When they arrived at Heathrow, they told Toorchen that Mila was going to visit an unspecified friend in the Midlands. While she set off to catch a train to Stoke, the two men headed for Toorchen's Surrey home.

Matthews forsook his more familiar haunt, the North Stafford Hotel, which was across the road from the station, for Mila's visit.

Instead he booked two single rooms at The George in Burslem. She teased him about his choice of a hotel with the same name as her husband. It was the sort of light touch that Matthews had previously encountered only when among fellow footballers. He evidently found it liberating and relaxing in a relationship with a woman who was well practised in putting men at ease. Mila reported that her five days and nights with Stanley passed as if by magic.

The success of inviting Mila to be with him in Stoke encouraged Matthews to go a step further. Early in 1968 he received invitations from South Africa and Canada to go there in the summer. He would ask Mila to join him on one of these trips. Two months together, he said, were necessary before they decided on their future. For the first time, he said, he considered divorcing Betty – something so alien to his culture that, instinctively, he stepped back from it. The communal safety of the traditional working-class family, with stigma attached to anyone who broke up this unit, and of a football club were all he had ever known.

Things changed for Matthews with the end of his playing days and his luckless foray into management. When he lifted his head he could not help but notice the changed attitudes of the so-called permissive society of the 1960s being slavered over by a palpitating media. Maybe a new life with Mila was possible, even if it did mean walking out on Betty.

Matthews made another of his business runs to Czechoslovakia in late January 1968, most of which he spent with Mila in the spa town of Karlovy Vary, Carlsbad to its English visitors, where they discussed the trip to Canada. She made out later that problems abounded. Jiří Winter would have to sign her application for an exit visa and the Canadian organisers would have to send her return air tickets and guarantee picking up her expenses, otherwise the Czechoslovak authorities would not grant their permission. On the other hand the StB, who knew all about this trip, may have waved it through. It is referred to in a June 1968 update to her file, which also records her giving up her job at the US Embassy in April and being allowed to stand down as a collaborator. She is not signed off completely, though. It remained possible that her collaboration and maintaining her regular contacts might, in the words of the update, 'still make sense'.*

The departure for Canada did involve one very real difficulty as far as Matthews was concerned: the perils of Heathrow's departure lounge. He was well aware of the freelance news agency who made their money from stories about well-known travellers passing through the airport – better still if they had an interesting companion.

Mila, who said she received Jiří's blessing on the grounds he still thought her relationship with Matthews was doomed, arrived in London from Prague to find Stanley in a state of great agitation. Terrified of headlines about a Matthews marital scandal, he imagined every other Heathrow employee and passenger was a reporter keeping him under surveillance. The tension returned when they stepped off the plane at Toronto to be surrounded by reporters wanting to talk to him about football. In case Mila did not understand that she should stand aside, one of the organisers of Matthews's trip marched her through arrivals into a car. She was driven on her own to a hotel, the same one Stanley was staying at but where they were booked into separate rooms. 'We gotta keep you under wraps,' she said the escort told her.

It was not until a week later, when they headed west on a two-day train journey to Winnipeg, where Matthews was playing, that they finally felt able to relax. There were uneasy moments, such as when Matthews was spotted by a Southport-born train

---

* The decision was taken to keep her file at the 1st Special Department of the Ministry of the Interior for at least ten years. This continuing association may have facilitated her many travels with Matthews, including the Canada trip, in the coming years.

steward, but Mila would describe this period as having all the trimmings of a traditional honeymoon. They spent a few nights in a cabin, lent to them by an admirer of Matthews's, at Clear Water in Manitoba on the edge of Riding Mountain National Park. Mostly they did very little. The one outing both remembered was a fishing expedition in a boat with an outboard engine, which flummoxed him but not her. Parting at Heathrow was, she said, exquisite torture. They agreed that they had to tell their spouses that they wanted divorces.

For Mila divorce was something of a routine by now, one that she happily admitted to. After their marriage she made light of the fact that Stanley was husband number five. As she had done before her trip to be with Stanley in Stoke in 1967, Mila said she wasted no time in confronting her current husband with her latest wish, and this time it was an end to their marriage. Again Jiří remained calm. Instead of tantrums or broken crockery, he assailed Mila with questions about how certain she was that Matthews would leave his wife. He did not agree immediately to letting her go.

He was right that Matthews was agonising over what lay ahead, although this was not because he had a problem with leaving Betty. His daughter, Jean, said that when her father left her mother in 1968 – 'I just upped and left,' he said – she, Jean, had no idea it was going to happen even though, it became clear, the marriage had been doomed for some time. 'Warmth and affection had once been part of it,' Matthews said soon after the break-up, 'but that was long ago.' He once said that in the ten years before they split she had not once called him Stan. She would speak to him through other people, even when they were gathered as a family: 'Ask your father if he'd like another cup of tea.'*

---

* Matthews's old friend, Peter Buxton, was one of the few people who ever stumbled upon the unhappiness in Matthews's marriage – or at least stumbled upon it and went public with it. It was in the 1960s and shows how effective Matthews had been in keeping his melancholy secret. The two were having lunch when Matthews said he was going off to

Apportioning blame for the failure of the marriage is a doomed exercise. Maybe it was Betty Matthews's fault but it could also be argued that Matthews needed it to fail, worked subconsciously towards that end, because a successful union would have distracted him from his obsession: to be a great footballer. The poet W. B. Yeats maintained that 'perfection of the work' was possible only at the expense of 'perfection of the life'. A family member said: 'In all fairness, Mila probably had the best years of Stanley; Betty had the hard years.'

What worried Matthews now was actually telling Betty. He knew she would take it badly despite the moribund state of their relationship. The pain of breaking it to his children, for whom his devotion never wavered, was another factor, although both of them were now independent of their parents. On top of this, the whole paraphernalia of arranging a divorce and the more immediate problem of meeting up with Mila, had the potential to subvert his enthusiasm for a new life. Finally there was outside opinion. This was still a consideration for anyone contemplating divorce, regardless of the sixties supposedly being swinging, and was many times worse for someone well known who cared about his public image. Matthews said he cringed with embarrassment whenever he thought of the publicity.

One person he felt he could confide in was his mother, now nearly eighty. This proved correct. He said Ada's reaction when he told her of a possible divorce from Betty was to observe that it had been coming a long time. According to Matthews, his mother even devised an outrageous contingency plan in the event of the divorce from Betty dragging on, which it did, and Mila needing a stopgap fiancé to enable her to leave Czechoslovakia. Ada put

Canada: 'And in all innocence I asked, "Is Betty going?" Stan seemed to be stumped by the question and mumbled, "No, you know she prefers to stay in Blackpool." I said jokingly, "She wants to watch out letting a handsome young man like you roam the world. Someone will be running off with you." Some time later I found why Stan seemed to be put out. Mila, his new love, went to Canada with him and Stan was quite convinced I had learned his secret.'

forward Matthews's older brother, Arthur, a dedicated bachelor who would not be tempted to hold on to Mila.

When Matthews broke the news to Charlie Chester of his wish to marry Mila, the comedian came up with a different solution. He, too, knew 'things weren't right at home', as Matthews put it, but felt a loyalty to Betty because she was particularly friendly with his wife, Doretta. Chester suggested Matthews keep Mila as a mistress, a common enough practice in show business but one that Stanley was instinctively against and felt would further complicate his life.

In Prague, Mila maintained in *Back in Touch*, another plan was being brewed, one that gave weight to Jiří's being 'a normal, young and healthy man'. The idea devised by Mila and her female friends was to set him up to be caught *in flagrante delicto* with a beautiful actress. The actress was well known to one of Mila's circle. She was not only irresistibly attractive, the friend assured Mila, but would undoubtedly accept the task of testing Jiří's fidelity to destruction.

On the night of 20–21 August 1968, real events of historic moment reduced this living-room conniving in Prague and Stoke to irrelevance. The world awoke to the Soviet-led invasion of Czechoslovakia, a brutal response to the Prague leadership's attempts at political liberalisation. And Stanley and Mila awoke right in the middle of it.

He had arrived in Prague, on another supposed business trip, the day before the invasion. Mila had brought her father to the airport to make an introduction she regarded as one more important step in her new relationship. The meeting went well and, in a happy mood, she and Stanley then drove to Karlovy Vary for a three-day break at the Interhotel Grandhotel Moskva. Early the next morning Matthews went downstairs to go for a run. He found the lobby packed with fellow guests. Some talked excitedly, others listened to radios and the rest crowded around a television set. When he returned the hubbub was even greater.

Unable to understand what was going on, Matthews called Mila to come to the lobby. She was told that tanks and troops of the Soviet Union and other Warsaw Pact countries had crossed the border and were spreading out across the country. 'Demonstrations were taking place all the time,' Matthews said later, 'and I saw people crying in the streets.' He said he saw Soviet tanks and a helicopter dropping propaganda leaflets.

The situation for Matthews, although trivial compared to that of Czechoslovakia, was complicated, if not entirely without its merits. With Prague airport closed to civilian traffic and other transport possibilities extremely limited, he had no chance of an immediate return to England. A group of tourists from Yugoslavia who were able to leave agreed to cable Betty to say that he was all right but could not say when he would return to Blackpool. His 'business affairs' on hold, he then settled back to spend more time with Mila, an arrangement, she said, 'with which he seemed more than content'.

News reports that Matthews was cut off in Czechoslovakia appeared in the UK soon after the invasion. They quoted Betty's reaction to her husband's apparent plight. She was, naturally, very worried and was waiting for a glimmer of news. 'I don't know where he is or when he'll be back,' she added. 'He said he would be away about a week, but he had not booked a return flight.' Three days after this, a cable, sent by the Yugoslavs from Maribor, reached Betty: 'I am fine and well. Don't know when leaving Prague. Love Stan'. Succinct and neatly phrased, it suggested he was in Prague, rather than Karlovy Vary, without exactly saying so. 'It is rather confusing,' Betty said, 'but it sounds as though he is still in Prague.'

The next cable Betty received came from Matthews in Karlovy Vary on Thursday 29 August. Understandably, it did not explain why he was in the health resort. 'Planes and trains at a standstill,' it told her. 'Home as soon as possible.'

A far more intriguing communication is a surviving letter

from Mila, handwritten on Interhotel Grandhotel Moskva
notepaper, to Jiří, or Jiricku (Georgie) as she called him:

Jiricku

I hoped I would again be able to call home, but no luck, one
cannot even send telegrams to Prague, so I'm writing. I would
so like to come home but Stan refuses to move from here until
planes leave from Prague. He refused to travel through West
Germany and also rejected my proposal to travel to Vienna
via Prague and then on by plane. He is afraid to be stuck there
because he has no plane reservation and has no money. When
he flew from England there were checks at the airport and he
was afraid of taking with him more than fifteen pounds because
he had already spent his fifty-pound quota and so he left the
rest with a friend. He's getting on my nerves and we're almost
without any cash. Is there any way you could send me some?
I keep listening to the radio and keep on translating things to
him, he wants to see everything and sees himself as a small hero.
I've even bought some cards to pass the time. Every day I go to
enquire at the airline office. I'm also not sure whether I could
drive off by car, especially when I would have him in the car. He's
terribly rebellious and he could get into conflict with an eventual
patrol checkpoint. I met a friend here and so I asked her to call
you. I so wish to be home at last, I'm so sad here in these times.
I had hoped to be able to telephone you and seek your advice
what to do.

Please send my love to my parents and mother. I shall come
back come what may, either at the end of the week or by Monday.

Best greetings

Yours Trude

The tone of the letter suggests that although Jiří clearly knew
his wife was with Matthews he was supposed to think her role
was not recreational, rather, most probably, that of an interpreter.

The criticism of Matthews may have been part of this charade. Jiří would have been understandably reluctant to part with money had she confessed she was having a frolickingly good time with her lover.

Counterbalancing the letter's peevishness is a note from Mila to Matthews, handwritten in English on one side of a business card that has 'Gertrud Winterova' printed on the other:

> I've become terribly possessive. I'd have to have all of you, not just a part. I couldn't help myself and I couldn't share you.

The note is undated but is conceivably her guilty reaction to having traduced him in her longer letter to Jiří. Its amorous content is consistent with her much later recollection of being with Matthews at the time of the Soviet invasion: '. . . we were so bound up with each other the rest of the world could have stopped for all we cared.'

Matthews eventually left Karlovy Vary on a train for Nuremberg in West Germany on Sunday 1 September. In the highly dramatised retelling of their story in *Back in Touch** Matthews said he boarded the train reluctantly after a warning reached him from local officials that he would be ill advised to stay. There was no possibility of Mila going with him. She had with her neither a passport nor a valid exit visa. He said the wrench of their parting made them both physically sick. They laid tentative plans for their next meeting, this time outside Czechoslovakia. She told him about a friend of hers in West Germany, a dentist. If Matthews managed to reach her on the phone and she mentioned a visit to the dentist it would mean she was trying to escape.

After two train journeys and a flight from Frankfurt, Matthews

---

* Someone who knew Mila told me the book 'is like a Mexican soap opera, almost everything is made up'.

made it home to Blackpool. At Manchester airport he spotted a newspaper headline he knew to be incorrect. Matthews, it announced, was still stuck behind the Iron Curtain. 'It's nice to be home,' Matthews said, 'but then it always is.' He also made out that because of language difficulties he had been in the dark about the invasion when it happened. No mention, of course, of his live-in interpreter.

When Mila arrived back in Prague she said she immediately set about arranging to leave the country. How and when she eventually achieved this is difficult to piece together from the information in the only two 'records' of what happened: her StB file and *Back in Touch*.

The relevant passage in the file, dated January 1973, comes under the general heading: 'Report on the Emigration of Collaborator GRETA, archive file nr 626887'. Under the specific heading, 'Method of Escape', it says:

> The above named emigrated on 4.12.1968 without her husband during a trip abroad to England, which had been legally approved. She had planned this trip to be with her lover, the English football player Stanley MATTHEWS, who had invited her to spend a holiday in England. At the time she no longer worked at the US Embassy since April 1968 and was a housewife. From what we know it can be assumed that none of the Americans working at the embassy knew of her emigration and it is assumed that none of the Czech employees knew either, also because she was no longer employed at the embassy. The motive for her emigration is most probably based on her efforts to gain better social standing and financial security, which was characteristic of her.

In *Back in Touch* Mila gave 9 November 1968 as the day on which: 'Stanley flew into Frankfurt . . . and we have lived together ever since.' This may or may not conflict with the StB file. Possibly she did receive legal approval to emigrate on 4

December 1968 for a trip to England but still managed to slip out of the country before this. A much later entry in her file suggests the StB lost track of her around this time. It gives the date she left the country as 3 December 1970.

In their version of events, neither Stanley nor Mila made any mention of a trip to England. She said the authorities had given permission for a train to go to Vienna. To fit with her timetable of how things unfolded this must have been in September or October. She identified the amount each person was allowed to take out of Czechoslovakia, nine dollars, as a particular difficulty of travelling on from Vienna, a true enough claim although most people heading for the West at this time took with them currency bought on the flourishing black market. She clearly felt able to press on with plans to secure a place on the train after she told Stanley, when he got a call through, that she was going to see her dentist. She said she enlisted the help of contacts at the US Embassy to have the still-current exit visa she had used to go to Canada approved for the journey to Vienna. For the first time, she added, her husband lost his temper over her leaving him but relented when he realised her mind could not be changed. Jiří even accompanied Mila, with her father, to the station.

People who were living in Prague in 1968 have cast doubt on Mila's dramatic account of her flight by train to Austria and then on to West Germany. They suspect embellishment because there was no need to be surreptitious. It was not until the end of 1969 that the authorities clamped down on freedom of movement. But why let this spoil a good story. Mila was clearly intent on making her unverifiable account as vivid as possible. She called the train on which she made her escape a 'dissident special' after noting how many of her fellow passengers were known opponents of the regime. She even had the driver diverting from the normal route and crossing the border at a point not yet guarded by the occupiers. Jan Krcmar, a working journalist at the time Warsaw Pact tanks arrived in Prague, found this all too fanciful. 'Lots of people moved in and out in those first days before the regime really tightened things up,' he said. 'One could get an exit visa – permit – with hardly any red tape until some time in September/October 1969.'

Matthews said he had wanted to tell Betty about Mila when he returned from Karlovy Vary but lost his nerve because there were guests at the house. This made it just as well that he had given Mila his brother Arthur's number. It was he who, Mila said, took the call from her with the news she had arrived in Austria from where she would move on to West Germany. Having escaped from Czechoslovakia, she was in a skittish mood and contemplated announcing herself to Arthur as his wife-to-be. She refrained because he did not sound the flirtatious type.

A group of Czechs who had left on the same train as Mila gave her a lift in a borrowed car to Karlsruhe in south-west Germany close to the French border. Here she worked with the brisk efficiency that distinguished her as a very different character from Matthews, which was undoubtedly one of the things he found attractive. By the time he flew out for their latest reunion, not long after she had arrived in Karlsruhe, she already had an apartment there and an administrative job on the local US Army base. For the first time they lived together, albeit briefly, in a place they could call their own. 'I very nearly stayed for good,' Matthews said.

Chapter 20

'He should be played by Michael Caine with Meryl Streep as Mila'

Stanley Matthews moved agitatedly around his study at his Blackpool home. An open briefcase was on the floor. Into it, during 'a mad half-hour of packing', he stuffed those papers he imagined were important and could remember where they were: legal documents, including contracts and endorsements, share certificates and various bank statements. He gathered up a few personal effects, left the house and headed for the airport. 'I flew away,' he said, 'not knowing when, or even if, I would ever return.'

This graphic recollection was of the moments after making up his mind, in the final days of 1968, to leave Betty. Something had snapped, he said. He could no longer bear the mental torture of being pulled towards a future with Mila Winterova while being bound to what he described as a dead marriage. Peter Whelan, the playwright, who met Matthews much later when he explored the possibility of making a film about Stanley and Mila, reckoned in this walking away from Betty he showed the same determination he had as a player.

'He was the tongue-tied, working-class hero Mila had never heard of and she, the elegant, educated graduate of Prague

University,' Whelan said, understandably unaware of Mila's true background. 'He had to battle through the difficulties of the communist occupation and at home with the long, drawn-out divorce from Lady M [Betty]. But he got there.' Matthews would say much later that he was as proud of his love for Mila as anything he achieved in football.

Matthews knew that leaving Betty to join Mila would mean having to live abroad. Not only did he feel a certain degree of shame, he feared the publicity. He was sure his action would be bitterly opposed by Betty and that, once Mila was revealed as the reason he had abandoned her, public opinion would almost certainly side with his wife. He was afraid that the press, had they found out, would resort to one of their favourite stereotypes, the man in the triangle being a heartless predator. And oh what joy for circulation figures if the heartless one just happened to be as famous as Sir Stanley Matthews.

Their first few weeks together in West Germany must have been strange and potentially destabilising, especially for Matthews. For all his travelling he still personified the provincial Englishman. Even the much more gregarious Mila had never known anything quite like this. And while he was obviously infatuated, was she at this point? For most of her adult life her guiding principle, as lover and collaborator, seemed to be to switch to whoever was offering the best deal. Now she found herself making the kind of commitment for which she had shown no obvious aptitude.

As well as sorting themselves out emotionally the rock face of practical problems in their immediate path must have appeared daunting. Matthews had acted shrewdly in gathering up his financial papers – Mila remembered that among what looked like the contents of a wastepaper basket were 15,000 £1 shares in Rolls-Royce – but dealing with his money affairs from abroad would not be straightforward. Two divorces would have to be negotiated, again from afar, and the question of where they would live was something that exercised Stanley in particular. He felt West Germany was too exposed to a prying media.

Matthews had left still not having discussed a divorce with Betty. Jean said none of them had any idea about his relationship with Mila, nor that he had been torn apart agonising over whether to join her. The family thought he had suffered a breakdown or was ill. They even suspected a little while later that he had found religion.

As Matthews predicted, Betty was crushed by his disappearance. And when she eventually found out another woman was involved her despondency turned to anger. She wrote letters, filled with bitterness, and made phone calls to try to arrange meetings with Matthews's brothers. As her rancour spilled over, Matthews's side of the family, with the exception of his children, mostly did what they could to avoid her. In time, she gave up and moved south. With both her children going overseas she went to live in Kent near to her close friend Doretta, the wife of Charlie Chester.

Once Matthews had settled in with Mila he wrote to his solicitor telling him to explore the possibility of a divorce. The likelihood of this happening quickly was soon dispelled. Under the laws as they were then constituted, Matthews had no grounds to petition for divorce even if he had confessed in his letter that he had run away to be with Mila. And even if he had, it would have made no difference. It soon became clear that Betty, regardless of what her husband was up to, was not about to petition. As someone who was close to the family at the time said: 'She just loved him so much. She always believed Stanley had lost his marbles and would one day come back to her.'

As Matthews knew, and feared, had the truth about his liaison with Mila come out at this stage it would have been a sensation. The Profumo Affair, involving a cabinet minister and the mistress of a high-ranking official at the Soviet Embassy, and the salacious minutiae of the Duchess of Argyll's divorce from her second husband had already captivated newspaper readers in the 1960s. Matthews's romance might have lacked the titillation of these two stories but the nation's most famous footballer forsaking his wife for a mysterious lady from Eastern Europe would undoubtedly have given many thousands of people a great deal of vicarious pleasure.

Avoiding discovery preoccupied Matthews, particularly, for some time. The next step after leaving England was to find a hideaway. As far as he was concerned, this ruled out anywhere on the mainland of Western Europe where the media were active and inquisitive. If possible it would be somewhere warm, which was why he and Mila, acting on a recommendation by a work colleague of hers, came to be on a flight to Malta.

On a small island such as Malta it did not take the local press long to discover Matthews's presence. As he had hoped, though, the journalists were far more accommodating and less relentless than those on the mass-circulation papers of the big European countries. Reluctantly at first, and in return for keeping Mila's name out of television interviews and newspaper reports – the word put about was that he was on the island, alone, for business reasons – Matthews agreed to cooperate with the media. He even accepted an offer by one journalist to play a game of football for a Christian Brotherhood team, hence the religious-convert theory. As a result of playing for them he formed a friendship with the Brothers, two of whom were English, and he started using them as a postal address. The only religion involved was football.

Eloping to Malta would prove a masterstroke for their relationship. The warm climate, the gentle pace of life and the locals' inclination to be friendly rather than suspicious, so different from anything Mila was used to, brought her an unaccustomed peace. If her feelings for Matthews had been speculative when she first met him there seems no doubt that they were becoming ever more sincere. They leased a flat in

Mosta and withstood the many vexations that might have driven them apart.

Irritations remained, though. Her controllers in Czechoslovakia were still on her case. She had not yet received permission from them to take up permanent residence in Malta. Her StB file shows that as late as October 1972 she had a request for permission refused and it was not until January 1977 that she was finally cleared to live on the island. In practical terms this does not appear to have meant much.

One other irritation was that the British press did not take long to find out that Matthews had fled to Malta. This meant he had to work hard to hide the fact he was not on his own. In town he would often tell Mila to cross the road so they would not be seen walking together. And after shopping expeditions, spent pretending they were strangers, they would approach their car from different directions. They would get in only when they thought no one was watching.

Another pressure was dealing with what Matthews's solicitor confirmed was going to be a drawn-out divorce with Betty refusing to petition. A decree absolute would not be made until 1975, as a result of a change in the law, and until that moment they had to live with the uneasy feeling that their being together was incomplete.

Especially in the early days, the bond between them was also tested by some stressful events. One of these was a failed business venture Matthews entered into in Malta. Another was his first encounter with a member of the family since he had left home, a visit from his daughter. The story of this meeting provided *Back in Touch* with more colourful copy.

Matthews had kept in touch with Jean but still had not told her about Mila and was alarmed when she wrote to inform him she was coming to Malta. In fact, the whole Gough family – Jean, her husband and their two children – were on their way for a holiday before moving to South Africa. Matthews's overworking imagination persuaded him she was on a reconnaissance mission on behalf of Betty.

He recalled his sense of panic when he went to meet them at Malta's international airport. By now he had also convinced himself Betty would actually be with them. When the flight's arrival was announced he hurried up to the observation platform. Still not satisfied that his wife was not on board after Jean, Bob and their two children, Matthew and Samantha, had walked off the plane, he waited until the last passenger disembarked before going down to greet them.

He then drove them to the villa where they were staying. What followed might have been lifted from a romantic comedy. As Matthews told it, Mila had filled the fridge with provisions, which he had to take credit for. The problem was that, as well as everyday stuff, 'he' had bought items such as peppers and sauerkraut. These were things he would have barely known about – and, if he had, would have been well aware that the Goughs did not eat them. He found himself being cross-examined, with Bob especially suspicious that they were not being given the full story. In his desperation to get away, he gave up making excuses for not being able to join them for a meal and agreed to come around the next day for lunch.

As he suspected, this was another ordeal with Jean and Bob probing to find out why he had come to a Mediterranean island, apparently alone. The subterfuge lasted until, during an awkward discussion about a night out together, Jean came to the point by wondering why he did not bring his lady friend with him. Matthews was taken aback but said he would, while hanging on to a fragment of the deceit by making out that whoever she was was no more than an acquaintance whose husband was busy. This last veil slipped away, albeit unacknowledged, when the lady friend detained the non-dancing Stanley on the dance floor for much of the evening.

Soon after this Mila met the wider family, including Matthews's

mother, Ada, when Stanley took her with him on a trip to Stoke
to see his solicitor. She was greeted warmly but when in public,
she said, she felt as though it was Canada all over again. She was
happy when they returned to Malta where they had bought a
bungalow overlooking the fishing village of Marsaxlokk. It was
in the process of being built when they found it, which meant
they could order their own added extras: a swimming pool and
tennis court for him, as much garden as possible for her. They
called it Idle Hours.

Clearly money was no great problem for Matthews. All those
extra-curricular opportunities while still playing professionally
and other acts of acuity, such as sweeping up vital documents
when he left England, were paying off. Also, with the name
Stanley Matthews remaining a prestigious brand associated
with quality and excitement, his earning potential barely
diminished after he retired. He received a flow of lucrative offers
from sponsors and other agencies to play and coach all over the
world. He said that part of his success in staying fit was Mila's
skill as an amateur physio. This included expert knowledge of
pressure points.[*]

Matthews's exceptional physical condition for someone his age
meant he continued playing football in Malta. Not only did he do
this for the Christian Brothers, he also turned out regularly for a
post office side in Paola, a small town not far from Marsaxlokk.
His greatest footballing triumph on the island, though, came in
September 1970 as an assistant to the manager of the Paola club,
Hibernians FC.

Father Hilary Tagliaferro, an Augustinian priest who for
years had combined his spiritual duties with taking an active
role in Maltese football at a number of levels, had just given up
managing Hibernians, with some success – three years earlier

---

[*] He picked up some of this himself, which enabled him to ease Kevin Keegan's back pain
before an international at Wembley in 1979.

they had even held Manchester United, complete with George Best and Bobby Charlton, in a European Cup competition that United went on to win. Having heard that Matthews had not only settled on the island, but had done so in nearby Marsaxlokk, Father Hilary invited him to support Hibernians' inexperienced new manager, Joe Attard, including for the two legs of a European Cup Winners' Cup tie against Real Madrid. The home tie in early September came as close as a goalless draw can to being classified a massive triumph – for Maltese football and Stanley Matthews.

Two things helped Hibernians frustrate Real Madrid at the Empire Stadium in Gzira: a pitch of compacted sand, unsullied by a single blade of grass, that rewarded local knowledge; and tactics, which included frittering away time, that were suspiciously worldly for a team from a small island. And the retribution might have been much worse two weeks later when Hibernians faced the unequal task of trying to do even better in the Bernabéu. Real's imposing home had unnerved greater sides than a collection of Maltese part-timers, who on this occasion included a waiter, dockyard worker, civil servants and the unemployed.*

Rules governing foreigners' involvement in Maltese football and Matthews's reluctance to have a high-profile role in the game on the island – he was, after all, trying to avoid publicity not court it and may have judged his trip to Madrid a mistake – meant his association with Hibernians did not last. But the unlikely footballphile Father Hilary did manage to coax him into one other major contribution to the game in Malta.

The friendly but determined priest, who wryly suggested

---

* At one point during the 5-0 defeat, the fifty-five-year-old Matthews resolved to leave his pitch-side seat and play. He said he made this decision while the team were being given the runaround in the first half. He changed his mind during the interval when he saw how eager his substitutes were to be given a game at the Bernabéu, a chance they were unlikely to have again.

God was telling man something when he created the world in the shape of a football, was aware that Matthews had reasons for his reclusive existence, but also knew that any project to do with football was the one thing he might consider. And so he asked him if he would coach youngsters at a national sports education centre he was setting up in Marsa, with the result that Matthews turned up regularly at the centre on Saturday mornings for the next three years. 'He was not a real coach,' Father Hilary said, 'like me he wanted to play more than teach, but he had a great passion for the game.'

Living in Malta with the woman he loved, in a home called Idle Hours and with plenty of opportunities to coach and play football were still not reasons enough for Matthews to settle permanently on the island. If Malta had a drawback as a bolthole it was that it swarmed with Brits who might recognise him. The solution to his restlessness lay in the many profitable offers that still came his way from much further afield. In 1971, he accepted one of these, setting off with Mila on a three-month coaching trip to his old haunt – and favourite place, according to Mila – South Africa. The Snoyman family were largely responsible for facilitating this visit. Lubbe and his brother Phil Snoyman set up PR and sponsorship opportunities. They also allayed Mila's fears that she would not be accepted by friends who knew Betty. Lubbe Snoyman made sure she felt included and helped to organise a safari for her and Stanley and a number of sightseeing excursions.

Some years later Dennis Snoyman, Lubbe's son, talked about the family's friendship with Matthews, the sort of man he was and his relationship with Mila. 'With us Snoymans, Stanley felt he could be himself,' he said. 'People he liked and trusted he'd let into his world. He was very comfortable with Phil and my father.

'Stanley did definitely come out of his shell more after meeting Mila. She changed his life, seemed to have a lot of influence on his thinking. I met both wives; they were two very different people. I'd describe Stanley as an honest man. He didn't speak to a lot of people, kept everyone at arm's distance, and tended to just let a few selected friends into his space. I seem to recall once or twice he got irritated with other people, but I wouldn't say he was bad tempered and he didn't have a dark side to him that I knew of.'

In South Africa in 1971 Stanley and Mila, in the relatively early stages of their relationship, still took care not to be seen together. Mila said she hated this but accepted it had to be the case. She thought it miraculous that the press had yet to rumble that they were linked. Even the solicitors, 'locked in battle in England', as she put it, were only vaguely aware of who she was. But the trip did provide an opportunity to remove the last vestiges of the pretence they had kept up in front of his daughter Jean and her family.

Bob Gough had gone to South Africa soon after the holiday in Malta. He and Jean, wanting to escape England's cold winters, had chosen this as the place at Matthews's suggestion. Once Bob found work, Jean and the children joined him and were living in Bryanston, near Johannesburg, when Stanley and Mila arrived. This time when they all met no attempt was made by Stanley and Mila to hide the true nature of their relationship. Mila said it was the start of a friendship with Jean's family that grew stronger over the years.

This gave Matthews even more reason to accept an offer, put to him by the *Sunday Times* of Johannesburg just before they returned to Malta, to come back with Mila in 1972 to coach for a year.

It was between these 1971 and 1972 visits to South Africa that Matthews confronted Mila with the rumour that she was a Communist spy. He had picked it up on a solo trip from Malta to Stoke to talk to his solicitors about his divorce. Mila said he broke it to her sheepishly that the story doing the rounds was that not only was she a spy but she had three different names and was being investigated by British counter-espionage. She feigned shock and dismissed it as 'utterly preposterous', which Matthews readily accepted. Presumably she justified this reaction on the grounds she had suspended her work as an active agent in 1968.

It was not, though, the end of the matter. When they arrived back in Johannesburg they discovered Betty was also in town. And not only was she staying with Jean and Bob, which put the Goughs out of bounds to Stanley and Mila, but was the prime suspect for the spy story having reached South Africa. For a time this soured relations with Matthews's closest friends in South Africa, the Snoymans. Mila observed that Lubbe's wife, Dawn, previously so amicable, was ignoring her and, although she managed to persuade her the story was untrue, their damaged friendship took a while to return to where it had been.

What Matthews preferred to recall of that 1972 visit was the start of something he found truly fulfilling: coaching in Soweto, the township that so vividly represented the nation's oppressed majority. Contrary to some claims he was no apartheid buster and his involvement in Soweto was not his idea. Rather, it came from his sponsors, Coca-Cola and the newspaper backing his trip. Their wish was to be seen reacting positively to the growing international opposition to South Africa's white regime.

The idea was that Matthews should form his own team of emerging players, in other words young blacks, who were to be called Sir Stan's Men. It did not take long before he developed a genuine empathy with this group.* A young helper was co-opted. His job was to drive a minibus on an almost daily basis around the local schools picking up players. They were the raw material

---

* 'Matthews was a friend, a brother, a father, everything to me,' Gilbert Moiloa, the team captain, said. 'As team captain I was able to visit him at the Mariston Hotel in Johannesburg even though as a black man I was not permitted by law to do so. He would even come to my house in Soweto at night. He had no fear of the risks involved. He never spoke politics; his politics was football.'

from which Matthews formed his small squad of 'great little footballers'. His involvement gave him a real sense of purpose and another reason for wishing to revisit South Africa on a regular basis. Before he and Mila left in 1972 the nucleus of Sir Stan's Men was in place. The frequency with which Stanley and Mila visited South Africa meant that, effectively, they now had two homes: Idle Hours in Malta and a long-stay apartment at the Mariston Hotel in Johannesburg, a favourite base for British expats, including a number from show business such as the actor David Tomlinson and the entertainer Dickie Henderson. For three years Matthews commuted the thirty kilometres from Johannesburg to Soweto, where, he said – stretching a point – he lived as a black man with a white face.

No sooner were he and Mila back in the country for their second extended visit in 1973, their bags barely unpacked, than an emissary from Sir Stan's Men arrived at the Mariston to say the players were waiting for him at the football stadium in Soweto. A hectic schedule of matches followed. At first they played against other teams in Soweto and in nearby townships. As they improved they had to travel all over South Africa and beyond to find opponents good enough for them: to Durban, Bloemfontein and eventually outside the country to Botswana, Lesotho and Swaziland. Mila would often accompany them, filling a role, Matthews said, that was part mascot, part nurse-maid, part mum.

In 1975 Sir Stan's Men even travelled to South America, visiting Rio de Janeiro in defiance of worldwide support for South Africa's isolation. England was first mooted as a destination but, with stories about the still-sensitive issue of Matthews's divorce proceedings now appearing in the UK press, without mention of Mila, Brazil took its place.

The tour was scrutinised from all sides. The United Nations, football's world governing body Fifa and the South African Non-Racial Olympic Committee (Sanroc) all looked askance at the expedition, even though it was by a black team to a country with the largest black population outside Africa. The massed opposition meant that, in order to avoid intervention, Sir Stan's Men agreed not to play any official fixtures. There was no question of breaking this commitment with João Havelange, Fifa's Brazilian president, who briefly met the team, on hand to check they stuck to it.

South Africa's white regime also had their misgivings about the tour. As a result two policemen accompanied the team, secretly at first, along with an entourage that also included Stanley and Mila, confident that their relationship would escape close inspection so far from home, and Lubbe Snoyman. The policemen's cover did not last long. The team captain Gilbert Moiloa said they found out the identity of the two white men, who always seemed to be hanging around them, about two days after arriving in Rio. 'These guys followed us to a nightclub where we got drunk and talked politics,' he said. Moiloa evidently sampled other delights of Rio's nightlife, bringing women back to his room in the hotel – a recreational extra carefully documented by the policemen. 'They had photos of me and a woman,' he said, 'and [when the team returned home] I fled South Africa for Botswana to avoid being arrested.' This suggests the woman was white, which, under the South African regime's rules of engagement between the sexes, would have made it illegal for Moiloa to consort with her.

Matthews would recount some years later that while in Brazil he had to deal with the problem of at least one team member being involved with a white hooker, paid for out of the pocket money Sir Stan's Men received for their food. It is possible that at this point he also wondered how on earth a working-class lad from an industrial town in England came to be in South America, accompanied by a woman who wasn't his wife, sorting out an incident between a black lad and a white prostitute.

Had they been English policemen escorting the team, they

would have been far more interested in another meeting
Matthews had – with Ronnie Biggs, who had taken part in the
Great Train Robbery in England in 1963. He was now living
as a fugitive in Rio having escaped from Wandsworth prison
in 1965. Matthews said a message from Biggs arrived at his
hotel and, having socialised with a number of famous people
during his career, he thought it time he met someone infamous.
As English people do abroad, they had tea together and talked
about the club Biggs supported, Charlton Athletic. Matthews
said that as he left Biggs told him the banknotes the robbers
stole were going to be burnt: 'It wasn't like we nicked them off
poor people.'

Matthews was the main reason the tour was a success. He
was manifestly popular with the players. He also enjoyed their
admiration, particularly after he participated in a practice
session with university students that turned into the closest they
came to playing a match. 'He took part for about twenty minutes,'
Ruskin Malobela, an inside-forward, said. 'To see a sixty-year-
old white man with such skill was amazing. Even though he was
old, Stan still had the ability to dribble and outrun many of us.'

The year after the Rio visit, rioting in Soweto, precipitated
by the government's attempt to enforce the use of Afrikaans
in schools, made the township too dangerous a place for
Matthews to continue his visits. The disturbances brought an
end to a project that might have seen Sir Stan's Men elevated to
professional and national league status. That they weren't 'was
very, very harsh', Moiloa said. 'The league said no because we
were named after Stanley Matthews.' Moiloa said they argued
in vain that Kaizer Chiefs were named after Kaizer Motaung, a
former player and founder of the Chiefs, and Orlando Pirates
took their name from Edwin Orlando Leake, Soweto's first
administrator.

How good a coach Matthews was is a matter of some debate.
Eddie Lewis, a Football League player in the 1950s and 1960s

with clubs that included Manchester United, West Ham and Leyton Orient, coached successfully in South Africa while Matthews was out there. Lewis remembered Matthews cutting him dead after Orient set back Stoke's ultimately successful 1962 promotion run by beating them 1-0, but found him easygoing and friendly when they met again in Johannesburg at a lunch given by Phil Snoyman. When it came to coaching, Lewis bracketed Matthews with other great players. 'Stan wasn't a good coach,' he said. 'I mean he could show them how to dribble but he didn't have many ideas. He mainly let them play with the ball and gave the kids skills. Look at him, Bobby Moore and Bobby Charlton, everything with them was their instinct – they never thought about what they did – yet people like me and others [who became coaches] had to think about it.'

Happy Dlamini, another of Sir Stan's Men, said of Matthews's coaching: 'The only time he got a bit angry was when we didn't play football according to his plan. Then he'd shout at us in his football language with his teeth closed, which made it difficult to understand exactly what he was saying.' Not playing 'according to his plan' agrees with Matthews's own recurring lament that the players had wonderful skills that they thought were wasted if they were made to play in defence. Matthews was glad his players saw that in Rio, where football matches, both organised and chaotic, took place all the time, teams at every level placed as much emphasis on defence as they did on attack.

Regardless of whether Matthews was a good coach or why exactly it was he went into Soweto and other townships – to satisfy sponsors or a desire to right wrongs – he did make an impression. In 2008, Archbishop Desmond Tutu, a central figure in the collapse of South Africa's white rule, said this to the British film-maker Geoff Francis:

It had a significance: a white man who had been at the top of his trade coming into the townships at a time when racial discrimination was at its most intense. It was something that had all kinds of ramifications in the fact that it also helped to strengthen our hope for the future. So, it wasn't just, as it were, maybe a sporting gesture or a gesture of magnanimity; it had a very, very profound significance in that although you might not have thought that might be the case, it did make a dent in the apartheid armoury because it said there's something quite ridiculous that you should have someone come all the way, ten thousand miles, to do something that was not normal in that country.

On Friday 20 June 1975, nearly seven years after Matthews had left his Blackpool home to be with Mila Winterova in West Germany, a decree nisi was made in an English court ending his marriage to Betty.

Mila said it was still the case when this happened that very few people knew she and Stanley were a couple. One person who very definitely did know was Betty – and had done for some time. Her fierce determination to hold on to Stanley was the reason the divorce took the time it did. It would almost certainly have caused further delay had not a reform of the law allowed Matthews to petition simply on the grounds of irretrievable breakdown, based on having lived separately for five years. Betty's feelings were understandable even if, according to some family members, they did turn into something disconcertingly hard-edged. At one point she threatened to talk to the press about her husband's relationship with Mila, but may have decided against this on the grounds that it would have ended any prospect of reconciliation. The wife of Matthews's old Stoke teammate Freddie Steele told of meeting Betty at a function at which she said: 'I am the real Lady Matthews, not that other lady.' She then broke down in tears. Her unhappiness was only thinly disguised in a greeting she once used to Helen Viollet. She asked whether Helen's husband, Dennis, ever saw 'Sir'.

In due course, Betty moved back to the Midlands. She had been joined in Kent by Jean and the rest of the Gough family when they resettled in England from South Africa. Then, when the Goughs returned to Stoke for Bob's business, she followed them. She lived in a retirement apartment in Stafford – close to Jean and her family – until she died at the age of ninety-five, still shattered by having lost Stanley. 'I am very sad today,' she said when he died in 2000. 'I was married to Stan for forty years; we had a wonderful marriage. I knew him during our younger days. He was the light of my life, the only man I ever loved.'

As Mila related it, she and Stanley were in Johannesburg, at the Mariston Hotel, when his solicitor rang from Stoke to tell him about the decree absolute. He then insisted on waiting until he received written confirmation before sharing her enthusiasm for planning their civil marriage straightaway in South Africa.

The ceremony took place in a register office in the small town of Nigel just to the south-east of Johannesburg. They went there to arrange the marriage in three days' time before deciding, all of a sudden, not to wait even though they were dressed, Mila said, like a pair of dropouts. They were married that afternoon by a morose-looking registrar, with the young female receptionist as their witness and in a room so sparsely furnished that they had to share a single chair.

This would have been wonderful material if Peter Whelan had ever made that television film about Stanley and Mila. Newspapers reported that the film did not happen because Matthews put 'too high a price on his love for Mila'. Whelan said this was not necessarily the case. The TV company's factual drama budget might not have been equal even to a modest cost. It seems possible another reason was that Mila discouraged the project for fear of what the film-makers might unearth about her past.

Whelan did get as far as discussing the project with Matthews in some detail. 'When Stan and I talked it through he always seemed most enthusiastic,' Whelan said. 'I recall us laughing over a dream casting of it. He said he should be played by Michael Caine . . . and I, not to be outdone, suggested Meryl Streep as Mila. We were enjoying ourselves . . . Stan very much so.

'I never met Betty and only met Stan in the company of Mila. Of course, Mila's vivacity and sense of fun certainly had a way of bringing him out. The Stan I knew briefly was a very happy man.'

Chapter 21

'It was all I could do to keep my composure
seeing him like that'

Aged sixty and married for a second time, Stanley Matthews was still more than a decade away from completing the circle of his life that would bring him back to Stoke-on-Trent and a home just a few miles from where he had been born. For the moment sufficient energy churned within him to feed his inclination, regardless of whether he had a ball at his feet, always to be on the move – a tendency that received every encouragement from the new Lady Matthews who was happy to travel as much as he was. What had been a solitary form of escape became a shared enjoyment. The name of the bungalow in Malta, Idle Hours, was apt only in the sense that it stood empty for so long.

South Africa, including the townships, remained a favourite place for Matthews to visit and coach, but the disbandment of Sir Stan's Men in 1976 and Fifa's decision the same year to expel South Africa from the international football fold changed things. Fifa's action was the cue for a number of foreign coaches and some players, who did not want to damage their careers, to leave the country. Matthews also started to look around for other destinations, although, given that he had no career to protect, he was less fussed than those still in their prime. 'I'm not sure Stan even cared about these things,' Peter Raath, the South African football historian, said. 'He had been defying the Nationalist Government for years by entering Soweto.'

Later, Matthews's name would appear on the United Nations' Register of Sports Contacts with South Africa, first published in May 1979 and known as the UN blacklist. This added to the problems of visiting the country but, again, Matthews took a relaxed view of being listed. He said his conscience was clear given that the offending contacts were chiefly his sessions coaching black players. 'I coach where I am invited, if I want to,' he said. 'There are 2,800 people on the UN blacklist, including Frank Sinatra – so I am in good company, very good company.'

His blacklisting did cause one unfortunate incident. This was when he flew to Zimbabwe to be the main guest at a sportsman of the year dinner honouring the country's cricket captain, the white player Dave Houghton. Matthews arrived only to find that, at the last minute, he had been barred from attending because of his links with South Africa. Instead, he and Mila dined elsewhere in Harare, not far from where Houghton was being honoured. Matthews said he was disappointed but not as disappointed as on some other occasions: 'Like when you play for England and lose a match.'

Interestingly, the United Nations' wrath was not so severe that the organisation reckoned Matthews to be completely beyond redemption. Unesco awarded him the 1986 Pierre de Coubertin Fair Play Trophy, which, because he was then living in Canada, he asked Bob and Jean Gough to accept for him at a ceremony in Paris.

Matthews's brushes with the UN did have one happy postscript. Sam Ramsamy, a South African living in exile in England, was responsible for drawing up the blacklist and was the one who refused to give permission for Matthews to attend the dinner in Harare. In the end, though, the two became friends. 'At the time we blacklisted him I wasn't very happy with him and he wasn't very happy with me,' Ramsamy said. 'But we had a blanket ban. A lot of these sportsmen didn't go to South Africa because they supported apartheid; money was what attracted them. But the apartheid government used their visits to indicate they supported the regime.'

Their friendship developed over a property deal. When Ramsamy returned to South Africa, after Nelson Mandela's release, he instructed an estate agent acquaintance who had found Matthews an apartment in Johannesburg to do the same for him. As Stanley and Mila were now trying to dispose of their apartment, in Rosebank Village, the agent suggested Ramsamy and his wife take a look at it. They liked it, bought it and invited Stanley and Mila to visit them there. 'We stayed in touch,' Ramsamy said. 'On one occasion he left me half a dozen champagne glasses with his photograph and name, which I still have.

'When I started chatting with him I got to know he wasn't a political person. He was altruistic in the sense that he loved passing on his knowledge of football to anybody and everybody.'

Stanley and Mila did settle down briefly back in Malta. To an extent the pause was a celebration of being able to live on the island without the need for furtiveness. They were now a properly married couple and Mila was no longer regarded as some shadowy figure from Eastern Europe, even if she was still being monitored by the secret police who once controlled her. They relished the normality previously denied them. Their network of friends, formerly vetted to exclude anyone thought capable of being indiscreet, widened, although they socialised sparingly.

Mila's life was made easier in one other way after she submitted a new application to Prague in 1975 to live permanently in Malta. Strictly speaking she had been on the run up until this point. In 1972 she had been refused permission to live in Malta and her StB file shows her latest request was not granted until

1977. But a tacit agreement with the Czechoslovak authorities seems to have existed from 1975 that she could live where she liked and travel as she pleased. As well as being the year of her marriage to Matthews, 1975 was also the year she was granted British citizenship under the name Gertrud Leonore Matthews. At last able to return to Prague without fear of arrest, Mila made a melancholy early trip back to attend her father's funeral.

Matthews remained boundlessly active, playing golf and tennis and swimming in their pool. A much younger friend recalled being outdriven, outputted, outwitted and outplayed at every hole by him during a round at Marsa golf course – and then watching his vanquisher sip fruit juice while he swilled a gallon of beer.

There was also Matthews's football, which he continued playing well into his sixties. He wrote to his old Stoke City teammate Dennis Viollet, who was living in Florida: 'By the way, I still play. I go out every Sunday morning and play for the post office team. It's not the greatest of standards but it keeps me fit.'*

To start with, Stanley and Mila may have thought in terms of a long, if not permanent, pause in Malta. His resolve gradually weakened, though, worn away by the flow of requests from all over the world for his services. To be so much in demand wrenched at any roots that had started to go down. Malta had been a wonderful retreat when he and Mila needed one to protect what he in particular regarded as their clandestine relationship. Now he was no longer fixated on keeping her a secret. On the contrary, he seemed eager to be seen with her. What better way to do this than by travelling openly with her as a football ambassador. Don Taylor, who collaborated with the couple on *Back in Touch*, said he sat with Matthews while he

---

* As Stanley played, Mila contented herself in the garden. Its colourful display had already helped to attract the makers of the 1973 film *The Mackintosh Man*, starring Paul Newman, who used it as a location – Newman and Stan got on famously, Mila said – and now she worked at making it even more of a show.

contemplated a number of invitations to go abroad and took a phone call from the great Wales player John Charles asking him to play in an exhibition match with Stan Mortensen in Bangor, North Wales. 'Within hours he was closeted with his travel agent, planning dates, flights and itineraries,' Taylor said. 'The excitement was enormous.'

With the difficult political situation in South Africa limiting what he could do there, Matthews was happy to consider any offer that came his way. In 1980, when he and Mila arrived back in Malta having been away for several weeks, they found a letter waiting for them from Australia. It was from Bill Webb, an expat from Lancashire who had played as a semi-pro for Wigan Athletic and Morecambe and was now living in Ipswich, Queensland. He had written asking Matthews to come over on a private visit to hold coaching clinics for children. Australia was a country Matthews had been particularly fond of since his visit with Blackpool in 1958. Subsequently, a rumour had circulated that he planned to settle in the country. He would play for the Sydney club Prague, a name that had not yet acquired a special resonance for him, while his son would receive the best tennis coaching available.

It never happened but the letter from Bill Webb revived happy memories. He wrote straight back. He apologised for not replying sooner and said that he would certainly undertake the trip if they could agree terms. Webb raised funds by ringing around clubs and associations he knew would be interested in welcoming Matthews. 'We offered a figure plus airfares and accommodation in Brisbane for him and Mila and he was quite happy with that,' Webb said. The Queensland Soccer Federation, however, turned down Webb's offer to involve them in Matthews's visit. 'They didn't want to know because the whole thing was what they described as a private matter,' Webb said. 'Stanley was very understanding. He knew we weren't a big organisation with money behind us and went out of his way to be as helpful as he could.'

As far as South Africa was concerned, Matthews's visits with
Mila were now as much as anything to see the Goughs, who in
1972 had presented him with another grandchild, and his friends
the Snoymans. A young reporter on Johannesburg's afternoon
newspaper, the *Star*, recalled what became an almost annual
event, a summons to one of the Snoyman car workshops where
the press would be served fish and chips while interviewing
Matthews about his agenda for this particular stay. The reporter
said it grew harder by the year to find an angle for what was no
more than another 'Sir Stanley back in town' story. Matthews
went there in 1982 and 1983 but as far as football was concerned
he was increasingly a peripheral figure.

In Canada, Stanley and Mila set up semi-permanent residence
first in Toronto and then in Burlington, which is in the Greater
Toronto Area on the western end of Lake Ontario. Matthews
had enjoyed his visits to Canada as a player and regarded North
America as a place where football was likely to expand rapidly,
a view that may have been unduly influenced by his spending
so much time with a relatively small group of soccer-minded
people. One of these was the ultra-wealthy businessman Steve
Stavro, who was Matthews's Snoyman figure in Canada. Stavro
made the country even more attractive to Matthews, one of the
few footballers whose name was familiar to Canadians, by his
readiness to sponsor the Englishman to live there with his new
wife and publicise the game.

Just as he was latterly in South Africa, Matthews was now
more likely to be seen at functions and promotional events
in Canada than he was playing or coaching, although his
commitment to fitness remained as intense as ever. He did
do some punditry for CBC television, including alongside the
stylish Canadian anchorman Ernie Afaganis during the 1982
World Cup, but this was not something at which he excelled,
quite the contrary according to some accounts. Stan Adamson,
a leading figure in Canadian football, remembered that for most

of the time Matthews was quite a removed figure. He and Mila lived quietly and, to start with, mostly unrecognised in a ninth-floor apartment, with views over the water, at Admiral's Walk, a prestigious new building on Burlington's Lakeshore Road.

Jim Waterman and his wife, Jean, were among the few who did instantly recognise the newly arrived couple. The Watermans originated from Staffordshire, Jim had taught in Cannock, and they had the next-door apartment to the grandly named Flagship suite where Stanley and Mila lived. Jean remembered being struck by Mila's introduction when they first met in the communal laundry. 'I'm Lady Matthews,' Mila said. In contrast to this rather stilted piece of social positioning, Stanley had no airs in this regard. Jim Waterman used to drive him to games and said his chest swelled with pride when Matthews introduced him as 'my buddy, Jim'. The Watermans remembered Stanley and Mila as being friendly and always happy to pop round for a drink, but were generally as retiring as they could be with so many people wanting to meet them as news of their whereabouts spread.

Most of these visitors had a football connection, some of them dropping by simply to pay homage. Terry Kelly, a lawyer and president of the Ontario Soccer Association, told of the day he took two hard-drinking Irish international players to see Matthews in Burlington. On the way they stopped off for lunch. 'I couldn't believe it, both of them refused to have a drink as a mark of respect to Matthews,' he said. 'It made me realise the regard he was held in.'

Kelly and his companions would have been entertained in a spotlessly kept home. Another story Jean Waterman told was of the time Stanley and Mila went away for several weeks. After a while, people in the apartments above and below the Flagship suite complained of a strong, disinfectant-type smell. When it became overwhelming someone managed to gain access to the Matthews apartment and found mothballs scattered over the furnishings like hailstones.

Hygiene and neatness in all things were part of the Matthews code. His appearance, for example, was always something that had mattered to him, and if anything became more important the older he got. Jim Waterman did catch him out once when he encountered his knight-of-the-realm neighbour, bin in hand, returning from the garbage chute wearing garishly coloured underwear.

Mostly, though, Matthews took meticulous care of how he dressed. He liked suits made by the Savile Row tailor Chester Barrie. A friend recalled the pair of them going for fittings at the company's factory. Even when he dressed down or played sport he liked to look snappy. 'He used to wear jeans – and he's the only man I know who looked smart in them,' Jean, his daughter, said. 'He'd go to dinners in jeans and jacket and look really dapper.' A photograph of him in tennis kit, standing next to Mila, is a vision in pristine white from his knitted skullcap to his immaculate trainers via polo-necked top, zip-up jerkin and carefully pressed shorts. He had a collection of natty hats and when without one it was a rare occasion that he was not scrupulously coiffured. A former fellow player once quipped when attending a function with an elderly Matthews: 'Don't want to get too close to Stanley. Wouldn't want to crack his hair.'

Maybe attention to how he presented himself only seemed to concern him more in later life. As a younger man he was invariably photographed dressed for football, which limited the opportunities to show off his sartorial flair. By the time he arrived in Canada, with Mila, in the ambassadorial role partly funded by Stavro, his invitations were mostly to dos that required him to dress up. He was asked to play one last game of football in 1985, a veterans' match between Brazil and England in Rio de Janeiro, after which he needed a cartilage operation on a knee. From then on his public appearances were invariably at events that required jacket and tie, all of which he attended vying to be the sprucest one there.

The year 1985 was a particularly good one for putting on his finery. He celebrated his seventieth birthday on both sides of the Atlantic. The Stanley Matthews Tribute Dinner on the actual day of his birthday, 1 February, was a major social happening in Toronto. It took place in the Grand Ballroom of the Sheraton Centre. Tickets were fifty dollars a head, proceeds going to the Canadian Soccer Association Youth Programme. The former Scotland international Graham Leggat was MC.

Ten days later Matthews returned to Stoke for a birthday ball whose organising committee included Jackie Mudie and Peter Buxton. It was held in the King's Hall, which had also been packed forty-seven years earlier for a protest meeting 'to urge the retention of Stanley Matthews by Stoke City.

This was the first time he had visited his hometown for a large, formal event since he had fled the country seventeen years earlier. Any apprehension he might have felt about how he would be received proved misplaced. Stoke, he realised, would be happy to see him and the second Lady Matthews whenever they wanted to come.

This point was made even more forcefully in 1987 when he was invited back, with Mila, on two occasions. Once more King's Hall was the venue on 30 June that year when Sir Stanley Matthews, one time pupil of Wellington Road School in Hanley, as unassuming an educational establishment as it is possible to imagine, was honoured by Keele University. Three others were similarly recognised on the same day: the playwright Alan Ayckbourn, the astronomer Professor Sir Francis Graham-Smith and Sir Brian Urquhart, a former Under-Secretary General at the United Nations.

Gurnos Jones, professor of organic chemistry at Keele, gave an appreciation of Matthews before Stoke's footballing knight received his honorary Master of the University degree. In an entertainingly droll address, Jones said that as 'a narrow specialist' Matthews was, perhaps, unsuitable for the degree. He insisted, Jones said, 'on winning games from his place on the wing, rather than tackling back to help his defence like a modern automaton'. On the other hand, throughout his life he had been an ambassador of sporting skill and of fair play, including in Soweto, and since his retirement had 'carried the name of Stoke and England to all corners of the globe'.

Three months later Matthews was back in Stoke, with Mila, flown over from Canada by the city council to open a pedestrian precinct and unveil a statue of himself. The local paper reported this exercise cost the council £4,284, which elicited the almost mandatory protest letter from a reader incensed that ratepayers had had to stump up without being consulted. Mostly, though, Matthews's presence at the inauguration of the life-size work, created in bronze by local sculptor Colin Melbourne, seems to have been appreciated as something that gave the area a fillip.

The statue stands in Parliament Row, less than half a mile from Matthews's childhood home in Seymour Street. It captures him aged forty-six when he helped Stoke return to the First Division. He has a ball at his feet, most of the time. It has been known to disappear, although the light-fingered find it more difficult now the ball has been secured with a metal spike. The inscription on the plinth, composed by David Miller who wrote the 1989 authorised biography of Matthews and gave an address at the unveiling, reads, in part: 'His name is symbolic of the beauty of the game, his fame timeless and international, his sportsmanship and modesty universally acclaimed. A magical player, of the people, for the people.'

In his speech, Miller told a story to illustrate Matthews's love for his hometown and its traditions. The year was 1950 when Matthews was in Brazil with the England team for the World Cup. The British Ambassador asked him at a reception if he knew what that was, pointing to a large Ali Baba vase. 'Yes,' Matthews said straightaway and with aplomb. 'There are only about fourteen of them left in the world. It's a rare Wedgwood.'

Not to be outdone, South Africa was about to stage its own Matthews-themed celebration. Matthews's friend Phil Snoyman orchestrated the plans for a Sir Stanley Matthews tribute dinner at the Carlton Hotel, Johannesburg, in January 1988, with Stanley and Mila the guests of honour. An estimated four hundred guests paid more than £100 a ticket for the five-hour banquet.

Unexpectedly, given the array of professional entertainers signed up for the event, the most-reported contribution came from Abdul Bhamjee, the flamboyant public relations officer of the National Soccer League who would be jailed for fraud in the 1990s. Bhamjee made the headlines on two counts. First he delivered a controversial speech, in which he called the United Nations 'a bunch of idiots' for blacklisting Matthews; he then bid generously for a portrait of Matthews with the idea of having it hung in the NSL boardroom, which, reportedly, did not go down well with other league officials.

The publicity given to Bhamjee was not quite what the organisers must have hoped for when planning this celebration of Matthews's long association with football in South Africa.

In 1989 Stanley and Mila, after fourteen years of being married but with no permanent address, ended their itinerant existence. Matthews's friend Huston Spratt, who lived in Stoke, took a telephone call from Canada. 'Stanley rang up to say he and Mila were coming back to live in England,' Spratt said. 'He told me he had nowhere to stop and could I help.' Spratt asked a friend who owned the Borough Arms Hotel in Newcastle under Lyme whether he could put up a couple who were due to arrive soon from abroad. 'When I let on that it was Sir Stanley Matthews and his wife, my friend offered to have them for nothing for as long as they liked.'

Matthews said that after two decades living and coaching overseas 'the pull of my roots became too strong'. He might have added that up until now not everything would necessarily have been right for such a return. His relationship with Mila might never have prospered had it not been allowed to start out on neutral ground. When the two of them met in middle age they had experienced only turbulence in their lives. The destabilising effect of living in the eye of the great European storm that beset Czechoslovakia in the middle of the twentieth century had been as real for Mila as the disrupting impact of fame had been for Stanley. Neither really had had the chance to adjust to living normal lives, to test their ability to truly love a fellow adult. Now, having passed this test, they were ready to settle down into what would prove as idyllic a home life as either had known since early childhood.

Matthews knew from his recent trips back to Stoke that his dramatic flight from England in 1968 was too long ago to have any lingering news mileage and that no one apart, possibly, from his first wife would rather he stayed away. He and Mila would go on making regular trips to sunny resorts, their favourite being Tenerife, somewhere his brother and sister-in-law, Ron and Mavis Matthews, recommended, but his greater need in old age was a home in the place he felt most comfortable. 'I think he enjoyed the Potteries people,' Stanley Junior said. 'He found them down to earth.' As Peter Buxton noted, back in Stoke he discovered 'a new zest for enjoyment'.

Much later, Nick Hancock, the comedian and Stoke resident, had his own droll take on Matthews's return to a town whose advantages as somewhere to set up home are kept well hidden. Speaking at the unveiling of the sculpture of Matthews in Stoke, Hancock noted that the footballer had lived in many places with more obvious charms: 'But he came back here and if he doesn't deserve a statue for that I don't know what he deserves one for.'

Quite apart from anything else Stoke was where most of the surviving members of Matthews's immediate family still lived. His mother, Ada, was no longer alive, nor was the second of the brothers, Arthur. But Jack and Ron, the oldest and youngest brothers, were there and Jean and Bob Gough would soon move back to the area.

The house Stanley and Mila bought in Stoke was on the other side of town from where Matthews had grown up and was at some remove, too, in terms of character, even if it did need a good deal of repair work. The grade II listed cottage, 1 The Views, on New Road, Penkhull, was where the scientist Sir Oliver Lodge, inventor of the spark plug, was born in 1851. It had a spacious downstairs, where Stanley had his study in which stood the wood and ivory throne presented to him in Ghana in 1957, four bedrooms upstairs and gardens front and rear. But the previous owner, an elderly lady, had largely neglected its upkeep. Matthews, with none of the necessary practical skills, took no credit for the restoration work. He said the interior refurbishment and the landscaping and replanting of the gardens, which were overgrown and full of rubble, were Mila's triumph. She had a great talent for such things. In 2000, after Matthews died, it went on the market for £300,000.

Stanley and Mila particularly liked being in the garden at the back on summer evenings. An enclosing screen of trees gave complete privacy and shut out any impression of being near to an urban centre. Their enjoyment of each other's company was nicely illustrated by a story Jean told about the times she and Bob were asked to dinner. As soon as they had finished eating her father would say: 'Don't you think you ought to be going?'

Evidence that no lingering resentment existed at Stoke City from Matthews's run-ins with the club or from his switch of allegiance to join Port Vale as manager arrived in 1990 when he was invited to be Stoke FC's president. It was not an honour that was likely to go to his head, nor did it. He summed up the enjoyment it gave him by saying: 'I have a couple of box tickets and I have a cup of tea before I go out, I have a cup of tea at half-time and I have a cup of tea at full-time – and when they win I'm very happy, everybody's winning. So that's the only enjoyment

I get out of it.' When a radio reporter once suggested he was a figurehead for the club, he said: 'I don't know about figurehead. I enjoy going down and seeing a lot of expert players or whatever.'

If this relaxed attitude suggests he was unwinding in all areas of his life the reality was rather different. As word spread that he was back living in Stoke he was much in demand for speaking engagements and other functions. He enjoyed these chances to get out and renew old acquaintances – as well as make a bit of pocket money. He said he 'got by' as a public speaker. His formula was mainly to reminisce about his experiences and throw in the odd joke. Among these was telling the audience he was a non-drinker and non-smoker before adding: 'Two out of three ain't bad.'

He received help in ordering his schedule from a friend, Pat Brogan, a boxing promoter who lived in Cheshire and was as close as anyone ever came to being his agent. Matthews had got to know Brogan a little before returning permanently to England with Mila. One of their meetings was in 1983 at the funeral of Roy Chapman, a player Matthews had signed while at Port Vale and whose son, Lee, would be a successful centre-forward for Leeds United. When Peter Buxton recommended Brogan to Matthews as someone who might take care of the requests for his services the two men soon formed a semi-formal association.

Their road trips provided Brogan with a fund of stories. One involved an event in Norwich at which Matthews and John H Stracey, the British boxer who held the WBC world welterweight title in the mid-1970s, were guests. Brogan drove them there, Matthews sitting in the front and Stracey in the back seat complaining of a terrible headache. Once again Matthews eagerly applied his knowledge of pressure points, passed on by Mila. 'The next thing I know', Brogan said, 'is that he tells John to give him his foot. So John dangles his foot over the seat and over Stan's shoulder and here I am driving along with Stanley

Matthews sitting beside me massaging John H Stracey's big toe and John's sitting there with his eyes shut saying, "Ooh, I feel better now".

Brogan said event organisers were prepared to pay four-figure sums for appearances by Matthews, but 'I never took a penny off Sir Stanley. I had too much respect for him.' Instead Matthews repaid Brogan in other ways. 'When I was ill I told Stan about my problem. He was on the phone to people in America to get me properly diagnosed and the best treatment. In the end I had the surgery done in England. And when I came round from the operation the first person on the phone to me was Stan.' Acts of kindness and common decency such as this were the recurring theme of Brogan's stories and those of so many others that poured out at the time of Matthews's death.

Paul Walters was a middleweight boxer managed by Brogan. He mentioned to Brogan one day that his grandfather, whose eightieth birthday was coming up, had watched Matthews play and would love to meet him. 'Without telling Paul,' Brogan said, 'I told Stan, "Listen, this fighter of mine, it's his granddad's eightieth birthday and he's always wanted to meet you." So Stan says, "Come and pick me up at half past seven." I picked him up and took him along to the hotel and Stan sat there chatting to the old man and eating chips off his plate. Paul was nearly in tears his granddad was so pleased.'

On another occasion Brogan arranged for a radio interviewer to meet Matthews in the Grand Hotel, Leicester. 'The guy doing the interview knocked on the door,' Brogan said, 'and Stan opened it in his underpants and invited him in. Stan then told him to sit on the bed with his tape recorder and asked him if he wanted a cup of tea. The interviewer guy said, "I couldn't believe Sir Stanley was doing this for me." Stan made him the tea and then sat on the bed and gave him a half an hour interview.'

A book of press cuttings that Jean Gough produced as a tribute to her father included several stories sent in by readers of the Stoke newspaper attesting to his kindness, far too many for them to be addressing a phoney or aberrant characteristic. One was from an expat couple in Canada. They had written to Matthews asking whether he could assist their ailing uncle, a lifelong Stoke fan still living in the town, to make one last visit to watch the club play. 'Imagine our feelings when our uncle phoned to say that he had been picked up by limo and had watched the game from the directors' box. He never did know how it happened but the excitement in his voice told it all.'

These stories, surely, reflected the intrinsic generosity of his nature, which, because of his unusual life, he had difficulty expressing until achieving contented seniority. But if acts of kindness towards people he had never met were mainly a feature of his later years, manifestations of his modesty were evident throughout his life, no less so in old age than when he was playing. A football writer told the story of when his wife, at Wembley for the opening ceremony and match of Euro 96, queued to collect tickets. She noticed an elderly gentleman waiting behind her and insisted he go ahead of her, which he did, reluctantly. The girl at the window had difficulty finding his ticket and asked him his first name. After he told her she found it immediately: 'Oh here it is . . . Sir Stanley Matthews, eh? You should have said!'

The final public display, during Matthews's lifetime, of the affection the people of Stoke felt for him was the celebration of his eightieth birthday at the Trentham Gardens Hotel in 1995. By now a formula existed for such anniversaries. It started with the formation of a committee. Brogan was one of the organisers of this event. The convivial occasion, attended by around eight hundred people, included a presentation to Matthews by Graham Kelly, chief executive of the FA, of a replica of his 1953 FA Cup winner's medal. As ever, Brogan remembered the occasion with an anecdote. It concerned the local businessman who made a substantial winning bid for an item in the charity auction. The next day Brogan received a frantic call from Matthews who had seen on the news that the businessman had been arrested. The offence had nothing to do with the birthday celebration but Matthews was worried, unnecessarily as it turned out, that the money for the item would not be paid.

The first public evidence of Matthews's failing health came in May 1997 when he was taken to hospital in Stoke with chest pains. Mila summoned help in the early hours of the morning but Matthews refused to be carried or pushed in a chair to the ambulance. He insisted on walking. Although he had also been suffering from flu and bronchitis, he had not, Mila said, given up his daily exercise regime. 'Stan still thinks he's fifty,' she said. He was taken to Stoke's City General Hospital, where three weeks before he had opened the new cardiac department. His brief stay meant he had to forgo being guest of honour for England's international friendly against South Africa at Old Trafford.

Two years later, on 27 July 1999, heart trouble would claim Mila's life at the age of seventy-six before it did Stanley's. She had suffered a minor scare that required hospital treatment earlier in the year but she had been apparently restored to full health. Matthews had left the house early to go for a routine check-up of his own and Jean found Mila when she dropped round to take her to join Stanley for a shopping expedition. She had died sitting in a chair with the television on. By the time Stanley called to find out where Mila had got to a doctor was at the house. He was able to spare Jean the task of breaking the devastating news to Matthews. A small gathering attended the funeral at Bradwell crematorium in Stoke six days later. Matthews left with Jean without saying anything. In the short period between her death and his own, Matthews added a few words to his autobiography. He said she had given him true happiness and with her he had experienced the unmitigated joys of a bond that was true, sincere and loving.

Apart from Matthews's immediate family, Geoff Oakey, a

friend who became Matthews's driver in his final years, was as close to Stanley as anyone at this time. Oakey said that, regardless of how late it was, whenever he delivered Stanley home, Mili, as he called her, would appear in the porch in her dressing gown to give him a hug. The nearest he heard them come to a row was over Mila's heavy smoking. One day in the car Stanley complained when she lit up, to which Mila said she never told him what or what not to do.

Oakey said that Matthews shut himself away after Mila's death. When some weeks later he received a call from Matthews he could barely recognise his croaking voice. Stanley told him it was the first time he had phoned anyone since Mila's death. Jean and her husband eventually persuaded Matthews to go on holiday to the apartment he and Mila had bought in Tenerife. Oakey, as ever, drove him to Luton airport. He noted that Matthews insisted that he observe Mila's stricture not to go faster than 50mph.

Since his heart trouble in 1997, Matthews had remained under constant observation by his specialist in Stoke. This continued while he was in Tenerife, the specialist receiving results of regular blood tests Matthews underwent on the island. These started to show a marked decline in his condition, something his friends could see for themselves. A member of the Lions Club of Santiago del Teide, who went with others to present Matthews with a certificate honouring his support for the charity, said that he was almost unrecognisable. 'It was all I could do to keep my composure seeing him like that,' the friend said.

Jean and Bob joined Matthews in Tenerife for his eighty-fifth birthday. They were told not to bring any of the many hundreds of cards that had already arrived at Penkhull. While the Goughs were there Matthews had a fall at his apartment. The accident seemed innocuous. A chair gave way as he tried to stand up and he tumbled backwards. 'The medical checks suggested he had only bruised his back and neck,' said the friend from the Lions

Club, 'but anyone who knew him before would have realised he was going downhill fast.' All Matthews wanted now was to return to England. He vetoed the idea of a check-up at the local hospital in case they stopped him flying.

When Oakey went to the airport to collect Matthews, the procedure was a familiar one. The attendant, who also knew the routine, directed him to his usual parking spot that was ideal for a quick getaway. This time, though, rather than being first off the plane, Matthews was the last to appear, pushed in a wheelchair by Jean. He muttered to Oakey something about not being at all well and getting him home as quickly as possible.

He was transferred to the North Staffordshire Nuffield private hospital in Newcastle under Lyme where, on Wednesday 23 February 2000, with Jean and Bob at his bedside, he died aged eighty-five. A spokesman for the hospital said: 'Sir Stanley Matthews died peacefully this evening after a short illness related to health problems that had first seriously affected him three years ago.' That same evening the England team wore black armbands when they walked out to play Argentina in a friendly at Wembley. The match, preceded by a minute's silence, ended 0-0.

England performed well but had no one skilled enough to create the sort of mayhem Matthews had in his last match against South American opposition, the 4-2 defeat of Brazil forty-four years earlier, also at Wembley.

Stanley Matthews's death marked the start of a new Matthews story. The man became a legend and the memories, accurate and fanciful, will be told and recycled well into the future. One aspect of the immediate legend-making was picked up on by the academic Garry Whannel. He remarked on the reluctance of obituarists to record Matthews's abandoning his first wife for Mila Winterova. This, Whannel said, 'stems partly from the culture of respect and reticence within which the conventions of obituary writing are framed, but it is also the case that it did not fit neatly within the very well-established frame of reference within which Matthews was cast as the ultimate working-class sporting gentleman.'

At a more mundane level, Matthews's many mementoes, artefacts and other possessions provided his most tangible legacy. Some of these are displayed in the Sir Stanley Matthews Lounge at the Britannia Stadium; others have proved particular favourites among the growing number of investors in sporting memorabilia. A letter sent by Stoke City in March 1945, thanking the RAF for releasing Matthews to play in a match, fetched £380 at auction and a four-inch high Royal Doulton toby jug in Matthews's image, which was one of only three, went for a world record £32,200.

His trophies and articles of playing kit also attracted robust bidding and continue to do so. Boots have done especially well – although not without controversy.

In February 2010 a pair of boots described as having been worn by Matthews in the 1953 FA Cup final were sold by auctioneers Bonhams of Chester for £38,400, five times more than expected. A forklift truck driver reportedly blew his redundancy money buying the still-muddied size sevens that were missing a stud but still had their laces. Matthews had given these boots to an old friend, Wilf Coomer, a keen Blackpool fan, after the '53 final. Coomer's son entered them for the auction.

Intriguingly, though, the National Football Museum in Preston claimed *they* possessed the holy footballing relic that is the footwear worn by Matthews in the Wembley final. The back-story here was that Matthews gave them to a Staffordshire cricket club who auctioned them in the 1960s. The winning bidder then loaned them to the museum.

And yet another boot, singular, 'belonging to Sir Stanley, possibly used in the 1953 Cup final', was lot 392 when the family sold off the bulk of Matthews's belongings in October 2000. It fetched £640. Other items at this auction, which took place at the Britannia Stadium, Stoke City's ground opened by Matthews in 1997 and where his ashes are buried, ranged from medals to a brass bedstead to a trouser press. Paperbacks by, among others, Dick Francis, Jack Higgins and Wilbur Smith also went under the hammer. Someone even bought his passport, giving his residence as Malta, for £500.

The crucifix now hanging in the church of St Peter ad Vincula in Stoke was one of the few things not sold. Mila had carried it with her when she left Czechoslovakia in 1969. She held on to it during her travels with Stanley – an attempt to part with it in Canada failed after the car taking it away broke down, which she decided was the work of providence – and it ended up hanging in the dining room in Penkhull. When the house was cleared, the family presented the cross to the church where Matthews's funeral had taken place. It is on display there with the accompanying text that tells a story at variance with the one in Mila's secret police file.

In October 2001 the Stanley Matthews Foundation unveiled the £250,000, monument to Matthews that stands outside the Britannia Stadium.

A striking and critically acclaimed example of commemorative art, it consists of three nine-foot figures representing the ages of Matthews the footballer: as a young player, in which he is seen beating his opponent; in his prime as a star of Blackpool and England, in which he is taking the ball forward; and as a veteran back at Stoke, in which he is crossing the ball from the byline. They are arranged in an S-formation to emphasise the fluidity of Matthews's movement.

Local craftsmen and Stoke City fans Andy Edwards, Julian Jeffery, who had the idea for the monument, and Carl Payne worked on the triptych in full public view in the foyer of the Britannia Stadium. They encouraged locals to tell them anecdotes to increase their understanding of Matthews and were even happy to be given a hand applying the clay. All the detail was meticulously researched with the sculptors going as far as talking to the man who cut Matthews's hair.

'Historically it is absolutely correct,' Payne said. 'People who knew Stan donated his old football boots so we could get it authentic – right down to the last eyelet. All the balls are in the right era and the strip, even the rope around the shorts of Sir Stan when he was a young lad and made his debut for Stoke.' Edwards, interviewed while the monument was a work in progress, said: 'We aim for Victorian standards of craft and we look to the Greeks and further back to the Egyptians as storytellers . . . this is a document, it's a diagram, so if you want to know what the boots looked like that Stanley Matthews wore or how long his shorts were you could measure them.'

Fashioned from local clay, it is as close as Stoke and the country could have hoped to come to holding on to Stanley Matthews.

Epilogue

'And did those feet in ancient time'

Stanley Matthews's funeral on Friday 3 March 2000 had many of the appearances of a state occasion – only this was Stoke-on-Trent with little or no history of staging solemn events of national interest. And rather than in a soaring, ancient cathedral the service took place in the church of St Peter ad Vincula, a stolid, dependable structure built in 1830. Still, one national newspaper reckoned that after funerals for royalty and Sir Winston Churchill this was the biggest the country had seen.

Matthews's death had brought forth telegrams and letters of condolence from Buckingham Palace, 10 Downing Street, numerous football bodies and associations, many hundreds of ordinary people and from around the world. The Queen's Telemessage was sent to Jean Gough at her home in Gnosall, Staffordshire. It praised Matthews's ability as a footballer and as an example of sportsmanship and fair play. It finished 'Elizabeth R'. Prime Minister Tony Blair added in his own hand, under two typed paragraphs, that he had met Matthews a number of times. 'We really will not see his like again,' he wrote. The letter from the Hungarian Football Federation said: 'We played several times against him in the 50-ies in wonderful games at Wembley and in the Nepstadion.' In fact they played against him only once and this being a letter of condolence it graciously scrubbed over the score, 6-3 to Hungary at Wembley in 1953.

The family handed over the organisation of the funeral to Stoke City FC. On a raw, occasionally rainy day, a cortege of nine cars made its way to the church, at its head the hearse with a floral recreation of Matthews's No. 7 shirt propped in the rear window. Crowds estimated at more than 100,000 lined the fourteen-mile route that started in front of a full stand at the Britannia Stadium. The procession, which lasted ninety minutes, paused along the way at Matthews's primary school, at his statue in the centre of Hanley, which was surrounded by wreaths, at the now-derelict Victoria Ground, where he played all his home matches for Stoke, and at the house in Penkhull where he and Mila had lived for ten years.

Another large crowd waiting outside the church applauded spontaneously when the hearse arrived ten minutes before the service, which one newspaper neatly described as 'another Matthews final'. Inside, a congregation of nine hundred, including three hundred Stoke City fans, who had collected their passes on a first-come-first-served basis on the previous evening, filled the pews. Several fans draped their club scarves over the gallery balcony. Matthews's first wife, Betty, was among the large turnout of family members. The front rank of former players included four who also acted as pallbearers, Gordon Banks, Sir Bobby Charlton, Sir Tom Finney and Nat Lofthouse.

The service, strong on tradition, rang with appropriate lines – and not just those composed by the speakers. The congregation sang 'And did those feet in ancient time' and 'I am the Lord of the Dance, said he'. The Old Testament reading included the words, 'they will run and not grow weary'.

Peter Coates, the majority shareholder in Stoke City FC, gave the first address. He said attending a function with Matthews was like going out with royalty, 'we got the red-carpet treatment. He was friendly, modest, self-effacing and never criticised players.

He was highly intelligent and was a shrewd judge. This city had master potter Josiah Wedgwood, literary figure Arnold Bennett, Victorian scientist Oliver Lodge and Spitfire designer Reginald Mitchell. But nobody played the same part in the lives of people in this city as Stan. He was a working-class hero.'

Other tributes followed from Jimmy Armfield, Gordon Taylor, chief executive of the Professional Footballers' Association, and Matthew Gough, Matthews's grandson.

Armfield recalled that as right-back at Blackpool he spent a lot of time looking at the back of a tangerine shirt with the number seven on it, which was fitting because this was how most opposition defenders also remembered Matthews. 'That speed off the mark, the feint, the flick, the dribble, the balance that tormented defenders around the globe, it seemed to come easy to Stan,' Armfield said. 'That was Stan. He was never Sir Stan to us because it never seemed to ring true. He was the first real football man.'

Taylor said that Matthews had more than paid his dues in the fight to end the maximum wage, his talent stepped over inter-club rivalries. As a young Bolton fan, Taylor watched the 1953 Cup Final. 'It was just like football heaven,' he told the congregation, 'Stan's personal Everest.' Taylor also read out a message from South Africa: 'Please, please pay a tribute to Sir Stan's family that he was responsible for producing so many good players in our country.'

Outside the church after the service Finney said: 'We see so little of his type today and when people say he wouldn't have been able to do that today, as far as I'm concerned that's rubbish. He had so much skill and ability. That was his great skill, his gift.'

An editorial writer in a national newspaper once damned a political speech by saying that it would be read long after Milton and Shakespeare were forgotten, but not until then. Matthews consigned just about every other footballer who has composed a few lines of his own out on the right wing to the same sort of wait.

Timeline

Club Career

STOKE CITY

Season	League		FA Cup	
	Appearances	Goals	Appearances	Goals
Manager: Tom Mather				
1931–2	2	–	–	–
1932–3	15	1	–	–
1933–4	29	11	4	4
1934–5	36	10	1	1
Manager: Bob McGrory				
1935–6	40	10	5	–
1936–7	40	7	2	–
1937–8	38	6	3	–
1938–9	36	2	2	–
1939–40*	3	–	–	–
1945–6	–	–	8	–
1946–7	23	4	5	1

*Football League/FA Cup matches suspended during Second World War.

BLACKPOOL

Season	League		FA Cup	
	Appearances	Goals	Appearances	Goals

Manager: Joe Smith

Season	Appearances	Goals	Appearances	Goals
1947–8	33	1	6	–
1948–9	25	3	3	–
1949–50	31	–	3	–
1950–51	36	–	8	–
1951–2	18	1	1	–
1952–3	20	4	7	1
1953–4	30	2	7	–
1954–5	34	1	1	–
1955–6	36	3	1	–
1956–7	25	2	4	–
1957–8	28	–	1	–

Manager: Ron Suart

Season	Appearances	Goals	Appearances	Goals
1958–9	19	–	6	–
1959–60	15	–	–	–
1960–61	27	–	1	–
1961–2	2	–	–	–

STOKE CITY

Manager: Tony Waddington

Season	Appearances	Goals	Appearances	Goals
1961–2	18	2	3	1
1962–3	31	1	–	–
1963–4	9	–	4	1
1964–5	1	–	–	–

ENGLAND

Status/Date	Opponent (Venue)	Result (Matthews goals)
HC 29.9.34	Wales (Ninian Park)	W4-0 (1)
FR 14.11.34	Italy (Highbury)	W3-2
FR 4.12.35	Germany (White Hart Lane)	W3-0
HC 17.4.37	Scotland (Hampden Park)	L1-3
HC 17.11.37	Wales (Ayresome Park)	W2-1 (1)
FR 1.12.37	Czechoslovakia (White Hart Lane)	W5-4 (3)
HC 9.4.38	Scotland (Wembley)	L0-1
FR 14.5.38	Germany (Berlin)	W6-3 (1)
FR 21.5.38	Switzerland (Zurich)	L1-2
FR 26.5.38	France (Paris)	W4-2
HC 22.10.38	Wales (Ninian Park)	L2-4 (1)
FR 26.10.38	Rest of Europe (Highbury)	W3-0
FR 9.11.38	Norway (St James' Park)	W4-0
HC 16.11.38	Northern Ireland (Old Trafford)	W7-0 (1)
HC 15.4.39	Scotland (Hampden Park)	W2-1
FR 13.5.39	Italy (Milan)	D2-2

Manager: Walter Winterbottom*

FR 18.5.39	Yugoslavia (Belgrade)	L1-2
HC 12.4.47	Scotland (Wembley)	D1-1
FR 18.5.47	Switzerland (Zurich)	L0-1
FR 25.5.47	Portugal (Lisbon)	W10-0 (1)
FR 21.9.47	Belgium (Brussels)	W5-2
HC 18.10.47	Wales (Ninian Park)	W3-0
HC 5.11.47	Northern Ireland (Goodison Park)	D2-2
HC 10.4.48	Scotland (Hampden Park)	W2-0
FR 16.5.48	Italy (Turin)	W4-0

FR 26.9.48	Denmark (Copenhagen)	**D**0-0
HC 9.10.48	Northern Ireland (Belfast)	**W**6-2 (1)
HC 10.11.48	Wales (Villa Park)	**W**1-0
FR 2.12.48	Switzerland (Highbury)	**W**6-0
HC 9.4.49	Scotland (Wembley)	**L**1-3
WCF 2.7.50	Spain (Rio de Janeiro)	**L**0-1
HC 7.10.50	Northern Ireland (Belfast)	**W**4-1
HC 14.4.51	Scotland (Wembley)	**L**2-3
FR 21.10.53	FIFA XI (Wembley)	**D**4-4
WCQ/HC 11.11.53	Northern Ireland (Goodison Park)	**W**3-1
FR 25.11.53	Hungary (Wembley)	**L**3-6
WCF 17.6.54	Belgium (Basle)	**D**4-4
WCF 26.6.54	Uruguay (Basle)	**L**2-4
HC 2.10.54	Northern Ireland (Belfast)	**W**2-0
HC 10.11.54	Wales (Wembley)	**W**3-2
FR 1.12.54	West Germany (Wembley)	**W**3-1
HC 2.4.55	Scotland (Wembley)	**W**7-2
FR 15.5.55	France (Paris)	**L**0-1
FR 18.5.55	Spain (Madrid)	**D**1-1
FR 22.5.55	Portugal (Oporto)	**L**1-3
HC 22.10.55	Wales (Cardiff)	**L**1-2
FR 9.5.56	Brazil (Wembley)	**W**4-2
HC 6.10.56	Northern Ireland (Belfast)	**D**1-1 (1)
HC 14.11.56	Wales (Wembley)	**W**3-1
FR 28.11.56	Yugoslavia (Wembley)	**W**3-0
WCQ 5.12.56	Denmark (Molineux)	**W**5-2
HC 6.4.57	Scotland (Wembley)	**W**2-1
WCQ 8.5.57	Rep of Ireland (Wembley)	**W**5-1
WCQ 15.5.57	Denmark (Copenhagen)	**W**4-1

FR = Friendly; HC = Home Championship; WCQ = World Cup qualifier; WCF = World Cup finals

*Before Walter Winterbottom's appointment in 1947, England teams were coached on a match-by-match basis by appointees of the Football Association.

Matthews made 30 other international appearances for which caps not awarded: 23 Wartime matches (1939–45); 6 Victory matches (1945–6); Bolton Disaster match v Scotland (1946). **He also played in 13 Inter-League matches for the Football League between 1934 and 1935 and 1956 and 1957.**

Author's Note

Having set out thinking I was about to write the biography of an uncomplicated, if extravagantly talented, footballer from Stoke-on-Trent, I encountered a character far more complex and a life far less simple than I could have possibly imagined. One consequence was that I needed a great deal more assistance piecing together Stanley Matthews's story than had seemed likely. In fact there are two stories: the one about the professional football career that transcended any that had preceded or, in many respects, has succeeded it; and the Cold War love story that provided a compelling postscript to Matthews's life as a footballer who apparently had antifreeze in his veins. Of those who helped me in my endeavour, members of his family including his children, Jean Gough and Stanley Matthews Junior, and his brother and sister-in-law, Ron and Mavis Matthews, are due particular thanks. As a result of my many visits to the British Newspapers Library in Colindale, north London, I met Frank Foy, who must stand in the front rank of meticulous researchers and whose help was invaluable. Jan Krcmar, a colleague from my days working for Reuters, gave me huge assistance with that significant part of Matthews's story that had Czechoslovakia at its centre. Others to whom I do scant justice by giving only a brief mention include Rex Adams, Ian Addis, Harold Alderman, Jimmy Armfield, David Barber,

Pat Brogan, Peter Collins, Richard Collins, David Conn, Philip Cornwall, Ed Cropley, Erika Danisova, Mark Gleeson, Roy Hay, Derek Hodgson, Colin Jose, Terry Kelly, Graham Kelly, Jimmy McIlroy, David Miller, John O'Brien, Martin Pavlata, Daniela Pavlatova, Carl Payne, Peter Raath, Sam Ramsamy, Don Ratcliffe, Bill Slater, Huston Spratt, David Steele, Kelvin Steele, David Steinke, Father Hilary Tagliaferro, Anthea Toorchen, Barbara Toorchen, Erica Toorchen, Tim and Jean Waterworth, Simon Walker, Bill Webb, Gerry Wolstenholme.

I would also like to thank Jonathan Conway of Mulcahy Conway Associates, without whose intervention I would not have written this or either of my earlier books, and, from Yellow Jersey Press, Matt Phillips and Caroline McArthur, whose calm and diligent assistance eased this book's passage from first manuscript to what you now hold in your hands.

Jon Henderson
May 2013

Select Bibliography

Books

Armfield, Jimmy, *Right Back to the Beginning* (London, 2004)

Bennett, Arnold, *The Card* (London, 1911)

Downing, David, *The Best of Enemies: England v Germany* (London, 2000)

Finney, Tom, *Tom Finney: My Autobiography* (London, 2003)

Francis, Geoff, *The Black Man With A White Face* (Milton Keynes, 2011)

Giller, Norman, *Billy Wright: A Hero For All Seasons* (London, 2003)

Gribble, Leonard, *They Kidnapped Stanley Matthews* (London, 1950)

Harvey, Charles, *Almanack of Sport 1966* (London, 1966)

Huggins, Mike, and Williams, Jack, *Sport and the English, 1918–1939* (London, 2006)

Matthews, Stanley, *Feet First* (London, 1948)

Matthews, Stanley, *Feet First Again* (London, 1952)

Matthews, Stanley, *The Way It Was* (London, 2000)

Matthews, Stanley, and Mila, *Back in Touch* (London, 1981)

McKinstry, Leo, *Sir Alf* (London, 2010)

Miller, David, *Stanley Matthews: The Authorized Biography* (London, 1989)

Rippon, Anton, *Gas Masks For Goal Posts* (Stroud, 2005)

Newspapers
Evening Sentinel (Stoke-on-Trent)
West Lancashire Evening Gazette (Blackpool)
Various other regional and national titles

Index